FIFTY KEY CONTEMPORARY THINKERS

Nc   ide surveys the
mc   y-first centuries
wit

-
-
-
-
-
-

W   o new sections
on   referencing and
up   exts, this is an
ess   t drives today's
wc   ed to find such
an   ideas around.

Jo   ocial theory at
M   blished widely
on

RELATED TITLES

Fifty Key Contemporary Thinkers, 1st edition
John Lechte
1994

FIFTY KEY CONTEMPORARY THINKERS

From Structuralism To Post-Humanism

Second Edition

John Lechte

Routledge
Taylor & Francis Group

LONDON AND NEW YORK

First published 2008
by Routledge
2 Park Square, Milton Park, Abingdon, Oxon, OX14 4RN

Simultaneously published in the USA and Canada
by Routledge
270 Madison Ave, New York, NY 10016

Routledge is an imprint of the Taylor & Francis Group, an informa business

© 2008 John Lechte

Typeset in Bembo by
Taylor & Francis Books
Printed and bound in Great Britain by
Antony Rowe Ltd, Chippenham, Wiltshire

British Library Cataloguing in Publication Data
A catalogue record for this book is available from the British Library

Library of Congress Cataloguing in Publication Data
A catalog record for this book is available from the Library of Congress

ISBN 978-0-415-32693-3 (hbk)
ISBN 978-0-415-32694-0 (pbk)
ISBN 978-0-203-39057-3 (ebk)

For Peetra and Simon with all my love

CONTENTS

PREFACE TO THE FIRST EDITION

This book follows the very admirable model provided by Diané Collinson's *Fifty Major Philosophers* (1987). Thus I offer the reader both an overview of each thinker's work together with biographical information. Like Ms Collinson, I also aim to introduce, sometimes in a fairly detailed way, one or more aspects of the *oeuvre* in question, and particularly as this relates to that aspect of thought inspired by structuralism. And I often engage with that thought – differ with it, or appreciate its insights. My hope is that the reader will get a real sense of the flavour, style, and, in many cases, the truly innovative character of the thought in question.

My task, however, was both easier and more difficult than Diané Collinson's, for while I did not have to treat the entire history of the Western canon of philosophy in writing my entries, I had to choose fifty *contemporary* thinkers. And although, of course, one can debate about who should be in the philosophy canon, there is less doubt about the fact that a canon has been extraordinarily influential, even to the point where people are speaking Plato, Hobbes or Sartre without knowing it. To some extent, then, Diané Collinson's task was to make explicit forms of thought which have already formed us. My task, by contrast, has been to distil key elements in the work of thinkers who are sometimes not yet widely known, but who are becoming so. Most people will at least have heard of Plato; but will they have heard of Saussure? Most will know that idealism is located somewhere in Plato's philosophy; but do they know that 'difference' is a key notion in Saussure? Clearly, I believe that the answer is 'no' in both cases.

It is not only the general reader's knowledge that I am actually alluding to here, but also my own. For the contrast that I am trying to bring out is that between a relatively stable canon with which I am familiar, if not in detail, and a series of thinkers whose thought is often still evolving, both because many are still writing and thus have not completed their work, and because, by definition, it is not possible to have a deep familiarity with thought that is essentially contemporary and innovative. In other words, whether I have chosen the most important or illuminating angle on the thinkers in question will be, and should be, a cause for debate.

In response to this difficulty, my wager on behalf of the reader is that the light that I do shine on the thought I have explicated is an informed one, but that even if it turns out to be but one possible way of understanding the thinker in question, this is still informative and educative in the sense that I intend. And this sense is that to (be able to) disagree with me is to understand me.

What of the choice of thinkers, however? Here, the subtitle of the book should convey the orientation of the choices I have made. The thinkers chosen serve to deepen an understanding of the post-Second World War structuralist orientation in thought, which arose largely, if not exclusively, in France. In my expositions, I have tried not to belabour this point; for each of the fifty thinkers treated is irreducible to a movement. Although the focus is primarily on the post-war period, it is not exclusively so: I have tried to include thinkers who chronologically, might have been of another generation (Saussure, Freud, Nietzsche), but who have been of seminal importance, and are of great contemporaneity, intellectually speaking. 'Contemporary', therefore, means more than chronologically contemporary.

As the orientation of the book is largely towards presenting those thinkers who represent a structural post-structural, modern–postmodern, orientation, I have also included a number of indisputably important thinkers (Adorno, Habermas) who are unsympathetic, or at least less sympathetic, to this orientation.

As to the material presentation of the book, I have grouped the thinkers in nine categories: early structuralism; structuralism; structural history; post-structuralist thought; semiotics; second generation feminism; post-Marxism; modernity; and finally, post-modernity. A short introductory note, intended to give the reader a broad overview of the intellectual orientation concerned, precedes each group of thinkers. Some may see these groupings as too reductive. My view is that they signal an orientation only, and help the reader to appreciate the global significance of this collection, a significance which should not go unnoticed and which, used intelligently, can assist understanding at a more individual level.

For each thinker, I have aimed to provide information about recent as well as early work in the listing of major works, as I have also attempted to provide recent further readings.

Finally, I should address briefly the question as to how this book might be used. It would have been farcical, I believe, to have claimed to have presented these fifty key contemporary thinkers in a way which obviated the need for the reader to do additional reading to consolidate his or her, understanding. This book offers a way in to understanding the thinkers concerned; it is not a substitute for reading them oneself. After Heidegger, I am not providing learning; I am trying to let learning take place.

John Lechte

PREFACE TO THE SECOND EDITION

A second edition of *Fifty Key Contemporary Thinkers* indicates a certain success with the first edition. Indeed, given the choices with regard to thinkers, the high level of sales is very gratifying.

The Second Edition contains ten new entries on Agamben, Badiou, Bergson, Butler, Haraway, Heidegger, Husserl, Maturana, Virilio and Žižek, along with the radical revision of entries on Barthes, Benjamin, Deleuze, Derrida, Kristeva, Lacan and Lyotard, and significant revision of, or addition to, entries on Arendt, Baudrillard, Bourdieu, Chomsky, Freud, Foucault, Irigaray, Le Doeuff, Merleau-Ponty and Serres, with minor editing being done on the remaining entries.

Each first edition entry has been fully reviewed, particularly with regard to up-dating the referencing system, 'Major writings' and 'Further reading'. The second edition is therefore quite different in content from the first.

Choices and Categories

Changes have been made regarding classification: three new categories of Phenomenology, the Post-Human and Vitalist-Inspired Thought have been added, while Structural History has been deleted. This, it is hoped, will add clarity to the reader's intellectual map of the fifty thinkers concerned.

As to the rationale for these classifications, it is clear that Phenomenology has been as important to Post-Structural thought, as Early Structuralist thinkers were for Structuralism. The category of Post-Human is justified because key thinkers today (Haraway, Maturana, Serres) are working at the cross-roads of cybernetics, post-Darwin biology, information technology and an earlier humanism, even if they can be critical of all, or of aspects, of such developments, as is Paul Virilio. The category of Vitalist-Inspired Thought makes it possible to do justice to those thinkers who focus on drives and the body in their thought, including those such as Nietzsche and Deleuze from the first edition, who are now more comfortably in this category.

What is the rationale, then, for the choice of the ten new thinkers, and within which movement in thought do they fall? Very simply, the judgement is that each has made a very significant impact on thinking and each connects, directly or indirectly, with the movements in thought outlined above. Of course, these choices may be contested, but I have chosen thinkers whose work has systematically placed a new set of ideas, or a key idea, before an audience, whether the latter be large or small. Thus, having a truly substantive idea, or set of ideas, to present was the most important criterion invoked when selecting the thinkers as the subject of new entries.

As with the first edition, the purpose of the book is not to serve as a substitute for reading the original material but to make the original more accessible to a wider public.

Note on the Text

All 'Major writings' and 'Further reading' have been thoroughly updated and referencing has been changed to the Harvard system. Subheadings have also been added to facilitate reading.

John Lechte
May 2007

ACKNOWLEDGEMENTS

I would like to thank Peetra, my wife, for her infinite understanding during the preparation of this second edition.

Also, thanks are due to Rosie Waters at Routledge for her extraordinary patience as the preparation of the manuscript overshot numerous deadlines.

INTRODUCTION

Fifty Key Contemporary Thinkers *as a Reference Book*

No one can fail to be struck today by the plethora of reference and self-help books available on the market. One need only cite, in this regard, the expansion of the Routledge Key Guide series itself, for which *Fifty Key Contemporary Thinkers* was a founding text. We are thus clearly witness to a sociological and intellectual phenomenon of some import. Rather than leap to the conclusion that mass education entails the induction into universities of students without the requisite cultural capital, or to the conclusion (à la Virilio) that in a world dominated by speed there is no time available to become acquainted with original, or primary texts, I prefer to consider the situation from another angle. It is that, while, on the one hand, works of reference and other secondary sources can become a substitute for the original, it could be that such sources also provide a bridge to the original. In Michel Serres's terms, the reference text becomes a means of translation – the indispensable third element – between the world of everyday life and the world of primary, and often demanding, texts.

Target texts can include those which, in modernity, had a certain avant-garde quality (the texts of Joyce, for sure, but also those of Derrida in the era of *Glas* (1974)); but they can also include canonical texts that function as the vehicles of a certain cultural heritage (again, Joyce is an example, but also Freud and Husserl). In addition, the primary text will also introduce students to a world of erudition and scholarship (some of Agamben's texts are exemplary here), and not just directly with regard to learning the importance of method, reasoning and evidence, but also indirectly, in the encounter with foreign terms and phrases leading to the subsequent realisation that world is not 'mono', either in language or thought. Such an encounter, when it takes place, can expand symbolic and imaginary capacities.

Reading and Invention

To be a bridge, then, not a substitute: this is the aspiration of *Fifty Key Contemporary Thinkers*. Let us acknowledge that (only extreme naiveté could fail to recognise it) such an aspiration is thwarted at every turn. To begin with, reading itself is in decline, at least when it comes to non-fictional theory. Other media (television, the internet) are beginning to take up the slack. In the late-1980s, Gregory Ulmer proposed a counter to this in his book, *Teletheory* (1989), which aimed to provide a strategy, not only for teaching theory in the age of the internet, but also invention. 'Academics', he said in effect, 'do not despair. Do not think that the rise of electronic media will signal the end of book culture; rather consider the possibility that electronic culture can deliver book culture by other means'. We do not have to choose, then, between book culture *or* electronic culture, but need to work with electronic culture. Or, if book culture, based on the alphabet, heightens a capacity for analysis, electronic culture heightens a capacity for 'patterned thinking' (using images), or 'euretics': 'The thesis is', says Ulmer, 'that new electronic technologies relate to euretics the way alphabetic literacy relates to analytic thinking' (Ulmer 1989: 71). Put simply, if hermeneutics is interpretative and analytical (making sense of what is already there), euretics is the opposite: it is inventive; creates the material for analysis. If interpretation and alphabetic culture are analytic, euretics is synthetic.

Thus, were Ulmer's insights to have wide acceptance and application in an academic context, we would realise that only by giving greater reign to euretics will it be possible to renew hermeneutics, or the analytical impulse so necessary for reading the thought of demanding thinkers such as those I cover in *Fifty Key Contemporary Thinkers*. This at least is the idea; the problem is to realise it. And in this regard, there is, no doubt, still enough inertia in universities to make life difficult for the teachers of invention.

Difficult Reading

Another problem we must address when it comes to the reading of key contemporary thinkers is that such reading is difficult. Of course; but why should we ponder this banality? The reason is that a sociological dimension is at play here. When reading is difficult in today's environment it becomes an obstacle to accessing certain thought, thought which is perhaps not just difficult in terms of its logic or language (mathematics is also difficult in this sense), but is difficult as different, is demanding as different, maybe, as learning a second language is demanding because it is fundamentally different from the mother tongue (has anyone noticed how the teaching of languages in universities has fallen off these days?). Another culture, another language – other thought – are difficult because they are different, as an artwork can be difficult because it is different, in the sense that it establishes its own rule, just as the unconscious, for Freud, establishes its own rules of grammar and syntax. It thus takes effort to work one's way into art and the unconscious.

Confronting difference, then, is demanding; difficulty is demanding. What are the chances of making the call heard to meet the challenge of difficulty? We often hear, do we not, the catch cry: 'no gain without pain'. Is this not an indication that commitment to difficulty is still possible? Here, it is necessary to take into account the cultural context of Western democratic and capitalist societies.

The parameters are made explicit by Michel Serres when he points out that (post) modern life is so different from life of the past that it is as though an entirely new humanity were on the horizon, one that can not only be self-creating through science and technology, but one (in the West) that no longer comprehends, let alone experiences, permanent suffering. It is as though the avoidance of suffering and the attainment of a comfortable lifestyle were addictive. One always wants more: more comfort, more luxury. Could consumer society function, were this not so?

'No gain without pain' only applies to specific goals, therefore, not to a way of life. Difficult reading, by contrast, is not part of a consumer lifestyle. Access to the thought that lies behind the challenge of difficult reading will only become accessible when such reading is rendered less difficult and onerous. For better or for worse, *Fifty Key Contemporary Thinkers* finds its niche here. As intermediary, and vehicle of translation, it also reduces the level of difficulty, difficulty that a post-modern sensibility cannot tolerate.

The Field of Thought in the Work of Fifty Thinkers

Movements and Moments in Thought and Understanding Them

Clearly, it is possible to view the thinkers surveyed uniquely according to the movement or moment in thought to which each has been nominated. Mauss, then, is an early structuralist who pressed towards valorising relations rather then essential qualities. Feminist thinkers, like Irigaray, provide the women's movement with its theory of difference in a push for ever more subtle political recognition. Habermas and Žižek are post-Marxist thinkers because there is a Marxist impulse in their writing evoked by the notion of critique. The obvious is that structuralism as a movement has seen its star decline, while aspects of phenomenology, which has heavily influenced post-structuralist thought, along with post-humanism, and even vitalism, are still on the rise. On the rise, too, is post-Marxism, when we include Badiou (who was influenced by Althusser) and Žižek amongst its ranks. It is now becoming more plausible, after the wave of economic rationalism, to mount a critique of globalisation and corporatisation. Such a critique is no longer the province of crackpots and cranks.

This kind of approach is all well and good, and can function as an organisational reference point, but it remains captive to fashion and to the conscious presentation of self and its representations. More interesting, I believe, is the attempt to get at the unconscious of thought, much as Michel Foucault did, through an archaeological method. One of the questions the archaeological approach raises is whether it is essentially epistemological and the therefore beholden to a subject–object dichotomy. Foucault's response was that it is so beholden, hence the disappearance from his work of epistemology or the *épistemé* after the publication of *The Archaeology of Knowledge* in 1969.

Epistemology and the Subject

Epistemology could not really link up with the Foucault's method because it is part of the practice of a self-conscious ego. How is the ego (or subject) itself formed in relation to the emergence of the social sciences? Such is archaeology's question. This question by-passes the self-consciousness of the social sciences and perhaps, in a certain way, communicates with ontology. Ontology and epistemology should not be confused here.

In any event, a common thread running through the work of many thinkers is the issue of whether subjectivity is an a priori entity given in advance, or whether it is enacted ('performed', Judith Butler will say), and entirely contingent: an event in history. Chomsky, Žižek, Husserl and possibly Freud are part of a group who, consciously, attribute to the subject an a priori status in the Cartesian sense. Žižek's cartesianism is certainly qualified and consists in a commitment to the notion of the subject as an empty space ready to be filled with 'pathological' (i.e. singular) content. For Chomsky, of course, language capacity is there from the start. It is innate. Chomsky thus stands out here; for even those like Žižek who subscribe to some kind of a priori form of the subject still refuse to give it any concrete content.

For his part, Badiou embraces totally a notion of the subject as axiomatic, founded in truth and the event. This subject is not a product of knowledge or of interpretation. It is entirely detached from epistemology. Indeed, on this basis, epistemology cannot, ironically, incorporate a subject in the strict sense. An ideological subject is a different matter. It may well go hand in hand with epistemology.

In the background here (less for Badiou than Deleuze) is the issue of whether it is logically legitimate to invoke a principle of individuation, or of subjectivity, prior to individuation itself. '[S]uch a research perspective', according to Gilbert Simondon, 'gives an ontological privilege to the already constituted individual' (Simondon 1989: 10, Simondon's emphasis). Do pre-existing models of subjectivity do it justice? Does a model of love, or of beauty, do justice to its uniqueness? The model, or blueprint, approach to subjectivity and individuation comes, according to advocates of 'nothing prior', to determine their reality. As well as being designated as idealist, this approach is also seen as reductionist and analytical: it assumes that the essential nature of individuation (the model) will clearly manifest itself in a variety of instances – that despite the apparent complexity the reality is definable and essentially simple and already given.

A key facet of contemporary debates surrounding subjectivity is thus located here. In science, this links up with complexity theory, which emphasises the emergent aspect of entities. That is, entities as 'emergent', evolve: they come into being, rather than being already constituted. Certainly, on this account, there is no knowing subject prior to its emergence. To speak about the subject of knowledge, then, is to presuppose what needs to be explained.

Structure and Emergence

The new entries in the second edition of *Fifty Key Contemporary Thinkers*, have shifted the centre of theoretical gravity away from that of the first edition – with its central points of reference of structure, code and differential relations all modelled on language – to the question once again of the nature of the human. Here, as Agamben says very poignantly in confronting the remnants of Auschwitz, the human being is not an essence, but is 'always beyond or before the human, the central threshold through which pass currents of the human and the inhuman, subjectification and desubjectification, the living being's becoming speaking and the logos' becoming living' (Agamben

2002: 135). In other words, even though the human is not an essence and so still thwarts an essentialist discourse, it is important, first, to address the question of the nature of the human and, second, to recognise that to be without essence is not to be nothing. Even to be no more than bare life in the concentration camps is not to be nothing: it is still to be human and to bear witness even in the impossibility of bearing witness.

However, and by contrast to Agamben on the human, to the extent that social science (anthropology, linguistics, psychoanalysis, literary theory) was the predominant vehicle of structuralism, as this was portrayed in the first edition, epistemology was the field at stake. Emergence is not outside this field, but it gives it a shake forcing a re-evaluation of first principles. Julia Kristeva's notion of a subject-in-process is perfectly in keeping with this. What Kristeva objected to in phenomenological accounts of the subject was precisely that it pre-supposed what it needed to explain. In positing a transcendental ego–subject, phenomenology, in Kristeva's eyes, could not show how such a subject came into being, how it evolved and changed, how it could only really be accounted for by the notion of emergence, even if Kristeva herself never uses that term. The phrase she does use at one point in her *oeuvre* when talking about love, is 'open system', referring to the fact that the psychic space of the subject in love is open to change and modification, and as such is able to expand and enrich imaginary and symbolic capacities.

Kristeva, then, shows herself to be very much a transitional figure in relation to the two editions of *Fifty Key Contemporary Thinkers*. For the tendencies towards a dynamic and emergent subject evident in her work from 1974 – tendencies which see a break with any kind of static, structuralist view of the subject as the product of discourse – are well within keeping with the refusal of static, explanatory princi-ples evident in key thinkers collected in the second edition.

Ontology

In Heidegger's language (a language that begins to supplant that of the social sciences as the dominant kid on the block), the social sci-ences are 'ontic': concerned with particular objects which they endeavour to know. They are concerned with beings (existence), not with being. Thus a further shift in the centre of gravity is observable in the second as compared to the first edition. Whereas structuralism, as we have already implied, was hegemonic in the first edition (even those who opposed it tended to situate themselves in relation to it), the late-1990s and the thinkers who emerged then with renewed visibility (cf. in particular, Agamben, Levinas. Žižek) seemed to recognize that, once again, the foundation of the social sciences is at issue after decades of the withdrawal of interest in this area. Knowledge itself becomes relativised, not just in the sense of being 'situated', as Donna Haraway argued, but in the sense that knowledge does not give access to more fundamental aspects of thought, such as the question of being. In short, ontology also makes a renewed appearance on the scene after holding the interest, in the decades after May '68, of only a handful of devotees.

This is not to suggest that there was, or is, a rush back to an essentialist position on society, culture, or the nature of the human; but it does mean that epistemology is put back in its place of subordination after being dominant in the period of anti-humanism. Badiou's thought is, in many respects, exemplary. For even though he links being with knowledge (within which interpretation is dominant), this is basically to emphasise the importance of truth (the opposite of interpretation) and the event: that occurrence with no concept which must be given a concept, one that challenges existing modes of thinking and doing. Badiou, like other thinkers in the second edition, is not a self-conscious ontologist; but it is clear that the level at which his thought operates is derived from a rejection of the hegemony of knowledge, and that pushes him towards the level that Heidegger called, 'being'. So even though Badiou continually takes issue with Heidegger on a range of ideas, he still finds himself called upon to say that: 'There is no doubt we are indebted to Heidegger for having yoked philosophy once more to the question of being [ontology]. We are also indebted to him for giving a name to the era of the forgetting of this question, a forgetting whose history, beginning with Plato, is the history of philosophy as such' (Badiou 2004: 39). Heidegger, the controversial Heidegger, thus opens up the path to deeper questions than those raised by epistemology.

The Spectacle

We live, according to the writings left by Guy Debord, in a society of the spectacle. This is a society of surfaces, or representations without depth. Most of all, the society of the spectacle is a society of commodification, where everything is on display and has attached to it an exchange-value represented by price.

Taking Marx's theory of the commodity as a point of departure in defining the society of the spectacle, Debord makes the commodity into a play of appearances, or, to be more precise, of images. The society of the spectacle, then, is a system of social relations mediated by images (Debord 1992: 16, para 4) – images which have become detached from their essential position: the true has become the false (Debord 1992: 19, para 9). The image, then, is a detached appearance that has ceased to refer to what is truly substantial. It goes to the heart of the 'unreality' of the real society (Debord 1992: 17, para 6) without, however, being something simply added on to social reality. For the spectacle is how society is organised at its most profound level. Moreover, as it is the result of the existing mode of production, the spectacle is produced by this mode of production. Therefore, as Debord explains: 'reality rises up in the spectacle, and the spectacle is real' (Debord 1992: 19, para 8).

To ask whether the spectacle is true and entirely pervasive is probably the wrong question. For the spectacle is true just as marketing and commodification are true; that is, they undoubtedly exist. It is not just that we live under the umbrella of commodification – seen in truly spectacular fashion (no pun intended) in the $104 million dollar price tag paid in May 2004 for Picasso's painting, 'Boy With a Pipe' – but that commodification and the ego are inextricably tied to each other. 'Ego' here, does not imply narcissism, or that the world is dominated by narcissism. Rather, a commodity as a thing that can be represented fulfils the desire of the ego. The ego itself is, in this sense, part of the spectacle. Its world is spectacular. The world of the spectacle is the very opposite of a sacred, ineffable, spiritual world, or a world of ideas. It is also quite clearly the opposite, of the world of the unconscious.

Unlike the world of representation, which the ego constructs in spectacular fashion, access to a sacred, spiritual world, or to a world of ideas, comes through exposure, an exposure that is also an opening up to ideas, to the sacred, to the spiritual, to the ineffable, just as in Levinas's terms one is exposed to the other.

I'm implying, of course, that the spectacle, fuelling the ego as it does, becomes an obstacle (unless one seeks guidance) in the way of opening oneself to ideas, and therefore to the ideas in *Fifty Key Contemporary Thinkers*. It is not just a matter, though, of pointing to Debord's thesis which explicitly names the spectacle, showing, as Debord admits, that his book, in naming and representing the spectacle is also part of the ego network that it denounces. To behold the spectacle is to reinforce the spectacle which is itself a beholding (representation). It is my estimation that archaeology as Foucault practised it, the Freudian notion of the unconscious, as well as Heidegger's philosophy, can provide a way out of this dilemma. For I believe that each of these approaches by-passes the ego, and thus allows access to ideas which constitute the environment of being.

The ultimate goal of the second edition of *Fifty Key Contemporary Thinkers*, then, is to be an intermediary also in the sense of enabling readers – against the spectacle – to open themselves to the ideas of a truly amazing group of thinkers, thinkers who can change our lives.

References

Agamben, Giorgio (2002), *Remnants of Auschwitz: The Witness and the Archive*, trans. Daniel Heller-Roazen, New York: Zone Books.

Badiou, Alain (2004), *Theoretical Writings*, trans. Ray Brassier and Alberto Toscano, London and New York: Continuum.

Debord, Guy (1992), *La société du Spectacle*, Paris: Gallimard.

Derrida, Jacques (1974), *Glas*, Paris: Galilée.

Simondon, Gilbert (1989), *L'Individuation psychique et collective*, Paris: Aubier.

Ulmer, Gregory (1989), *Teletheory: Grammatology in the Age of Video*, New York and London: Routledge.

FIFTY KEY CONTEMPORARY THINKERS

THINKERS

From Structuralism To Post-Humanism

EARLY STRUCTURALISM

To give an insight into the factors which set in motion the structuralist movement, we can already see certain tendencies in the relational understanding of exchange in Marcel Mauss. The focus on relations begins to destabilise the presuppositions of more essentialist and positivistic forms of thought. A focus on society as a system where certain phenomena constitute a 'total social fact', or on the epistemological basis of knowledge (Bachelard), begins to shift the emphasis away from an explanation of society focused on its content and more towards a focus on form as structural (that is, as differential and relational). The history of science is no longer the expression of a mind. Instead, through an epistemological configuration, history constructs the intellectual framework that comprehends it. In addition, changes in the present experience of a society or an individual change the meaning of the past. The past can no longer be understood in its own terms because now the past is to be understood in terms of the concerns of the present.

GASTON BACHELARD (1884–1962)

Gaston Bachelard – epistemologist, philosopher of science, and theorist of the imagination – influenced key figures in the structuralist and post-structuralist generation of the post-war era. Through Jean Cavaillès, and especially in light of the work and guidance of Georges Canguilhem, Michel Foucault found his particular orientation in researching the history of knowledges. Again, with Louis Althusser finding inspiration in Bachelard's concept of 'discontinuity' – which he translated into 'epistemological break' – a generation of Marxist philosophers was stimulated to rethink the notions of time, subjectivity, and science.

Gaston Bachelard was born in 1884, in rural France, at Bar-sur-Aube and died in Paris in 1962. After being employed in the postal service (1903–13), he became professor of physics at the Collège de Bar-sur-Aube from 1919 to 1930. At the age of 35, Bachelard engaged in further studies – this time in philosophy, for which he completed an *agrégation* in 1922. Still later, in 1928, he published his doctoral thesis, defended in 1927: *Essai sur la connaissance approchée* (*Essay on Approximate Knowledge*) and his complementary thesis, *Etude sur l'évolution d'un problème physique, La propagation thermique dans les solides* (*Study on the Evolution of a Problem in Physics: Thermal Propagation in Solids*). In light of this work, in 1940 Bachelard was called upon to take up the chair of history and philosophy of science at the Sorbonne, a position he held until 1954.

The New Framework of Science

Three key elements of Bachelard's thought made him both a unique philosopher and thinker and also rendered his work crucial to the post-war generation of structuralists. The first element concerns the importance placed on epistemology in science. If, in this regard, scientists were to have a defective understanding of their own practice, the application of their work would be fundamentally impeded. Epistemology is the domain where the significance of scientific endeavours is comprehended. As Bachelard wrote in *The Philosophy of No*: 'The space in which one *looks*, in which one *examines* is philosophically very different from the space in which one sees' (Bachelard 1968: 63). This is because the space in which one sees is always a represented space, and not a real space. Only by recourse to philosophy can one take account of this. Indeed, Bachelard goes on to advocate 'a systematic study of *representation*, the most natural intermediary for determining the relationships of noumenon and phenomenon' (Bachelard 1968: 64).

Theory and Practice in Science

Closely aligned to the interaction between reality and its representation, is Bachelard's unswerving advocacy of the dialectical relationship between rationalism and realism – or empiricism, as it could also be called. Thus in perhaps what became, for a wider public, his most influential book, *The New Scientific Spirit*, this veritable poet of epistemology argues that there are fundamentally two prevailing metaphysical bases: rationalism and realism. Rationalism – which includes philosophy and theory – is the field of interpretation and reason; realism, on the other hand, provides rationalism with the material for its interpretations. Simply to remain at a naive and intuitive level – the experimental level – in grasping new facts is to condemn scientific understanding to stagnation; for it cannot become aware of what it is doing. Similarly, if one exaggerates the importance of the rationalist aspect – perhaps even claiming that, in the end, science is nothing but the reflection of an underlying philosophical system – an equally sterile idealism can result. For Bachelard, therefore, to be scientific is to privilege neither thought nor reality, but to recognise the inextricable link between them. In the following memorable expression, Bachelard captures what is at stake: '*Experimentation must give way to argument, and argument must have recourse to experimentation*' (Bachelard 1985: 4, Bachelard's emphasis). All of Bachelard's writings on the nature of science are motivated by this principle. Trained as a scientist and as a philosopher, Bachelard exemplified the position he strove to represent in his writing. As may be expected, a book like *Le Rationalisme appliqué* (*Applied Rationalism*), is geared to demonstrate the theoretical basis of different types of experimentation. A profound rationalism is thus always an applied rationalism, one that learns from reality. This is not all, however. For Bachelard also agrees that the empiricist can learn something about reality from the theorist when it happens – as with Einstein – that a theory is developed prior to its experimental correlate. Here, theory *needs* its experimental correlate in order to be confirmed. With the emphasis he placed on epistemology, Bachelard brought science and philosophy together in a way seldom seen before. The human and natural sciences in fact find their intermediary here, in the man who, in the end, comes to write a 'poetics' of science.

History of Science

The second major aspect of Bachelard's work which has been particularly influential as far as structuralism is concerned is his theorisation of the history of science. In a nutshell, Bachelard proposes a non-evolutionary explanation of the development of science, where prior developments do not necessarily explain the present state of science. For example, according to Bachelard, it is not possible to explain Einstein's theory of relativity as developing out of Newtonian physics. New doctrines did not develop out of the old, says Bachelard, 'but rather, the new *enveloped* the old'. And he continues: 'Intellectual generations are nested, one within the other. When we go from non-Newtonian physics to Newtonian physics, we do not encounter contradiction but we do experience contradiction' (Bachelard 1968: 60). On this basis, the concept that links later discoveries to a prior set of discoveries is not continuity, but discontinuity. There is thus a discontinuity between Euclidean and non-Euclidean geometry, a discontinuity between Euclidean space, and the theories of location, space and time put forward by Heisenberg and Einstein. Again, Bachelard points out that in the past, mass was defined in relation to a quantity of matter. The greater the matter, therefore, the greater the force thought to be needed to oppose it: velocity was a function of mass. With Einstein, we now know that mass is a function of velocity, and not the reverse. The main point made here is not that previous theories were found wanting and therefore opposed, but that new theories tend entirely to transcend – or are discontinuous with – previous theories and explanations of phenomena. As Bachelard explains:

> No doubt there are some kinds of knowledge that appear to be immutable. This leads some people to think that the stability of the contents is due to stability of the container, or, in other words, that the forms of rationality are permanent and no new method of rational thought is possible. But structure does not come from accumulation alone; the mass of immutable knowledge does not have as much functional importance as is sometimes assumed.
>
> (Bachelard 1968: 54)

In fact, Bachelard argues, it is the – sometimes radical – changes in the meaning of a concept, or in the nature of a research field which best characterise the nature of scientific endeavour. What is new in science, therefore, is always revolutionary.

As an addendum to the Bachelardian conception of scientific development, it is important to note that all scientific thought, 'is, in its essence, process of objectification' – a sentiment with which Pierre Bourdieu (a former student of Bachelard's) would entirely agree. Moreover, in speaking about the scientific thought of the modern era, Bachelard notes that it is fundamentally oriented to seeing phenomena relationally, and not substantively, or as having essential qualities in themselves. This observation clearly signals a feature present in contemporary structuralist thought. Thus, Bachelard confirms, 'the properties of the objects in Hilbert's system are purely relational and in no way substantial (Bachelard 1968: 30–31).

When he argues that 'the assimilation of the irrational by reason never fails to bring about a reciprocal reorganization of the domain of rationality' (Bachelard 1968: 137), Bachelard confirms the dialectical nature of his approach – one that is recalled, albeit in a different context and with different aims, by Julia Kristeva and her concepts of the 'semiotic' and the 'symbolic'. Thought is always 'in the *process* of objectification' (Bachelard 1968: 176, emphasis added); it is never given and complete – never closed in upon itself and static, as some scientists used to assume.

The Simple and the Complex: Against Descartes

Connected to this view of thought is Bachelard's anti-Cartesian stance. Whereas Descartes had argued that to progress, thought had to start from the point of clear and simple ideas, Bachelard charges that there are no simple ideas, only complexities, this being particularly in evidence when ideas are applied. 'Application is complication', Bachelard claims. Moreover, while the best theory seems to be the one that explains reality in the simplest way, our author retorts that reality is never simple, and that in the history of science attempts to achieve simplicity (e.g., the structure of the hydrogen spectrum) have invariably turned out to be over-simplifications when the complexity of reality is at last acknowledged. As a notion derived from Descartes, simplicity does not adequately cope with the fact that every phenomenon is a fabric of relations, and not a simple substance. As such, phenomena can only be grasped through a form of synthesis that corresponds to what Bachelard, in 1936, called *surrationalisme* (Bachelard 1936). Surrationalism is an enrichment and revitalisation of rationalism through reference to the material world, just as, through dream, surrealism, from another direction, aimed to revitalise realism through dream.

Imagination

Another dimension of Bachelard's thought which has been influential is his work analysing forms of the imagination, particularly the images related to the themes of matter, movement, force, and dream, as well as the associated images of fire, water, air, and earth. Bachelard, in works like *La Terre et les rêveries de la volonté* (*The Earth and Reveries of Will*) include numerous references to the poetry and literature of the Western cultural tradition, references which he uses to illustrate the *work* of the imagination. The work of the imagination is to be distinguished from the perception of the exterior world translated into images.

The work of imagination, as our author says, is more fundamental than the image-perception; it is thus a question of affirming the 'psychically fundamental character of creative imagination' (Bachelard 1948: 3). Imagination is not here a simple reflection of exterior images, but is rather an activity subject to the individual's will. Bachelard thus sets out to investigate the products of this creative will – products which cannot be predicted on the basis of a knowledge of reality. In a certain sense, therefore, science cannot predict the trajectory of the imagination, for the latter has a specific kind of autonomy. Being subject to will means that the imagination – as for some of the surrealists – has to do with semi-conscious day-dreaming (*rêverie*) rather than with the unconscious processes (condensation, displacement, etc.) of dream–work. Indeed, this factor, together with his interest in archetypes, places Bachelard much closer to Jung than to Freud. Also reminiscent of Jung is the emphasis Bachelard gives in his analysis of the imagination to the four 'primary' elements of fire, water, air, and earth seen to be eternally present in a poetical alchemy. A certain mystical element is thus on the horizon (cf. Jung's *Psychology and Alchemy*). Furthermore, Bachelard's insistence on the primacy of the already given subject–object relation, which he takes, although not always willingly, from phenomenology, means that while the imagination might produce images (most often sublimations of archetypes), the work of creativity is not itself seen to produce the subject–object relation. In effect, the subject here is his Majesty the ego, as Freud said; for there is an assumption of autonomy that verges on being absolute. An element of closure, apparently absent from his scientific writings, thereby enters into Bachelard's writings on imagination.

The imagination, then, is the field of the image, and as such is to be distinguished from the translation of the external world into concepts. The imagination produces images and is its images, whereas thought produces concepts. Without a surrealism that emerges in order to revivify the image, the world of the image would wither and die, so much would it be closed in upon itself. Similarly, were it not for a certain surrationalism, thought and its concepts would also wither – sick from its very completeness and simplicity. Rather, 'openness' and 'complexity' sum up Bachelard's position. In his pleiade of elements – a little too Jungian – the concept falls to the masculine side of things, whereas the image tends towards the feminine. Similarly, the concept corresponds to the *image* of the day (for it is equivalent to 'seeing'), while the image corresponds to the *image* of the night. Dominique Lecourt's astute little book on Bachelard draws attention precisely to this feature of the thinker's work: 'In short, to reiterate Bachelard's terms, between his scientific books and his books about the imagination, it is as the Day is to the Night' (Lecourt 1974: 32).

For the most part, Bachelard himself is coy about whether the two elements in fact come together, that is, about whether the image emerges in science, and science in the realm of images. Bachelard's writing, almost despite itself, has nevertheless come to be seen as a source of inspiration for those intent on breaking down the barrier between concept and image, so that new images can become the basis of new scientific concepts, while new concepts can emerge on the basis of new images.

Transparency and Opacity / Day and Night

More specifically, Bachelard's writings point to the fact that neither a concept nor an image is transparent, and that this opacity signals that an element of subjectivity is always in play in human affairs. This means that human beings are spoken as much as they are speaking in the frameworks of science and the symbolic that constitute their lives. As Lecourt again puts it: 'no one can read these divergent texts without sensing a *unity* which is to be looked for there beneath the contradiction' (Lecourt 1974: 32, Lecourt's emphasis). 'Unity'? – or 'synthesis'? The answer is not unimportant. For whereas unity connotes homogeneity and risks becoming a simple unity, synthesis, as Bachelard said, is to do with relations. The latter can exist between *different* elements (provided the difference is not radical), and presupposes divisions of some sort. Unity, on the other hand, tends to erase relations. In the end, Bachelard's *oeuvre* tends to embody the notion of synthesis that he propounded in his early writing. Of necessity, though, this was a synthesis that he could not see, a necessary blindness constitutive of the place (existentially speaking) from which he wrote. In this sense, then, the Night might well be seen to take precedence over the Day in this exceptional *oeuvre*.

References

Bachelard, Gaston (1936), 'Le Surrationalisme', *Inquisitions*, 1.
—— (1948), *La Terre et les rêveries de la volonté: essai sur l'imagination des forces*, Paris: Corti.
—— (1968), *The Philosophy of No: A Philosophy of the New Scientific Mind*, trans. G. C. Waterston, New York: Orion Press.
—— (1985), *The New Scientific Spirit*, trans. Arthur Goldhammer, Boston: Beacon Press.
Lecourt, Dominique, (1974), *Bachelard ou le jour et la nuit (un essai de matérialisme dialectique)*, Paris: Maspero.

See also: **Bourdieu, Foucault, Freud**

Bachelard's major writings

(2002 [1948]) *Earth and Reveries of Will: An Essay on the Imagination of Matter*, trans. Kenneth Haltman, Dallas: Dallas Institute of Humanities and Culture Publications.
(2000) *The Dialectic of Duration*, trans. Mary McAllester Jones, Manchester: Cinamen.

(1990 [1961]) *The Flame of a Candle*, trans. Joni Caldwell, Dallas: The Dallas Institute of Humanities and Culture Publications.

(1988a [1970]) *The Right to Dream*, trans. J.A. Underwood, Dallas: The Dallas Institute of Humanities and Culture Publications.

(1988b [1943]) *Air and Dreams: An Essay on the Imagination of Movement*, trans. Edith and Frederick Farrell, Dallas: The Dallas Institute of Humanities and Culture Publications.

(1984a [1940, 1951]) *Lautréamont*, trans. Robert Duprée, Dallas: The Dallas Institute of Humanities and Culture Publications.

(1984b [1934]) *The New Scientific Spirit*, trans. Arthur Goldhammer, Boston: Beacon Press.

(1983 [1942]) *Water and Dreams. An Essay on the Imagination of Matter*, trans. Edith

(1972 [1938]) *La Formation de l'esprit scientifique. Contribution à une psychanalyse de la connaissance objective*, Paris: Vrin. Eighth edn.

(1971) *On Poetic Imagination and Reverie: Selections from the Works of Gaston Bachelard*, trans. Colette Gaudin, Indianapolis: Bobbs-Merrill.

(1970 [1928]) *Essai sur la connaissance approchée*, Paris: Vrin (principal thesis for the Doctorate in literature).

(1968 [1940]) *The Philosophy of No. A Philosophy of the New Scientific Mind*, trans. G.C. Waterston, New York: The Orion Press.

(1966 [1949]) *Rationalisme appliqué*, Paris: PUF.

(1965 [1960]) *La Poétique de in rêverie*, Paris: PUF.

(1964a [1957]) *The Poetics of Space*, trans. Maria Jolas, New York: Orion Press.

(1964b [1938]) *The Psychoanalysis of Fire*, trans. Alan C.M. Ross, Boston: Beacon Press; London: Routledge & Kegan Paul.

(1963 [1953]) *Le Materialisme rationnel*, Paris: PUF.

(1950 [1936]) *La Dialectique de la durée*, Paris: Boivin.

(1948) *La Terre et les rêveries de la volonté: essai sur l'imagination des forces*, Paris: Jose Corti.

(1937) *L'Expérience de l'espace dans la physique contemporaine*, Paris: PUF.

(1933) *Les Intuitions atomistiques: essai de classification*, Paris: Boivin.

(1932) *Le Pluralisme coherent de la chimie moderne*, Paris: Vrin.

(1932) *L'Intuition de l'instant: étude sur la 'Siloë' de Gaston Roupnel*, Paris: Stock.

(1929) *La Valeur inductive de la relativité*, Paris: Vrin.

Further reading

Chimisso, Christina (2001), *Gaston Bachelard: Critic of Science and the Imagination*, London: Routledge.

Lecourt, Dominique (1974), *Bachelard ou le jour et la nuit*, Paris: Grasset.

McAllester Jones, Mary (1991), *Gaston Bachelard: Subversive Humanist. Texts and Readings*, Madison: University of Wisconsin Press.

Smith, Roch Charles (1982), *Gaston Bachelard*, Boston: Twayne.

Tiles, Mary (1984), *Bachelard, Science and Objectivity*, Cambridge: Cambridge University Press.

MIKHAIL BAKHTIN (1895–1975)

Mikhail Bakhtin is, according to some estimations, one of the greatest theoreticians of literature of the twentieth century (Todorov 1984: ix). Both the historical range of his writing and the political conditions under which he wrote (particularly the political repression under Stalin) have made Bakhtin a social philosopher of some magnitude.

Born in November 1895, Bakhtin took a degree in classics and philology at the University of Petrograd in 1918. Largely for political reasons, he lived much of his life in self-imposed obscurity, taking up a professorship at the remote Mordovia State Teachers College in 1936, where, apart from one interruption in the 1940s due to rumours of a political purge, he taught until 1961. Despite his low political profile, Bakhtin was arrested in 1929 for alleged involvement in the underground Russian Orthodox Church and sentenced to six years' internal exile in Kazakhstan where he worked as a bookkeeper. By the 1960s, Bakhtin had become a cult figure in Russia, his 1929 work on Dostoyevsky having been rediscovered and his best-known book on Rabelais – initially submitted as a doctoral thesis in the 1940s – being published for the first time in the Soviet Union in 1965. With the renewed interest in his work, Bakhtin began working in the early 1970s on a number of projects – such as one on the philosophical bases of the human sciences – which remained unfinished at his death in March 1975.

Work Method and Periods of Thought

Bakhtin's intellectual trajectory and his practice of writing are quite exceptional. Not only did he often rework partially completed pieces and continue to elaborate already formulated concepts in a different way – so that his trajectory is less a straight line than a spiral – but, in addition, there is a controversy concerning the authorship of a number of books suspected of having been written by him, but published under the names of his friends, V.N. Voloshinov and R.N. Medvedev. The most notable of these are *Freudianism and Marxism and the Philosophy of Language* by Voloshinov, and *The Formal Method in Literary Studies* by Medvedev.

Questions of attribution aside, most scholars agree that Bakhtin's work can be divided into three main periods. (1) Early essays on ethics and aesthetics; (2) Books and articles on the history of the novel; (3) Posthumously published essays which again take up the themes of the second period. Despite the careful scholarship that is now being undertaken to show the depth of his thought, it remains true that, outside a circle of specialists, Bakhtin is best known in the West, first, for his notion of carnival, which comes from his study of Rabelais; second, for the concept of the dialogical, polyphonic novel that derives from Bakhtin's study of Dostoyevsky; and finally, for terms, such as 'chronotope' and 'novelistic discourse' which derive from his collected essays on the theory of the novel (see Bakhtin 1981).

Rabelais and Carnival

In his Rabelais study, the first of his works to be translated into English, Bakhtin focuses on the carnival as it existed in the pre-to mid-Renaissance period (Rabelais (1494–1553) wrote his most important works in the early 1530s). Rabelais, for Bakhtin, continues the carnival tradition, while adding his own innovations. What then is carnival?

The most important aspect of carnival is laughter. However, carnival laughter cannot be equated with the specific forms it takes in modern consciousness. It is not simply parodic, ironical, or satirical. Carnival laughter has no object. It is ambivalent. Ambivalence is the key to the structure of carnival. The logic of carnival is as Kristeva has shown, not the true or false, quantitative and causal logic of science and seriousness but the qualitative logic of ambivalence where the actor is also the spectator, destruction gives rise to creativity, and death is equivalent to rebirth.

Carnival, then, is neither private nor specifically oppositional, as it is in the period just prior to, and during, Romanticism. In no sense is carnival to be understood as an event that is officially sanctioned, or simply as a holiday period – a break from the normal labour of everyday life; nor is carnival a festival which reinforces the prevailing regime of everyday life, with its power hierarchy, and striking contrast between rich and poor. Carnival, in short, is not the result of officialdom (which is always serious) reinforcing its own power on the principle of 'bread and circuses'. Rather, the people are the carnival, and officialdom, like everyone else, is subject to its rituals and its laws – the Church as well as the Crown. To put it in a nutshell: carnival is not simply negative; it has no utilitarian motive. It is, to repeat, ambivalent.

Consequently, rather than a spectacle to be observed, carnival is the hilarity lived by everyone. And this raises the question as to whether there can be, strictly speaking, a theory of carnival. For there is no life outside the carnival. The people in it are both actors and spectators simultaneously. And as the festival laughter of carnival is also directed against those who laugh, the people in it are both subjects and objects of laughter. This laughter is general, has a philosophical basis, and embraces death (cf. the themes of macabre laughter and the grotesque) as well as life. As such, carnival laughter is one of the 'essential forms of truth concerning the world' (Bakhtin 1984a: 66). Bakhtin remarks, however, that with the modern era, laughter has been reduced to one of the 'low genres'. Carnival itself, on the other hand, embraces lowness. Degradation, debasement, the body and all its functions – but particularly defecation, urination and copulation – are part and parcel of the ambivalent carnival experience. The body, then, is part of this ambivalence. It is not closed in and private, but open to the world. Similarly, the proximity between the womb and the tomb is not repressed, but, like reproduction, is celebrated, as 'lowness' in general is celebrated. The body only becomes 'finished' (that is, private) according to our author, in the Renaissance.

Carnival figures, such as the clown, who exists on the border between art and life, experiences, such as madness, and the figure of the 'mask', which does not hide but reveals, all illuminate the ambivalent, all-embracing logic of carnival. Of the mask, Bakhtin writes that it is 'connected with the joy of change and reincarnation, with gay relativity and with the merry negation of uniformity and similarity' (Bakhtin 1984a: 39). The mask in the eighteenth century of course became a symbol – especially in the work of Rousseau – of everything that was false and inauthentic. The mask, in effect, was always the mask of hypocrisy. With carnival ambivalence, the mask is always *obviously* distorting. That it is covering up and transforming its object is clearly understood. The mask undermines the notion of being as identical with itself; it both reveals and plays with contradiction, and in so doing begins to encapsulate the ambivalence of the carnival as practice. As Bakhtin says: 'The mask is related to transition, metamorphosis, the violation of natural boundaries, to mockery and familiar nicknames. It contains the playful element of life' (Bakhtin 1984a: 40). For Kristeva, the mask signals the loss of individuality and the assumption of anonymity, and thus the assumption of a multitude of identities. Hence the mask always plays with the symbolic so as to unhinge it from its fixed and rigid forms. The mask is the incarnation of movement and change. It is never serious unless we understand that to refuse to give seriousness absolute power is a serious matter. The exhortation of the carnival is, as a result, that we should enter the game of life, masked: that is, ambivalently, irreverently, and with a spirit of laughter.

Carnival, in its ambivalence, focuses attention on the people as the arena of participation. As participation, it is the circumvention of representation. Carnival, then, makes the people the most important element in life. The people, as participants in the carnival as participation, come to embody the universal. This is why the universal is practical and tends to escape objectification. Again, while carnival laughter can find a place for seriousness (even if this be to mock it – 'not a single saying of the Old Testament was left unchallenged', says Bakhtin (Bakhtin 1984a: 86) – seriousness cannot find a place for laughter). If we equate seriousness with objectification (all seriousness is self-conscious), this would mean that laughter cannot be objectified, cannot be theorised.

Carnival logic (the logic of ambivalence) is not restricted to the limitation of binary oppositions which set limits, but is equivalent of the power of continuum (positive *and* negative). The carnival logic is revealed closer to home when we realise that any speech act is essentially bivalent (both One and Other), so that, for instance, the seriousness of academic discourse is based on the repression of ambivalence.

Polyphony: The Dialogical Text

In his study of Dostoyevsky, Bakhtin argues that the Russian writer's fiction has a 'polyphonic' structure in that – like carnival – it includes the other's voice within itself. For example, with a text like *The Brothers Karamazov*, 'the other's discourse gradually, stealthily penetrates the consciousness and the speech of the hero' (Bakhtin 1984b: 222).

For Bakhtin, novelistic discourse should not be understood as the word of communication studied by linguistics, but is rather the 'dynamic milieu' in which the exchange (dialogue) takes place. In terms of linguistics, the word for Bakhtin is translinguistic: the intersection of meanings rather than a fixed point, or a single meaning. While parody, irony, and satire are, for instance, clear examples of the word in Bakhtin's sense (we must resort to the translinguistic/semiotic dimension in order to interpret them), Dostoyevsky's work leads us to the same kind of insight by way of the dialogical word which includes the other's word within itself. This is a polyphonic word in the sense that polyphony, too, has no fixed point but is the interpenetration of sounds. Polyphony is multiple, not singular it includes what would be excluded by a representation of it.

Bakhtin reads Dostoyevsky in the spirit of carnival with its double logic. Justice therefore cannot be done to Dostoyevsky's writing by reducing it to a story with characters, as is typical of the closed structure of the epic, and also fundamental to what Bakhtin called a 'monological' text. Most simply understood, a monological text has a single (mono-), homogeneous, and relatively uniform logic. It lends itself very easily to an ideological appropriation; for the essential aspect of ideology is the message conveyed, and not the *way* the message arises and is articulated within the milieu of the word. For Bakhtin, Tolstoy's works are most often monological in this sense. By contrast, in *The Brothers Karamazov*, not only words create meaning but also the contextual relationship between them (e.g. Ivan's 'poem', 'The Legend of the Grand Inquisitor', and Smerdyakov's confession).

All of Bakhtin's approach directs attention to the way the novel is constructed – its *mise-en-scène* – rather than the intrigue, or story, or the particular views, ideology, or feelings of the author. Quite simply: the author becomes the site of the *mise-en-scène* of the novel. The polyphonic novel makes this more explicit than other forms, but in almost every novelistic genre, there are a number of languages in operation, each one utilised by the author. As Bakhtin explains:

> The author is not to be found in the language of the narrator, not in the normal literary language to which the story opposes itself . . .– but rather, the author utilizes now one language, now another, in order to avoid giving himself up wholly to either of them; he makes use of this verbal give-and-take, this dialogue of languages at every point in his work, in order that he himself might remain as it were neutral with regard to language, a third party in a quarrel between two people.
>
> (Bakhtin: 1981: 314)

Bakhtin and Structuralism

Although Bakhtin formally distanced himself from structuralism and semiotics, his refusal to embrace the ideology of the author's intentions as a way of explaining the meaning of a work of art, places him much closer to a structural approach than might at first appear. For Bakhtin, the author is an empty space where the drama would take place – or better: the author is the dramatisation itself. In this sense, Bakhtin founded a dynamic view of structure, certainly one with more dynamism than what developed in Russia under the aegis of the Russian formalists. Indeed, Bakhtin's concern to emphasise the open-ended, unfinished quality of Dostoyevsky's novels (and even the unfinished quality of much of his own writing, both published and unpublished), together with his concern to show that (static) form was never separable from (dynamic) content, means that his is a structural approach that refuses to be limited by a privileging of the synchronic over the diachronic. Similarly, in his critique of Saussure's distinction between *langue* and *parole*, Bakhtin claims that Saussure ignores speech genres, and that this renders doubtful the usefulness of *langue* in explaining the essential working of language. Furthermore, Bakhtin rejects what he sees as the structuralist tendency to analyse texts as though they were completely self-contained units whose meaning could be established independently of context. Rather, any attempt to understand *parole* must take into account the circumstances, assumptions and the time of the enunciation of the utterance. In effect, Bakhtin urges that account must be taken of the contingency of language.

Chronotope

The concern for the contingency of language led Bakhtin to formulate his theory of the 'chronotope'. As the term implies, both space and time are at issue, and Bakhtin sought to reveal the way in which the history of the novel constituted different forms of the chronotope. Inspired by Einstein's theory of relativity, Bakhtin defines the chronotope as the 'intrinsic connectedness of temporal and spatial relationships in literature'. He goes on to show the variations in the chronotope in the history of the novel. The novels of Greek Romance, for example (second and sixth centuries AD), are characterised by 'adventure time' which is played out through the obstacles (storm, shipwreck, illness, etc.) preventing the union between the two lovers taking place. The plot is often played out over several geographical locations, and the manners and customs of the people within these locations are described. In the idyllic novel (e.g. Rousseau), space and time are inseparable: 'Idyllic life and its events are inseparable from this concrete, spatial corner of the world where the fathers and grandfathers lived and where one's children will live' (Bakhtin 1981: 225). The idyllic world is thus self-sufficient, homogeneous and identical with itself – almost outside time and change. This implies that in the polyphonic, dialogical novel, time is a heterogeneous, almost unrepresentable element. Furthermore, time will tend to render (Euclidean) space more fluid, so that the time of relativity becomes a possible analogy.

Clearly, the chronotope is a mechanism for classifying various genres of the novel as well as a means of constituting a history and theory of the novel. And it should be remembered that for all his interest in the particular details of the speech and other events of everyday life, Bakhtin was a thinker who used the broadest canvas possible to develop his theory of literary production. In fact the effect of Bakhtin's use of macro-categories like 'chronotope' and 'genre' is to render invisible the unique, the singular, the individual and the unclassifiable. Some critics, such as Booth, have suggested that Bakhtin generalises at the expense of a detailed exegesis of the great variety of works concerned. Moreover, in his description of genres like 'Greek romance' or the 'Idyllic novel', he adopts a formal approach very like that of the early structuralists (e.g. Propp), emphasis being placed on the individuality and distinctiveness of the homogeneous structure of the genre, with the result that the indivi-duality of the works which make it up becomes invisible. One might go further and suggest that the problem of genre is that it risks turning individual works of art into myth. For myth exhibits a homogeneous, and relatively undifferentiated structure; this allows it to be communicated to a vast audience who, it is true, may then appropriate it in their own way.

Perhaps if Bakhtin had a more dynamic view of structure, and had seen the structure of genres as a kind of grammar which constituted the precondition of specific works done under its aegis, he would not have given the impression of the lack of rigour which comes with a procrustean attempt to place all the works of an era under the same classificatory umbrella.

References

Bakhtin, Mikhail (1981), *The Dialogic Imagination, Four Essays by M. M. Bakhtin*, trans. Caryl Emerson and Michael Holquist, Austin: University of Texas Press.
—— (1984), *Rabelais and his World*, trans. Hélène Iswolsky, Bloomington: Indiana University Press.
—— (1984a), *Problems of Dostoevsky's Poetics*, trans. Caryl Emerson, Min-neapolis and London: University of Minnesota Press.
Todorov, Tzvetan (1984b), *Mikhail Bakhtin: The Dialogical Principle*, trans. Wlad Godzich, Manchester: Manchester University Press.

See also: **Kristeva, Lévi-Strauss**

Bakhtin's major writings

(1984a [1929]) *Problems of Dostoyevsky's Poetics*, trans. Caryl Emerson, Man-chester: Manchester University Press.

(1984b [1940]) *Rabelais and His World*, trans. Hélène Iswolsky, Bloomington: Indiana University Press.

(1981) *The Dialogic Imagination, Four Essays by M.M. Bakhtin (1965–75)*, trans. Caryl Emerson and Michael Holquist, Austin: University of Texas Press.

(1987) *Speech Genres and Other Late Essays*, trans. Vern W. McGee, Austin: University of Texas, second paperback printing.

(1976 [1927]) with V.N. Volishonov, *Freudianism: A Marxist Critique*, trans. I.R. Titunik, New York: Academic Press.

(1929 [1973]) with V.N. Volishonov, *Marxism and the Philosophy of Language*, trans. L. Matejka and I.R. Titunik, New York: Seminar Press.

Further reading

Clark, Katerina, Holquist, Michael (1984) *Mikhail Bakhtin*, Cambridge, Mass. and London: The Belknap Press of Harvard University Press.

Gardiner, Michael (ed.) (2003), *Michael Bakhtin*, London, Thousand Oaks, CA: Sage, 4 vols.

Kristeva, Julia (1982), 'Word, dialogue and novel' in *Desire in Language: A Semiotic Approach to Literature and Art*, trans. Thomas Gora, Alice Jardine and Leon S. Roudiez, Oxford: Basil Blackwell.

Morson, Gary Saul and Emerson, Caryl (1990), *Mikhail Bakhtin: Creation of a Prosaics*, Stanford: Stanford University Press.

Todorov, Tzvetan (1984), *Mikhail Bakhtin: The Dialogical Principle*, trans. Wlad Godzich, Manchester: Manchester University Press.

MARCEL MAUSS (1872–1950)

It would be hard to underestimate the intellectual significance of Marcel Mauss for at least two generations of French thinkers. Beginning with Bataille, Dumézil, and Lévi-Strauss, Mauss has also been a crucial reference point for a new generation which would include Bourdieu, Baudrillard, Derrida and Foucault. While Mauss's theory of the gift and the nature of exchange in so-called archaic societies has particularly occupied thinkers inspired by structuralism, like Lévi-Strauss, the debt of others like Bourdieu and Foucault is more related to Mauss's thinking about techniques of the body. *Habitus* is a term that Mauss remarked upon prior to its reworking by Bourdieu; and Foucault's notion of a 'technology of the body' could be easily derived from Mauss's view that bodily techniques are, effectively, a 'technique without an instrument' – the French term, *technique* connoting technology, not just the technical. A technique of the body is thus a technology to the extent that it can be transferred across areas of activity, and because, to do this, it must be at least partially objectified (i.e. formalised).

Life and Intellectual Trajectory

Mauss, a nephew and pupil of Émile Durkheim, was born in Epinal in 1872, and died in Paris in 1950. Like his uncle, he grew up in a Jewish orthodox atmosphere. In 1895, he came third in the *agrégation* in philosophy, after which he studied Greek, Latin, Hebrew and Ancient Iranian at the École Pratique des Hautes Études.[1] By 1902, Mauss had become a *maître assistant* at the École Pratique des Hautes Etudes, Fifth Section, where he taught in the 'history of religions of uncivilized peoples'. At the outbreak of the First World War, Mauss volunteered for service and served as an interpreter in the British army, and was decorated for bravery with two citations and two military crosses. His experience in the army gave Mauss the opportunity to study the different bodily techniques observable in British, Australian and French troops. Later, in his writings on the techniques of the body, Mauss remarked on the capacity of Australian soldiers for sitting on their haunches during rest periods, while he, a Frenchman, had to remain upright; for he, like many Europeans, lacked this ability. Unlike his uncle, Mauss was more of a Bohemian with socialist aspirations; he collected exotica, championed the work of Debussy and Picasso and was always open to new ways of understanding social and cultural forms. In 1925, Mauss set up the Institut d'Ethnologie, and in 1930 he was elected to the Collège de France until his retirement in 1940.

In 1899, Mauss published, with H. Hubert, *Sacrifice: Its Nature and Function*. Mauss's renown and influence, however, came largely through articles he published in the Durkheimian sociological journal, *L'Année sociologique*, rather than through any monograph. He was also a highly respected and engaging teacher. According to Georges Dumézil, who had very little time for Durkheim – Mauss's mentor – Mauss rarely prepared his courses, but he had a taste for the universal supported by an enormous knowledge which knew few boundaries.

Gift and Exchange

Due no doubt in part to Claude Lévi-Strauss's famous *Introduction to the work of Marcel Mauss* (Lévi-Strauss 1983: IX-LII), Mauss's best-known work is his *Essai sur le don* (trans. *The Gift*) first published in the 1923–24 volume of the *Année Sociologique*. Although, ostensibly, the gift can be distinguished from a commodity (the basis of exchange in a money economy) in that it apparently does not entail reciprocity, in fact, Mauss argues, the gift implies a threefold obligation: to give, to receive and to reciprocate. Thus, in light of the ethnographies of a wide range of societies – but particularly those describing the potlatch in America, the *kula* in the Pacific and the *hau* in New Zealand – Mauss shows that the gift is the very foundation of social life – so refined and differentiated are the forms of behaviour that are carried out in its wake. The gift, then, is never a simple exchange of goods. It involves honour and a particular use of time; it is a mechanism touching upon every aspect of life ensuring the circulation of people (women) as well as goods. Thus exchange can be seen in marriage, festivals, ceremonial rites, military service, dances, feasts, fairs and the like. Even when exchange has to do exclusively with objects of some kind, it has to be recalled that objects are not simply the dead, inanimate things they are assumed to be in highly differentiated, capitalist societies. Rather, objects have a 'soul', a spirituality, so that an object is not simply an object; conversely, while human beings have a spirituality – most often called *mana* – about them, they are also objects which can therefore be part of the exchange system.

Prestige of the Giver: Potlatch

Instead of the accumulation of wealth for the purpose of accumulating more wealth that is characteristic of capitalist societies, societies of the gift are characterised by expenditure – giving – and the gaining of prestige. The essence of the North American potlatch, for example, is the obligation to give. Prestige and honour are gained and maintained by the one who can expend to the greatest possible extent, thus placing the receiver under an obligation to match the prodigality of the giver. At least this is so for as long as the potlatch does not turn into an orgy of pure destruction, that is, into a pure expenditure without return. In general, however, gifts must be reciprocated with interest, thereby raising the stakes ever higher.

As to the nature of things exchanged in the system of the gift, it would be wrong to assume that these are limited to material goods. Indeed, a key point made by Mauss is that virtually everything – services, sexual favours, festivals, dances, etc. – is drawn into the system. For an individual or group not to engage in the obligations implied by the gift system is to run the risk of war.

While a capitalist society is not structured according to the general social obligations attached to the gift, it is, says Mauss, reasonable to say, in light of historical evidence, that Western systems of law and economy originally emerged from institutions similar to those of societies dominated by the gift. In modern capitalist societies, then, an impersonal and calculating attitude developed, whereby a notion of monetary equivalence came to supplant the moral obligation and battle for prestige integral to the gift. Rather than invading the whole of life's activities, the development of law and a money economy allowed exchange to be formalised and limited to the public domain through the separation of the public from the private sphere.

Mauss concludes his study by summarising a number of key points. First of all, he notes, the gift still permeates 'our own' societies, but in a much reduced form. Special religious occasions, weddings and birthdays can still generate a substantial gift-giving and the sense that one should reciprocate with interest, that 'we must give back more than we have received' (Mauss 1990: 65). Not to be able to reciprocate can leave the receiver in a position of inferiority *vis-à-vis* the giver. Whether the meaning of charity and social welfare should perhaps be viewed in this light is an open question; for while there may be an element of reciprocity and pride at stake, charity is also backed by a utilitarian motive that is absent in gift-exchange. Those societies whose social structure is entirely based on the gift, however, have no space which is not subject to exchange. Human beings are also part of this exchange system. This is a notion of exchange that has to be clearly separated from utilitarian motives. Much more than economic exchanges in so-called highly differentiated societies with a marked distinction between public and private, the gift is an end in itself; for even though it is indeed a question of a person's *mana*, or indefinable quality of prestige which is at stake, this is inseparable from the act of giving (and receiving) itself. 'To give is to show one's superiority' (Mauss 1990: 74). Because it animates the social structure, touching every facet of life, the gift is an example of what Mauss calls a 'total social fact'. Thus while occurring at an individual, or group, level the gift exchange is, *par excellence*, a social fact. Individual and group fortunes are inextricably tied to the fortunes of the society as a whole. To understand the implications and significance of an individual act of gift-giving, it is thus necessary to understand the nature of the whole social structure. The very triangular structure of the gift, entailing giving, receiving and reciprocating, clearly evokes the idea of the total social fact.

Mana

The notion of *mana*, deemed to be linked to the indefinable quality of prestige in the system of the gift, had been discussed in Mauss's earlier essay on magic (Mauss 1972). There, the author remarks that *mana* is one of the troubling concepts of which anthropology had thought it had rid itself. *Mana* is a vague term, obscure and impossible to define rigorously. There are indeed, Mauss comments, a veritable 'infinity of manas' (Mauss 1972: 111). *Mana* is not simply a force, a being, but also 'an action, a quality and a state'. The word is at one and the same time, 'a noun, an adjective, a verb' (Mauss 1972: 108). *Mana* cannot be the object of experience because it absorbs all experience. In this, it is of the same order as the sacred. For Mauss, this is to say that *mana* has a spirituality which is equivalent to collective thought, which is the equivalent of society as such.

For its part, magic is irregular and tends towards something that is prohibited by society. Magic is a private, secret and singular act. It is isolated, mysterious, furtive and fragmented. It encapsulates the non-social side of the social world, and is indeed at one and the same time a threat to the social and the limit which gives it meaning. Magicians can be women, children or foreigners – any 'non-professional' being.

Mana and magic thus raise the issue of the precise nature of the social bond. For Lévi-Strauss the very fact that *mana* is difficult to define suggests that it is essentially indefinable; or rather, because *mana* can take on a multiplicity of meanings, it is a 'floating signifier' – an indefinable 'x' – analogous to the 'zero' phoneme brought to light by structural linguistics. Such a phoneme has no meaning in itself, but can take on a variety of meanings, depending on the context, and its differential relationship with other terms. This implies that *mana* can only be interpreted synchronically, at a given moment, rather than in an evolutionary sense where meaning would be derived from the past – that is, diachronically. Equating *mana* with the 'floating signifier' was Lévi-Strauss's way, at the time of his famous 1950 essay on Mauss, of claiming Mauss for structuralism.

A number of additional consequences follow from a structural interpretation of *mana* and the gift. For instance, light can be thrown on the nature of the social evoked by *mana* and the gift as a 'total social fact' if the social is understood to be analogous to the structure of language. In this way, the social would not be immediately revealed by the presentation of social facts, any more than the grammar of a natural language is immediately present to the consciousness of a native speaker. Similarly, Lévi-Strauss argues, the fact of exchange is not immediately present in empirical observation, which only furnishes three obligations: give, receive and reciprocate. The notion of exchange explains the relationship between the three elements; it does not exist transparently in the facts, but must be constructed from the facts.

Techniques of the Body

In another important study, Mauss's historical and contextual approach to social phenomena is perhaps even more pronounced. Thus in his discussion of the 'techniques of the body' (Mauss 1973: 70–88), he calls on the notion of *habitus* (Mauss 1973: 73) in order to throw light on the way that bodily activities are specific to a given culture and society. Two elements must be present for there to be a bodily technique: first, the technique must be efficacious and so capable of producing a desired result; and, second, it must be inscribed within a tradition which makes its transmission possible. In short, a technique is something that can be transmitted. For Mauss, bodily techniques are not spontaneous nor are they simply anatomical or physiological. To illustrate the degree to which supposedly natural acts can in fact be the result of the technique, Mauss relates how he actually taught a child who was suffering from a cold to spit.

Every bodily technique has its form. The error of the past has been, Mauss argues, to think that there is a technique only when there is an instrument. Bodily techniques are effectively like technology without an instrument. The framework of a technique allows one to explain the significance of the multitude of small actions carried out by each individual every day of their lives. Technique brings all these taken-for-granted instances into an explanatory framework so that they cease to be arbitrary and the result of pure chance. Michel Foucault's concept of 'techniques of the self' seems to be clearly presaged in Mauss's insights in this domain. The pertinence of Mauss is particularly in evidence for the contemporary understanding of practices when we recall that he distinguishes specific categories of behaviour from techniques of the body – from so-called mechanical acts of a 'physical-chemical' type. These are also traditional and efficacious acts in the sphere of religion, symbolic acts, juridical acts – acts relating to communal life, moral acts; in other words, acts which for Mauss cannot be reduced to a purely physical event.

Modern thought, however (cf. Foucault, Bourdieu, Althusser) has questioned the opposition between a supposedly self-conscious symbolic act, and a physical technique. In fact, following Pascal's description of acquiring faith – 'Kneel down, move your lips in prayer, and you will believe' (quoted in Althusser 1971: 158) – the claim is made that even the most symbolic act is inextricably bound to a physical technique – even to the extent that the technique is seen to be prior to the symbolic meaning. And as if to confirm that he himself doubted the validity of keeping the symbolic aspect separate from the physical, Mauss concludes his reflection on bodily techniques by saying that

> I believe precisely that at the bottom of all our mystical states there are techniques of the body which have not been studied but which were perfectly studied in China and in India, even in very remote periods. ... I think that there are necessarily biological means of entering into 'communication with God'.
>
> (Mauss 1973: 87)

Mauss, let it be reiterated, is a largely unacknowledged source of this aspect of contemporary thought concerned with the body.

Individuality

Finally, we should note with Lévi-Strauss that Mauss, even more than Durkheim, showed that an individuality, while not reducible to the social, always has a social expression. In short, because social facts are only manifest in individuals, society is in the individual as much as, or even more than, the individual is in society. In reality, therefore, the tedious debate about whether the individual is prior to society, or whether society is prior to the individual comes to an end with Marcel Mauss. It now remains for those who have come after him to recognise this.

Note

1 This and the following biographical details on Mauss are derived from Anthony Richard Gringeri, Jr. (1990).

References

Althusser, Louis (1971), *Lenin and Philosophy and Other Essays*, trans. Ben Brewster, London: New Left Books.

Mauss, Marcel (1990), *The Gift: The Form and Reason for Exchange in Archaic Societies*, trans. W.D. Halls, London: Routledge.

Gringeri, Jr., Anthony Richard (1990), 'Twilight of the Sun Kings: French anthropology from modernism to postmodernism, 1925–50', unpublished Ph.D. thesis, Berkeley: University of California.

Lévi-Strauss, Claude (1983), 'Introduction à l'oeuvre de Marcel Mauss' in Marcel Mauss, *Sociologie et anthropologie*, Paris: Presses Universitaires de France. 'Quadrige', eighth edn.

—— (1972), *A General Theory of Magic*, trans. Robert Brain, London and Boston: Routledge & Kegan Paul.

—— (1973), 'Techniques of the body', trans. Ben Brewster, *Economy and Society*, 2, 1.

See also: **Bataille, Bourdieu, Dumézil, Lévi-Strauss**

Mauss's major writings

(2003) *On Prayer*, trans. Susan Leslie, New York and Oxford: Durkheim Press/Berghahn.

(1990 [1923–24]) *The Gift: The Form and Reason for Exchange in Archaic Societies*, trans. W.D. Halls, London: Routledge.

(1983) *Sociologie et anthroplogie*, Paris: Presses Universitaires de France, 'Quadridge'.

(1981 [1899]) (with Henri Hubert) *Sacrifice: Its Nature and Function*, trans. W.D. Halls, Chicago: University of Chicago Press.

(1973 [1935]) 'Techniques of the body', trans. Ben Brewster, *Economy and Society*, 2, 1.

(1972 [1902–3]) *A General Theory of Magic*, trans. Robert Brain, London: Routledge.

Further reading

Allen, N.J. (2000), *Categories and Classifications: Maussian Reflections on the Social*, New York and Oxford: Berghahn Books.

Bloor, David (1982), 'Durkheim and Mauss revisited: Classification and the sociology of knowledge', *Studies in the History and Philosophy of Science*, 13, 4.

Carrier, James (1991), 'Gifts, commodities, and social relations: A Maussian view of exchange', *Sociological Forum*, 6, 1 (March).

Carrithers, Michael, Collins, Steven and Lukes, Steven eds (1985), *Category of the Person: Anthropology, Philosophy, History*, Cambridge: Cambridge University Press. As well as essays on Mauss, this book contains a translation of Mauss's 'A Category of the human mind'.

Gane, Mike, ed. (1992), *Radical Sociology of Durkheim and Mauss*, London: Routledge.

Goderlier, Maurice (1999) *The Enigma of the Gift*, Cambridge: Polity.

Lévi-Strauss, Claude (1987), *Introduction to the Work of Marcel Mauss*, trans. Felicity Baker, Routledge & Kegan Paul: Boston.

Ritter, Henning (1990), 'The ethnological revolution: On Marcel', trans. John Burns, *Comparative Civilizations Review*, 22 (Fall).

PHENOMENOLOGY

While phenomenology initially aspired to gain access in thought to the things themselves, and focused on the role of consciousness, it also aspired to be rigorous and scientific and to return to what was essential. To do this, Husserl developed a methodological strategy called the *epochē*, which involved bracketing out, or disconnecting from the natural, everyday contingent world.

Subsequently, Heidegger brought back the everyday world into consideration as the realm of beings, or of existence, which is distinct from but related to, being. It is the plethora of philosophical questions that related to this approach (questions of language, technology, science, art, thinking) that provided a key impetus to the trajectory of post-structuralist thought.

MARTIN HEIDEGGER (1889–1976)

Martin Heidegger is as famous for changing the focus of philosophy and modern thought toward the notion of being as he is infamous for joining the Nazi party in the 1930s, becoming the *Rektor* of the University of Freiburg from 1933 – the year of Hitler's appointment as Chancellor – to 1934, and witnessing the withdrawal of Edmund Husserl's license to teach. Although he was subsequently critical of the way, as he saw it, that Nazi thought degenerated compared to its ideals, Heidegger was, concerning 'the final solution', always guarded and ambiguous about it in his public statements and writings. Because of the nature of his political involvement, Heidegger's biography is significant. We shall thus provide some details of this.

Elements of Heidegger's Biography

Born in 1889 in Messkirch, Baden, Germany, where he would be buried in 1976, Heidegger attended, in 1903, a Jesuit gymnasium in Constance. Subsequently, he would renounce his preparation for the novitiate and his Catholicism, but in his youth he seemed destined for things theological rather than philosophical.

In 1913, Heidegger completed his PhD dissertation entitled 'The Doctrine of Judgement in Psychologism', for which he was awarded a *summa cum laude*. Five years later, he presented his Habilitation dissertation, 'The Doctrine of Categories and Signification in Duns Scotus' and was made a *Privatdozent* in philosophy at Freiburg, meaning that he had a license to teach, but did not receive a regular salary.

During the Great War, Heidegger did various stints in the army, largely working with a meteorological unit.

In 1923 Heidegger was appointed as an associate at the University of Marburg. One of his students was Hannah Arendt (1906–75), with whom he had an affair.

Heidegger was eventually appointed professor of philosophy at Freiburg in 1928 and joined the Nazi party on 3 May 1933. Soon after, in July, Heidegger wrote to the ministry of education supporting anti-Semitism. In addition, he secretly denounced to authorities the professors of chemistry (Staudinger) and philosophy (Baumgarten).

During the War Heidegger continued to teach, giving courses on Nietzsche and nihilism in 1940, on Hölderlin's nationalist poem, *Der Ister* in 1942, and on Nietzsche's statement 'God is dead' in 1943. But he had his license to teach withdrawn at the end of hostilities due to his complicity with Nazism. The prohibition was lifted in 1949 and Heidegger was made professor emeritus at Freiburg.

In the 1950s and 1960s, Heidegger further developed his philosophy of language, poetry, thinking and Greek Philosophy. In September of 1966, 1968 and 1969, Heidegger gave three seminars, which cover the majority of his work, in Le Thor in Provence, France. These were attended by young philosophers such as Giorgio Agamben. The poet, Paul Celan, who was incredulous about Heidgger's Nazi past and wanted him to explain it, met Heidegger for the first time in Freiburg in July 1967.

Heidegger's Thought

Being and Beings

In a famous formulation, Heidegger distinguishes between being (*das Sein*) and beings (*das Seiende*), which is then equated with *Dasein* (being there; more colloquially: existence). His idea of difference is linked to this distinction: that is, the terms of ontological difference consist of the difference between being and existence. Heidegger's point is that there is a being of (all) particular beings in the world and that being cannot be reduced to a particular being. We are then not going to find being in a representation, objectification or scientific formulation; for the latter are applicable to beings as existence, *Dasein*, not to being as such. How to think being thus becomes the question of philosophy as thought (not as reason or calculation). It is this insight, the philosopher claims, which has been covered up in the West, at least since Roman times.

Science

Inspired by Husserl's pioneering work, Heidegger's work challenges the dominance of the quest for facts (existence) for their own sake – whether these be about the world or about the human. The reason for this is that a search for facts cannot do justice to the illumination of being, nor, as with Husserl, can such a focus allow for a consideration of the essence or foundation of things. Heidegger goes even further than Husserl; for while Husserl challenged facts, or at least put them out of play, he did not challenge the dominance of science. Indeed, Husserl wanted philosophy to be scientific. Heidegger, by contrast, is opposed to the sway science holds; for science does not think; it objectifies. In this vein, Heidegger is opposed to the dominance of epistemology and aesthetics, because these, in their own way, are systems of objectification and constitute the foundation of a sub-jectivism, a factual domain. Even Nietzsche fails the test here and has his philosophy classified as being ultimately subjectivist. Heidegger further argues that a return to tradition is necessary to reveal what it hides and to show how it can be used to reveal something new. In this regard the Heideggerian term, *Destruktion*, (destruction) is important and can be translated as 'de-construction' (see Inwood 1999: 181ff.), because it is not a matter of simply destroying tradition, but of making evident the congealed elements it brings to illumina-tion as well those things it seeks to obscure. The link to Derrida's term, 'deconstruction', should be noted here.

Thus, Heidegger's explicit aim in his most famous work, *Being and Time*, is to enable being to come into unconcealment after the domination of science – both natural and social – had added to its concealment.

Heidegger's philosophy of being also attempts to go beyond the 'subject–object' dichotomy found in the social sciences as 'ontic' sci-ences. The latter – each in its own speciality – would be concerned with society and nature as objects of knowledge and, in this light, these objects need to be explained and controlled. As explanation seeks the cause of an object's existence, there is always a strong functionalist and even reductionist tendency in the 'ontic' sciences.

Although Heidegger's thought is steeped in a thinking and a re-thinking of the unthought of the classical Greek philosophy of being, and of truth as *aletheia* (as an unveiling and a bringing into uncon-cealment), there are in his writings schematic statements regarding the state of the sciences in modern, industrial and in what we would now call post-industrial society based on information transfer and cybernetics. For instance, he frequently suggests that given the failure to grasp the link between technē and being, thinking has become logistical and thinks technology only as a means, particularly in its American incarnation.

Heidegger suggests that the nature of science is captured in Nietzsche's view that modernity is not dominated by science but by the scientific method. 'Method' becomes the basis upon which objects of knowledge and research are constituted. 'Method' is the 'project' of calculation which has organised the world in advance and made it accessible to experimentation and control. Again, 'method' is the condition of possibility of cybernetics (synthesis of man and machine) and information technology. Science also installs humanity in a 'closure'. 'Closure' means that humanity risks becoming totally turned in upon itself the more it believes in the domination by humanity for humanity of the world through method. Nothing, hypothetically, is to remain outside the human purview. In effect, the unshakeable faith in the sciences characteristic of modernity leads to the separation of humanity from its true destiny, which is always beyond it. Heidegger thus raises the prospect of a world of calculation and method which, as such, cannot think being because being is beyond the sciences. Being is a question, or a call, that can come to us despite being hidden by the obviousness of the 'being there' (*Dasein*) of everyday living. But being is also a gift, or a giving, bequeathed to humanity, and rendered visible in language by the '*es gibt*' of the German idiom of the English, 'there is'.

Technology and Thought

The age of technology is one that does not allow technology to appear as technology – to appear as it is, essentially speaking. For technology as an efficient means and, as incidental and contingent, is always involved with something other than itself. But technology is also intimately implicated with humanity understood as physically existing. Technology, indeed, assures the existence of the species, as it might assure the existence of every living creature on the face of the globe. There are as many ways of existing as there are human beings. Each mode of existence is different from, and yet equal to, any other. Equality and difference are thus by no means foreign to each other. Or rather, at the level of existence, everything is equivalent: one form of living is equal to another form of living – to the point where animal existence is equivalent to (although not necessarily the same as) that of human existence. Only when things are viewed from an essential perspective can one begin to discriminate between forms of existence.

The present age is pragmatic and instrumental, one where technics is charged with insuring that the outcome of every action is favourable to existence. In the political arena we see this when bureaucracy, or the bureaucratic ethos, ensures the survival (both physically and politically) of a political actor.

'The philosophical question', says Heidegger, 'must bear its necessity within itself; it must – if sufficiently unfolded – make this necessity itself visible' (Heidegger 1994:94). The philosophical question, unlike the anthropological question (the question of the social sciences – which Heidegger also calls the 'technologised sciences' (Heidegger 1972:59)), is always originary because of its concern with the question of being, or with the 'event of [the] Appropriation' (*Ereignis*) of being. Philosophy – in its proximity to thought and to language as poetry – is itself originary. Nothing, then, will be prior to the philosophical question (this is its necessity), whereas, anthropologically speaking, there is always something prior. The relationship between a prior reality and the theory of that reality is characteristic of the necessity of anthropology: that is, of sciences which place the human at the origin of culture and society. This necessity is often determining: it includes, as we have seen in relation to method, notions of explanation, calculation, inference, function and instrumental causality – the *causa efficiens* [the efficient cause] (Heidegger 1977:6). For Heidegger, *causa* comes from the verb *cadere*, to fall. The *causa efficiens* is also linked to language as a pure means of communication, as opposed to language as poetry. Here, Heidegger is challenging the dominance of the instrumentalism implied in a correspondence theory of truth.

Again, philosophy's necessity is centred on a questioning of anthropological necessity because the latter is linked to the correspondence theory of truth (truth as adequation as opposed to truth as *aletheia*). To truth as adequation – characteristic of the modern era – Heidegger poses truth as the coming into unconcealment of being: truth as *aletheia* – the bringing forth of something from obscurity into the clearing of illumination.

The disclosure or – in art – 'bringing forth out of concealedness', or poiesis, Heidegger links to technē as a mode of knowing and, from one angle at least, to the nature, or being of technology, a nature which is nothing technological. To bring something into illumination, and thus out of unconcealedness is to bring it into presence. The question – the one that we effectively started out with – is: what is the relation of philosophy to being and to truth, if it is not one where philosophy is dependent on being in the way that social science is dependent on its object? Is the autonomy of philosophy the other side of the dependency of anthropology? If there is dependency it suggests a prior set up of thought and its object. Heidegger is pains to argue against such a dependency saying that being and thought are two sides of one and the same coin. Rather than moving in propositions, thought is contained in the 'movement of showing', even though Heidegger, in a text such as *On Time and Being* (1972), seems frustrated by the apparent necessity of presenting his ideas in propositions. For, it is precisely the logic giving rise to propositions that the notions of being and time seek to challenge.

Although true thinking is aligned with showing and involves giving up metaphysics, thinking also takes place in metaphysics. Heidegger, for instance, often speaks, as we have said, in propositions. Propositions are the vehicles of his discussion of causality. In his 'The Word of Nietzsche' he points out that 'metaphysics is an epoch [withholding] of being itself', and it is also nihilism (Heidegger 1943: 110). Accordingly, thinking, *qua* thinking, has to give up – has to sacrifice – metaphysics.

Language, Thinking and Being

For Heidegger, poetry is connected to poiesis (knowing as making) and it has a privileged position in the realm of the arts. Language here is not essentially a lucid, undistorted communication between a sender and a receiver, as the utilitarian view would have it; rather, language as poetry is a thinking where poetry alone brings what is into view, into unconcealedness. Poetry discloses what is. 'Language itself is poetry in the essential sense' (Heidegger 1971: 74). 'The nature of poetry is the founding of truth' (1971: 75). Art, too, has a poetic origin. Language is poetry to the extent that poetry lets language be seen as language. Poetry reveals language as language, and thus language as the entity which brings being into unconcealment.

Closely connected, in Heidegger's thought, to the question of language as language (poetry) is 'neighbourhood' as the relation between poetry and thought. As well as being a 'naming' and so a revealing, poetry calls upon us to think. This calling is bound up with the Saying of language – language as Song.

Such a view is illuminated in Heidegger's response to Stefan George's poem, 'Words' (*'Das Wort'*) (Heidegger 1982: 139–56). Here, Heidegger's question is: can a linguistic approach do language justice? Can it tell us what language is in its essential being? A related question, one which concerns Heidegger in all of his writings in response to language, is: is there a word, or a saying, which could capture the being of language – language in its deployment, in its unfurling or unfolding, in its being enacted as language? Heidegger is not looking for a word about language, nor is he making language an object for science. For the question of language, like every profound question puts the questioner in question. The questioner is always already in language in speaking about it. Speaking about language is another instance of language speaking. Every science based on the modern, Cartesian version of the logos is in this situation. Heidegger does not want to engage with the being of language linguistically, scientifically – as method – because to think the word linguistically is to think it within the framework that conceals rather than reveals the nature of language as language.

To know language in its being is to know it neither as expression, nor as representation, nor, as we find in Noam Chomsky's explanation, as a psychological faculty. The aim is to avoid an encounter with poetic language in terms of anything exterior to it. The essence (*das Wesen*) of language brings us to the impossibility of finding the word for the essence of language. Poetry is the name of this impossibility.

Thus, Heidegger addresses this theme in a reading Stefan George's poem 'Words', which contains the following lines:

> And straight [away] it vanished from my hand,
> The treasure never graced my land ...
> So I renounced and sadly see:
> Where the word breaks off no thing may be.
>
> (Heidegger 1982:140)

The poet, Heidegger says – taking particular note of the poem's title and of these last two lines – has been on a journey searching for the word for the being of words: this is the treasure. The poet, not being able to find the word for the being of language, sees the treasure – which he lives within – slip from his grasp. He therefore renounces his project, sadly. But there is no sadness without joy, argues Heidegger. Is this renunciation equivalent to a silence regarding the word for the being of language? Is silence the word of language in its being? Heidegger answers that it is not. It is simply that the word for the being of language can find no equivalent of itself in the modern scientific logos.

Like the poet in the poem, Heidegger's meditation must make a sacrifice. It must think the word without having recourse to a representation of language. In certain respects it is an impossible meditation. Here we already sense a proximity between poetry and meditation as thinking. What truly calls on us to think is beyond us; but in its being beyond: thought is. How do we treat the reality of the word in the full awareness of the impossibility of ever thinking it essentially as an object of knowledge? Heidegger answers that we must listen to poetry. Poetry is the monologue of the enactment of language. Thus the impossibility of finding a word for language is also the possibility of letting language appear as language in poetry. The discipline of linguistics, by contrast is only satisfied by finding the word for language as language. It has a problem with poetry for it sees language as a code, and thus as an arbitrary system of differences, where (despite Saussure) what is essential to language does not appear.

We arrive at the point where language is giving in the sense that being is given to humanity in language, in the poetic word. To say: 'language gives' and that giving is essential to what it is, is to say that language is original: it gives and is given. There is nothing prior to language.

Giving

In *On Time and Being* (1972) and elsewhere, the notion of being becomes *Ereignis*: the Appropriating event. In this event, Heidegger says that being and time are related in a very specific way: being does not 'pass away' like a man who has died; nor does time encapsulate being. Rather, 'there is [*es gibt*: lit. 'it gives'] Being and there is time' (Heidegger 1972: 5). Yet if being is not a being, neither is it the totality, or unity of beings; it is not the One gathering the Many into its bosom, as is echoed, in amongst other places, Durkheim's notion of the social as the sacred. Rather, being is the '*es gibt*' as such: not the gift, but giving as such, which Heidegger also calls 'sending' (*schicken*, which echoes, as commentators have noted, *Geschick* (destiny) and *Geschichte* (history)) thus evoking the idea of time as a 'destining' (a 'beyond' or an 'ec-stasis'). Being is what is given – or is sent to us – as a destining. Destining is the receipt of the gift of being and the concomitant emergence of being into unconcealment. This is the 'presencing' of being. Presencing extends to what has been, so that 'Not every presencing is the present' (Heidegger 1972:13).

Consequently, we see that Heidegger is a thinker who, like Freud with the unconscious, Bergson with intuition, Deleuze with the virtual and Derrida with différance, does not equate thought with use, representation or objectification – that is, with the ego, writ large or small. 'Being' in Heidegger's thought cannot but be an extreme

challenge, both in its political overtones and its philosophical originality, in this, the first decade of twenty-first century capitalism.

References

Heidegger, Martin (1943), 'The Word of Nietzsche: "God is Dead"' in
(1977) *The Question Concerning Technology and Other Essays*, trans. William
Lovitt, New York: Harper Torchbooks.
—— (1971), 'The Origin of the Work of Art' in *Poetry, Language, Thought*,
trans. Albert Hofstadter, New York: Harper Torchbooks.
—— (1972), 'The end of Philosophy and the Task of Thinking' in *On Time
and Being*, trans. Joan Stambaugh, New York: Harper Torchbooks.
—— (1977), *The Question Concerning Technology and Other Essays*, trans.
William Lovitt, New York: Harper Torchbooks.
—— (1982), 'Words' in *On the Way to Language*, trans. Peter Hertz, *et al*,
New York: Harper and Row.
—— (1994), *Basic Questions of Philosophy. Selected 'Problems' of 'Logic'*, trans.
Richard Rojcewicz and André Schuwer, Bloomington and Indianapolis:
Indiana University Press.

See also: **Agamben, Badiou, Derrida, Husserl, Levinas, Merleau-Ponty,
Žižek**

Heidegger's major writings

(1996 [1927]) *Being and Time*, trans. Joan Stambaugh. Albany: State University of New York Press.
(1994 [1984]) *Basic Questions of Philosophy: Selected 'Problems' of 'Logic'*, trans.
Richard Rojcewicz and André Schuwer, Bloomington and Indianapolis:
Indiana University Press.
(1993a [1970]) with Eugene Fink, *Heraclitus Seminar 1966–1967*, trans.
Charles H. Seibert, Evanston, Illinois: Northwestern University Press.
(1993b) *Martin Heidegger's Basic Writings: From* Being and Time (1927) *to* The
Task of Thinking (1964), ed. David Farrell Krell, London: Routledge.
(1993c) *Basic Concepts*, trans. Gary E. Aylesworth, Bloomington and Indianapolis: Indiana University Press.
(1992a [1942–43]) *Parmenides*, trans. André Schuwer and Richard Rojcewicz, Bloomington: Indiana University Press.
(1992b [1989]) *The Concept of Time* (bilingual edition), trans. William
McNeill, Oxford, UK and Cambridge, Mass.: Blackwell.
(1991 [1961]) *Nietzsche* (two paperback volumes), ed. David Farrall Krell,
New York: Harper & Row.
(1990 [1929]) *Kant and the Problem of Metaphysics*, trans. Richard Taft, Bloomington: Indiana University Press.
(1988 [1930–31]) *Hegel's Phenomenology of Spirit*, trans. Parvis Emad and
Kenneth Maly, Bloomington: Indiana University Press.

(1984 [1928]) *Metaphysical Foundations of Logic*, trans. Michael Heim, Bloomington and Indianapolis: Indiana University Press.

(1990 [1929]) *Kant and the Problem of Metaphysics*, trans. Richard Taft, Bloomington: Indiana University Press.

(1982 [1927]) *Basic Problems of Phenomenology*, trans. Albert Hofstadter, Bloomington: Indiana University Press.

(1979 [1925]) *History of the Concept of Time: Prolegomena*, trans. Theodor Kisiel, Bloomington: Indiana University Press.

(1977 [1950, 1954]) *The Question Concerning Technology and Other Essays*, trans. William Lovitt, New York: Harper & Row.

(1975 [1954]) *Early Greek Thinking*, trans. David Ferrell Krell and Frank A. Capuzzi, New York: Harper & Row.

(1974 [1957]) *Identity and Difference* (bilingual edition), trans. Joan Stambaugh, New York: Harper and Row, Harper Torchbooks.

(1972 [1969]) *On Time and Being*, trans. Joan Stambaugh, New York: Harper and Row, Harper Torchbooks.

(1971a [1959]) *On the Way to Language*, trans. Peter D. Hertz and Joan Stambaugh, New York: Harper and Row, Harper Torchbooks.

(1971b) *Poetry, Language, Thought*, trans. Albert Hohofstadter, New York: Harper & Row.

(1970 [1950]) *Hegel's Concept of Experience*, trans. J. Glenn Gray and Fred D. Wieck, New York: Harper & Row.

(1968 [1954]) *What is Called Thinking*, trans. Fred D. Wieck and J. Glenn Gray, New York: Harper & Row.

(1967 [1962]) *What is a Thing?*, trans. W.B. Barton, Jr. and Vera Deutsch, Chicago: Henry Regnery Company.

(1966 [1959]) *Discourse on Thinking*, trans. John M. Anderson and E. Hans Freund, New York: Harper & Row.

(1959 [1953]) *An Introduction to Metaphysics*, trans. Ralph Manheim, Yale and London: Yale University Press.

(1958 [1956]) *What is Philosophy?* (bilingual edition), trans. William Kluback and Jean T. Wilde, New Haven, CT: College and University Press.

Further reading

Fóti, Véronique M. (1995), *Heidegger and the Poets: Poiēsis/Sophia/Technē*, New Jersey: Humanities Press, Paperback Edition.

Fynsk, Christopher (1993), *Heidegger: Thought and Historicity*, Ithaca and London: Cornell University Press.

Inwood, Michael (1999), *A Heidegger Dictionary*, Oxford, UK and Malden, Mass.: Blackwell Publishers.

Ott, Hugo (1993), *Martin Heidegger: A Political Life*, London: Harper Collins.

Schürmann, Reiner (1990), *Heidegger on Being and Acting: From Principles to Anarchy*, trans. Christine-Marie Gros in collaboration with the author, Bloomington: Indiana: University Press, Midland Book Edition.

Zimmerman, Michael. E. (1990), *Heidegger's Confrontation with Modernity: Technology, Politics, Art*, Bloomington and Indianapolis: Indiana University Press.

EDMUND HUSSERL (1859–1938)

Edmund Husserl, born in Prossnitz, Moravia, in 1859, was a contemporary of Freud (born 1856), of Ferdinand de Saussure (born
1857), of Émile Durkheim (born 1858) and of Henri Bergson (also
born 1859). Husserl died in April 1938 in Freiburg, where he taught
as professor of philosophy from 1916 to 1928. It was from Freiburg
University on 6 April 1933 that Husserl was suspended by Nazi
decree, and where Martin Heidegger, on 21 and 22 April 1933
respectively, was elected *Rektor* of the University of Freiburg and
joined the Nazi party.

Husserl began his academic career in mathematics. He studied
under the famous mathematicians, Kronecker and Weierstrass at the
University of Berlin from 1878 to 1881. In 1883, he took his PhD
with a thesis on variation calculus, from the University of Vienna. In
the autumn of 1887, Husserl published his *Habilitationsschrift, Über den
Begriff der Zahl, Psychologische Analysen* ('On the Concept of Number,
Psychological Analyses'). After which, in 1891, his work on Arithmetic entitled: *Philosophie der Arithmetik* (Philosophy of Arithmetic)
appeared. Characteristic of these works is Husserl's interest in foundations from a subjective or psychological perspective. Later, this
perspective evolved into the focus – after Brentano (1838–1917) – on
consciousness, as consciousness *of* something, in phenomenological
reflection. So, Husserl became concerned with foundations (of logic,
of the sciences), but not in an objectivist or positivist sense, rather in
the sense of establishing rigorous criteria for phenomenological
reflection centred in consciousness as 'consciousness of', also known
as 'intentionality'.

Eidetic Science

In light of these facts about Husserl's life and career, it is appropriate
to recall that in enunciating his notion of phenomenology, Husserl
distinguished between the science of facts and eidetic sciences, or
sciences concerned with essences, or the transcendental realm.
Arguably – especially in light of Husserl's influence on Heidegger and
the rest of his age – this was Husserl's most profound philosophical
gesture. In effect, Husserl reintroduced, in a growing climate of philosophical relativism and the influence of science, a concern for the
essential. And he did it in the face of the scepticism regarding the
essential as developed by the empiricist tradition. The moment
empiricism tries to justify itself, Husserl showed, it inevitably entered

the sphere of the essential. Truly consistent empiricists must thus eschew all discussion and debate concerning 'foundations' or the essential.

At stake, with regard to Husserl's insight, is less the philosophical status of empiricism and more the distinction between the factual and essential realms. Everything factual – including facts of nature – is contingent and so could have been otherwise. In a key passage, Husserl explains that:

> Individual existence of every sort is, quite universally speaking, '*contingent*'. It is thus; in respect of its essence it could have been otherwise. Even though definite laws of Nature obtain according to which if such and such real circumstances exist in fact then such and such definite consequences must exist in fact, such laws express only *de facto* rules which themselves could read quite otherwise.
>
> (Husserl 1982: 7, Husserl's emphasis)

Clearly, the essential is not contingent. As factual, biological existence, humanity is a contingent species. Each individual might not have been born, or the circumstances over which one has no control might have been different. Husserl's phenomenology itself is testimony to the dominance of the pragmatic and empirical approach to things. In other words, phenomenology's *raison d'être* is, with its ideal aspect, to be an alternative to relativist, and ultimately sceptical position of empiricist and pragmatic philosophies, philosophies wedded to the contingent, the accidental, and the natural, objective world. Empiricism can never provide certainty, while phenomenological reflection strives to transcend the world of contingent experience.

Phenomenological reflection – or phenomenological consciousness – is not psychological (a psychological experience). In psychology the psyche is given as an event in nature, while, for the phenomenologist, phenomenological consciousness remains within pure reflection (it asks questions about psychological consciousness in general). Furthermore, if consciousness were simply psychological consciousness – different for each individual – the possibility of objective knowledge would be ruled out. The search for certainty would have to be abandoned before it began. Phenomenology thus becomes a modified version of Descartes's cogito (putting out of action the reality/objectivity of the natural world, and focusing on what is certain).

In sum: phenomenology is a science, but not a natural science; it involves pure consciousness, but is not a psychology, and also comes to be called transcendental subjectivity; it is a transcendental science. Let us expand on this.

The Essential and Contingent Worlds

In everyday parlance – for mathematicians as for anyone else – 2 + 2 = 4 ... This is so in *everyday* parlance, which we shall begin by defining as the parlance of *today*, of the present moment understood unreflectively. In everyday parlance, 2 + 2 is not the same as (or identical to) 4, but is *equal to* 4. Or, to follow Husserl, a + b is not the same as, but is *equal to*, b + a. This principle goes to the heart of the synthetic truth of arithmetic, essentially speaking. 'Essentially' here means that the truth of arithmetic is a synthetic truth; the ideal possibility – the ideal basis – of arithmetic is its synthetic nature, whether or not a given, empirical individual recognises this. Within the narrow confines of arithmetical addition, the left-hand side – synthetically speaking – is *not* the right-hand side, but is *equal to* the right-hand side. The principle of equality is thereby enunciated in this arithmetical illustration, a principle that governs our experience of the present.

The essential, then, is what cannot be doubted. To make contact with it, phenomenology has recourse to a foundational principle: the *epochē* (also called bracketing or disconnection from the factual world). Husserl also used two other terms in an attempt to save phenomenology from being understood as a form of introspection. These are *noema* – intentional objects as described by phenomenology – and *noesis*: the attitude towards intentional objects. By engaging the *epochē*, with the aid of these concepts, the existential, contingent and factual world is put out of view in order to direct attention onto the *eidos*, or the essential, giving rise to eidetic philosophy – or eidetic science, as Husserl preferred to call it. Whether or not it is possible to specify exactly what is signified by 'eidetic', it is indisputable that Husserl attempts to effect a separation between the natural and social sciences dealing with the factual world, and the sphere of eidetic philosophy dealing with the *eidos*, or the essence of things.

Even a cursory knowledge of developments in contemporary thought shows that the nature and rationale for such a separation has been challenged – not only by the social sciences seeking to give greater explanatory power to 'material conditions', but also by philosophy itself. The separation is deemed to come under pressure from both sides, as it were: the eidetic will be affected or 'contaminated' by the factual sciences, just as the latter will be riven by presuppositions deriving from an essential realm. As Merleau-Ponty said as early as

1945, 'The most important lesson that the reduction teaches us is the impossibility of a complete reduction' (Merleau-Ponty 1992: xiv).

The reading by Husserl of empiricist and pragmatist philosophers, together with the emergence of social science (especially experimental psychology), prompted him to investigate the foundational, essential, or 'non-real' basis of the contingent, factual, spatio-temporal world. In an uncharacteristically straight-forward manner, Husserl says, in the short Introduction to *Ideas*, that:

> In contradistinction to that [to a science of realities], *pure or transcendental phenomenology will* become established, *not as a science of matters of fact, but as a science of essences* (as an *'eidetic'* science); it will become established as a science which seeks exclusively to ascertain 'cognitions of essences' and *no 'matters of fact' whatever.*
> (Husserl 1982: xx, Husserl's emphasis)

Thus, reality – even human, bodily reality – becomes a generally 'accidental' reality. While the 'accidental' or the contingent realm always exists, it is fleeting and transitory in its manifestations and effects. Despite the effort to separate out the 'natural' from the 'eidetic' standpoint, Husserl is far from denying their interdependence. Nor does he claim the eidetic as a stance adopted uniquely by the professional philosopher; rather, he sees it as part of the thought process of anyone intent on knowing the world. For no such knowing relationship can take place outside an a priori conceptual framework. To ask, for instance, about the origin of nature, is necessarily to have recourse to notions of causality and logical inference, not to mention the concepts of object and subject. Studying this a priori, eidetic realm produces new 'data', things that were unknown before reflection took place.

As an illustration, we refer to the field of experimental psychology and determine the difference between the approaches of eidetic phenomenology and the experimental scientist. Through his experiments based on observation as well as on a frequently unacknowledged epistemological framework that gives rise to a method, the psychologist comes in touch with psychological experiences. As an observer, the psychologist relies on his senses as the channel through which sense data can be absorbed and interpreted. As an empiricist, the same observer is wedded to the self-evident basis of the relationship between knowledge and sense experience. Indeed, here, knowledge and sense experience become one. The question that such positivist research never raises – as Husserl and thinkers after him recognised – is that of how it is possible for the individual sense experience of one researcher to be confirmed by the individual sense experience of another. In order that this be so, a realm is implied which transcends the experience of two different researchers, a realm authenticating, as it were, the experience of both.

As Husserl saw it, the empiricist attitude included a refusal to acknowledge the possibility, or even necessity, of a transcendent realm opening out onto eidetic 'intuition', as Husserl called it. Against empiricism, Husserl argues that all knowledge is couched in just such a transcendent framework.

It is a mistake to think that because Husserlian phenomenology 'operates exclusively in acts of reflection' (see Husserl 1982: 174) and in consciousness that it is ultimately a philosophy founded in psychology. Rather, it is a question of the *foundation* of psychology as an experimental science, not one of philosophy's foundations in the regional discipline of psychology. Psychology deals with entities in the world, and thus lacks the universal and transcendent status of philosophy as phenomenology. On the other hand, phenomenology, as reflection, is a philosophy of consciousness, which, as the phenomenological tradition has never tired of repeating after Husserl, is always consciousness *of* something, and never consciousness in itself. Consciousness, then, is transcendent. It is also pure reflection in the sense that it is not 'contaminated' by the world. Husserl thus speaks of 'a pure consciousness' that 'no longer has the sense of an event in Nature' (Husserl 1982: 127) and of 'the exclusion of Nature' (1982: 131) in the phenomenological reduction, together with

> all the sorts of cultural formations, all works of the technical and fine arts, of sciences ... aesthetic and practical values of every form. Likewise, naturally, such actualities as state, custom, law, religion. Consequently, all natural sciences and cultural sciences, with their total stock of cognition, undergo exclusion precisely as sciences which require the natural attitude.
>
> (Husserl 1982: 130–31)

Later, Husserl will say that the sciences are 'dogmatic' (1982: 141) in the sense that they take for granted their founding presuppositions, and fail to develop a critical stance towards these presuppositions.

Difficulties with the Purity of Consciousness

Even though the world is not reduced to pure consciousness, but simply excluded from the sphere of essential reflection, phenomenology's

Achilles heel has proved to be just this claim to the purity of the transcendental realm, even while the necessity of transcendental reflection has been its strength. In contradistinction to a philosophical materialism, phenomenological consciousness is independent of worldly being and nature; for these are correlates of consciousness and only accessible via consciousness (Husserl 1982: 116). The world and nature are thus excluded, through the phenomenological *epochē*, *qua* world and *qua* nature from essential reflection, while at the same time they provide the basis for that reflection.

As knowledge for Husserl is also a fact of nature, it is not the epistemological level (implying a subject–object relation) which can give rise to the essential, eidetic consciousness. In short, knowledge is part of the lived experience of a psychological being. It is only by transcending this that a pure eidetic science can be established. The question arises, though, as to how it is possible to achieve certainty about whether or not the transcendental realm has been reached. Might there not always be a transcendence of a higher power to which recourse can be made in light of any claim to transcendental purity? The empiricist, or factual scientist, might go even further and say that the whole enterprise is hopeless precisely because there is no ultimate principle of validation to which recourse could be made. The starting and end points, therefore, can only be those given by sense experience.

In response to such scepticism, Husserl proposes two things: first, that a totally innocent empiricism is unsustainable. Indeed, empiricism is in fact a philosophy with an a priori foundation. It must, for instance, have recourse to the principle of non-contradiction and to the rules of the syllogism in forming propositions, as it must have recourse to the principles of induction and deduction. Moreover, secondly, if the empiricist cannot 'appeal to eidetic insight', there can be no universal, and thus no philosophical defence of empiricism. For such a defence is essentially transcendental. As a result, the inaugurator of phenomenology states that, 'by contesting the validity of purely eidetic thinking, one arrives at a skepticism which, as genuine skepticism, cancels itself out by a countersense' (Husserl 1982: 37).

The Cultural Context: Is it Important?

Much hinges on Husserl's insistence on the ontological priority of the eidetic realm. The stakes here are cultural and political, as well as philosophical, as the following question serves to highlight: Is the European tradition of philosophy ethnocentric, given its claim concerning the essential nature of the transcendental realm? Husserl addresses this question towards the end of his *Origin of Geometry*:

> One will object: what naïveté, to seek to display, and to claim to have displayed, an historical a priori, an absolute, supertemporal validity, after we have obtained abundant testimony for the relativity of everything historical, of all historically developed world-apperceptions, right back to those of 'primitive' tribes. Every people, large or small, has its world in which, for that people, everything fits well together, whether in mythical-magical or in European-rational terms, and in which everything can be explained perfectly. Every people has its 'logic' and, accordingly, if this logic is explicated in propositions, 'its' a priori.
>
> (Husserl 1989: 175)

Does this not mean that it is inadmissible to 'privilege' a single, European way of understanding cultural forms?

Husserl's answer to this objection is clear and to the point, whether one agrees with it or not. It is that knowledge which is specific to a given time and place (knowledge deriving from myth or magical powers, for example) – 'all merely factual' knowledge, in effect – is, as we have seen, unable to account for its foundation. Moreover, the failure to account for the foundation means that the presuppositions underpinning a given form of scientific endeavour also remain unthematised and invisible, even when the necessity of these presuppositions is no less incontestable. How, Husserl thus puzzles, does one establish that there are different knowledges, different histories, different cultural presuppositions, if not through some sort of transcendence? The objection, then, has two levels: one concerns the 'facts of the case' (the fact of different logics and thus of historical relativity); the other concerns the preconditions of this knowing. For Husserl, 'facts' presuppose non-factual preconditions. There are no autonomous facts in themselves because the establishment of the relativity of factual knowledge entails a comparative approach that raises the question of how insight into, or knowledge of, the relativity of knowledges is possible. Put another way, it is necessary to know how differences in knowledges could be established from a particular position. On this basis, the claim that, *de facto*, Eurocentrism colours all attempts to found universal premises, does not, *de jure*, invalidate the necessity for such universal premises. Even if attempts at universalism are found wanting, the well-foundedness of a universalist insight is not thereby refuted.

42

Consequently, Husserl endeavours to prove that transcendental-ism cannot be avoided simply by arguing against it. For an abso-lutely anti-transcendentalist philosophy is precisely inconceivable. To question it is still to maintain a transcendent or a meta-linguistic position.

Essential and Inessential: Can These Remain Separate?

To follow Husserl in his encounter with sceptical empiricism is also to work towards recognising the line dividing the essential Idea from the inessential, contingent moment. The contingent moment is also the existential moment: the moment of worldly existence that so fascinated the existentialists. Such a dividing line – such a border – current thinking has argued, is susceptible to breaches of all kinds. The integrity of the essential realm is at risk. Contingency intrudes into the essential and threatens its purity. Chance, too, plays a part in the rupture of boundaries, and so the repressed (the negative) returns. All this is appreciated. And yet ... (Husserl might respond) this division cannot but be maintained; this is precisely why it can be threatened.

For even if the unthinkable negative (in the form of the repressed) stands at the door ready to contaminate an ideal purity, the possibility of purity being breached is itself a philosophical – i.e., transcendental – insight.

Husserl's defenders can point out that the very notion that, ulti-mately, a transcendental philosophy cannot found itself without risk-ing an infinite regress (for there is always a transcendence of transcendence) is also a transcendental (ideal) insight. In short, the very limits to (transcendental) thought are themselves generative of thought because such limits constitute a real insight.

References

Husserl, Edmund (1982), *Ideas Pertaining to a Pure Phenomenology and to a Phenomenological Philosophy*, trans. F. Kersten, Dordrecht, Netherlands: Kluwer Academic Publishers.
—— (1989), *The Origin of Geometry*, trans. David Carr with an Introduction by Jacques Derrida, Lincoln and London: The University of Nebraska Press.
Merleau-Ponty, Maurice (1992), *Phenomenology of Perception*, trans. Colin Smith London: Routledge.

See also: **Agamben, Derrida, Heidegger, Levinas, Merlau-Ponty**

Husserl's major writings

(1982 [1913]) *Ideas Pertaining to a Pure Phenomenology and to a Phenomenological Philosophy*, trans. F. Kersten, Dordrecht, Netherlands: Kluwer Academic Publishers.

(1981) *Husserl, Shorter Works*, ed. Peter McCormick and Frederick A. Elliston, Notre Dame, Indiana: University of Notre Dame Press; Brighton, Sussex: Harvester Press.

(1980 [1952]) *Phenomenology and the Foundation of the Sciences*, trans. Ted E. Klein and William E. Pohl, The Hague: Martinus Nijhoff.

(1977 [1950]) *Cartesian Meditations: An Introduction to Phenomenology*, trans. Dorian Cairns, The Hague: Martinus Nijhoff.

(1977 [1959]) *Phenomenological Psychology*, trans. John Scanlon, The Hague: Martinus Nijhoff.

(1973 [1939]) *Experience and Judgement: Investigations in a Genealogy of Logic*, trans. James S. Churchill and Karl Ameriks, Evanston, Illinois: Northwestern University Press.

(1970 [1913]) *Logical Investigations*, 2 vols, trans. J. Findlay, London: Routledge and Kegan Paul.

(1970 [1954]) *The Crisis of the European Sciences and Transcendental Phenomenology*, trans. D. Carr, Evanston, Illinois: Northwestern University Press.

(1969 [1929]) *Formal and Transcendental Logic*, trans. Dorian Cairns, The Hague: Martinus Nijhoff.

(1964a [1950]) *The Idea of Phenomenology*, trans. Walter P. Alston and George Naknikian, The Hague: Martinus Nijhoff.

(1964b [1928]) *Lectures on Internal Time Consciousness*, trans. J.S. Churchill, Bloomington: Indiana University Press.

Further Reading

Bernet, Rudolf, Iso Kern, and Eduard Marbach (1993), *An Introduction to Husserlian Phenomenology*, a translation of, *Edmund Husserl: Darstellung seines Denkens*, Evanston, Illinois: Northwestern University Press.

Lyotard, Jean-François (1991 [1954]), *Phenomenology*, New York: State University of New York.

Mohanty, Jitendranath (1970), *Phenomenology and Ontology*, The Hague: Martinus Nijhoff.

EMMANUEL LEVINAS (1906–1995)

In her biography of Jean-Paul Sartre, Annie Cohen-Solal relates that because the subject of her book had, by 1930, developed a kinship with phenomenology, 'he bought a recent book by Emmanuel Levinas, *Théorie de l'intuition dans la phénoménologie de Husserl* [1930], eagerly leafed through it, constantly recognizing his own thoughts in its pages' (Cohen-Solal 1987: 91). Such would be the way that the person to become one of France's most influential philosophers was himself indebted to the scholar of phenomenology, Emmanuel Levinas. Of equal importance is the way Levinas influenced a later generation of thinkers – people such as Blanchot, Derrida, Irigaray and Lyotard. Of particular interest to this generation has been Levinas's rethinking of the concept and reality of the Other (*Autrui*). In ethics, as we shall see, Levinas has said that he is concerned with the Other, 'prior to any act' (Levinas 1989a: 290).

Levinas was born into a Jewish family in Kovno in Lithuania in 1906, and he died in Paris in 1995. As his parents saw their future belonging to the Russian language and literature rather than to the Lithuanian language, the young Emmanuel came to read both Russian and Hebrew. Lithuania was, in the early twentieth century, a centre of Talmudic studies, and this has also left its mark on Levinas's *oeuvre* in the form of his own Talmudic readings and other writings in Jewish theology. As an avid reader of Dostoyevsky, Tolstoy, Pushkin and Gogol, Levinas became absorbed by the ethical issues raised by these writers, particularly the issue of responsibility for the Other in Dostoyevsky. Dostoyevsky and the great Russian writers were, to Levinas's mind, a good preparation for reading Plato and Kant.

His reading of the writers mentioned led Levinas, in 1923, to Strasbourg in France to study philosophy under Charles Blondel and Maurice Pradines. At the time, Bergson's philosophy was making an impact, particularly with his theory of duration, an impact which also reveals itself in Levinas's thinking. While at Strasbourg, Levinas made friends with Maurice Blanchot who introduced him to the writing of Proust and Valéry. A collection of Levinas's writings on Blanchot was published in 1975.

Career

In 1928–29, Levinas attended Husserl's lectures in Freiburg, and he also read Heidegger's *Being and Time*. The book of his *doctorat de troisième cycle* thesis on Husserl's theory of intuition appeared in 1930 – the same book that was to captivate Sartre (see Levinas 1998a). In the same year that his thesis was published, Levinas received French citizenship. He was thus eligible, at the outbreak of the Second World War, to be mobilised, and served as an interpreter in Russian and German until he was made a prisoner of war in 1940. Almost all of Levinas's family remaining in Lithuania were killed by the Nazis. During his captivity in Germany, Levinas began his book, *Existence and Existents*, which was published in 1947.

After the war, Levinas became director of the École Normale Israélite Orientale. In 1961, his *Doctorat d'état* thesis, *Totalité et infini*, was published and led to his appointment as professor of philosophy at the University of Poitiers. He was subsequently appointed to the University of Paris-Nanterre in 1967, and then to a chair in philosophy at the Sorbonne in 1973. He retired from the Sorbonne in 1976.

'There is'

Levinas's intimate acquaintance with Husserl's phenomenology provided the basis for a detailed consideration of the 'givenness' of existence, as for example, in the impersonal (in English) form of the verb to be: 'there is', or its French equivalent, *il y a*, or again (in German), *es gibt*. Levinas gives this most everyday of everyday expressions a powerful twist by linking it with horror. 'There is' is impersonal and given; it is neither exterior nor interior; it is, says Levinas, the 'sheer fact of being' (Levinas 1989b: 31). 'There is' – the givenness (cf. *es gibt*) of being – is the equivalent of the night, of ambiguity, of indeterminateness. 'There is' comes to thought, confronts it before revelation or the concept orders it in any way; it slips through transcendence and indeed defies the ego, and all personal forms of the symbolic. As such, Levinas argues, 'The rustling of the *there* is ... is horror.' And he continues by noting the way 'it insinuates itself in the night, as an undetermined menace of space itself disengaged from its function as a receptacle for objects, as a means of access to beings' (Levinas 1989b: 32). Although Levinas would refuse the vaguest hint of a psychoanalytic explanation, it is as though the 'there is' as horror were a trauma for consciousness, and an impossibility for symbolic processes. However, we should also remember that horror here is always already given: it is thus unavoidable, as being is unavoidable. It is not to be understood, then, as equivalent to the Heideggerian anxiety before the acknowledgement of nothingness. 'To be conscious is to be torn away from the *there is*' (Levinas 1989b: 32). This is because consciousness has to form itself into a subjectivity constructed by a certain framework of rationality. Levinas is interested in the underside of this rationality which is not simply the irrational, or the unspeakable void, but is a positive force that cannot be excluded. Put another way: subjectivity forms itself according to the universal principles of Western philosophy; the 'there is', by comparison, is a contingency – the particular which eludes the universal. The 'haunting spectre' as seen in Shakespeare's *Macbeth*, is being as the 'there is', and it is this, precisely, which horrifies Macbeth. Night, crime, phantom and horror here come together to give the shadow of being.

The Other and the Dominance of the Same

What exactly is at stake in the Levinasian project if, as Levinas proposes, neither a phenomenological nor a psychoanalytical framework can do justice to horror as being as an Otherness? To answer this question, we note that from the time of his lectures given at the College of Philosophy in 1946–47 on time and the Other, to his later work on God and the idea, otherness – alterity – has been at issue. Thus, time as alterity, existence as alterity, the other person (*autrui*) as alterity, language as alterity, and God as alterity – these words point to a project of great subtlety and determination. For Levinas effectively wants to bypass thought in philosophy. His trajectory leads, he argues, away from ontology, epistemology, or reason, to a point where alterity is confronted in all its 'nudity' (to use a term dear to Levinas) – a point where its irreducibility can be acknowledged.

The transcendence of Western philosophy is against this enterprise if by transcendence we mean that which can be conceptualised, theorised, visualised, objectified – universalised. Levinas, by contrast, uses transcendence in the sense of rupture, and opening up to the Other, as opposed to the Western tradition's reduction of the Other to the Same in its drive to objectify and universalise. The dominance of the Same makes the universal the goal of thought. The universal is, by definition, independent of any given set of concrete circumstances. It is thus disembodied and idealist. In keeping with the tenor of the phenomenological project, the aim is to reduce the gap between thought and embodiment – or, as in the case of Heidegger, between being and existence.

The point, Levinas says, is to go 'beyond being', beyond 'egoisms struggling with one another' (Levinas 1998b: 4). Not to *be* otherwise, but *otherwise* than being, which entails: otherwise than essence, because being and essence go together. This is Levinas's proposition, implying that there is more than being for humanity and it has to do with the primacy of a responsibility for the other (see Levinas 1998b: 3–14).

The Other Thought in the West

In attributing a kind of primacy to otherness or alterity, rather than to the thinking, unified, ego, Levinas has, of course, met the objection which says that, in the end, whether one likes it or not, the Other of the universal – the alterity which calls to us – is inevitably the Other of Western thought itself, an Other waiting to be put into conceptual form and universalised, an Other which Western thought needs. This Other of Western thought would be inescapably another version of the Same – ultimately a formal Other (the Other of negation) and not true alterity at all. Feminists meet a similar objection when they argue, as Irigaray does, that the feminine is an alterity which must be thought of independently of the patriarchal order of identity (= the Same).

Interestingly, in an interview given in 1985, Levinas points out that when he wrote his lectures published as *Time and the Other* in 1948, he thought that femininity was the modality of alterity that he was looking for (Levinas 1989c: 10). Knowledge, too, Levinas recognises, reiterates the relationship of the Same to the Other in which the Other is reduced to the order of the Same (Levinas 1984: 12). Despite this, Levinas still searched, until his death in 1995, for a way of presenting the irreducible Other in philosophy, an Other indeed foreign to the order of the Same. No doubt one should pause on the resonances of the notion of 'search' here; for what Levinas in fact presents is the trace of his search for a way of rendering the Other intelligible without resorting to the language of idealism.

The Other and Others

Levinas never ceased to emphasise that the Other arises in relation to others and not immediately in relation to the universality of the law. This relation is the unique relation of ethical responsibility. Ethics is the practical relation of one to an other – a relation which is prior to ontology. The Absolutely Other is the other person (*autrui*). The Other is a 'nudity' – not the nudity emerging in light of an unveiling; rather, says Levinas, true nudity is the face (of the Other) as an epiphany which solicits us; it is that face which comes to us from the exterior. 'The face *is* by itself and not by reference to a system' (Levinas 1961: 47). The Other is also the infinite in me to the extent that he or she brings about a rupture in the self as an entity identical with itself. The self even poses itself *for the other* rather than for itself. The nudity of the other as a practical exterior unassimilable to ontology entails that the relationship between Self and Other is dissymmetrical; in other words, it bypasses the symmetry of intersubjectivity so forcefully outlined in idealism. Levinas likens this dissymmetry to synthetic, non-spatialised time – the time that cannot be represented by clocks, but which corresponds to the internal experience of time captured in Bergson's notion of 'duration'.

The dimension of time that interests Levinas more than any other is the future. Unlike the past, the future cannot so easily be assimilated to another present. Instead, the future is the present's difference with itself: this is the future as absolutely new, and so absolutely Other. The future is time without a concept.

Language: The 'Saying' and the 'Said'

An intriguing aspect of Levinas's philosophy of alterity concerns language, not language as 'the said', but as 'the saying'. 'Saying' is a complex notion that cannot simply be understood linguistically, that is, representationally. For then it would again enter the realm of the said. The 'saying' does not 'consist in giving signs' (Levinas 1998b: 48), and it signifies prior to essence. Saying is a mode of exposure, or of disclosing, oneself to the other. This is a central theme in Levinas's philosophy, and he frequently returns to it. A structuralist account of language, therefore, would not be of interest to Levinas, because of the linguistic heritage implied and the emphasis on the said.

To stress this point, Levinas also defines signification in general as infinity – that is, as the existence of alterity. His insight is that language cannot be reduced to a system of logic or representation. Like the future, the infinite, and the face, language becomes an extended epiphany. It is the astonishment of the Other speaking in me – the Other speaking in me which enables me to become a self in language; in other words, through language, the Other enables me to have an identity.

Through the face of alterity, Levinas says, God is reached:

> The face 'signifies' beyond, neither as an index nor as symbol, but precisely and irreducibly as a face that *summons me*. It signifies *to-God* (*à Dieu*), not as sign, but as the questioning of myself, as if I were summoned or called, that is to say, awakened or cited as myself.
>
> (Levinas 1983: 112)

God and the Infinite

In his last works, Levinas is more insistent in equating God with the infinite. It is almost as though theology comes to take the place of a

Western philosophical outlook in order to ensure alterity once again finds its place in thought – a place beyond ontology.

With his emphasis on the practical importance of ethics as being distinct from ontology, Levinas opens up a new vista within philosophy. Within philosophy? This is perhaps the question we should pose to the one who revealed the solipsism of reason, and who showed that previous philosophies of the subject reduced alterity to the order of the Same. Another question which arises is: how is Levinas, the interpreter of Husserl and Heidegger, to be understood given that he speaks clearly within the history of philosophy, but endeavours to escape from it although, it is true, his writing clearly gestures towards theology? For Levinas, to speak within the history of philosophy seems to imply that the very tradition he challenges might have within it a hitherto unsuspected suppleness – much as Levinas himself showed that language is vested with hitherto unsuspected possibilities. In other words, Levinas may well have shown that philosophy is in fact not reducible to ontology.

References

Cohen-Solal, Annie (1987), *Sartre: A life*, trans. Anna Cancogni, New York: Pantheon Books.

Levinas, Emmanuel (1961), *Totalité et infini: essai sur l'extériorité*, The Hague: Martinus Nijhoff.

—— (1983), 'Beyond intentionality', trans. Kathleen McLaughlin in Alan Montefiore ed., *Philosophy in France in France Today*, Cambridge: Cambridge University Press.

—— (1984), *Transcendance et intelligibilité*, Geneva: Labor et Fides.

—— (1989a), 'Ethics and politics' (Levinas in discussion with Alain Finkielkraut) trans. Jonathan Romney in Sean Hand ed., *The Levinas Reader*, Oxford: Basil Blackwell.

—— (1989b), 'There is: Existence without existents', trans. Alphonso Lingis in Sean Hand ed., *The Levinas Reader*, Oxford: Basil Blackwell.

—— (1989c), 'Intretien' [realised in February 1985] in Jean-Christophe Aeschlimann ed. *Répondre d'autrui Emmanuel Lévinas*, Neuchâtel: Editions de la Baconnière, Collection, Langages.

—— (1998a), *The Theory of Intuition in Husserl's Phenomenology*, trans. André Orianne, Evanston, Illinois: Northwestern University.

—— (1998b), *Otherwise than Being, or Beyond Essence*, trans. Alphonso Lingis, Pittsburgh: Duquesne University Press.

See also: **Bergson, Blanchot, Derrida, Heidegger, Husserl, Irigaray, Lyotard**

Levinas's major writings

(2004) *Paul Celan*, Saint-Clément-de-Rivière: Fata Morgana.

(1998a [1930]) *The Theory of Intuition in Husserl's Phenomenology* (Studies in Existential Philosophy), trans. André Orianne, Evanston, Illinois: Northwestern University.

(1998b [1974]) *Otherwise than Being, or Beyond Essence*, trans. Alphonso Lingis, Pittsburgh: Duquesne University Press.

(1993 [1987]) *Outside the Subject*, Stanford: Stanford University Press.

(1991 [1963]) *Difficult Freedom: Essays on Judaism*, trans. Sean Hand, Baltimore and London: Johns Hopkins University Press.

(1990a [1977]) *Nine Talmudic Readings by Emmanuel Levinas*, trans. Annette Aronowicz, Bloomington: Indiana University Press.

(1990b [1948]) *Time and the Other*, trans. Richard Cohen, Pittsburgh: Duquesne University Press.

(1989) *The Levinas Reader*, ed. Sean Hand, Oxford, Basil Blackwell. Contains Levinas's writings on existence, ethics, aesthetics, religion and politics.

(1987a) *Collected Philosophical Papers*, ed. A. Lingis, The Hague: Martinus Nijhoff.

(1987b [1961]) *Totality and Infinity*, trans. A. Lingis, Pittsburgh: Duquesne University Press.

(1985 [1982]) *Ethics and Infinity*, trans. Richard Cohen, Pittsburgh: Duquesne University Press.

(1984) *Transcendance et intelligibilité*, Geneva: Labor et Fides.

(1978 [1947]) *Existence and Existents*, trans. A. Lingis, Dordrecht, Boston and London: Kluwer Academic Publishers.

(1975) *Sur Maurice Blanchot*, Montpellier: Fata Morgana.

Further reading

Cohen, Richard (2001), *Ethics, Exegesis, and Philosophy: Interpretation after Levinas*, Cambridge: Cambridge University Press.

Davis, Colin (1996), *Levinas: An Introduction*, Cambridge: Polity Press.

Huchens, B.C. (2004), *Levinas: A Guide for the Perplexed*, New York: Continuum.

Llewelyn, John (1995), *Emmanuel Levinas: The Genealogy of Ethics*, London, New York: Routledge.

Nordquist, Joan (compiler) (1997), *Emmanuel Levinas: A Bibliography*, Santa Cruz, CA.: Reference and Research Service.

Smith, Michael B. (2005), *Toward the Outside: Concepts and Themes in Emmanuel Levinas*, Pittsburgh: Duquesne University Press.

MAURICE MERLEAU-PONTY (1908–1961)

Even though he remained a French 'philosopher of consciousness', Maurice Merleau-Ponty separated himself gradually from the phenomenology of Jean-Paul Sartre, and also from that of Husserl.

Specifically, Merleau-Ponty brought Saussure into his reflections and teachings on language in the late 1940s and early 1950s. During the 1950s, he was also well aware of Saussure's influence on the work of Lévi-Strauss and formed a close alliance with the latter, who eventually became his colleague at the Collège de France.

Merleau-Ponty was born in 1908. Like Roland Barthes's father, Merleau-Ponty's father was also killed in the First World War. He attended the Lycées Janson-de-Sailly and Louis-le-Grande, and in 1930 he successfully completed his *agrégation* in philosophy at the École Normale Supérieure (rue d'Ulm). Like many intellectuals of his generation, Merleau-Ponty attended Kojève's lectures on Hegel. He was also associated for a short time with the Catholic journal, *Esprit*. When the Second World War broke out, Merleau-Ponty served in the infantry and was tortured by the Germans. During the Occupation he was associated with the ill-fated, independent Resistance group, 'Socialism and Freedom', the group which also counted Jean-Paul Sartre as one of its members. In 1945, Merleau-Ponty's major work was published: *Phenomenology of Perception*. In 1949, he was appointed to the chair of child psychology at the Sorbonne, and in 1952 he was the youngest candidate ever to be elected to the chair of philosophy at the Collège de France, a position he held until his sudden death in May 1961.

From 1945 to 1952, Merleau-Ponty was a close friend and collaborator of Jean-Paul Sartre, and one of the founding editors of *Les Temps Modernes*. The year 1952 marked Merleau-Ponty's disillusionment with the Korean War and Sartrian politics, and he thus resigned from the editorial board of what was to become Sartre's journal. The substance of his differences with Sartre is contained in Merleau-Ponty's book, *Adventures of the Dialectic*, published in 1955. Here, his former comrade-in-arms develops an exhaustive analysis of Sartre's relationship to communism, at the same time as he questions the privileging of the subject–object relationship in Sartre's version of phenomenology. As Vincent Descombes explains, without an 'inter-world', the subject–object dichotomy leads to solipsism: 'If the subject-object dichotomy were correct, then all meaning would issue from men, and all meaning *for myself* would issue from *myself*' (Descombes 1980: 72).

From 1952, Merleau-Ponty began to develop a conception of political activity which freed itself from Sartre's naive flirtation with hard-line communism. More importantly, though, Merleau-Ponty began to sketch out a philosophical trajectory which confirmed the importance of lived experience in grasping the nature of language, perception, and the body. An outline of the main aspects of the link between perception and thought opened up in the *Philosophy of Perception* will help to clarify what is at stake here.

Phenomenology of Perception

In the Preface to the work in question, Merleau-Ponty confirms the influence of Husserl on his own philosophy. Thus, like Husserl, Merleau-Ponty emphasises the importance of the phenomenological reduction, or *epochē* (abstention; also called 'bracketing' and 'disconnection') introduced in order to open access to 'essences'. The latter are to be grasped, not as the transcendental essences given in available scientific disciplines, or in the general abstract knowledge (such as that relating to space and time) an individual may have about the world. Rather, the phenomenological *epochē* gives access to the immanent essences of the consciousness of 'lived experience'. The *epochē* is a disconnection from the given natural world in all its objectivity. This disconnection, Husserl is quick to say, is not in any sense a denial of the natural world. Indeed it, and all the knowledge provided by the sciences which study its various aspects, is entirely accepted. However, the consciousness of lived experience – the consciousness which is always a consciousness *of* something – is fundamentally different from an acceptance of the givenness of the world, or scientific knowledge. Fixing attention firmly on consciousness and its ego, to study, as Husserl says, 'what we find immanently within *it*', in order to arrive at the insight that:

> *consciousness has, in itself, a being of its own which in its absolute essence, is not touched by the phenomenological exclusion.*
>
> (Husserl 1982:65, Husserl's emphasis)

The study of the essence of things in consciousness opens up the field of the science of phenomenology (Husserl 1982: 66). The point is: (1) that consciousness is constituted as an autonomous realm, and (2) that it is the object of phenomenological inquiry (= science). As, presumably, the inquiry takes place within consciousness, the upshot is consciousness conducting a science of itself. The tension here is not lost on Merleau-Ponty in his later work.

Like Husserl, Merleau-Ponty's point of departure is the *epochē* (bracketing of the factual world). For him, however, the aim is not to remain within the structure of Descartes's philosophy of doubt, as Husserl did in providing an explanation of phenomenology, but rather to go to the heart of embodied experience, which is what perception is. Pitting himself directly against the abstractness and emptiness of the Cartesian cogito – 'I think, therefore I am' – Merleau-Ponty shows that 'to be a body is to be tied to a certain world'; and he adds: 'our body is not primarily *in* space: it is of it' (Merleau-Ponty 1992: 148, Merleau-Ponty's emphasis). In effect, our body is always already in the world; therefore, there is no body in-itself, a body which could be objectified and given universal status. Perception, then, is always an embodied perception, one that is what it is only within a specific context or situation. Perception in-itself does not exist.

In his own explanation of his philosophical trajectory, Merleau-Ponty confirms the primacy of lived experience by saying that the 'perceiving mind is an incarnated mind' (Merleau-Ponty 1989a: 3). Furthermore, perception is not simply the result of the impact of the external world on the body; for even if the body is distinct from the world it inhabits, it is not separate from it. Indeed, the very imbrication of the perceiving organism and its surroundings is what lies at the basis of perception. This means that there is no perception in general – a notion which would turn it into an abstract universal; there is only perception as it is lived in the world. It is precisely the 'lived' nature of perception and the body which makes phenomenological research viable and necessary. As a result of the incarnate nature of perception, the perceiving subject is always changing, always going through a process of rebirth. Consciousness, for its part, does not relate to the world in the manner of a thinker in relation to a series of objects. There is no subject in general, in effect, one entirely autonomous and separate from its objects, as Descartes argued. Rather, consciousness is perceptual; consequently, the certainty of ideas is based on the certainty of perception. This certainty always remains to be established and confirmed by phenomenological investigation; for the phenomenologist, there are no ideal, universal certainties at the level of ideas. Descartes's cogito is thus what Merleau-Ponty's phenomenology is opposing more than anything else. To sum up: 'I perceive' is not equivalent to 'I think', nor can it be universalised. The incarnate status of the perceiving subject opens the way to a phenomenological description of the Living Present. Within such a description – that is, within the phenomenological *epochē* – the perceived thing is equivalent to what is said about it. Merleau-Ponty elaborates:

> The perceived thing is not an ideal unity in the possession of the intellect, like a geometrical notion, for example; it is rather a

totality open to a horizon of an indefinite number of perspectival views which blend with one another according to a given style, which defines the object in question.

(Merleau-Ponty 1989b)

Given the status of perception as incarnate, what is the real *raison d'être* of phenomenological description, and, indeed, reflection? Merleau-Ponty's answer is that, if left to itself, perception 'forgets itself and is ignorant of its own accomplishments' (Merleau-Ponty 1989b: 19). But the issue is not, as Merleau-Ponty seems to think, that we risk going back to an unreflected moment prior to philosophy, but that a distinction has been made quite unambiguously between the perception of an incarnate perceiving subject and the philosophy of perception – as though, after all, one were forced to accept at least some version of the universal, 'I think', just at the point where the primacy given to the 'I perceive' seemed to deal it a truly mortal blow. Such would be the typically insurmountable problem faced by a philosophy of consciousness which wants to maintain a sense of its own self-presence (contained in the 'I think'), while at the same time launching into a description of the heterogeneous level of the subject incarnate. Within his phenomenological framework, Merleau-Ponty has presented a fundamental rift between consciousness and 'Lived Experience', a rift which must remain repressed.

Saussure and Language

If this were the end of the story, however, there is no doubt that the philosopher of perception would have long ceased to be of interest to a post-war generation brought up on the aporias of philosophies of consciousness, just as Merleau-Ponty's teachers (like Brunschvicg) have ceased to be of interest. The enactment of the subject, rather than its positing (albeit in only partially elaborated form) and, more importantly, language, and Merleau-Ponty's attempt to make it central to his later philosophical concerns via the aegis of a reading of Saussure, inspired early structuralism. For instance, Algirdas-Julien Greimas was one who attended Merleau-Ponty's inaugural lecture at the Collège de France in 1952, and came away with a sense that Saussure, and not Marx, held the key to a genuine philosophy of history (see Dosse 1991: 62–63).

Although it is often said that Merleau-Ponty took from Saussure's theory of language what he wanted in order to confirm his phenomenology, it should also be said that he highlighted two Saussurian principles which would come to be the focus of structuralist theories of language and semiotics. These are that meaning in language arises through a diacritiçal relationship between signs, and that a diachronical study of language cannot explain the nature of current usage. Thus in his unfinished work, *The Prose of the World*, Merleau-Ponty writes that 'Saussure shows admirably that . . . it cannot be the history of the word or language which determines its present meaning' (Merleau-Ponty 1974: 22). What the phenomenologist finds in the structural linguist is a theory which seems to emphasise the subject's lived relation to the world. Again, Merleau-Ponty writes that Saussure's notion of the primacy of the synchronic dimension of language for understanding the nature of language as such, 'liberates history from historicism and makes a new conception of reason possible' (Merleau-Ponty 1974: 23). To view language synchronically, Merleau-Ponty argues, is to view it as enacted, and not as an abstract, universal entity, subject to gradual evolution over time. Language here is fundamentally the 'living present' in speech. To speak, to communicate – to use language – is in part equivalent to becoming aware that there are only successive living presents. Indeed, any discourse *on* language must come to grasp itself as an enactment of language. A linguistics worthy of the name, therefore, comes to recognise that language can only be understood from the inside. In other words, language can no more be reduced to a history of linguistics than history can be reduced to historical discourse.

Nevertheless, in by-passing Saussure's theory of *langue* (language as a system) which explains *how* speech is enacted, in favour of *parole* (the enactment itself), Merleau-Ponty is unable to show that language is doubly articulated: the level of the signifier is relatively independent of the level of the signified. And while Merleau-Ponty, with his emphasis on the 'living present', had focused on the signified (the enactment of meaning), structuralist linguistics would, almost from the moment of Merleau-Ponty's death in 1961, oppose the phenomenologist's emphasis on the embodied transparence of the signified,[1] only to become dazzled by language's opacity as a system of signifiers.

Furthermore, in focusing almost exclusively on the level of *parole* as the embodiment of language, the phenomenologist is unable to explain satisfactorily how a move can be made from the individual, 'I speak', to the fact that another speaks. The usual (Sartrian) claim that the 'I speak' entails a recognition that 'we speak' fails to show how the 'I' is not simply being raised to the power of the 'we' – a 'we' which is effectively rendered homogeneous in the process. This issue is but the tip of the iceberg. For phenomenology (Merleau-Ponty's included) has notoriously found it difficult to cope with the general problem of otherness – of which the 'I speak' issue is an instance. Having rejected any theory of the unconscious, phenomenology treats every subjective (even if embodied) instance as a unity, present to itself. Then, in the illusion of pluralising it, it raises this instance to the power of 'we'. This 'we' then becomes a unity: the unity of the collectivity. Otherness and heterogeneity are thus done away with in a veritable wave of the phenomenologist's homogenising wand. It is perhaps to Merleau-Ponty's credit, however, that through his creative audacity the limit of phenomenology becomes visible in his work.

Note

1 For example, Merleau-Ponty writes: 'A friend's speech over the telephone brings us the friend himself, as if he were wholly present in that manner of calling and saying goodbye to us' (Merleau-Ponty 1987: 43).

References

Descombes, Vincent (1980), *Modern French Philosophy*, trans. L. Scott-Fox and J. M. Harding, Cambridge: Cambridge University Press.

Dosse, François (1991), *Histoire du structuralisme I. Le champ du signe, 1945–1966*, Paris: éditions la découverte.

Husserl, Edmund (1982), *Ideas Pertaining to a Pure Phenomenology and to a Phenomenological Philosophy. First Book: General Introduction to a Pure Phenomenology*, trans. F. Kersten, Dordrecht, Boston and London: Kluwer Academic Publishers.

Merleau-Ponty, Maurice (1974), *The Prose of the World*, trans. John O'Neill, London: Heinemann.

—— (1987), 'Indirect language and the voices of silence' in *Signs*, trans. Richard C. McCleary, Evanston, Illinois: Northwestern University Press.

—— (1989a), 'An unpublished text by Maurice Merleau-Ponty: A prospectus of his work', trans. Aleen B. Dallery in James M. Edie ed., *The Primacy of Perception*, Evanston, Illinois: Northwestern University Press.

—— (1989b), 'The primacy of perception and its philosophical consequences', trans. James M. Edie in James M. Edie ed., *The Primacy of Perception*, Evanston, Illinois: Northwestern University Press.

—— (1992), *Phenomenology of Perception*, trans. Colin Smith, London: Routledge.

See also: **Heidegger, Husserl, Lacan, Lévi-Strauss, Saussure**

Merleau-Ponty's major writings

(2004) *Maurice Merleau-Ponty's Basic Writings*, ed. Thomas Baldwin, London and New York: Routledge.

(2002) *Husserl at the Limits of Phenomenology, Including Texts by Edmund Husserl*, Evanston, Illinois: Northwestern University Press.

(2000 [1947]) *Humanism and Terror: The Communist Problem*, trans. John O'Neill, New Brunswick, NJ: Transaction Publishers.

(1974 [1967]) *The Prose of the World*, ed. Claude Lefort, trans. John O'Neill, London: Heinemann.

(1973) *Consciousness and the Acquisition of Language* (Sorbonne course for the year, 1949/50), trans. Hugh J. Silverman, Evanston, Illinois: Northwestern University Press.

(1973 [1955]) *Adventures of the Dialectic*, trans. Joseph Bien, Evanston, Illinois: Northwestern University Press.

(1968 [1964]) *The Visible and the Invisible*, ed. Claude Lefort, trans. Alphonso Lingis, Evanston, Illinois: Northwestern University Press.

(1964a) *The Primacy of Perception*, ed. James M. Edie, Evanston, Illinois: Northwestern University Press.

(1964b [1960]) *Signs*, trans. Richard C. McCleary, Evanston, Illinois: Northwestern University Press.

(1964c [1948]) *Sense and Non-Sense*, trans. Hubert L. Dreyfus and Patricia Allen Dreyfus, Evanston, Illinois: Northwestern University Press.

(1963a [1953]) *In Praise of Philosophy*, trans. John Wild and James M. Edie, Evanston, Illinois: Northwestern University Press.

(1963b [1942]) *The Structure of Behaviour*, trans. Alden L. Fisher, Boston: Beacon Press.

(1962 [1945]) *Phenomenology of Perception*, trans. Colin Smith, London: Routledge.

Further reading

Barabas, Renaud (2004), *The Being of the Phenomenon: Merleau-Ponty's Ontology*, trans. Ted Toadvine and Leonard Lawler, Bloomington: Indiana University Press.

Langer, Monika M. (1989), *Merleau-Ponty's Phenomenology of Perception: A Guide and Commentary*, Basingstoke: Macmillan.

Matthews, Eric (2006), *Merleau-Ponty: A Guide for the Perplexed*, London and New York: Continuum.

Priest, Stephen (1998), *Merleau-Ponty*, London and New York: Routledge.

Schmidt, James, (1985), *Maurice Merleau-Ponty: Between Phenomenology and Structuralism*, Basingstoke: Macmillan.

STRUCTURALISM

Two aspects of the structural approach stand out: (1) the recognition (Chomsky not withstanding) that differential relations are the key to understanding culture and society; and, (2) that, as a result, structure is not prior to the realisation of these relations. Saussure, even if he did not recognise the full implications of what he was arguing, inspired the view that to focus on material practices is the way to come to grips with the full, and most anti-essentialist, meaning of 'structure'.

Structuralism also takes language as a system of differential relations as the model most insightful for understanding society, culture, and thought.

EMILE BENVENISTE (1902–1976)

Born in Cairo in 1902, Emile Benveniste was professor of linguistics at the Collège de France from 1937 to 1969, when he was forced to retire due to ill-health, tragically caused by aphasia. He died in 1976.

After being educated at the Sorbonne under Ferdinand de Saussure's former pupil, Antoine Meillet, Benveniste's early work in the 1930s continued Saussure's interest in the history of Indo-European linguistic forms, particularly the status of names. Because of the specialist, technical nature of this early work, Benveniste was little known outside a relatively narrow circle of scholars.

This situation changed with the publication of the first volume of his *Problèmes de linguistique générale* in 1966. A second volume appeared in 1974. The book brings together Benveniste's most accessible writings of a period of more than twenty-five years, and looks at language as a linguistic and semiotic object, as an instrument of communication, as a social and cultural phenomenon, and as a vehicle of subjectivity.

Those Inspired by Benveniste

In the wake of this work, Benveniste became an important figure in the evolution of the structuralist tendency in the social sciences and humanities. Lacan, for instance, recognises in his *Ecrits* that it is Benveniste who deals a behaviourist interpretation a mortal blow with the insight that, unlike the communication of bees, human language is not a simple stimulus–response system. And Kristeva, for her part, has seen that Benveniste's theory of pronouns – especially the relationship between 'I' and 'you' – or what is called the I–you polarity – is of fundamental importance for developing a dynamic conception of subjectivity. Roland Barthes, similarly, clearly saw Benveniste's writings on the 'middle voice' of the verb as being of seminal importance for understanding the position of the writer today – the writer who now writes intransitively (middle voice).

More recently, Giorgio Agamben has made recourse to Benveniste's theory of the subject of the enunciative act (*énonciation*) in order to formulate a theory of witnessing the impossibility of witnessing in relation to Auschwitz (Agamben 2002: 137–65).

Énonciation *(Act of Stating)* and Énoncé *(Statement)*

In his work on pronouns, Benveniste developed a theory of the difference between the *énoncé* (statement independent of context) and the *énonciation* (the act of stating tied to context). Given the phenomenon of 'shifterisation', as elaborated by Roman Jakobson, no meaning of an *énoncé* containing pronouns and other markers of the shifter (such as 'here', 'there', 'this', 'that', etc.) can be understood without reference to context, equivalent here to the act of enunciation. Granted that it is difficult to give an example of an *énonciation* because in fact an *énoncé* is always the necessary vehicle of any example (an example being an instance of a speech act taken out of its context), it is important to recognise that the subject in language is inseparable from its realisation. In other words, the subject is not equivalent to the status attributed to it in the formal, grammatical structure. In terms of the latter, the subject is always the fixed, static entity given in the *énoncé*. In sum, then, Benveniste's insight is that any linguistics which wants to do justice to the dynamics of language must see it as a 'discursive instance' – as discourse, in short. Discourse is the enactment of language.

Pronouns

A key element of Benveniste's theory of language as discourse is his theory of pronouns, and in particular, the theory of the I–you polarity. Grammatically, this polarity constitutes the first and second person pronouns, with he–she–it constituting the third person. Benveniste's insight is that the third person functions as the condition of possibility of the first and second person; the third person is a 'non-person', a status revealed by the neutral voice of narration, or description – the voice of denotation. Kristeva, came to see this polarity as the key to understanding the dynamics of the subject–object (I = subject, you = object) relation in language. The upshot is that, now, the I–you polarity has meaning uniquely in relation to the present instance of discourse. As our author explains when discussing the 'reality' to which *I* or *you* refers:

> *I* signifies 'the person who is uttering the present instance of the discourse containing *I*.' This instance is unique by definition

and has validity only in its uniqueness. ... *I* can only be identified by the instance of discourse that contains it and by that alone.

(Benveniste 1971: 218)

You, for its part, is defined in the following way:

by introducing the situation of 'address', we obtain a symmetrical definition for *you* as the 'individual spoken to in the present instance of discourse containing the linguistic instance of *you*'. These definitions [Benveniste adds] refer to *I* and *you* as a category of language and are related to their position in language.

(Benveniste 1971: 218)

More generally, Benveniste sees language as essentially a dialogue between two or more parties, unlike a signal system where there is no dialogue. Again, in language a message can be passed on to a third person, in contrast to a signal system where the 'message' goes no further than the receiver. Finally, human language is a form that makes possible an infinite variety of contents, while a simple communication system based on a signal is invariably limited to what is programmed (e.g. the signal system of bees relates exclusively to honey). An important implication deriving from these insights is that human language can be used in an ironical way, or in a way requiring the constant interpretation and reinterpretation of the potentially multiple meanings latent in the *énonciation*. This means that human language has an undeniable poetic and fictive side. Connected to this is the further implication that, *qua énonciation*, human language never repeats itself exactly, as is the case with a signal system.

Thought and Language

While he did not ever claim that thought and language were identical, Benveniste would not accept either the position of Hjelmslev, for whom thought was entirely separate from language. For his part, Benveniste pointed out that in practice it is impossible to separate thought from language for, at minimum, language must be the vehicle for thought. As Benveniste says, 'whoever tries to grasp the proper framework of thought encounters only the categories of language' (Benveniste 1971: 63).

Revising Saussure and Semiotic Systems

Although a strong advocate of the importance of Saussure for the history of modern semiotics and linguistics, Benveniste also recognised the need to modify Saussure's theory, in particular in terms of the relationship Saussure drew between linguistics and semiotics. Linguistics, Saussure said in the *Course in General Linguistics*, would one day be subsumed by semiotics, the discipline which studies sign-systems. Such a prediction, Benveniste recognised, needs to be carefully thought through. In doing this, Benveniste notes that linguistic systems such as Morse code, Braille or sign language for the deaf and dumb can be translated between themselves, while semiotic systems are characterised by their non-redundance and therefore are not mutually translatable. As our author explains, 'there is no "synonymy" between semiotic systems; one cannot "say the same thing" through speech and through music, which are systems each having a different basis' (Benveniste 1974: 53). Again, two semiotic systems may well have the same constituent base and yet still be mutually untranslatable – such as, to cite Benveniste, the red in the traffic code and the red in the French tricolore. Consequently, Benveniste concludes, there is no single system of signs which would transcend all other systems; the possibility of an all-embracing semiotics which would include linguistics is therefore greatly reduced. The reverse is perhaps much more likely, namely that the linguistic system is the basis of translation of all semiotic systems.

Semiotics, Semantics and Society

Further to his analysis of the difference between the semiotic and the linguistic systems is Benveniste's discussion of the difference between the semiotic and the semantic dimensions of language. The semiotic (*le sémiotique*) dimension is the mode of significance proper to the sign. Fundamentally, the semiotic exists when it is recognised. It is independent of any reference. The semantic aspect, on the other hand, is to be understood, rather than recognised. As a result, it is entirely referential and engendered by discourse.

Benveniste also became influential during the 1960s with his writings about the nature of language. Like Lévi-Strauss, he pointed out that language is constitutive of the social order, rather than the other way round. Furthermore, it was Benveniste who showed that language's unique and paradoxical aspect in its social setting is its status as a super-individual instrument which can be objectified (hence linguistics), and which, as an instance of discourse, is constitutive of individuality. Indeed, the I–you polarity implies that the individual and society are no longer contradictory terms; for there is no individuality without language and no language independently of a community of speakers. Although Benveniste recognised that it is perfectly possible to study the history of national languages – just as it is possible to study the history of societies – it is not possible to study the history of language as such, or the history of society as such, because it is only within language and society that history is possible.

> For humanity, language (*langue*) and society are unconscious realities. ... Both are always inherited, and we cannot imagine in the exercise of language and in the practice of society that, at this fundamental level, there could ever have been a beginning to either of them. Neither can be changed by human will.
>
> (Benveniste 1971: 72)

Consequently, important changes certainly occur within social institutions, but the social bond itself does not change; similarly, the designations of language can change, but not the language system. This, Benveniste tried to impress upon those who, like Freud in some of his writings, would explain language and society at the level of ontogenesis. The risk is that the 'primitive' form (of society, language, culture) is made to serve as an explanation for the more advanced form. In this sense, 'primitive' societies were deemed by Rousseau, and certain anthropologists who were influenced by him, to be the 'childhood' of mankind, and so hold the key to a knowledge of the foundations of Western society. Benveniste, in 1956, to his credit, demonstrated that Freud, too, was not free of the temptation to call upon an ontogenesis in order to explain dream, primal words and language in general. Benveniste's response is to point out that:

> confusions seem to have arisen in Freud from his constant recourse to 'origins': origins of art, of religion, of society, of language. ... He was constantly transposing what seemed to him to be 'primitive' in man into an original primitivism, for it was indeed into the history of this world that he projected what we could call a chronology of the human psyche.
>
> (see Benveniste 1971: 72)

By drawing attention to the risks involved in allowing ontogenesis to have a strong influence in social theory, Benveniste shows himself to be one of those who opened the way towards a structuralist (and later post-structuralist) approach to the analysis and interpretation of social phenomena. He showed conclusively that language has no origin precisely because it is a system. There can, therefore, be no primitive language. Language changes, but it does not progress. Linguistically, every natural language without exception is complex and highly differentiated. With Benveniste, then, the ethnocentrism of early ethnography is dealt a significant blow.

References

Agamben, Giorgio (2002), *Remnants of Auschwitz: The Witness and the Archive*, trans, Daniel Heller-Roazen, New York: Zone Books.

Benveniste, Émile (1971), *Problems in General Linguistics*. trans. Mary Elizabeth Meek, Coral Gables, Florida: University of Miami Press, 'Miami Linguistics Series No. 8'.

—— (1974), *Problèmes de linguistique générale*, Vol 2, Paris: Gallimard, TEL.

See also: **Agamben, Barthes, Kristeva, Lacan, Lévi-Strauss, Saussure**

Benveniste's major writings

(1994) *Le Vocabulaire des institutions indo-européennes 2: Pouvoir, droit, religion*, Paris: Minuit.

(1987) *Le Vocabulaire des institutions indo-européennes 1: Économie, parenté, société*, Paris: Minuit.

(1974) *Problèmes de linguistique générale*, Vol 2, Paris: Gallimard, TEL.

(1973) *Indo-European Language and Society*, trans. Elizabeth Palmer, London: Faber & Faber, 'Studies in General Linguistics Series'.

(1971 [1966]) *Problems in General Linguistics*, trans. Mary Elizabeth Meek, Coral Gables, Florida: University of Miami Press, 'Miami Linguistics Series No. 8'. Trans. of Vol. 1 of *Problèmes de linguistique générale*, Paris: Gallimard, TEL.

(1966) *Titres et noms propres en iranien ancien*, Paris: Klincksieck, 'Travaux de l'Institut d'Etudes Iraniennes de l'Université de Paris, I'.

(1948) *Noms d'agent et noms d'action en indo-européen*, Paris: A. Maisonneuve.

(1935) *Origines de la formation des noms en indo-européen*, Paris: A. Maisonneuve.

(1935) *Les Infinitifs avestiques*, Paris: A. Maisonneuve.

Further reading

Lotringer, Sylvèrer, and Gora, Thomas (1981), 'Polyphonic linguistics: The many voices of Emile Benveniste', special supplement of *Semiotica*, The Hague: Mouton.

PIERRE BOURDIEU (1930–2002)

Pierre Bourdieu was born in 1930 in Denguin in the south-west of France in the Pyrenees mountains. This is significant because of the relation of the south to Paris. French in the region there is spoken with a southern accent, and Bourdieu often spoke of being treated like a foreigner in Paris, an experience which enabled him to see things from a different perspective: as an outsider, or even foreigner.

Like Jacques Derrida his direct contemporary, Bourdieu attended the prestigious Parisian Lycée, Louis-Le-Grand in 1950–51, and completed his *agrégation* in philosophy at the École Normale Supérieure (rue d'Ulm) in 1955. As part of his military service, Bourdieu taught in Algeria, and so experienced French colonialism at first hand. This experience was formative, and the effort to understand it set the philosopher on the path of anthropology and sociology. Later, between 1959 and 1962, Bourdieu taught philosophy at the Sorbonne, where he worked with Raymond Aaron, who saw his potential. In 1964, he became director of studies at the École des Hautes Études, and the director of European Sociology. In 1981, he was elected to the chair of Sociology at the Collège de France and gave his inaugural lecture there in 1982.

Bourdieu's Oeuvre

Certain things stand out in Pierre Bourdieu's *oeuvre* as a practice of sociology: a concern to analyse inequality and class distinction at a structural rather than at an ideological level, but without succumbing to the (as Bourdieu puts it) 'objectivist' illusion of structuralism; a refusal of scholasticism, or the purely abstract study of phenomena independently of any context; a concern to enable science to go beyond its reliance on the model for grasping the nature of social life, and so come to grips with practice, or practices, and their relation to practical knowledge; a desire to go beyond the clichés, stereotypes, and classifications of the universally unquestioned *doxa*, and, as a consequence, to make explicit the power relations inscribed in social reality, in a social field. Finally, Bourdieu's epistemology is characterised by a refusal to be caught between the either–or issue of singular truth or historicism, while aiming to do justice to truth and its context (see Bourdieu 2004: 1–3; 21–31).

Always of interest to the media, Bourdieu caused a certain furore in 1996 when he published a critique of television and journalism, saying that television, in the pretence of being open to the world was in fact a form of censorship because, with its various and strict formats, it limited what could be said and communicated (see Bourdieu 1996).

Class

Since undertaking fieldwork in Algeria in the 1960s, Bourdieu was committed to revealing the underlying modes of class domination in capitalist societies as these appear in all aspects of education and art. His abiding thesis is that the dominant class does not dominate overtly: it does not force the dominated to conform to its will. Nor does it dominate in capitalist society through a conspiracy where the privileged would consciously manipulate reality in accordance with their own self-interest. Rather, the dominant class in capitalist society is, statistically, the beneficiary of economic, social and symbolic power, power which is embodied in economic and cultural capital, and which is infused throughout society's institutions and practices and reproduced by these very institutions and practices.

The Academic Milieu

In his book, *Homo Academicus* (1988), Bourdieu says that the École des Hautes Etudes in Paris remains one of the rare marginal, yet prestigious, institutions in the French academic system, one which fostered original thought and research. This was important for Bourdieu early in his career, because higher education in France tends to be structured around academically prestigious individuals and institutions (like the École Normale Supérieure – rue d'Ulm). 'Academically prestigious' does not necessarily mean scholarly and intellectually challenging. Rather, it means that academic accolades tend to go to those who know, whether consciously or not, how to work the patronage system, and make best use of any inherited privileges, or cultural capital, they might have. Academic privilege and the institutional power that goes with it are contrasted by Bourdieu with scholarly and intellectual renown. While the latter might entail a certain imagination, originality and critical acuity, the former requires 'the most authentic proof of *obsequium*, unconditional respect for the fundamental principles of the established order' (Bourdieu 1988: 87).

The view of the academic milieu as 'fair' and 'competitive' and supposedly charged with 'pushing back the frontiers of knowledge', and selecting 'the best minds' for the task, is the kind of common-sense orthodoxy that Bourdieu's sociological research and reflection aimed to dispel. Indeed, for Bourdieu, what is self-evident, and taken for granted, what goes without saying – our common-sense ideas, or our imprecise unscientific language – are founded on a misrecognition (*méconnaissance*) of unequal power relations and a concomitant *reproduction* of privilege.

Epistemology

To a large extent, Bourdieu's underlying theoretical stance was presented in his early essay, *An Outline of a Theory of Practice* (Bourdieu (1972) [1977]). There, in the context of ethnographic studies, Bourdieu delineates a three-tiered framework of theoretical knowledge, where the most reflexive level will eventually be employed to classify 'the classifiers', to 'objectify the objectifying subject', and to judge the very arbiters of taste themselves. The first element of this framework is 'primary experience', or what Bourdieu also calls the 'phenomenological' level. This level is known to all researchers in the field because it is the source of their basic descriptive data about the familiar, everyday world – either of their own society or of another. The second level, almost as familiar, is that of the 'model' or of 'objectivist' knowledge. Here, knowledge 'constructs the objective relations (e.g. economic or linguistic) which structure practice and representations of practice'. Thus at a 'primary' level, the researcher might note that at every wedding, birthday or Christmas people exchange presents. At an objectivist level, the researcher might theorise that, despite what common sense suggests, gift exchange is a means of maintaining prestige and confirming a social hierarchy, and perhaps also an instance of the way exchange as such is a mode of social cohesion. The point Bourdieu emphasises about such knowledge is that it is fundamentally the knowledge of the detached, neutral observer who is engaged in developing a theory of the practice implied in the primary data. When it comes to studying language or gift-exchange in particular, the knowledge of the detached theorist is significantly limited. Clearly, if language is studied only from the position of the listener (often the position of detachment), and not also from the position of speaker, a defective form of knowledge is derived. Bourdieu thus argues that an adequate theory of practice must include a theory of the actor's position. The major defect of the objectivist approach to practice is that it is too rigidly detached from the subtleties of everyday activities. It therefore fails to account for elements integral to practice – such as 'style', 'tact', 'dexterity', '*savoir-faire*', and particularly, 'improvisation'. Similarly, in constructing a model of practice – e.g. exchange of gifts – objectivist knowledge cannot account for 'misfires', or 'strategies' which might undermine the universality of the model. In other words, time is left out of the model along with the notion of 'strategy'. 'Strategy', says Bourdieu, 'allows for individual intervention against the model.' This, the structuralist position as enunciated by Lévi-Strauss, failed to do. To be sure, relations, and not substances, characterise social and cultural life – as Saussure's theory of language led researchers to see. However, to remain at this level, as Bourdieu claims first-wave structuralism tended to do, is to remain at the level of the model, or objectivist knowledge.

Bourdieu proposes, then, that a theory of objectivist knowledge will, at the same time, be a more rigorous and illuminating theory of practice. He claims that a truly rigorous theory of practice is accomplished by taking up the position of the realisation of practice. A tall order it might well be thought. Bourdieu, though, is not to be denied. And from the position of theory in the *Outline*, he goes on to produce, in the period 1979–92, four important works on education and taste – *Distinction*, *Homo Academicus*, *State of Nobility* (*La Noblesse d'état*) and *The Rules of Art* – works in which a number of Bourdieu's key concepts are deployed. '*Habitus*', 'field' and 'cultural capital' are cases in point.

Habitus

Although sometimes mistaken for specific routines of everyday life, or as a synonym for socialisation, *habitus* is in fact part of Bourdieu's theory of practice as the articulation of dispositions in social space. The space is also a social field in that the positions in it form a system of relations based on stakes (power) that are meaningful and desired by those occupying the positions in social space. *Habitus* is a kind of expression of the (unconscious) investment social actors have in the power stakes so implied. *Habitus* is a kind of grammar of actions which serves to differentiate one class (e.g. the dominant) from another (e.g. the dominated) in the social field. In *Distinction* Bourdieu refers to *habitus* as a system of schemas for the production of particular practices. Thus if 'good taste' entails that the university professor will have a marked preference for Bach's *Well Tempered Clavier*, while 'middle-brow' manual and clerical workers will prefer *The Blue Danube*, the validity of good taste is only undermined when it is revealed that the professor (especially of law or medicine) is himself the son of a professor who had a private art collection and whose wife was a good amateur musician. For, the professor is marked as someone who has not only 'achieved' a certain amount in the field of education, but also as someone who has inherited cultural capital. This is to say that, in particular cases, the family environment can provide a significant amount of knowledge, under-standing and 'taste' which is not formally learned, but is uncon-sciously acquired.

A specific *habitus* becomes evident when a range of variables (occupation, education, income, artistic preferences, taste in food, etc.) are shown, statistically, to correlate with each other. Thus, in con-tradistinction to the manual worker, the professor of law will tend to have had a private school education, prefer Bach (and more generally, the form of art to its content), have a high income, and will prefer a simple, if elegant, cuisine of lean meats, fresh fruit and vegetables. This correlation is what Bourdieu says constitutes a specific (in this case bourgeois, or dominant) set of dispositions, or a *habitus*. A *habitus* is generative of a set of dispositions common to a class. With the knowledge of a class *habitus*, it is not possible to predict exactly what a member of the dominant, or the dominated, class will do at a par-ticular time and in a particular situation. To do so would be to eliminate time and agency and to reaffirm the primacy of the model over practice, the very thing that the *Outline* had criticised in the early 1970s. Bourdieu has also said that *habitus* has to do with a 'sense of one's place' which emerges through processes of differentiation in social space, and that it is a system of schemas for the production of practices, as well as a system of schemas of perception and appercep-tion of these practices. The boundaries between one *habitus* and another are always contested because they are always fluid – never firm.

Bourdieu's Approach as a Whole

Bourdieu worked hard to refine this key concept of his *oeuvre*, for it is the basis on which he laid claim to originality as a sociologist. Because the economistic approach of Marxism is too reductionist, and because early structuralism was too objectivist, and because, finally, conspiracy theories of class domination give too much weight to primary experience – as exemplified, for instance, in specific, everyday acts of naked self-interest – Bourdieu worked to refine his theory of practice in order that it may be both scientific and behol-den to practice. To be scientific here, is to account for contingency, agency, and time.

The success of Bourdieu's approach is another matter. For it could be argued that any link with theory is bound to freeze practice in its tracks. To be sure, *habitus* might be a disposition, but what exactly is the relationship between this disposition and contingent acts? Statistical regularities, Bourdieu replies; in other words: scientific knowledge. But of what use (cultural, political, social, etc.) is this knowledge? When it is used by groups for political purposes it risks becoming purely ideological, a dimension of symbolic power: the power to represent.

While it is true that Bourdieu's notion of entering the game of practice without being carried away by it, is suggestive, and while his more tragic image of science as real freedom to the extent that it is the 'knowledge of necessity' offers a possible basis for a deeper understanding of the scientific, and thus sociological, enterprise, Bourdieu's work is still reliant on a fundamental division between theory and practice, or between theory and reality. This division itself needs to be reworked if Bourdieu's work is to encompass the dynamism of Freud's.

Again, in a postscript in his monumental study, *Distinction*, Bourdieu takes to task the 'cultivated' disposition of the philosopher as exemplified even in Jacques Derrida's 'unorthodox' reading of Kant on aesthetics. To oppose philosophy philosophically is merely to reinforce the privileged status of the 'philosophical field', says Bourdieu. It is still to pay homage to a body of canonical texts which are relatively inaccessible to the outsider. It is still to forget the 'objective conditions' of philosophy, where prestige is awarded to the erudite and denied to the neophyte. It is, moreover, characteristic of intellectuals to have the *habitus* of the privileged, even though they tend to be the dominated fraction of the dominant class.

All this is fine up to a point. The importance of being aware of the social conditions of philosophy – and art – should put a break on any sanctimonious assertion of its autonomy. Nevertheless, Bourdieu himself was clearly trained in philosophy, just as his work also relies on the canon of privileged texts for its inspiration. Bourdieu thus tacitly recognises that this canon is the only one we have at the moment, and that, for better or for worse, we are led to seek inspiration there, even though there can be no absolute confirmation of its truth and legitimacy. Drawing attention to the objective conditions of different kinds of discourse is no doubt Bourdieu's greatest contribution to sociological thought. However, this sociology risks standing still if it does not also develop new theoretical insights in light of this contribution.

References

Bourdieu, Pierre (1972 [1977]), *An Outline of a Theory of Practice*, trans. Richard Nice, Cambridge, London, New York and Melbourne: Cambridge University Press.

—— (1988), *Homo Academicus*, trans. Peter Collier, Cambridge: Polity Press.

—— (1996), *Sur la télévision*, Paris: Liber/Raisons d'agir.

—— (2004), *Science of Science and Reflexivity*, trans Richard Nice, Cambridge: Polity Press.

See also: **Derrida, Lévi-Strauss, Saussure**

Bourdieu's major writings

(2005 [2000]) *The Social Structures of the Economy*, trans. Chris Turner, Cambridge, UK and Malden, Mass.: Polity Press.

(2004 [2001]) *Science of Science and Reflexivity*, trans Richard Nice, Cambridge: Polity Press.

(2003 [1998]) *Firing Back: Against the Tyranny of the Market*, trans. Loïc Wacquant, New York: New York Press.

(2001 [1998]) *Masculine Domination*, trans. Richard Nice, Stanford: Stanford University Press.

(1999 [1993]) *Weight of the World: Social Suffering in Contemporary Society*, trans. Priscilla Parkhurst Ferguson, Stanford: Stanford University Press.

(1996a [1992]) *Rules of Art: Genesis and Structure of the Literary Field*, trans. Susan Emanuel, Cambridge: Polity Press.

(1996b [1989]) *The State Nobility: Elite Schools in the Field of Power*, trans. Lauretta C. Clough, Stanford: Stanford University Press (trans. of *La Noblesse d'état: Les Grandes Ecoles et esprit de corps*, Paris: Minuit).

(1994) with Jean-Claude Passeron and Monique de Saint Martin, *Academic Discourse: Linguistic Misunderstanding and Professional Power*, trans. Richard Teese, Stanford: Stanford University Press.

(1993) *The Field of Cultural Production: Essays on Art and Literature*, ed. Randal Johnson, Cambridge: Polity Press.

(1992) with Loïc J. D. Wacquant, *An Invitation to Reflexive Sociology*, Chicago: University of Chicago Press.

(1991a [1978]) 'Sport and social class' in Chandra Mukerji and Michael Schudson (eds), *Rethinking Popular Culture*, Berkeley: University of California Press.

(1991b) *Language and Symbolic Power*, ed. John B. Thompson, Cambridge: Polity Press.

(1991c [1988]) *The Political Ontology of Martin Heidegger*, trans. Peter Collier, Cambridge: Polity Press.

(1991d [1968]) with Jean-Claude Passeron and Jean-Claude Chamboredon, *The Craft of Sociology: Epistemological Preliminaries*, trans. Richard Nice, Berlin and New York: de Gruyter.

(1990a [1987]) *In Other Words: Essays Toward a Reflexive Sociology*, trans. M. Adamson, Cambridge: Polity Press.

(1990b [1980]) *The Logic of Practice*, trans. Richard Nice, Cambridge: Polity Press.
(1988 [1984]) *Homo Academicus*, trans. Peter Collier, Cambridge: Polity Press.
(1986 [1979]) *Distinction*, trans. Richard Nice, London and New York: Routledge & Kegan Paul.
(1979a [1977]) *Algeria 1960: The disenchantment of the World: the Sense of Honour: the Kabyle House or the World Reversed: Essays*, trans. Richard Teese, Cambridge and New York: Cambridge University Press.
(1979b [1964]) with Jean-Claude Passereon, *The Inheritors*, trans. Richard Nice, Chicago: University of Chicago Press.
(1979c [1977]) *Algeria 1960*, Cambridge: Cambridge University Press.
(1977 [1970]) with Jean-Claude Passeron, *Reproduction in Education, Society and Culture*, trans. Richard Nice, London: Sage.
(1972 [1977]) *An Outline of a Theory of Practice*, trans. Richard Nice, Cambridge, London, New York and Melbourne: Cambridge University Press.
(1968) 'Structuralism and theory of sociological knowledge', *Social Research*, 35, 4 (Winter), 682–706.
(1962) *Sociologie de l'Algére*, Paris: PUF, second edn.

Further reading

Danaher, Geoffrey; Shirato, Tony; Webb, Jen (2002), *Understanding Bourdieu*, London and Thousand Oaks, CA: Sage.
Robins, Derek (2000), *Pierre Bourdieu*, London and Thousand Oaks, CA: Sage.
Robins, Derek (2005), *Pierre Bourdieu 2*, London and Thousand Oaks, CA: Sage.

NOAM CHOMSKY (b.1928)

If critical interest and acclaim are any indication, Noam Chomsky would have to be seen as one of the most significant and influential linguists of the twentieth century. Chomsky received his linguistic training under Leonard Bloomfield, whose behaviourist empiricism dominated American linguistics during the 1930s and 1940s, and from Zellig Harris, whose political stances during the 1950s pleased Chomsky more than his version of linguistic structuralism.

Chomsky's contribution to linguistics, and thence to modern thought, has been broadly threefold. In the first place, he moved the emphasis of linguistics from the strictly descriptive and inductive level (the level of the endless cataloguing of utterances from which conclusions about grammar could then be drawn) to the ideal level of competence and 'deep structure', the level which opens up a creative aspect in language. In short, Chomsky showed, within his technical expertise in linguistics, that language was more than its material execution. Second, he brought about a reconsideration of language learning by arguing that language competence is not acquired inductively through a behaviourist stimulus-response conditioning, but is the consequence of an innate cognitive capacity possessed by humans. In other words, linguistic freedom and creativity is not acquired, but always already exists as a governing a priori. Third, the distinction between 'competence' and 'performance' – even when it was poorly understood – has served as a metaphor for structural studies in other disciplines such as philosophy and sociology (cf., Habermas's notion of 'communicative competence', and Bourdieu's notion of '*habitus*' – notions which echo Chomsky's conception of agency).

The Liberal

It is worth noting that Chomsky has also become an outspoken, left-liberal intellectual who vigorously opposed America's involvement in the Vietnam War, and who has written nearly a dozen books dealing with international and domestic political issues of the day. After publishing a raft of books on American and world politics, including: *American Power and the New Mandarins* (1969); *The Backroom Boys* (1973); *Necessary Illusions: Thought Control in Democratic Societies* (1989); and *Deterring Democracy* (1991), Chomsky has also been productive since September 11, 2001, with books such as *Power and Terror: Post 9/11 Talks and Interviews* (2003); *Hegemony or Survival: America's Quest for Global Dominance* (2004) and *Failed States: the Abuse of Power and the Assault on Democracy* (2006).

Left-liberalism is not about changing the system (political, economic, social), but about radically reforming it from within. Although it is pragmatic and secular in the sense that, for it, the material world, here and now, must be changed, and therefore one must engage with this world as it is, left-liberalism is also critical of principles being too readily sacrificed in the interests of consensus. In short, as a left-liberal is unlikely to be elected to government, he or she can afford to occupy the moral high ground. For Chomsky, and for many liberals, the American government is truly at odds with the people. This is simultaneously a cause for despair and for hope. It provokes despair because the people are kept powerless by subterfuge and propaganda; it is a cause for hope because, in fact, the majority are opposed to the government's mode of conduct, particularly foreign policy, but lack the means to change it. The liberal's task is to help the people to see that they can turn their virtual opposition into political capital.

In keeping with his left-liberal principles, Chomsky, in what seemed to many like a tremendous lapse of political judgement – he is himself a Jew (his father was in fact a Hebrew scholar) – wrote a Preface in 1980 to Robert Faurisson's notorious book against the existence of the Nazi gas chambers. Chomsky based his intervention on the (misguided) principle that to be a consistent liberal in politics all shades of opinion have a right to be heard, however repugnant these might seem. In other words, the liberal sticks to principle, no matter what!

The Man and Early Work

Noam Chomsky was born in Philadelphia in 1928. His early education was in an 'experimental progressive school', and at the Central High School, Philadelphia. At the University of Pennsylvania, he studied mathematics and philosophy, as well as linguistics under the influence of Zellig Harris. Although he gained his PhD degree at the University of Pennsylvania, most of the work for it was completed at Harvard University between 1951 and 1955. Since 1955, Chomsky has taught at the Massachusetts Institute of Technology, and he has been an Institute Professor there since 1976.

Through his father – who published *Hebrew: The Eternal Language* (1958) – Chomsky was introduced to historical linguistics. In fact, the son's first major piece of writing is his unpublished Master's thesis – also on Hebrew – entitled 'Morphophonemics of modern Hebrew' (1951). Given Chomsky's parallel interest in logic and mathematics, it was no doubt to be expected that the work of logicians (Goodman, Quine, Kripke, Lakatós, Hintikka) and analytical philosophers (Austin, Wittgenstein) would be of greater interest to him than philosophers or linguists from the so-called Continental tradition. Such an interest has at times given Chomsky's writings the sparse style imitative of the putative rigour of the natural sciences. As he himself has put it, like physics, the intellectual interest of linguistics resides less in phenomena (the products of language) and more in the explanatory power of its principles (Chomsky 1979: 58–59). 'Natural science', says Chomsky, 'as distinct from natural history, is not concerned with the phenomena in themselves, but with the principles and the explanations that they have some bearing on' (Chomsky 1979: 59). Such an approach – also evident in work in logic – entails that a certain style (use of notation), format (use of micro-examples), and method (idealisation) are taken to be axiomatic, and so generally to be beyond critical scrutiny. This has meant that although his work has been taken up elsewhere (e.g. France), Chomsky himself has often been unable to engage in a dialogue with linguists whose presuppositions are inherited from a different tradition.

Generative Grammar Linguistic Theory

Chomsky initially set out to explain how an ideal language-user could generate and understand new and unique grammatical sentences without ever having encountered them in practice. As a result, he set out to show that a finite and describable set of transformational rules constituted the 'competence' of the ideal language-user, and that this competence could generate grammatical sentences. 'Performance', which is equivalent to the finite number of grammatical sentences realised by actual language-users, provides evidence (a corpus), Chomsky said, for an investigation of competence, and he added that competence did not imply a conscious appreciation and invocation of generative rules on the part of the language-user; instead, it had to be seen as equivalent to the mode itself of the speaker's being in language. In other words, competence is the very condition of possibility of language: competence is constitutive of the speaker rather than the other way around.

In turning now to aspects of Chomsky's theory of language, we focus first of all on the notion of 'generative' grammar. Generative grammar is a kind of elementary system of rules that recursively define and give rise to sentence transformations. It is linked to the basic 'competence' of an ideal speaker–hearer, a competence which enables the production of a potentially infinite number of well-formed sentences. 'Generative' evokes the mathematical term, 'generator'. The latter gives rise to a 'generating function' (e.g. $2x + 3y - z$) which generates an infinite set of values. For his part, Chomsky defines a generative grammar as a set of rules which, in defining a set (of objects), 'may be said to generate this set'. And he continues:

> [A] (generative) grammar may be said to generate a set of structural descriptions, each of which, ideally, incorporates a deep structure, a surface structure, a semantic interpretation (of the deep structure), and a phonetic interpretation (of the surface structure).
>
> (Chomsky 1972: 126)

The structure (for this is indeed what it is) of a generative grammar may be – following Chomsky's approach in *Syntactic Structures* of three basic types (it being remembered that a grammar explains how sentences are generated):

1 *Finite state grammar*: this is linear only, so that sentences are generated by means of simple choices from left to right with each preceding choice limiting the scope of a succeeding choice.
2 *Phrase structure grammar*: this corresponds to parsing (the classification of constituent elements of the 'surface' structure of a sentence), and is concerned with the multiple meanings possible in the same phrase constituents: 'old men and women' (to take the example given by Lyons) can mean '(old men) and women', or, 'old (men and women)'.
3 *Transformational grammar*: this is a way of deriving a new constituent structure (e.g. active form into passive form) through a set of rules based both on the horizontal string of the base phrase structure (represented by a phrase-marker) and on the vertical 'tree' resulting when account is taken of how this string was derived.

Chomsky was able to show that both phrase structure grammar and transformational grammar are more powerful (i.e. can do more) than finite state grammar, and that transformational grammar is a more powerful grammar than phrase structure grammar. Transformational grammar is essentially Chomsky's own contribution to a general theory of grammar. The other two grammars – although previously not formalised – existed in linguistics prior to Chomsky's work. Only a transformational grammar can derive the basic rules constitutive of the ideal speaker–hearer of, for example, English. The logic behind transformational grammar is that if every utterance implied a unique rule as a condition of its acceptability, there would be too many rules to deal with. Clearly, the number of rules is not equivalent to the number of utterances; this is what any grammar implies. On the other hand, Chomsky points out that if one cannot show that many sentences – apparently different at a 'surface' level of phrase structure grammar – are in fact transformations of the same rule, the grammar becomes almost infinitely complex and contains little explanatory power. Phrase structure grammar would thus become too complex if it alone were charged with providing all the rules of the ideal speaker–hearer's sentence formation. In sum, then, a transformational grammar is a way of reducing sentence formation to the smallest number of rules possible. From a slightly different angle, the transformational grammar, providing the rules of competence, is equivalent to Chomsky's notion of 'deep structure'.

Language Competence

One further facet of Chomsky's theory of language needs to be considered before we move to a brief assessment of his work. It concerns his attempt to bolster his theory of generative grammar by linking it to a notion of 'cognitive capacity' (see for example Chomsky 1976: Ch.1)

Because he believes that we cannot explain language acquisition and language competence (which presupposes language creativity) inductively, or in terms of any version of stimulus–response theory, Chomsky resorts to the notion of an innate, specifically human, language capacity as a way of explaining the nature of human language. In particular, he has been much taken with the Cartesian view that language and mind are so inextricably linked that knowledge of the origin of language would at the same time open up a knowledge of the human mind. For the inventor of generative grammar, therefore, language is fundamentally part of human psychology – psychology to be understood as a theory of the faculties of the human mind. Language competence is thus less linguistic than psychological in origin; or, should we not rather say that the origin of language is the psychological subject? In these views, Chomsky has been particularly influenced by Descartes and the seventeenth-century rationalist, scientific tradition. Instead of giving language autonomous status – as came to be the case with Saussure's structuralist view of language – seventeenth-century rationalism saw language as an expression of the psychological subject. Apparently, Chomsky believes that only by identifying with this tradition can justice be done to the dynamic and creative essence of language and a relapse into some form of empiricist explanation of it avoided. Indeed, to Chomsky's eyes, Saussure's incipient (or even full-blown) empiricism makes him unacceptable to generative linguistics. According to the Cartesian linguist, Saussure ended up privileging *parole* (speech) over *langue* (grammatical structure).[1]

How Innovative is Chomsky?

What, then, are we to make of Chomsky's work? Let it be acknowledged that any profound evaluation of generative grammar will need to take account of Chomsky's considerable technical expertise in linguistics. That said, some things are clearly debatable, even to the outsider. Thus, even though the theory of generative grammar is undoubtedly one of the intellectual achievements of the twentieth century, it is limited in at least the following respects.

The first of these limitations concerns the notion of idealisation. In this regard, we recall that 'competence' refers to the 'competence of the idealised speaker–hearer'. The problem with this does not pertain to the fact that 'competence' is virtual (i.e. is never fully realised empirically), but with the fact that this competence is identified with a non-linguistic component, the ideal 'speaker–hearer', rather than with language itself. Here, idealisation is quite compatible with Chomsky's rationalist view that language is an expression of something else – namely, a cognitive capacity inseparable from individual psychology. The question arises as to what language must be for it to be an expression of individual psychology. But is language only an expression of something? That is, is it purely transparent? Modern semiotics and poetics would suggest that the answer is in the negative, for there is also poetic language: language as (relatively) opaque.

Let us suppose that Chomsky were to respond by saying that idealisation is a methodological exigency and is not to be confused with the way language is in itself. The difficulty here is that it is impossible to avoid the sense that idealisation is being linked with the principle of competence *per se* – competence being equivalent to an infinite (= ideal) number of sentences. Still another problem with idealisation is that it fails – as Kristeva has shown – to account for language as a *process* of realisation. Chomsky's level of 'performance' does not alter this. For performance simply focuses on utterances as already realised; it does not account for the *fact* of the process of their realisation: the level of discourse for Benveniste. As a result, Chomsky's is a static, rather than a dynamic view of language.

Yet another problem raised by Chomsky's linguistics stems from the emphasis placed on the competence of the native speaker as the model speaker of a language. Two issues (at least) need to be considered here. The first is whether the native speaker (the speaker of a mother tongue) is an adequate model of how language works. Although there may be advantages in relying on the native speaker in assessing grammaticalness, could it not be proposed that, ideally, speakers can acquire native competence in a number, or even many, languages? The fact that they do not cannot necessarily be attributed to the nature of language itself. Second, it could be suggested that an essential aspect of language is the possibility of its being translated. This aspect is necessarily overlooked in Chomsky's focus on the competence of the native speaker.

Finally, Chomsky's rationalism seems to be a vast over-reaction to the behaviourism and empiricism characteristic of the Anglo-American philosophical and linguistic environment in which Chomsky was trained. As a result, he often comes across as the embattled rationalist painfully trying to make some headway against the forces of empiricism. However, the important theoretical debates about language and philosophy today are clearly not limited to those that the rivalry between rationalism and empiricism has thrown up. That Chomsky's theoretical writing does not seem to have registered this is a serious limitation.

Note

1 The irony is that most critics of Saussure (e.g. Bourdieu) tend to argue that he privileged *langue* over *parole*.

References

Chomsky, Noam (1972), *Language and Mind* (enlarged edn), New York: Harcourt Brace Jovanovich.

—— (1976), *Reflections on Language*, London: Temple Smith in association with Fontana Books.

—— (1979), *Language and Responsibility, Based on Conversations with Mitsou Ronat*, trans. John Viertel, New York: Pantheon Books.

See also: **Benveniste, Kristeva, Saussure**

Chomsky's major writings

(2006) *Failed States: the Abuse of Power and the Assault on Democracy*, New York: Metropolitan Books/Henry Holt.

(2004) *Hegemony or Survival: America's Quest for Global Dominance*, New York: Henry Holt.

(2003) *Power and Terror: Post 9/11 Talks and Interviews*, John Junkerman and Takei Masakazu (eds), New York: Seven Stories Press.

(2002) On Nature and Language, Adrianna Belleth and Luigi Rizzi (eds), Cambridge: Cambridge University Press.

(2000a) *Rogue States: the Rule of Force in World Affairs*, Cambridge, Mass.: South Edn Press.

(2000b) *New Horizons in the Study of Language and Mind*, Cambridge and New York: Cambridge University Press.

(1997) *Media Control: the Spectacular Achievements of Propaganda*, New York: Seven Stories Press.

(1995) *The Minimalist Program*, Cambridge, Mass.: The MIT Press.

(1993) *Language and Thought*, Wakefield, R.I.: Moyer Bell.

(1988) *Language and Problems of Knowledge: The Managua Lectures*, Cambridge, Mass.: MIT Press.

(1980) *Rules and Representations*, Oxford: Basil Blackwell.

(1976) *Reflections on Language*, London: Temple Smith in association with Fontana Books.

(1975) *The Logical Structure of Linguistic Theory*, New York: Plenum Press.

(1972a) *Studies on Semantics in Generative Grammar*, The Hague and Paris: Mouton.

(1972b) *Studies on Semantics in Generative Grammar*, The Hague and Paris: Mouton.

(1972c) *Language and Mind*, New York: Harcourt Brace Jovanovich.

(1971) *Chomsky: Selected Readings*, J. P. B. Allen and Paul Van Buren (eds), London and New York: Oxford University Press.

(1968) with Morris Halle, *The Sound Pattern of English*, New York: Harper & Row.

(1966) *Cartesian Linguistics: A Chapter in the history of Rationalist Thought*, New York: Harper & Row.

(1965) *Aspects of the Theory of Syntax*, Cambridge, Mass.: MIT Press.

(1964) *Current Issues in Linguistic Theory*, The Hague and Paris: Mouton.

(1957) *Syntactic Structures*, The Hague and Paris: Mouton.

Further reading

Huck, Geoffrey and Goldsmith, John A. (1995), *Ideology and Linguistic Theory: Noam Chomsky and the Deep Structure Debates*, London and New York: Routledge.

McGilvray, James (2005), *The Cambridge Companion to Chomsky*, Cambridge and New York: Cambridge University Press.

Newmeyer, Frederick J. (1996), *Generative Linguistics: A Historical Perspective*, London and New York: Routledge.

Otero, Carlos P., ed. (1994-), *Noam Chomsky: Critical Assessments*, 8 vols, London and New York: Routledge.

Radford, Andrew (1981), *Transformational Syntax: A Student's Guide to Chomsky's Extended Theory*, Cambridge: Cambridge University Press.

Smith, Neil (2004), *Chomsky: Ideas and Ideals*, New York: Cambridge University Press.

Winston, Morton (2002), *On Chomsky*, Belmont, Cal.: Wadsworth/Thomson Learning.

GEORGES DUMÉZIL (1898–1986)

Along with Claude Lévi-Strauss, Georges Dumézil is recognised, in the social sciences, as one of the earliest exponents of a comparative structuralist method. This method, based on a carefully constructed system of classifications and analyses, allowed Dumézil to mark out, in Indo-European 'civilisation', three invariant social functions: sovereignty, war and production. More precisely, Dumézil sought to demonstrate the nature and connectedness – without denying the

differences – of the elements constitutive of Indo-European civilization. This demonstration takes place through an astonishing foray
into Indo-European religion and mythology, as these are rendered
manifest in epics, legends, and histories (cf. the founding of Rome).
Amongst Dumézil's privileged sources should be mentioned the
Indian *Mahabharata*, the *Iranian Avesta* (the sacred book of the Zor-
oastrians), the Scandinavian *Edda*, and, for Rome Virgil's *Aeneid*.
How did Dumézil come to be the scholar of Indo-European civilisation? And what is it, exactly, that Durnézil calls 'Indo-European
civilisation'?

Georges Dumézil was born in Paris in at the end of the nineteenth
century. According to his own account, he first became interested
in myth through reading Greek legends as a child. His father had
given him the well-known parallel German–French text by Niebuhr.
Also read at an early age by the future mythologist were the tales of
Perrault.

After his secondary schooling, Dumézil attended the prestigious
Parisian *lycée*, Louis-Le-Grand, then entered the École Normale (rue
d'Ulm) in 1916. Although his studies were interrupted by the First
World War (he was demobilised in 1919), Dumézil passed his *agrégation* in *lettres*, in December 1919, and was shortly afterwards named
'professeur' at the Lycée of Beauvais in the north of France, where he
taught until October of 1920.

Unable to tolerate the life of a secondary school teacher, Dumézil
resigned his post in order to devote himself to preparing his *doctorat
d'état – Le Festin d'immortalité. Etude de mythologie comparée indo-européenne*
(*The Festival of Immortality. A Study of Comparative Indo-European
Mythology*) – under the direction of the leading historical linguist of
the day, Antoine Meillet. He also thought to look out for a foreign
posting and was subsequently named as a reader in French at the
University of Warsaw. As living away from France at that time was
too painful, Dumézil resigned after six months returning to Paris in
the summer of 1921. Three years on a scholarship saw the completion of his thesis, defended in 1924.

Soon afterwards, the young scholar left for Turkey to take up a post
as professor of the history of religions at the University of Istanbul, a
post made possible by the secularising policies of Mustapha Kemal.
For six years (1925–31), Dumézil taught in Turkey – 'the best years'
of his life he said in 1986. Dumézil returned to France in 1933 to
take up a post as director of studies at the École Pratique des Hautes
Études, having spent two years at the University of Uppsala (where
he started to learn Scandinavian languages) as a reader in French.

In 1949, Dumézil was elected to the Collège de France to the chair of Indo-European civilisation, where he taught until his retirement in 1968. He then spent three years teaching in the United States, and was elected to the French Academy in 1978. He died in October 1986.

Comparative Mythology: Three Functions of Sovereignty, War and Production

Dumézil always insisted on the progressive and provisional character of his *oeuvre*, often comparing his numerous publications to annual reports. As a result many of his books are elaborations of works already published. The various volumes of *Myth et épopée*, for example, have been published in three and four editions, each carefully revised and corrected. In Dumézil's terms, Indo-European civilisation refers to the cultures of India, North Africa (especially Egypt and Iran), Europe (especially Rome), and Scandinavia. And in his earliest work, *Le Festin d'immortalité* published in 1924, and the result of his doctoral research, Dumézil begins his exploration of the way elements of different cultures within the Indo-European framework, contain within them echoes of others. In the case of *Le Festin d'immortalité*, the concern is to reconstitute the mythology of the sacred drink of Indo-European peoples, and to show how the sacred drink of ambrosia (the drink which permits the gods to be immortal) in the Occident corresponds to the Indian (Sanskrit) *amrita*. Although Dumézil distanced himself from this and other work done before 1938, it contains in embryo the programme of all his future research. As with his *Ouranos-Varuna: Étude de mythologie comparée indo-européenne* (1934) – where the god of Greek mythology (Uranus) is ranged with the Indian god (Varuna) and *Flamen-Brahman* (1935) – where the Roman god (Flamen) is ranged with the Indian Brahman – the comparison is deemed by Dumézil in 1938 not to work.

After 1938, Dumézil is inspired by the idea, derived from his research, that the three functions of sovereignty, war and production link together the diverse origins of the cultures constitutive of the Indo-Europeans. This tripartition becomes the focus of all of Dumézil's subsequent writing. The first two functions (sovereignty and war) are treated in individual studies: in books on sovereignty – such as *Mitra-Varuna: An Essay on Two Indo-European Representations of Sovereignty* (1940) – in books on war – such as *Aspects de la fonction guerrier chez les indo-européens* (1956) (reworked and republished as *Heur et malheur du gerrier* (1969)) – in books, such as *Jupiter, Mars,*

Quirinus in relation to Rome, which treat all three functions both in terms of specific areas, and in terms of the way the three functions occur in the context of the Indo-European mythology as a whole. The latter theme is examined in works such as *L'Idéologie tripartie des indo-européens* (1953) (incorporated into *L'Idéologie des trois functions dans les épopées des peuples indo-européens* (1968)). The significant absence from this series of studies is any work which specifically analyses the third function: productivity, fertility and the people in general. According to Dumézil, this function resists systemisation and is the most difficult to treat in isolation. What follows now is a brief and extremely schematic summary of the three functions as these are analysed by Dumézil in relation to a number of different cultures. Before proceeding, however, we note that Dumézil often called the three functions a 'tripartite' (or 'three-party') ideology. By ideology Dumézil means

> a conception and an appreciation of the great forces which animate the world and society, and their relations. Often this ideology is implicit and must be deciphered through the analysis of what is said overtly about the gods – and above all about their actions – about theology and, above all, about mythology.
>
> (Dumézil 1992: 240)

Clearly, if the three functions are an ideology, this means that their presence is not immediately apparent. Later, ideology in Dumézil's writing comes closer to the unconscious structure of society. We shall return to this.

Three Functions in Roman, Indian and Scandinavian Myths

The three functions in Roman myths are Jupiter (representing the priestly class), Mars (representing war) and Quirinus (representing agriculture or productivity). In India, the three functions are represented respectively in the Vedic – the oldest Indian religion – by Mitra-Varuna, Indra and Nâsatyâ. Similarly the three functions appear in Scandinavian myths as Odin, Thorr and Freyr. These Scandinavian gods bear a close resemblance to their Germanic counterparts, Thorr, Wodan and Fricco. From the North African perspective, Iran was historically attached to the Indian world before the Muslim conquest (the name 'Iran' is derived from 'Iran shahr'). Dumézil thus studies Indo-Iranian myths and language prior to the Vedic religion which produced Sanskrit, and he finds parallels between the Indian Mitra (equivalent to the first function: sovereignty) and the Iranian Vohu Manah (also equivalent to the first function). Dumézil shows that in the Vedas, Mitra is accompanied by two gods, Aryaman – protector of the community (second function of war) – and Bhaga in charge of repartition of the goods (the third function of production). In the theology of Zarathustra, Aryaman is replaced by Sroasa, protector of the Zoroastrian community (second function), and Bhaga by Asi, the patron of the just retribution of this world in the other (third function). For each part of the Indo-European domain, Dumézil's work forges links between the gods, heroes, and various mythical and theological figures, so as to demonstrate the presence of the three functions across what became religious, social and political boundaries. The point for Dumézil is that the tripartite function has its origin in Indo-Iranian culture, and that this tripartite structure progressively spread to every part of the Indo-European 'family' – as Dumézil called it on occasion. This exact division of functions has no counterpart elsewhere in the world. One of the objections against Dumézil's work has been that one is bound to find evidence of such a structure in Indo-European culture because it is basic to the very survival of human society. Dumézil countered by saying that the precise *form* of the tripartite division is not essential: it is quite possible to point to a deity elsewhere in the world in which the functions overlap or are quite different.

Dumézil: Product of the Nineteenth Century

Despite the undoubted originality of his scholarship and its links with the structuralist project of the 1960s, Dumézil was, in several important ways, a product of nineteenth-century comparative and historical linguistics. Antoine Meillet, his mentor and the supervisor of his thesis, and Michel Bréal, the first professor of comparative linguistics at the Collège de France in 1864, were both keen students of the founder of historical linguistics, Franz Bopp. Meillet's *L'Aperçu d'une histoire de in langue greque* (*An Overview of the History of the Greek Language*) published in 1913, was a formative influence, while Michel Bréal had translated from the German Bopp's *Grammaire comparée*. Bréal had done much more for the young Dumézil. He had published his *Dictionnaire étymologique du latin* (*Etymological Dictionary of Latin*). Through Bréal's dictionary, Dumézil came to experience the marvels of etymology and to develop his Indo-European passion: 'There, I discovered that in Sanskrit "father" [*père*] would have been "pitar", and mother [*mère*], "matar". That bedazzled me. It's the origin of my Indo-European passion' (Dumézil

1986: 16). Thus, as we shall see shortly, although Dumézil is, methodologically speaking, close to contemporary structuralism, his 'Indo-European passion' – the dream of discovering the origin of, and subsequent kinship between the three functions in Indo-European societies – places at least part of his enterprise squarely within the paradigm of nineteenth-century historical linguistics. On the other hand, Saussure himself (whose importance for structuralist thought is undoubted) also came out of the very same intellectual milieu, and Émile Benveniste, for some time Dumézil's opponent but later his strongest supporter, was also Meillet's student, and one of the inspirations of the contemporary structuralist movement.

Even though fascinated by etymology and the notion of origin, the influence on Dumézil of scholars such as Meillet and Bréal meant that he too – while using science to do so – came to study language as a social rather than as a natural fact. The goal was to detach the science of language from the science of nature, it was a question of studying the nature of social action through rites, myths and customs (see Milner 1986: 22–24).

Although loath to become embroiled in general questions about method, Dumézil was not, as he said, the least enamoured of the 'a priori' approach often taken in the studies of language and of myth. Indeed, Dumézil publicly expressed his repulsion at (in his view) Durkheim's 'a priori' approach both in *The Elementary Forms of Religious Life* and in *The Rules of Sociological Method*. In the former, Dumézil says, facts are made to fit an a priori schema; they are not the material from which schema itself arises. And within the work on method, written early in Durkheim's career, Dumézil mused about how any researcher could produce a text on method before he had actually published a piece of empirically based research. As a result, Frazer's *The Golden Bough*, as well as the writing and teaching of Marcel Mauss, was much more important for Dumézil than anything Durkheim wrote.

Social Facts: Structure and System

Despite his apparent leaning towards an inductive empirical approach in the social sciences, Dumézil, at the same time, argues strongly against the view that social facts are autonomous and meaningful in themselves. 'Structure' and 'system', and not facts in isolation, are at the heart of Dumézil's approach.

For Dumézil 'structure' and 'system' are interchangeable: structure says in Latin what system says in Greek. Coupled with Dumézil's comparative method, structure becomes the key to the Dumézilian effort to show that each religion, culture or society is an equilibrium. The composition of intrinsically meaningful elements does not come together by chance to form a sort of (possibly) defective whole. Rather, the whole is always already constituted by the relations between the elements themselves; the meaning of the whole being given by the fact of these relations. Here Dumézil is clearly ranged with the structuralist movement in thought. However, as opposed to Lévi-Strauss's search for the universals in human affairs, Dumézil made it clear that he was much more wedded to the particular, to the 'facts', as he called them. To leave the realm of facts is to 'do poetry', to enter a dream-world, Dumézil claimed. Because of his emphasis on facts, on the particular, Dumézil could not see how one could draw out of his work any kind of broadly based philosophical system, similar to the system of Lévi-Strauss (see Dumézil 1987: 120–22). In addition, Dumézil consciously resisted throughout his life all efforts to place him within a 'school' of thought, desiring – and very keenly – to be his own person in intellectual or scholarly matters. To be the member of a school, he believed, was to lose the autonomy essential to truly original and rigorous scholarship.

References

Dumézil, Georges (1986), 'Interview with François Ewald' in *Le Magazine Littéraire*, 229, April.
—— (1987), *Entretiens avec Didier Eribon*, Paris: Gallimard, 'Folio/Essais'.
—— (1992), *Myths et dieus des indo-européennes* (Selections presented by Hervé Coutau-Bégarie), Paris: Flammarion.
Milner, Jean-Claude (1986), 'Le Programme Dumézilien' in *Le Magazine Littéraire*, 229, April.

See also: **Benveniste, Lévi-Strauss, Saussure**

Dumézil's major writings

(2003) *Esquisses de mythologie*, Paris: le Grand livre du mois.
(1996 [1966]) *Archaic Roman Religion with an Appendix on the Religion of the Etruscans*, 2 vols, trans. Philip Krapp, Baltimore: Johns Hopkins University Press.
(1988a [1940]) *Mitra-Varuna: An Essay on Two Indo-European Representations of Sovereignty*, trans. Derek Coltman, New York: Zone Books.
(1988b) *Destiny of a King* (partial translation of *Myth et idéologie II*, 1971), trans. Alf Hiltebeitel, Chicago: University of Chicago Press.
Myth et épopée:.

(1986a [1968]) I *L'Idéologie des trois fonctions dans les épopées des peuples indo-européens*, Paris: Gallimard, fourth revised edn.
(1986b [1971]) II. *Types épiques indo-européens: Un héros, un sorcier, un roi*, Paris: Gallimard.
(1973) III. *Histoires romaines*, Paris: Gallimard.
(1983 [1956 and 1969]) *The Stakes of the Warrior* (a translation of *Heur et malheur du gerrier*), trans. David Weeks, Berkeley: University of California Press.
(1982) *Apollon sonore, et autres essais, Esquisses de mythologie*, Paris: Gallimard.
(1977 [1959]) *Les Dieux souverains des indo-européens*, Paris: Gallimard. Partially translated into English as:.
(1973) *Gods of the Ancient Northmen*, ed. Einar Haugen, trans. various, Berkeley: University of California Press.
(1976) *Fêtes romaines d'été et d'automne*, followed by *Dix questions romaines*, Paris: Gallimard.
(1968) *Idées romaines*, Paris: Gallimard.
(1941) *Jupiter, Mars, Quirinus*, Paris: Gallimard.
(1935) *Flamen-Brahman*, Paris, Annales du musée Guimet, petit collection.
(1934) *Ouranos-Varuna: étude de mythologie comparée indo-européenne*, Paris: Adrien-Maisonneuve.
(1924) *Le Festin d'immortalité. Etude de mythologie comparée indo-européenne*, Paris: Annales de musée Guimet (This was Dumézil's doctoral thesis.).

Further reading

Belier, Wouter (1991), *Decayed Gods Origin and Development on Georges Damézil's 'idéologie tripartie'*, Leiden and New York: E.J. Brill.
Bubuisson, Daniel (2006 [1993]), *Twentieth Century Mythologies*, trans. Martha Cunningham, London and Oakville, CT: Equinox Publications.
Scott Littleton, C. (1966), *New Comparative Mythology: An Anthropological Assessment of the Theories of Georges Dumézil*, Berkeley: University of California Press.

GÉRARD GENETTE (b.1930)

The work of Gérard Genette is of particular importance to literary theorists and semiologists. The abiding concern in Genette's substantial *oeuvre* which ranges over the literary spectrum from the Greek Classics to Proust, is to produce a general theory – based on classificatory schemas – of the *singularity* of the literary object. Keen to avoid a procrustean procedure of imposing categories on to literary works from the outside, yet refusing the naivety of literary criticism's empiricism, Genette has endeavoured – by way of a supple 'analytic method' – to produce a knowledge of the 'mystery' of the literary work without thereby destroying that mystery. Inspired by structuralist insights which took formal textual analysis to new heights in the 1960s, Genette has been careful to argue for the autonomy of the literary object. Thus, he says, in the end, Proust's great work, *A La recherche du temps perdu*, taken as whole, is irreducible: it 'illustrates nothing but itself' (Genette 1972: 68).

Born in Paris in 1930, and a product of the École Normale Supérieure – where he gained his *agrégation* in *Lettres classiques* in 1954 – Genette is a direct contemporary of Jacques Derrida, Pierre Bourdieu and Christian Metz. Derrida's reflections on writing in *Of Grammatology* in particular left their mark on Genette's articles of the 1960s in literary criticism and literary theory. He was one of the first to signal the importance of Derrida's notion of grammatology for a spatial view of literary works (Genette 1969: 17). In 1959–60, both Genette and Derrida taught in a *lycée* and prepared students for their entry into the École Normale Supérieure. He then became, in 1963, an *assistant* in French literature at the Sorbonne, then *Maître-assistant*. In 1967, he was appointed to the position of director of studies in aesthetics and poetics at the École des Hautes Etudes en Sciences Sociales.

With Tzvetan Todorov and Hélène Cixous, Genette started, in 1970 at the Éditions du Seuil, the very influential journal, *Poétique* as well as the literary collection of the same name. It was *Poétique* in fact which first published Derrida's important essay, 'White mythology: Metaphor in the text of philosophy' (see Derrida 1971).

Anonymity of the Writer/Author

In the collection of Genette's early articles published in *Figures I* (1966), an intimation of later themes may be observed. There is, for instance, the critique of psychologism, rejected because of its reductive and determinist impulse. A literary text is seen by the theorist to be literary precisely because it cannot be reduced to an author's psychological disposition. Following Blanchot, Genette agrees that the writer's place is a place of anonymity. To write is to hide, to wear a mask. At most the writer's lived experience is refracted – displaced – in the text: it is not reflected, or explored there. The literary theorist is interested in the process of displacement *per se*, rather than in the psychological condition (if this could ever be established) of the author. Genette thus joins Foucault, Barthes and others in taking the 'death' of the author as his point of departure.

Narrative

From *Figures III* (1972) onwards, the issue of the presence/absence of the author gives way to Genette's major concerns of the 1970s and the 1980s. These include: analyses of narrative (culminating in *Nouveau discours du récit* (1983)); the study of the imagination of language in *Mimologiques* (1976), the development of a theory of genres in Introduction a *L'architexte* (1979); to the formation of the notion of 'transtextuality' and 'hypertextuality' in *Palimpsests* (1982) and, finally, a study of the 'paratext' (the title Foreword, Afterword – elements in, but not of, the main text) in *Seuils* (1987). Genette has also published his reflections on a theme first signalled in *Figures II*, namely, the nature of fiction and the condition of 'literarity' in *Fiction and Diction*. What important insights thus emerge from Genette's writing in these two decades of sustained theorising and reflection?

Genette's contribution to a theory of narrative and the literary (i.e. aesthetically satisfying) object in general resides in the meticulous way he substantially broadens the reader-cum-critic's analytical purview. Many aspects of narrative writing have hitherto been taken for granted. A story 'works' for some reason, but few have asked penetrating questions about how and why this is so. Take narration. Genette shows – particularly with regard to Proust – how numerous aspects and levels constitute a narrative function: it is simply not reducible to a single instance of story-telling. If, for the purposes of illustration, we take the aspect of narrative 'voice', through Genette's analysis we realise that voice alone is constituted by the following elements:

1 *Narrative instance*: this refers to the fact that there is always an enunciative moment or context, in which the narration takes place. As such, the narrative instance is crucial for attributing meaning or significance, to what is uttered by the narrating voice. Here we are reminded of Benveniste's insight that to understand fully the way language works we must account for the *act* of stating (*énonciation*) as well as the statement made (*énoncé*). In themselves, narrative utterances (*énoncés*) are often simple and transparent (e.g. Proust's 'For a long time I went to bed early', cited by Genette). Only when the narrative instance is taken into account can the full weight of an utterance's singular narrative meaning be appreciated.

2 *Narrative time*: whereas place, or space, can remain indeterminate in narrative, time cannot – if only because it is inscribed in the tense of the verb and thus in language as a whole. In addition, the

narrative instance will have a specific temporal relation to the events recounted. Often narrative succeeds the events, but not inevitably. There are 'predictif' narratives (prophetic, apocalyptic, oracular) which refer to a future moment, as there are also narratives which describe events as they are happening, or which make the act of narration itself (e.g. *A Thousand and One Nights*) the focus of the story. Narrative time inevitably refers to the time of the narrative. One of the clearest examples of this is in the epistolary novel where the act of writing/narrating (e.g. in Rousseau's *La Nouvelle Héloïse*) is itself part of the narration. In this case, the time of the event recounted can be the time of the narration itself. Numerous variations on this theme are possible. For instance, there can be a narration narrated within another narration, as in Homer's *Odyssey*. Or again, in an epistolary novel, a prior letter which played its part in keeping the novel going can become the event narrated in a subsequent letter. Clearly, in order that the time of the story might coincide with the narration, both have to be 'in' the same time. An intriguing possibility flowing from the coincidence of the two times is that the end of narration becomes an event in the story – such as when at the end of a confession, the narrator is executed.

Since the nineteenth century, the most common form of narration has been the one in the third person and ulterior to the events recounted. As Genette notes, a curious feature of this narration is that it is 'intemporal': there is no index of the time of writing/narration.

3 *Narrative levels*: this refers to the relation between the act of recounting and the event recounted. Every recounted event is deemed to be at a level superior to the event of recounting. Balzac's short story *Sarrasine* exemplifies the possible variations in narrative level. Thus the narrator in the story narrates the events leading to his narration of the story about Sarrasine, then narrates the story of Sarrasine's infatuation with the young La Zambinella, before returning to the point of his narration, as it were. A story within a story, we might say; but for Genette it constitutes an illustration of narrative level.

These, then, are some of the features of 'voice' that Genette brings to light in his discussion of narrative. He also highlights 'metalepse' (narration of the movement from one narrative level to another), 'person' (the difference between the narrator who refers to himself as narrator, and a narration in first person), 'hero' (as narrator and as narrated), 'functions of the narrator' (to tell the story; to facilitate the internal organisation of the text; to ensure the narrative situation of narrator and reader; to ensure the affective, moral or intellectual status of the narrative; to give vent to an ideology), and the 'recipient' (*narrataire*) of the narration as this is marked within the narration itself.

In addition to 'Voice', Genette also defines and discusses four other aspects of narrative:

1 *Order*: the order of events in relation to the order of narration. An event can occur prior to the point, of narration (analepse), or an ulterior event might be evoked in advance (prolepse), or again, there might be a discordance between the two orders (anachronie).
2 *Duration*: the rhythm at which things happen.
3 *Frequency*: the extent of repetition in a narrative.
4 *Mode*: the point(s) of view, including the 'distance' of the narrator from what is being narrated.

To this point, we have focused on aspects of Genette's theory of narrative. Three terms specify the essential elements of every narrative act: (1) a story (*histoire*); (2) the narrative discourse (*récit*); and (3) the narration (the act of telling the story). Genette comments: 'As a narrative, the narrative discourse lives through its relation to the story it recounts; as discourse, it lives through the narration which proffers it' (Genette 1972: 74). Even at a general level, therefore, there is never simply a story which is told, but also a third element (narrative discourse) which, while not separable from the story or the act of its telling, is nevertheless not identical with them. Looked at linguistically, the narrative (*récit*) corresponds to the level of the statement made (*énoncé*), while narration would correspond to the act of stating (*énonciation*).

Mimesis and Diegesis

In discussing the narrative discourse in *Figures II*, Genette refers to the opposition between diegesis and mimesis which appears in Plato's *Republic* and Aristotle's *Poetics*. Diegesis in particular occurs frequently in Genette's discussion of narrative. For the Greeks, diegesis is the purely narrative aspect of fiction (an imperfect mimesis) to be distinguished from mimesis: the imitative or dramatic aspect. Diegesis, then, is the narrative discourse without direct speech or other dramatic effects. Today, the distinction between mimesis and diegesis has been lost to the advantage of diegesis. In Genette's work of the early 1970s, diegesis came to refer specifically to the narration of events. In *Sarrasine*, Genette sees the introduction to the telling of the story of Sarrasine and La Zambinella as 'extradiegetic' – that is, as not being part of the recounting proper of the events of a story. Not only is this a doubtful distinction (the uniqueness of *Sarrasine* is surely that it is a story of two stories), but the point of the notion of diegesis seems minimal in light of the story-narrative-narration trilogy.

Naming

In his work of the mid-1970s, *Mimologiques*, Genette sets about reading Plato's enigmatic theory of naming in the *Cratylus*. Unlike the majority of critics and interpreters of Plato, Genette takes seriously Plato's mimologism – that is, the idea that names, in some fundamental way, imitate that to which they refer. Although a structuralist approach emphasises language's conventional nature, Genette embarks on a long and detailed study of writers of the early modern and modern eras who have been influenced by the Platonic principle of 'eponymy'. 'The function of eponymy', says Genette, 'is to give a meaning to a name which is supposed not to have one, that is, to find in it one or two hidden names hypothetically endowed with meaning' (Genette 1976: 25). The 'meaning' will inevitably be a form of mimesis.

Texts and Intertexts

In *Mimologiques*, Genette studies the witting and unwitting inventiveness of those who have speculated about the origin of language over a period of three centuries or more, and who have, like Plato, presupposed, according to the principle of eponymy, a mimetic relationship between a name and what is named.

Palimpsests, in the rigour and extent of its analytical purview, is possibly Genette's most accomplished work. In it he classifies and analyses a vast range of ways one text is echoed within another. In Genette's use of the term, the palimpsest is a function; it is literature in the second degree, a 'transtextuality' comprised, in part, of the following aspects: 'intertextuality' – including citation, plagiarism and allusion; 'metatextuality' – the way one text is united within another without being cited, as when Hegel evokes Diderot's *Le Neveu de Rameau* in the *Phenomenology of Mind*; 'architextuality' – types of discourse, modes of enunciation, literary genres which transcend each individual text, but to which each individual text refers; and 'hyper-textuality'. The latter is the main focus of Genette's study, and is defined as: 'every relation uniting a text B, to an anterior text A. onto which it is grafted in a way that is not that of commentary' (Genette 1982: 13). Text B could not exist without text A, but it does not speak of it. An example is Joyce's *Ulysses* which clearly relates to Homer's *Odyssey*. One clear outcome of Genette's study is that it is doubtful as to whether any text really is the singularity it is often presented as being by literary history.

Literary Theory

As mentioned at the outset, Genette's *oeuvre* is, for better or for worse, a drive to construct a systematic and rigorous terminology for theorising the 'literarity of literature'. We thus have before us a project which seeks to objectify, and thus render transcendent, every aspect of the production and being of the literary text. Despite Genette's protestation that he also seeks to do justice to the mystery of the singularity of the literary text, it is often difficult not to become weighed down with a terminology that appears concerned above all to leave nothing to chance – that is, to leave nothing to the inde-terminacy at the heart of literature, and, more generally, at the heart of the art product.

References

Derrida, Jacques (1971), 'La mythologie blanche', *Poétique*, 5.
Genette, Gérard (1969), *Figures II*, Paris: Seuil.
—— (1972), *Figures III*, Paris: Seuil, Poétique.
—— (1976), *Mimologiques: voyage en Cratylie*, Paris: Seuil, Poétique.
—— (1982), *Palimpsests: La littérature au second degré*, Paris: Seuil, Points.

See also: **Barthes, Derrida**

Genette's major writings

(2005 [1999]) *Essays in Aesthetics (Figures IV)*, trans Dorrit Cohn, Lincoln: University of Nebraska Press.
(2002) *Figures V,* Paris: Seuil, Poétique.
(1999 [1997]) *The Aesthetic Relation*, trans. G. M. Goshgarian, Ithaca and London: Cornell University Press.
(1997a [1994]) *The Work of Art: Immanence and Transcendence*, trans. G. M. Goshgarian, Ithaca and London: Cornell University Press.

(1997b [1987]) *Paratexts: Thresholds of Interpretation*, trans. Jane E. Lewin, Cambridge and New York: Cambridge University Press.

(1995 [1976]) *Mimiologics (Mimologiques): voyage en Cratylie*, trans. Thaïs E. Morgan, Lincoln, Neb. and London: University of Nebraska Press.

(1993 [1991]) *Fiction and Diction*, trans. Catherine Porter, New York: Cornell University Press.

(1992 [1976]) *The Architext*, trans. Jane E. Lewin, Los Angeles: University of California Press.

(1989) *Paratexte*, Paris: Maison des Sciences de l'homme.

(1984) *Figures of Literary Discourse*, trans. Alan Sherdan, New York: Columbia University Press (Selections from *Figures I-III* (1966–72)).

(1983) *Narrative Discourse Revisited*, trans. Jane E. Lewin, New York: Cornell University Press.

(1982) *Palimpsests: La littérature au second degré*, Paris: Seuil, Points.

(1979) *Narrative Discourse: An Essay in Method*, trans. Jane E. Lewin, New York: Cornell University Press. Translation of *Discours du récit* and part of *Figures III*.

(1972) *Figures III*, Paris: Seuil, Poétique.

(1969) *Figures II*, Paris: Seuil.

(1966) *Figures I*, Paris: Seuil.

Further reading

Mosher, Harold, (1976) 'The structuralism of G. Genette', *Poetics*, 5, 1.

Smith, Barbara H. (1980), 'Narrative versions, narrative theories', *Critical Inquiry* (Autumn).

ROMAN JAKOBSON (1896–1982)

Roman Jakobson was born in Moscow in 1896 to a well-to-do family. A leading figure, as a young scholar, in both the Moscow and Prague linguistic circles, he is generally regarded as one of the twentieth century's foremost linguists, and a proponent of the structuralist approach to language, particularly because of his emphasis on seeing the sound-pattern (Jakobson's first and abiding area of linguistic inquiry) of language as fundamentally relational. The relations between sounds within specific contexts are what come to constitute meaning and significance. Within his very diverse and prolific writings (nearly 500 articles) on poetics, phonology, Slavic languages and folktale, language acquisition, epistemology and the history of linguistics, Jakobson unflinchingly endeavours to elucidate 'the different levels of linguistic structure' through 'a consistent elicitation and identification of relational invariants amid the multitude of variations' (Jakobson

1985: 85). A strictly relational approach is forced on the linguist because, first, 'every single constituent of any linguistic system is built on an opposition of two logical contradictories: the presence of an attribute ("markedness") in contraposition to its absence ("unmarkedness")' (Jakobson 1985: 85); and, second, the 'interplay of invariants and variations proves to be an essential, innermost property of language at each of its levels' (Jakobson 1985: 85).

Here, we can see the extent to which Jakobson influenced Lévi-Strauss's anthropology. For Lévi-Strauss's interest in language is inseparable from his effort to isolate 'marked' and 'unmarked' oppositions, and to analyse society as a relationship between 'invariant' model, and 'variable' history. Such influence was no doubt intensified by the common experience of teaching with Lévi-Strauss in New York during the Second World War at the New School of Social Research set up at Columbia University.

Jakobson's Intellectual Trajectory

In 1914 Jakobson entered the historico-philological faculty at the University of Moscow, and enrolled in the language section of the Department of Slavic and Russian. The study of language would be the key to understanding literature and folklore as well as culture in general. In 1915, Jakobson founded the linguistic circle of Moscow and became influenced by Husserl, with the result that Husserl's phenomenology became particularly important for helping him to think through the relationship between 'part' and 'whole' in language and culture. The poetic word revealed one of the clearest links between the part and the whole. Poetry comes closest to having a structure where the part is equal to the whole.

By the end of 1920, Jakobson had left Moscow and had taken up residence in Prague where, from its inception in 1926, he became an influential member of the Prague linguistic circle. It was in Prague that Jakobson became especially interested in the differences between the phonic and prosodic structures of Russian and other Slavic languages. In 1929, under the auspices of the Prague circle, Jakobson published his *Remarques sur l'évolution phonologique du russe comparée à celle des autres langues slaves* (*Remarks an the Phonological Evolution of Russian Compared with Other Slavic Languages*).

In the 1930s, Jakobson collaborated with his friend, Nikolai Trubetskoy in research on the sound-pattern of language. A follower of Saussure, it was Trubetskoy who directed Jakobson towards the idea that sounds in language function differentially: they have no intrinsic meaning. This set the way for Jakobson to elaborate his theory of the 'distinctive feature', more of which below.

During the late 1930s with the rise of Nazism and the prospect of war, Jakobson travelled to Sweden and Denmark. In Copenhagen he collaborated with Louis Hjelmslev and the Copenhagen linguistic circle. His pioneering work, *Kindersprache, Aphasie und allgemeine Lautgesetze* (*Child Language, Aphasia and Phonological Universals*) was written in Sweden in 1940–41, just before his departure for New York. Although victim during the 1950s of the prejudices of McCarthyism because of his connection with communist Eastern Europe, Jakobson eventually obtained appointments at Harvard and the Massachusetts Institute of Technology, and he remained in America until his death in Boston in 1982.

Language Function: Metaphor and Metonymy

Jakobson was one of the very first linguists of the twentieth century to examine seriously both the acquisition of language and the ways in which the language function could break down – as, for example, in aphasia. Of seminal importance here is the emphasis he placed on two basic aspects of language structure represented by the rhetorical figures of metaphor (similarity), and metonymy (contiguity). (Metonymy, Jakobson says, is not to be confused with synecdoche which, like the former, is sometimes defined as the part standing for the whole. However, with synecdoche, one has an internal relation of part to whole (sail for ship) while with metonymy, the relation is external (pen for writer)). To understand the way that various forms of aphasia affect the language function, is to understand how a breakdown occurs in the faculty of selection and substitution – the metaphoric pole – or in combination and contextualisation – the metonymic pole. The first implies an inability at a metalinguistic level: the second, a problem with maintaining the hierarchy of linguistic units. The relation of similarity is lost in the first and contiguity in the second.

Shifter

Although he did not invent the term, the 'shifter' is another aspect of language elaborated by Jakobson and is closely associated with the capacity for contextualisation. The shifter is in operation in personal pronouns (I, you, etc.), and demonstratives like 'this' and 'that', 'here' and 'there'. During language acquisition, the use of shifters – terms applicable to any specific context whatever – is one of the last abilities the child acquires. Shifters are specifically linked to the enunciative function of language: their meaning cannot be grasped independently of the context in which they are used. They constitute what Jakobson calls a 'duplex structure', meaning that their meaning simultaneously invokes the code ('I' is the first-person pronoun) and the message (specifies the actual speaker). Shifters make it possible for each person to use language individually; they thus constitute the place where history enters language. In other words, in order to understand a statement like, *L'état, c'est moi*, an account must be given of the context and the identity of the speaker (i.e. reference must be made to the message) as well as of the meaning of the words used at the level of the code. As Jakobson shows (Jakobson 1971a: 130–31), the situation can be more complex with the message referring to the code ('"I" is a pronoun') and the code referring to the message ('"I" means me, the speaker'). Moreover, code can refer to code ('"Jerry" is the name of the boy called Jerry'), and the message can refer to the message (He said, 'I am not coming'). More generally, shifters would constitute the link between '*langue*' (structure, or code) and '*parole*' (speech act), so that language would be the constant interaction between *langue* and *parole*.

Because of this duplex structure, Jakobson suggested that far from being more 'primitive' than the denotative, descriptive aspect of language, the use of shifters is one of the last capacities the child masters in the process of language acquisition. In aphasia, this capacity is the first to be lost. Looked at it from a slightly different angle, it could be said that the shifter is an empty category – a little like the floating signifier in the work of Mauss as interpreted by Lévi-Strauss. Through the use of shifters, the code can be adapted to a wide range of contexts, thus enabling the production of a relatively heterogeneous set of messages, and so becoming language's more or less direct link with history.

Such at least would be the kind of argument adduced by Jakobson when accused of ignoring the social and historical dimensions of language, poetry and art, and of supporting the principle of *l'art pour l'art*. In his own defence, and in defending the Russian formalists (with whom he was aligned in the 1920s) on this point, Jakobson claimed in the 1930s that neither he nor the other Russian formalists had 'ever proclaimed the self-sufficiency of art' (Jakobson 1980: 749). And he went on to say that,

What we have been trying to show is that art is an integral part of the social structure, a component that interacts with all the others and is itself mutable since both the domain of art and its relationship to the other constituents of the social structure are in constant dialectical flux. What we stand for is not the separation of art but the autonomy of the aesthetic function.

(Jakobson 1980: 749–50)

The Poetic Function and Distinctive Features

In sum, not poetry, but the poetic function – or *poeticity* – contained in the diversity of spoken and written forms was what interested Jakobson and his colleagues at this time. 'Poeticity' becomes a necessary part of the study of language when it is realised that language and reality – or words and things, sign and referent – do not coincide: that, in short, meaning in language is only minimally linked to referentiality. Very importantly, Jakobson goes on to say here that this fundamental antinomy between language and reality means that 'without contradiction there is no mobility of concepts, no mobility of signs, and the relationship between concept and sign becomes automatized. Activity comes to a halt, and the awareness of reality dies out' (Jakobson 1980: 750).

Although, for Jakobson, as for many others, poetry tends towards the metaphoric pole of linguistic endeavour, it was the sound pattern of poetry – and not the role of metaphor as such – initially illustrated in the differences between the sound patterns of Czech and Russian poetry, which first stimulated Jakobson's original researches in this area. In effect, the difference between Czech and Russian poetry, Jakobson discovered, was in the rhythm. It was from the study of poetic rhythm that Jakobson's 'phonology' developed. In particular, by focusing on the link between sound and meaning, Jakobson concluded that sound and meaning were mediated by difference – what he came to call the 'distinctive feature'. Or rather, because, in Jakobson's view, language is primarily a system of meanings, speech is not made up of sounds, but of phonemes: 'a set of concurrent sound properties which are used in a given language to distinguish words of unlike meaning' (Jakobson 1971b: 636). As this notion of phoneme still focuses on the intrinsic qualities of the linguistic element – although it hints at the differential aspect – Jakobson came to use the term 'distinctive feature', first presented in the work of the linguists, Bloomfield and Sapir. Distinctive features are 'the simplest sense-discriminating units such as sonority, nasality, etc' (Jakobson and Pormorska 1983: 25). These 'sense-discriminating units' which are only established differentially, become crucial in the constitution of meaning. Prior to Jakobson's work in this area, phonemes were thought to resemble 'atoms' of sound which did not in themselves call for 'opposites'. Further analysis revealed that even if phonemes in themselves did not call for opposites, a distinctive feature always does. Thus the apparently minimal, but ultimately critical, difference between phonemes constitutes the difference in meaning between 'boor' and 'poor'. What distinguishes 'boor' from 'poor' is the difference between /b/ and /p/: /b/ is partially voiced and /p/ is unvoiced. From this example, we can see a distinctive feature constituted by the difference between voiced and unvoiced features. The remaining phonemes of each word become redundant. With the words 'tome' and 'dome', the distinctive feature is the aspirated /t/ as opposed to the non-aspirated /d/. In sum, whether or not the difference between /p/ and /b/, or between /t/ and /d/, and other phonemes which present a similar potential ambiguity, appear in close proximity in a text, is less important than the fact that they exist within the linguistic universe, and that meaning depends on discriminating successfully between them. Thus when a speaker of American English is confronted with two names 'Bitter' and 'Bidder' (Jakobson 1971a: 462), the difference between /t/ and /d/ becomes crucial for hearing the names correctly, although when they occur in isolation from each other, the two sounds are often pronounced in the same way.

More controversial with regard to Jakobson's theory of distinctive features is his claim that the same features are present in every language, and that they constitute a category of linguistic invariables: 'The list of distinctive features that exist in the languages of the world is supremely restricted, and the co-existence of features within one language is restrained by implicational laws' (Jakobson 1983: 87). On this basis, distinctive features become one of the invariants of the communication system as such.

Sounds

The sounds of language, too, form the basis of Jakobson's theory of poetics. Once again though, the term 'sound' is a misleading one when dealing with Jakobson's approach, because sound is a purely physical entity. Jakobson rather compares speech to music which 'imposes upon sound matter a graduated scale' while 'language imposes upon it the dichotomous scale which is simply a corollary of the purely differential role played by phonemic entities' (Jakobson 1971a: 423).

In his study of poetic practice Jakobson was a pioneer in pointing to the way that oppositions of all kinds (phonemic oppositions, the opposition between sound and vision, oppositions in pitch and rhythm, etc.) – but especially oppositions between consonants – figured in the production of poetry. He was also one of the first to emphasise the importance of rhythm in the poetry of the Russians Mayakovsky and Khlebnikov. In short, few linguists before or since have analysed poetry with such success in revealing the structures of poetic discourse. In this, Jakobson brought together the 'literary' and the 'overall linguistic' dimensions through a notion of structure that united one to the other. Speaking at a conference in 1958, Jakobson affirmed:

> I believe that the poetic incompetence of some bigoted linguists has been mistaken for all inadequacy of the linguistic science itself. All of us here, however, definitely realize that a linguist deaf to the poetic function of language and a literary scholar indifferent to linguistic problems and unconversant with linguistic methods are equally flagrant anachronisms.
>
> (Jakobson 1971a: 51)

Predominance of Phenomenology

For all his innovation, however, Jakobson remained in certain ways locked within the phenomenological framework of language which influenced him in his early years as a linguist. As a result, he never deviated from retaining as the most pertinent model of language the transmission of a message from a sender to a receiver. Even if Jakobson repeatedly emphasised the need to consider the sender's (active) role in the circuit of communication, as well as that of the (passive) receiver, it remains true that the sender and receiver – psychological, rather than linguistic entities – constitute the indispensable givens of the system. The main problem with such a model is that it does not recognise that language, far from being the property of *a* hypothetical sender and a hypothetical receiver, is a fundamentally social fact – that is, it can only be understood correctly as a *system*, which, as such, is the pre-condition of individuality.

Moreover, while Jakobson was instrumental in drawing attention to the rhythm and sound of poetry, he did not see these aspects of poetry as being in any way a challenge to the ideal communicability and meaningfulness of the linguistic utterance. Rhythm even reinforced the notion of language as communication. Compared to those such as Barthes and Kristeva, who emphasise polysemy and the semiotic respectively, and for whom the notion of language as uniquely a means of communication is problematic, Jakobson often appears somewhat at odds with his psychologism. The latter sometimes belies Jakobson's effort to analyse linguistic phenomena linguistically.

References

Jakobson, Roman (1971a), 'Shifters, verbal categories and the Russian verb' in *Selected Writings – II: Word and Language*, ed. Stephen Rudy, The Hague and Paris: Mouton.

—— (1971b), *Selected Writings – I: Phonological Studies*, ed. Stephen Rudy, The Hague and Paris: Mouton.

—— (1980), 'What is poetry?' in *Selected Writings – III: The Poetry of Grammar and the Grammar of Poetry*, ed, Stephen Rudy, The Hague and Paris: Mouton.

—— (1985), *Selected Writings –VI: Early Slavic Paths and Crossroads*, ed. Stephen Rudy, The Hague and Paris: Mouton.

Jakobson, Roman and Pomorska, Krystyna (1983) *Dialogues*, Cambridge: Cambridge University Press.

See also: **Barthes, Hjelmslev, Kristeva, Lévi-Strauss, Saussure**

Jakobson's major writings

(1994) *Letters and other materials from the Moscow and Prague Linguistic Circles, 1912–1945*, ed. Jindřich Toman, Michigan: Ann Arbor, Michigan Slavic Publications.

(1988) *Major Works, 1976–1980*, ed. Stephen Rudy, Berlin and New York: Mouton.

Selected Writings, vols I–VI, ed. Stephen Rudy, The Hague, Paris: Mouton.

(1971a) I: *Phonological Studies*.

(1971b) II: *Word and Language*.

(1980) III: *The Poetry of Grammar and the Grammar of Poetry*.

(1966) IV: *Slavic Epic Studies*.

(1978a) V: *On Verse, Its Masters and Explorers*.

(1985) VI: *Early Slavic Paths and Crossroads*, Part I and Part II.

(1980) *The Framework of Language*, Michigan: Ann Arbor, Michigan Slavic Publications.

(1979) with Linda Waugh, *The Sound Shape of Language*, Bloomington, Indiana: Indiana University Press.

(1978b) *Six Lectures on Sound and Meaning*, Cambridge, Mass.: MIT Press.

Further reading

Bradford, Richard (1994), *Roman Jakobson: Life, Language, Art*, London and New York: Rouledge.
Holenstein, Elmar (1974), *Roman Jakobson's Approach to Language*, Bloomington, Indiana: Indiana University Press.
Steiner, Pete, (1984), *Russian Formalism: A Metapoetics*, Ithaca and New York: Cornell University Press.
Waugh, Linda (1976), *Roman Jakobson's Science of Language*, Bloomington, Indiana: P. de Ridder.

JACQUES LACAN (1901–1981)

Although Jacques Lacan was to change the whole orientation of psychoanalysis in France and elsewhere, his early education and training were quite conventional. Born in Paris of a bourgeois Catholic family in 1901, Lacan undertook – as was normal practice – a medical degree at the Sorbonne before pursuing further training in the 1920s under the celebrated psychiatrist, Gaëtan de Clérambault. From the latter, Lacan learned the art of observation; from the surrealists, he learned the art of a baroque self-presentation, beautifully evoked by Elisabeth Roudinesco in her history of psychoanalysis in France (Roudinesco 1990: 295–96).

Theory and Practice of the Unconscious: The Paranoid Critical Method

The point to be made here is that Lacan, despite a gap of forty years, indirectly returns, at least in part, in his work of the 1970s, to what drove him in the 1930s. This needs explanation.

While Freud, and later, Lacan, were interested in establishing the theoretical structure that makes known the preconditions of the unconscious, the surrealists were interested in imitating experiences of so-called madness and then making poetic and artistic capital out of such experiences. The surrealists resorted to delirium to achieve their artistic goals, while theoretical psychoanalysis dealt exclusively with articulated discourse – to the point where the structure of articulated discourse would become simultaneously the structure of the subject and of language (see Roudinesco 1990: 25).

When, in 1932, Lacan presented his thesis on paranoia and its relation to the personality through a case-study of 'Aimée', he had already been touched by Salvador Dalí's 'paranoid critical method', a method based on the capacity for things to reveal – to make visible – multiple significations, almost to the point of madness. Things – objects – become a giant pun to which Dalí's paintings bore testimony. Although hallucination is no doubt involved, paranoia pluralises interpretive possibilities. The plural dimension is posed as being 'in' reality; it is not just a delirious relation to reality. Such a paranoid relation, it is true, could only be assumed with difficulty by an individual subject in a non-delirious state; for to pluralise meaning is to challenge univocal identity and the imaginary disposition upon which identity relies.

Lacan, in the 1970s towards the end of his teaching, will later turn this paranoid relation into the *sinthome*, the enjoyment of meaning exemplified by Joyce's writing. The *sinthome*, 'joined to the unconscious' is 'what is singular in each individual' (Lacan 1987: 28). The letter, symbolic object *par excellence*, now becomes, after Joyce, a 'litter', and the focus of a certain enjoyment. The symptom is connected to the real through enjoyment. Enjoyment defies interpretation, and as such marks a gap in the Symbolic. Who, or what, however, is the locus of enjoyment? The answer seems to be: a presymbolic subject; or, as Žižek puts it, the subject prior to subjectivation. (Žižek 1989: 178). This is the subject in the real, the subject as *sinthome* – as enjoyment – prior to being the subject of desire. Whether there are problems of coherence and rigour in this formulation of things is of less importance than the fact that the symptom is deemed to have a 'totally contingent material element' (Žižek 1989: 183.) We will return to the symptom as *sinthome* when explaining Lacan's theory of the four discourses.

Against the Ego and For the Unconscious and Language

To rework the theory of subjectivity and sexuality as these derive from the Freudian corpus, Lacan re-read Freud so as to clarify and reinvigorate a whole series of concepts – not the least of which being the concept of the unconscious. What had most inhibited a knowledge of the subversiveness and revolutionary nature of Freud's work, Lacan contended in the 1950s, was the primacy given to the ego in understanding human behaviour. The theory of the ego as identical with itself, as homogeneous, and the privileged source of individual identity not only held sway in ego-psychology in America under the influence of Heinze Hartmann, but spilled over into all the disciplines in the social sciences and humanities. In effect, the early post-war period (especially in America and other English-speaking countries) was the era of humanism and the belief that human intention, understanding, and consciousness were fundamental. A certainty reigned in which the ego – for good or ill – was at the centre of human psychical life.

With the structuralist emphasis on language as a system of differences without positive terms in mind, Lacan highlights the importance of language in Freud's work, and links Roman Jakobson's terms in linguistics of 'metaphor' and 'metonymy' to Freud's concepts, respectively, of 'condensation' and 'displacement'. Metaphor, accordingly, is defined as the 'replacement of one word by another', while metonymy is the 'word-to-word connexion' (contiguity). Lacan can then equate the 'presence' of the unconscious in language with the effects generated by metaphor and metonymy – much as Freud, in *The Interpretation of Dreams*, relates the evidence of the unconscious in the dream to the working of condensation and displacement.

Language is not simply the bearer of thoughts and information, nor is it simply a medium of communication. 'Defective' communication is also significant. Misunderstandings, confusions, poetic resonances, and a whole host of features (such as slips of the tongue, absent-mindedness, the forgetting of names, misreadings, etc. – features analysed in Freud's *The Psychopathology of Everyday Life*) also emerge in and through language. These are the features through which the effects of the unconscious may be perceived and they are the basis upon which, Lacan, in a famous aphorism, links language and the unconscious: 'The unconscious is structured like a language'. The unconscious, then, disrupts conventional communicative discourse – not according to chance, but according to a certain structural regularity.

Mirror Stage

Even before the structuralist approach had become generally known, Lacan had, in 1936, developed the theory of the 'Mirror Stage' (Lacan 2006a: 75–81). The Mirror Stage concerns the emergence, between the ages of six to eighteen months, of the capacity of the infant (*enfans* = speechless) to recognise its own image in the mirror. This occurs before the infant is able to speak, and before it has control over motor skills. This act of recognition is not self-evident; for the infant has to see the image as being both itself (its own reflection), and not itself (*only* a reflected image). The image is not identical with the infant subject, and to become a human subject (that is, a social being) means coming to terms with this. The child's entry into language is entirely dependent on this recognition. So, too, is the formation of an ego (the centre of consciousness). Language and symbolic (i.e. cultural) elements now become fundamental whereas, before, it was generally held that biological (i.e. natural) factors were the basis of human subjectivity.

The mirror, therefore, is not simply a prosthesis but rather points to a universal and ideal relation that is constitutive of the Imaginary. And this is ironical to the extent that in his early seminars, Lacan locates the Imaginary purely and simply in experience, while the Symbolic alone is the source of a priori principles (cf. Lacan 1978: 50).

Real, Imaginary, Symbolic

While language, as the privileged part of the Symbolic order, is central to Lacan's psychoanalytic theory, it is but one element in a trilogy of orders constitutive of the subject in psychoanalysis. The other orders in the trilogy are the Imaginary and the Real. While the unconscious decentres the subject because it introduces division, at the level of the Imaginary (that is, in the discourse of everyday life), the effects of the unconscious are not acknowledged. At the level of the Imaginary, the subject believes in the transparency of the Symbolic; it does not recognise the lack of reality in the Symbolic. The Imaginary is not, then, simply the place where images are produced or where the subject engages in the pleasures of the imagination. In effect, the Imaginary is where the subject mis-recognises (*méconnaît* – is ignorant of) the nature of the symbolic. The Imaginary is thus the realm of illusion, but of a 'necessary illusion', as Durkheim said of religion.

One formulation of the Real given by Lacan, is that it is always 'in its place'. The Real is always in its place because only what is missing (absent) from its place can be symbolised, and therefore formalised. The Symbolic is a substitute for what is missing from its place. The symbol, word, etc. always entails the absence of the object or referent. This approach to the Real is elaborated in Lacan's essay on Edgar Allan Poe's short story, 'The Purloined Letter' (Lacan 2006b: 6–48).

However, at the level of the formation of the individual subject as sexed, what is missing is the mother's phallus. The story is that the infant's entry into language parallel's its separation from the mother. Before separation, there is a plenitude based on the union of mother and child. After separation, the mother becomes the child's first object – that is, its first experience of absence, or lack. For the mother, on the other hand, the child is a substitute for the missing phallus: she feels a sense of fulfilment in light of her close bond with the child. Without separation, however, the formation of language is inhibited. The father (as the agent of the father principle) is the element which tends to intervene in the mother–child relationship, so that in identifying with him, the child can come to form an identity of its own. In this scenario – whose metaphorical status should be noted – the mother's place (also the place of the feminine) tends to be that of the Real, the father evokes the Symbolic, while the Imaginary can be grasped from the child's place. At a more precise and specific individual level, the child's identity is the outcome of its coming to terms with sexual difference. First and foremost in this process of sexual differentiation is the recognition on the part of the child that its mother does not have a penis: she thus bears the indelible *mark* of difference. From this, Lacan demonstrates that the penis has an irreducibly symbolic status, a status he signals by speaking only of the phallus. The penis is real, but it is the (symbolic) phallus which is a signifier; in fact, the phallus, because of its role in signifying what is missing (or lacking), becomes the signifier of signification.

This experience does not simply derive from a knowledge (on the part of the child) of the mother's real lack of a penis, but derives also from the mother as an intimation of the child's own potential lack in castration. Consequently, the Symbolic, through the role of phallus as symbol *par excellence*, confronts the subject with its own vulnerability and mortality.

In the most general sense, the Symbolic is what gives the world its meaning and its law – if not its order. Indeed, in the 1950s, Lacan spoke about the Law as embodied in the Name-of-the-Father. Consequently, the Symbolic Order, exemplified by the Name-of-the-Father, constitutes society. Or rather, in the name of the dead father – following Freud's story in *Totem and Taboo* – the sons give up their right to possess their father's women. For Lévi-Strauss, whose work was of great interest to Lacan at the time, this is the moment of the institution of the law against incest.

Woman as Non-Existent

For some feminist writers, a patriarchal system which valorises masculinity and therefore most males is the predominant outcome of Lacan's Freudian anthropology. No doubt Lacan has only reinforced this impression in the eyes of many women with his provocative aphorisms, '*la* femme n'existe pas' [woman does not exist], and 'la femme n'est pas toute' [woman is not all]. The first statement is meant to indicate that there is no stereotype that captures a female essence; in fact there is no essence of femininity. And this is why sexuality is always a play of masks and disguises. To say that 'woman' does not exist, then, is to say that sexual difference cannot be contained in any essential symbolic form: it cannot be represented. The second statement plays on the notion that the woman does not have a penis, and is thus part of the emergence of the symbolic: the penis becomes a phallus which becomes the signifier of absence. Before saying with too great a haste that this picture of woman is a negative one (one that therefore benefits males), it has to be said that 'man' is no more disposed to accept this figure of woman as castrated than many women might be. Indeed, we need to take account of the resistance to the 'reality' of the myth of castration that emerges constantly in social life. This resistance is not marked in words or images, but precisely in the refusal to try to symbolise the sense of loss engendered by castration. Be this as it may, the question that still must be asked – although it cannot be answered here – is whether this 'story' that the psychoanalyst tells, partly in order to give psychoanalysis its coherence, finally spells oppression for women as social beings. A supplementary question might be: Does the choice have to be between a false symbolic figure of woman (as with the phallic mother), and an inexpressible (woman as) truth?

Cybernetics

Lacan recognised, in a far-sighted paper delivered in 1955 (Lacan 1978: 339–54), that cybernetics does not do justice to the Imaginary, even though it might allow the difference between the Imaginary and the Symbolic to appear (see 1978: 352.) Cybernetics can put us in touch with pure language – language as a syntax prior to semantics – but it does not easily allow for key features of the Imaginary: identification and conviction; images in a *Gestalt*; a sense of unity and fullness in an identity; intuition. Yet, there is a slide towards a privileging of the Symbolic. By way of the Symbolic, humanity as a whole must separate itself from its imaginary representations. Without the Symbolic, for instance, there would be no law against incest and thus no (primitive) society.

Mathemes

A further dimension of Lacan's theory, especially evident in his later seminars, such as *Encore*, is the attempt to give psychoanalysis a mathematical basis. Thus if a signifier only takes on meaning in relation to other signifiers, it can be symbolised by an '*x*'. A pure signifier, in other words, would be a letter in mathematical language in as far as this signifier is purely formal. Lacan, after the work of Jacques-Alain Miller, argues that the unconscious also was a pure signifier of this type, and is thus able to take on any meaning whatever; that is, it is entirely open to the context in which it is found. Such is the sense Lacan subsequently attaches to the letter in his reading of Edgar Allan Poe's short story, 'The Purloined Letter'. The letter (epistle) which is stolen assumes significance according to whether it is in the possession of the king, the queen, or the minister who stole it. Because the content of the letter is unknown (to the reader) – because it has no essential content – it begins to resemble the letter as the material support of language: a letter of the alphabet. In this sense, the unconscious becomes a form of writing detached from any natural object. As a mathematical formula, it is also teachable. For the inexpressible unconscious now becomes the object = x. During the 1960s and early 1970s, Lacan's teaching bore the influence of the mathematicians, Frege, Russell, Gödel and Cantor. More and more he moved away from the rhetorical mode that had dominated his teaching of the 1950s. In Roudinesco's view, 'Lacan's recourse to formalization and mathematics was a final attempt to save psychoanalysis from its hypnotic roots, but also, at the other end of the chain, from schooling, in a society where school tends to replace the church' (Roudinesco 1990: 561).

Four Discourses

Towards the end of the 1960s, Lacan formulated a theory of discourse. These are outlined clearly by Slavoj Žižek (Žižek 1999: 28–29). Discourse, then, could be of four types: the discourses of the Master, of the University, of the Analyst and of the Hysteric. The discourse of the Master is focused on truth and order, backed by power, without any messy remainders; it is characterised by a dominant signifier (S_1), far removed from the *sinthome* and the enjoyment of multiple meanings. The untidy residue is also called *object petit a*, and the other discourses are three different attempts to come to grips with this residue.

For the University, *object petit a* is the unknown, or untamed object which has to be brought into the domain of knowledge as order and coherence. It claims to let the facts speak for themselves, the repressed truth being that the University makes a claim to be Master.

The discourse of the Hysteric is based on a question to the Master, to whom the hysteric is in thrall: 'Why am I who you say that I am?' In other words, the Master has imposed a symbolic identity onto the hysteric, but the hysteric is not sure about this. A gap thus appears between language and reality, or between the signifier and an unsymbolisable existence. The hysteric wants to know how he or she can *truly* conform to the wishes of the Other, and is always in doubt about this.

For its part the discourse of the analyst is the inverse of the Master discourse. The analyst thus attempts to occupy the place of the *object petit a* (the messy surplus) and bring it into discourse. The discourse of the Analyst is founded on what habitually escapes discourse, and will, therefore, be concerned to bring into discourse the *sinthome* as enjoyment in language. This explains Lacan's interest in Joyce and the connection between Lacan's very early work on paranoia influenced by surrealism.

Indeed, it is possible to argue, as does Žižek (1999: 29), that the four discourses form a matrix that is still beholden to a network of communication and that Lacan's later foray into Joyce and mathematics was an attempt to break away from this and to give a certain autonomy to language as enjoyment and as basis of the subject's singularity.

References

Lacan, Jacques (1978) '*Le Séminaire, Livre II, Le moi dans la théorie de Freud et dans la technique de la psychanalyse*, Paris: Seuil.
—— (1987) 'Joyce le symptôme I' in Jacques Aubert, ed. *Joyce avec Lacan*, Paris: Navarin.
—— (2006a), 'The Mirror Stage as Formative of the I Function in Psychoanalytic Experience' in *Ecrits: The First Complete Edition in English*, trans. Bruce Fink in collaboration with Héloïse Fink and Russell Grigg, New York: Norton.
—— (2006b), 'Seminar on "The Purloined Letter"' in *Ecrits: The First Complete Edition in English*, trans. Bruce Fink in collaboration with Héloïse Fink and Russell Grigg, New York: Norton.
Roudinesco, Elisabeth (1990), *Jacques Lacan and Co. A History of Psychoanalysis in France, 1925–1985*, trans. Jeffrey Mehlman, Chicago: University of Chicago Press.
Žižek, Slavoj (1999), 'The Undergrowth of Enjoyment' in Elizabeth Wright and Edmund Wright, eds, *The Žižek Reader*, Oxford and Malden, Mass.: Blackwell..
—— (1989), *The Sublime Object of Ideology*, London: Verso.

See also: **Freud, Irigaray, Jakobson, Kristeva, Saussure**

Lacan's major writings

(2006 [1966]) *Ecrits: The First Complete Edition in English*, trans. Bruce Fink in collaboration with Héloïse Fink and Russell Grigg, New York: Norton.

(2005a) *Mon enseignement*, Paris: Seuil.

(2005b) *Le Corps*, Paris: Association Lacanienne internationale.

(2005c) *Des noms-du-père*, Paris: Seuil.

(2002) *Ecrits: A Selection*, trans. Bruce Finkin in collaboration with Hélöse Fink and Russell Grigg. New York: Norton.

(2001) *Autres Écrits*, Paris: Seuil.

(1990 [1973]) *Television: A Challenge to the Psychoanalytic Establishment*, trans. Denis Hollier, Rosalind Krauss and Annette Michelson, New York: Norton.

Le Séminaire (The Seminar):.

(2006) *Livre XVI, D'un autre à l'autre, 1968–1969*, Paris: Seuil.

(2006 [1991]) *Book 16, The Other Side of Psychoanalysis Livre XVII, L'envers de la psychanalyse*, Paris: Seuil.

(2005) *Livre XXIII, Le sinthome, 1975–1976*, Paris: Seuil.

(2004a) *Livre X, L'angoisse, 1962–1963*, Paris: Seuil.

(2004b) *Le moment de conclure, 1977–1978*, Paris: Association Lacanienne internationale.

(2002) *RSI, 1974–1975*, Paris: Association Lacanienne internationale.

(1993 [1981]) *Book III, The Psychoses*, trans. Russell Grigg, New York: Norton.

(1992 [1986]) *Book 7, The Ethics of Psychoanalysis*, trans. Dennis Porter, New York: Norton.

(1991) *Livre VIII, Le transfert*, Paris: Seuil.

(1988 [1975]) *Book I, Freud's Writings on Technique, 1953–1954*, trans. John Forester and Sylvana Tomaselli, New York: Norton.

(1978a [1973]) *Book XI, Four Fundamental Concepts of Psychoanalysis*, trans. Alan Sheridan, New York: Norton.

(1978b) *Livre II, Le moi dans la théorie de Freud et dans la technique de la psychanalyse*, Paris: Seuil.

(1975) *Livre XX, Encore, 1972–1973*, Paris: Seuil.

Further reading

Harari, Robert (2001), *Lacan's Seminar on 'anxiety': An Introduction*, trans. Jane C. Lamb-Ruiz, New York: Other Press.

Homer, Sean (2004), *Jacques Lacan*, London and New York: Routledge.

Rabaté, Jean-Michel (2003) *Cambridge Companion to Lacan*, Cambridge and New York: Cambridge University Press.

Voruz, Véonique and Wolf, Bogdan, eds (2007), *The Later Lacan*, Albany: State University of New York Press.

Žižek, Slavoj, ed. (2003), *Jacques Lacan: Critical Evaluations in Cultural Theory*, London and New York: Routledge, 4 vols.

CLAUDE LÉVI-STRAUSS (B. 1908)

Claude Lévi-Strauss was born into a Belgian Jewish family in 1908. Both his parents were artists, and so while he was learning to read and write, the future anthropologist had a paintbrush or crayon in his hand.

Although he completed an *agrégation* in philosophy at the Sorbonne in the early 1930s, the desire to escape from the philosophical orthodoxies then in vogue in Paris (neo-Kantianism, Bergsonism, phenomenology and, later, existentialism) prompted Lévi-Strauss in 1934 to accept a position as professor of anthropology at the University of Sao Paulo. Later, following military service in France, Lévi-Strauss fled, to escape persecution, to the United States where, from 1941 to 1945 he taught at the New School for Social Research in New York. In 1941, he met Roman Jakobson who was to be a formative influence in the linguistic and structuralist turn in Lévi-Strauss's postwar anthropology.

Intellectual Trajectory: Exchange
and Structure

Not only did Lévi-Strauss distance himself from the French philosophy of his day, he also distanced himself from orthodox interpretations of Durkheim, which played up the positivistic and evolutionist aspects of his thought. However, it was a reinterpretation of the work of Durkheim's disciple, Mauss, which played a major part in defining Lévi-Strauss's early intellectual trajectory.

In his classic work on the link between kinship and exchange – *The Elementary Structures of Kinship* (1949) – Lévi-Strauss describes the following custom. In inexpensive restaurants in the south of France, especially in the wine-growing regions, a meal normally includes a small bottle of wine. The quality and quantity of wine for each diner is the same: one glass of the lowest quality. Instead of pouring wine into his or her own glass, the owner will pour the wine into that of a neighbour. Despite the exchange, the quantity of wine remains the same (Lévi-Strauss 1969: 59–60). Exchange of wine becomes a means of establishing social contact, through reciprocity. Indeed, wine is the social element of the meal – gives it a group aspect – while food is the individual element, intended for the nourishment of the diner. In microcosm, then, the link between exchange and the 'total social fact' is revealed, since it is not what is exchanged that is important, but the *fact* of exchange itself, a fact inseparable from the very constitution of social life.

Two important aspects of Lévi-Strauss's anthropology are introduced here. The first is the principle that social and cultural life cannot be uniquely explained by a version of functionalism: cultural life is not explicable in terms of the intrinsic nature of the phenomena in question. Nor can it be explained empirically by facts deemed to speak for themselves. In short, although empirical research constitutes an important part of his work, Lévi-Strauss is not an empiricist. Rather, he has always maintained that he is first and foremost a structural anthropologist. Broadly, structural anthropology, inspired by Saussure, focuses on the way elements of a system combine together, rather than on their intrinsic value. 'Difference' and 'relation' are the key notions here. Moreover, the combination of these elements will give rise to oppositions and contradictions which serve to give the social realm its dynamism.

'Scope' is another important aspect of Lévi-Strauss's approach. For while many social researchers have limited their interpretations of social life to the specific society in which they have carried out fieldwork, Lévi-Strauss adopts a universalist approach, theorising on the basis of both his own and other anthropologists' data. Of all the general criticisms that have been levelled against Lévi-Strauss, the one which claims that he theorises from an inadequate fieldwork base is probably the most common in English-speaking countries. For these are also the countries with the strongest empiricist tradition.

Generally speaking, the stakes of Lévi-Strauss's work are high. They amount to a demonstration that when all the data are to hand, there is no basis upon which one could draw up a hierarchy of societies – whether this be in terms of scientific progress, or in terms of cultural evolution. This is because every society or culture exhibits features that are present in a greater or lesser degree in other societies, or in other cultures. Lévi-Strauss argues this way because he is persuaded that the cultural dimension (in which language is predominant), and not nature – or the 'natural' – is constitutive of the human. Symbolic structures of kinship, language and the exchange of goods become the key to understanding social life, not biology. Indeed, kinship systems keep nature at bay; they are a cultural phenomenon based on the interdiction against incest, and as such are not a natural phenomenon. They make possible the passage from nature into culture, that is, into the sphere of the truly human. To understand this more fully, we turn to Lévi-Strauss's notion of structure.

Structure

'Structure' for Lévi-Strauss is not equivalent to the empirical structure (whether, by analogy, it is deemed to be skeletal or architectural) of a particular society, as it is in Radcliffe-Brown's work. In fact, structure is not given in observable reality, but is always the outcome of at least three elements, and this ternary nature gives it its dynamism. Having said this, we should acknowledge that in Lévi-Strauss's *oeuvre*, there is in fact an ambivalence between the kind of structuralism which views structure as an abstract model derived from an analysis of phenomena seen as a (more or less) static system of differences – that is, the synchronic dimension is privileged – and the notion of structure as being fundamentally ternary, containing an inherently dynamic aspect. The third element of the ternary structure would be always empty, ready to take on any meaning whatsoever. It would be the element of diachrony, that is, the element of history and contingency, the aspect which accounts for the perpetuation of social and cultural phenomena. While Lévi-Strauss's own explanation of the 'structural' in structural analysis (Lévi-Strauss 1972: 31–54, esp. 33) tends towards focusing on the synchronic dimension, in practice his work clearly leads towards seeing structure as being essentially ternary and dynamic. We can confirm this point through reference to Lévi-Strauss's most important writings on kinship, myth, and art.

Mana: the Empty Signifier

Lévi-Strauss's *Introduction to the Work of Marcel Mauss* (Lévi-Strauss 1987), published shortly after the appearance of *The Elementary Structures of Kinship*, shows that while exchange in Mauss's *Essay on the Gift* is equivalent to the 'total social fact', Mauss failed to recognise that exchange was also a key to understanding the phenomenon of *mana*. Although Mauss had seen that exchange was a concept constructed by the anthropologist and that it did not have an intrinsic content, he treated *mana* differently. Like Durkheim, Mauss attributed to it the meaning it took on in indigenous societies, a meaning that sees *mana* as having an intrinsic, or sacred, content.

Lévi-Strauss, on the other hand, argues that the diversity of contents assumed by *mana* means that it has to be seen as empty, much like an algebraic symbol (Lévi-Strauss 1987: 55 and see 55–66 for a discussion of the 'floating' signifier), and able to take on any number of meanings – like the word 'thing' in English. In short, *mana* is a 'floating', or pure signifier with a symbolic value of zero. And it exists in a general sense (every culture will have examples of floating signifiers) because there is an abundance of signifiers in relation to the signified, since language must be thought of as having come into being all at once (it is a system of differences, and therefore fundamentally relational), while knowledge (the signified) only comes into being progressively.

The structural aspect of Lévi-Strauss's approach here is more implicit than explicit. It consists in the fact, first, that emphasis is not placed on the (hypothetical) content of *mana*, but on its potential to assume a multitude of meanings. It is an empty signifier, much as for Lacan the phallus has no intrinsic meaning, but is the signifier of signification. Second, and more importantly perhaps, *mana* is a third element intervening between the signifier and the signified, the element which would give language its dynamism and continuity. For if there were a perfect 'fit' between the level of the signifier and the level of the signified, there would be nothing more to be said, language would come to an end. The floating signifier, therefore, is a structural feature of language in general, an element that introduces into it an asymmetrical, generative aspect: the aspect of contingency, time and, in Saussure's terms, the level of *parole*.

Kinship

Although the title might suggest it, no explicit reference to Saussurian linguistics is to be found in *The Elementary Structures of Kinship*. The reason, no doubt, is that this, the first major work in structural anthropology, was written in New York in the 1940s, and so before the revival of interest in Saussure's work had taken place in Europe – let alone America. In *The Elementary Structures of Kinship*, marriage (the outcome of the universal interdiction against incest) in non-industrialised cultures is reduced to two basic forms of exchange: restricted exchange, and generalised exchange. The former, may be represented as in Figure 1.

$$X \rightarrow YY \rightarrow X$$

Figure 1 Restricted exchange

Here, reciprocity requires that when an X man marries a Y woman a Y man marries an X woman. Similarly, generalised exchange can be represented as in Figure 2.

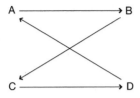

Figure 2 Generalised exchange.
  Source: Levéi Strauss, *The Elementary Structures of Kinship*, 1969: 178.

Thus, where an A man marries a B woman, a B man marries a C woman; where a C man marries a D woman, a D man marries an A woman. Almost all of *The Elementary Structures of Kinship* is a development of the variants of these two forms of matrimonial exchange.

Even to the untrained observer, what is striking about both forms of exchange is that reciprocity seems to entail a symmetrical structure (the only difference between restricted and generalised exchange being that the latter has twice the number of terms, thereby remaining entirely symmetrical). As Lévi-Strauss later realised, the question arises as to whether a symmetrical structure can be permanent; for after a period of time, groups X and Y in restricted exchange would, through marriage, merge into a single group. Similarly, even with generalised exchange – because of the symmetrical nature of the structure – a single group would eventually emerge. In other words, exchange, set in motion by the interdiction against incest, would encounter an insuperable limit, one that would place at risk the very continuation of social relations.

For exchange to remain viable as an institution, the presence of a third, heterogeneous element is always necessary. Such is indeed the theme of two important articles – one published in 1945 (Lévi-Strauss 1972: 31–54), the other in 1956 (Lévi-Strauss 1972: 132–63) – which clarify this point. In the first article, Lévi-Strauss points out that the child is the dynamic, asymmetrical element in the kinship structure:

> we must understand that the child is indispensable in validating the dynamic and teleological character of the initial step, which establishes kinship on the basis of and through marriage. Kinship is not a static phenomenon; it exists only in self-perpetuation. Here we are not thinking of the desire to perpetuate the race,

but rather of the fact that in most kinship systems the initial disequilibrium produced in one generation between the group that
gives the woman and the group that receives her can be stabilized
only by the counter-presentations in following generations.

(Lévi-Strauss 1972: 47)

In the article on dual organisations, Lévi-Strauss points out that every
apparent division into two groups in fact implies three elements precisely because of the requirements of self-perpetuation. Any truly dual
(i.e. symmetrical) structure leads to the dissolution of the groups
involved. There must, then, be a third element – whether real or
imagined – which introduces asymmetry and dynamism into the situation. Consequently, institutions having a '*zero value*' are an indispensable element in any society. Like *mana*, these institutions 'have no
intrinsic property other than that of establishing the necessary preconditions for the existence of the social system to which they
belong; their presence – in itself devoid of significance – enables the
social system to exist as a whole' (Lévi-Strauss 1972: 159).

Myth

The study of myth led Lévi-Strauss to refine his structuralist
approach. A clear enunciation of the principle that the elements of
myths gain their meaning from the way they are combined and not
from their intrinsic value, leads Lévi-Strauss to the position that
myths represent the mind that creates them, and not some external
reality. Myths resist history: they are eternal. Even different versions
of a myth are not to be thought of as falsifications of some true,
authentic version, but as an essential aspect of the structure of myth.
On the contrary, different versions are part of the same myth precisely because a myth is not reducible to a single uniform content,
but is a dynamic structure. Eventually, all the versions (diachronic
aspect) of a myth have to be taken into consideration so that its structure can become apparent. From another perspective, myth is always
the result of a contradiction – for instance, 'the belief that mankind is
autochthonous', 'while human beings are actually born from the
union of man and woman' (Lévi-Strauss 1972: 216). In effect, contradiction, as the unassimilable aspect of human society, generates
myths. Myth derives from the asymmetry between belief and reality,
the one and the multiple, freedom and necessity, identity and difference, etc. Looked at in terms of language, myth, says Lévi-Strauss, is 'language functioning on an especially high level' (Lévi-Strauss 1972: 210).

Moreover, if *langue* – the synchronic element of language – is equated with reversible time, and *parole* with I diachronic, or contingent, historical aspect, myth constitute; a third level of language (Lévi-Strauss 1972: 209). Myth is the (impossible) synthesis between diachronic and the synchronic aspects of language. It is the continual attempt to reconcile the irreconcilable:

> since the purpose of myth is to provide a logical model capable of overcoming a contradiction (an impossible achievement if, as it happens, the contradiction is real), a theoretically infinite number of [versions] will be generated, each slightly different from the others.
>
> (Lévi-Strauss 1972: 229)

Myth thus becomes the third dimension of language: in it a continuous attempt is made to reconcile its other two dimensions (*langue* and *parole*). Because complete reconciliation is impossible 'myth grows spiral-wise until the intellectual impulse which has produced it is exhausted' (Lévi-Strauss 1972: 229). Myth grows, then, because, structurally, the contradiction – the asymmetry – which gives it life, cannot be resolved.

Art and Structure

Like myth, the facial painting of the South American Caduveo Indians, described in Lévi-Strauss's autobiographical work, *Tristes Tropiques* (Lévi-Strauss 1974: 178–97), provide another illustration of structure as a dynamic, ternary phenomenon. There, facial painting designs are asymmetrical arabesques – a ternary structure geared to generate more designs. A purely symmetrical design, as well as being difficult to 'fit' to a real face, would fail to fulfil the purpose assigned to it. This purpose is like that of a figure in European playing cards. Each figure on a playing card must fulfil both a contingent function – it is an element in a specific game between players – and a structural (synchronic) function: it is an element occupying a particular place in the pack, and this place never changes. Caduveo facial painting tries to capture the symmetry of function (status in the group), and the asymmetry of part played (contingency)

> by the adoption of a composition that is symmetrical but set on an oblique axis, thus avoiding the completely asymmetrical formula, which would have met the demands of the role but run counter to those of the function, and the reverse and completely

symmetrical formula, which would have had the opposite effect.

(Lévi-Strauss 1974: 194)

The arabesques of the facial painting bring two conceptions of structure into sharp focus. For his part, Lévi-Strauss writes as though his own work were more focused on the static, symmetrical, binary notion of structure, while his actual analyses of social and cultural phenomena suggest that it is the second, ternary view of structure which has far greater explanatory and methodological significance.

Lévi-Strauss's Critics and His Achievements

Such an ambivalence with regard to the basis of his theoretical framework has led to misunderstandings. In particular, critics have been able to claim that history is neglected in structural anthropology, a fact that has been played up because, no doubt, of Lévi-Strauss's hostility to Sartre's Existentialism, a doctrine in which almost every act is historical (that is, contingent) (Pace 1983: 183–84 and chapter 6). Furthermore, Lévi-Strauss's insistence on the scientific status of anthropology (admittedly in order to defend the possibility of a social science detached from immediate political debates) sits oddly with his view that science cannot entirely escape being mythical, and the view that cultures are not hermetically sealed off from each other, but constitute an infinite series of transformations. And so while, for instance, science thinks *of* the concrete, native thought thinks *with* the concrete. Again, when Lévi-Strauss says in the 'Overture' to *The Raw and the Cooked* (Lévi-Strauss 1970: 7) that the book about myth is itself a myth, the very possibility of a detached science in the usual Western sense is brought into question. Lévi-Strauss, however, has often shown himself to be loath to take the consequences of this into account.

Unlike Julia Kristeva, or those inspired by Lacan's reading of Freud, there is little about subjectivity in Lévi-Strauss's *oeuvre*. It is as though he believed that Durkheim's battle to separate psychology from anthropology and sociology were still to be won, and that any concessions to a theory of subjectivity would be equivalent to conceding to the explanatory power of psychology over anthropology. But this battle is not still to be won. And the anthropologist's work suffers from the absence of any attempt to include within it a theory of the subject.

Nevertheless, the significance of Lévi-Strauss's anthropology, as mentioned earlier, cannot be limited to its analytical contents. Much more is at stake. For Lévi-Strauss shows the complexity of non-industrialised cultures which the West – often through its anthropologists (cf. Lévy-Bruhl and Malinowski) – had assumed to be equivalent to the childhood of mankind and who, through that fact, were deemed to be more primitive and more simplistic than the West in their thinking (primitive societies have myth; the West has science and philosophy, etc.). Lévi-Strauss's universalism should thus be understood to mean that transformations of the same myth (as in the Oedipus myth) throughout the world indicate that human beings belong to a single humanity, but that the presence of others is essential if we are to constitute our differences.

References

Lévi-Strauss, Claude (1969), *The Elementary Structures of Kinship*, trans. James Bell and John von Sturmer, Boston: Beacon Press, revised edn.

—— (1970), *Introduction to a Science of Mythology, Volume I: The Raw and the Cooked*, trans. John and Doreen Weightman, New York and Evanston: Harper Torchbooks.

—— (1972), 'Structural analysis in linguistics and anthropology' in *Structural Anthropology*, trans. Claire Jacobson and Brooke Grundfest Schoepf, Harmondsworth: Penguin Books.

—— (1974), *Tristes Tropiques*, trans. John and Doreen Weightman, New York: Atheneum.

—— (1987), *Introduction to the Work of Marcel Mauss*, trans. Felicity Baker, Boston: Routledge & Kegan Paul.

Pace, David (1983), *Claude Lévi-Strauss, The Bearer of Ashes*, Boston: Routledge & Kegan Paul.

See also Jakobson, Mauss, Saussure

Lévi-Strauss's major writings

(1997 [1993]) *Look, Listen, Read*, trans. Brian C.J. Singer, New York: Basic Books.

(1995 [1991]) *Story of Lynx*, trans. Catherine Tihanyi, Chicago: University of Chicago Press.

(1988 [1985]) *The Jealous Potter*, trans. Bénédicte Chorier, Chicago: Chicago University Press.

(1987) *Anthropology and Myth: Lectures, 1951–1982*, trans. Roy Wills, Oxford and New York: Blackwell.

(1987 [1950]) *Introduction to the Work of Marcel Mauss*, trans. Felicity Baker, Boston: Routledge & Kegan Paul.

(1985 [1983]) *The View From Afar*, trans. Joachim Neugroschel and Phoebe Hoss, New York: Basic Books.

(1982 [1975]) *The Way of Masks*, trans. Sylvia Modelski, Seattle: University of Washington Press.

(1978 [1964]) *Volume I: The Raw and the Cooked*, trans. John and Doreen Weightman, London: Jonathan Cape.

(1973 [1967]) *Volume II: From Honey to Ashes*, trans. John and Doreen Weightman, London: Jonathan Cape.

(1978 [1968]) *Volume III: The Origin of Table Manners*, trans. John and Doreen Weightman, London: Jonathan Cape.

(1981 [1971]) *Volume IV: The Naked Man*, trans. John and Doreen Weightman, London: Jonathan Cape.

(1978 [1973]) *Structural Anthropology, Volume II*, trans. Monique Layton, Harmondsworth: Penguin.

(1974 [1955]) *Tristes Tropiques*, trans. John and Doreen Weightman, New York: Atheneum.

(1972 [1958]) *Structural Anthropology*, trans. Claire Jacobson and Brooke Grundfest Schoepf, New York: Basic Books.

(1969 [1949]) *The Elementary Structures of Kinship*, trans. J. H. Bell and John von Sturmer, Boston: Beacon Press.

(1966 [1962]) *The Savage Mind*, (translated from the French), London: Weidenfeld & Nicolson.

(1963 [1962]) *Totemism Today*, trans. Rodney Needham, Boston: Beacon Press.

Further reading

Badcock, C. R. (1975), *Lévi-Strauss: Structuralism and Sociological Theory*, London: Hutchinson.

Pace, David (1983), *Claude Lévi-Strauss, The Bearer of Ashes*, Boston: Routledge & Kegan Paul.

CHRISTIAN METZ (1931–1993)

Born in 1931 in Béziers in the south of France, Christian Metz died tragically at the end of 1993. Metz opened the way in the 1960s to the establishment of film theory as a new intellectual discipline. Indeed, articles (written between 1964 and 1968) in Metz's *Essais sur la signification au cinéma* (1968) paved the way for the establishment of a department of cinema studies at the University of Vincennes (Paris VIII).

Along with other intellectuals of his generation who were inspired by the structuralist impulse (cf. Bourdieu, Derrida, Genette), Metz attended the École Normale Supérieure (rue d'Ulm) where he obtained an *agrégation* in 'classical letters' (French, Greek, Latin) after also obtaining a degree in German and a *maîtrise* in ancient history. Metz's academic training culminated in a *doctorat d'état* in general linguistics at the Sorbonne.

Parallel to his studies, Metz was engaged in the activities of cinephile and animator of ciné-clubs. Much of his knowledge of film history, and of specific films which often serve as examples for his theoretical work, actually come from these activities. In addition, Metz did translations from German and English, specialising in works on jazz. Strangely, perhaps, contact with such works on music has failed to leave any visible mark on Metz's film theory, music being a neglected aspect of his (and others') film and cinema studies.

The Film Theory Vacuum and the Structuralist Intervention

To appreciate the significance of Metz's impact, we need to recognise that before the mid-1960s little work had been done on analysing the nature of film (especially as image) or the institution of cinema (especially from the spectator's position). In short, while there was no shortage of film criticism, almost nothing had been done on film as a medium. In response to this, and in accordance with the evolution of his theoretical framework, Metz's work follows two broad lines of inquiry: the semiological study of film, and the psychoanalytic study of the cinema. Consideration of these two lines of inquiry will enable us to get an idea of Metz's work as a whole.

Langage, langue and parole

Inspired by his background in linguistics (in light of his *doctorat d'état*, Metz taught a course in general linguistics (1966–69) at the École des Hautes Études en Sciences Sociales before teaching film theory), Metz began to investigate film in light of Saussure's work on language – especially in terms of the categories of (in French) *langage* (language in general, or a specific, technical language), *langue* (so-called natural language: French, English), and *parole* (the level of speech or discourse). Just as a Saussurian approach to literary texts took the text's opacity (its status as a linguistic system) as its point of departure, so Metz began by taking the film's opacity as his point of departure. Almost immediately it became clear that such an operation was by no means straightforward; for while the literary analyst had both grammar and poetry as points of departure for investigating the opacity/transparence of literary texts, no such ready-made supports existed for the investigation of film – the medium *par excellence* of transparency. Transparency in film, Metz saw, was intimately tied to its realism – or verisimilitude. Not that film is more real than theatre. Just the opposite. The actors on stage might constitute a real presence for the spectator by contrast with the celluloid image of film, but theatre, in relation to the drama that is enacted, lacks the power of illusion based on verisimilitude which, Metz will come to emphasise, is the mark of film as a medium. At least this is so unless the theatre audience were primarily interested in the presence *per se* of a great actor.

Realism and the Impression of Reality

By comparison with theatre, the real power of film derives from its capacity to create an illusion of reality. 'Because the theatre is too real,' says Metz, 'theatrical fictions yield only a weak impression of reality' (Metz 1974: 10). Paradoxically, perhaps, the 'realism' of film is only achieved after a threshold of 'irreality' has been crossed. (The neologism, 'irreality' (rather than 'unreality'), is used here to refer to an imagined object, or one established by the imaginary in the psychoanalytic sense, not to the existence or non-existence of an object. See entry on Lacan.) This is tied to the requirement that the spectator suspend his or her disbelief because film as a medium – as a vehicle of representation – is an illusion in relation to the supposedly true reality beyond the representation. Of course 'a film is only a film ... but all the same': this is the attitude the suspension of disbelief is founded upon.

Metz's early essays thus reflect on the notion that film in general is a specific kind of illusion, one that is undeniably successful in seducing the spectator into suspending disbelief. Once immersed in the film world, once having accepted the principle that film is an illusion, or an 'impression' of reality, the image assumes all its seductive power. To present film largely from the spectator's position, as we have done here, is, however, to move too quickly. For Metz's early essays were less focused on film as experienced by the spectator (this focus would come later with a psychoanalytic study of cinema), and more on the way film signifies. In particular, Metz was interested in the way the film signifier, by comparison with other media – other signifiers – succeeds in presenting a narrative (diegesis), intrigue, description, drama, etc. The key point here concerns the way film as such presents a narrative structure, and not the way specific films unfold and may be interpreted in light of this unfolding. In other words, the point is not to interpret (particular) films (in which case the film signifier becomes incidental), but to analyse film as a structure of signification.

Film in general tends to defy analysis because being an 'impression of reality' is its defining feature. At all times in his early work, Metz keeps in view the fact that the filmic story, or subject-matter, is always realised through the image (the filmic signifier), and that the latter, although an essential element of fascination, is not what a film is about.

How then is it possible for a series of images to present a story which is, however minimally, always narrated (i.e. always presented through a diegesis)? A documentary film can resort to a voice-over in order to give the images presented in time an order and coherence. Some feature films, it is true, resort to the same device; but most do not. What is the basic syntax of the unfolding of the feature film – the film of fiction? Like Greimas's analysis of the basic meaning structure of actions in literary texts, where an attempt is made to construct a universal syntax of actions, Metz is concerned to construct the basic structure, or syntax, of film diegesis as it is realised in images (see Greimas entry in Lechte 1994). Neither Greimas nor Metz were interested in interpreting a specific text (they are not, to repeat, working only at the level of the signified), but set out to achieve a much more daunting objective: a description of the basic syntactic order of every possible text – be it of literary or of filmic form. While it is true that some light might be thrown on to the problem of the filmic signifier by way of a detailed analysis of particular films, and while it might be possible to throw light on to the structure of the filmic signifier through a knowledge of a select number of films, Metz's interest is primarily in film in general.

Discourse and the Subject of Enunciation

To say that a feature film – a film of fiction – unfolds by way of a narrative structure, is to say that it is a discourse, and thus, as Benveniste said, is an enunciation (*énonciation*) enacted by a subject of enunciation (*sujet de l'énonciation*) – or by, as Metz prefers, a 'narrating agency' (*instance racontante*). In effect, film images are always organised in a specific way; they are never simply given in a raw, descriptive form, although, to be sure, descriptive sequences can occur within the film diegesis. As a discourse, then, film has to be understood in terms of *parole* – or process – rather than *langue* – or system. On the other hand, Metz argues that film images correspond to statements (*énoncés*), or speech acts, rather than to words, precisely because, unlike words, images are of indefinite number and are created by the film-maker/speaker. Furthermore, film is not a language (*langue*) but an art of both connotation (unlike music or architecture) and expressivity (it uses natural objects which do not invoke a code). While 'a concept signifies, a thing is expressive', Metz points out (Metz 1974: 78. Translation modified).

Due to its reliance on the presentation of images in time and space, film tends to privilege the syntagmatic, or horizontal axis, over the paradigmatic, or vertical axis. Caution leads us to ask exactly why this is so. The answer is that although a page of graphic text might also appear to unfold syntagmatically, a word, as Lacan said, is a knot of (largely conventional) meanings which thus renders fragile the horizontal flow of language. An image (to repeat) is not a word, however. It is produced (in time and space) by the filmic discourse, a discourse that is not only realised through the direction taken by the camera, but also through the procedure of montage – the act of linking one image with another through contiguity. This is not to deny the existence of certain stereotypes (heroic cowboy) in film, nor to deny the use of symbols to create oppositions (e.g. white versus black corresponding to good versus evil). However, Metz, at least in his essays of the 1960s, points out that such paradigmatic features are extremely fragile. Another film-maker can come along and render the stereotype or symbol obsolete by changing the content of the signifying elements (black = good, for example).

The Syntagmatic Dimension of Cinema

Metz in any case chose to base his most rigorous construction of a film syntax on the syntagmatic axis of signification. This construction, which he calls *la grande syntagmatique* (the great syntagmatic chain), we shall now briefly summarise. The great syntagmatic chain is divided into eight autonomous segments. These are:

1 *Autonomous plan*: this is not a syntagm, but a syntagmatic type. It is equivalent to the exposure in isolation of a single episode of the intrigue. Inserts – e.g. a 'non-diegetic insert' (image outside the action of the story) – can also be equivalent to an autonomous plan.
2 *Parallel syntagm*: corresponds to what is often called a 'sequence of parallel montage'. Here, no precise relationship between syntagms is evident. This is an a-chronological syntagm.
3 *Accolade syntagm*: syntagm of evocations. For example, Metz points to the way that eroticism is evoked in Goddard's *Une femme mariée* through references to the 'global signified' of 'modern love'. This syntagm is also a-chronological.
4 *Descriptive syntagm*: here the relation between all the elements presented successively is one of simultaneity. For example, a face,

then the person to whom it belongs, then the room or office where the person is located (Metz gives the example of a view of the countryside, bit by bit). A descriptive syntagm is chronological.

5 *Alternating syntagm*: this syntagm corresponds to 'alternating montage', 'parallel montage', etc. Through alternation, the montage presents several series of events which are then understood to be happening simultaneously.

6 *Scene*: the scene properly speaking is equivalent to a continuous flow of images without any diegetic hiatus – one of the oldest cinematic constructions.

7 *Sequence by episodes*: discontinuity becomes a principle of construction. A linear syntagm produces a discontinuity of facts. Metz calls this 'the sequence properly speaking'.

8 *Ordinary sequence*: disposition of ellipses in dispersed order exemplified by jumping moments deemed to be without interest. The point about any sequence is that it is removed from the 'real conditions of perception'.

The Imaginary Signifier

By the mid-1970s, Metz had come to see that the semiotic approach to film tended to privilege the level of the structure of film discourse and to neglect the conditions of film reception – the position of the spectator. Furthermore, Metz realised that to account for the dynamics of the spectator's position at the same time entailed accounting for the cinema as an institution; for the cinema would hardly exist if it were not for the spectator's desire to 'go to the cinema'. This shift in focus from signification to film reception coincided with his interest in a psychoanalytical (i.e. Freudian and Lacanian) study of cinema.

Metz thus employs the key Lacanian concepts of the 'imaginary' and the 'symbolic' to explain the logic of the spectator's fascination with the image. Thus through an evocation of Lacan's 'Mirror Stage', Metz sees the spectator's captivation by the image as being equivalent to the child's identification of itself with its image in the mirror. Most importantly, this identification is pleasurable, a factor reinforced by the cinema institution's encouragement of the spectator. Clearly, the cinema institution has a vested interest in ensuring that the spectator experiences any individual film as a – to use Kleinian terms – 'good object': the object of fantasy that often forms the basis of a pleasant day-dream. A 'bad object', by contrast, is what the subject/spectator wants to avoid.

The spectator, then, has assimilated the positive cue associated with going to the cinema institution because he or she is part of that very institution. This is to say that the subject's imaginary is an integral part of the same institution. Film, in effect, becomes integrated into the subject's desire. The screen becomes equivalent to a mirror which offers an image of the subject's own desire. Because the cinema is structured in this way, Metz shows, discourse on the cinema is often part of the cinema institution. Only rarely, therefore, is cinema discourse critical of the cinema institution.

The theorist, by contrast, attempts to take up the position of the symbolic, but this position, as Metz recognises, is precarious, precisely because the theorist's own imaginary (read: desire) is also involved. In other words, film poses in an acute form the problem of distinguishing a judgement of what is good, or objective, from an expression of what is desirable.

In a sustained psychoanalytical study of the cinematographic signifier (that is, the materiality of film, not what it signifies), Metz attempts to compare cinema with the level of the primary process in Freud's theory. This brings the drive aspect into consideration: the way the image fascinates, that way the viewing of film approximates dream, and that way metaphor and metonymy approximate primary process thinking based on condensation and displacement. The drive aspect implies, first of all, that there is a pleasure in perceiving what passes on the screen, and that, furthermore, due to the irreality of film, the spectator's pleasure does not derive from an object properly speaking, but is narcissistic, that is, imaginary. The irreality of the cinematographic signifier invites a comparison between dream and the image in the mirror. Like dream, film has a hallucinatory quality which at the same time calls for interpretation; like the child's prototypical experience with the mirror as enunciated by Lacan, film images also please. Unlike the mirror, of course, the spectator's own body is not there on the screen. Also, the spectator is quite aware that the image is only an image. Nevertheless, argues Metz, identification is still crucial, only now the spectator '*identifies with himself*, with himself as a pure act of perception' (Metz 1982: 49, Metz's emphasis).

Dream and Hallucination

In the darkness of the cinema, the spectator acts out a number of Freudian scenarios, scenarios precisely deriving from the very nature of the film signifier's irreality. Scopic passion, voyeurism and fetishism in particular come to the fore. Each of these stimulate the drives which, to a certain extent, do not need a real object for achievement of satisfaction. Voyeurism evokes the primitive scene of the child being present while its parents have intercourse. The voyeuristic position is one of passivity, entailing a gap between eye and object. The fetish is equivalent to a substitute for the penis in castration. It is a way of denying the absence of the penis (= real object) and marvelling at the cinema as a grand technique of illusion. To the point of delusion and hallucination? Metz almost implies as much at certain points, so concerned is he to emphasise the fact that spectator, *qua* spectator, disavows cinematic irreality.

The same might be said of Metz's treatment of dream and cinema as we have just said of the treatment of the spectator as fetishist. The analogy is made to be too complete. For whereas dream and hallucination often lead to a confusion between reality and illusion (this is why Freud called a dream a psychosis (see Freud 1969: 29), the distinguishing mark of the cinematic signifier, it could be argued, lies precisely in its being experienced *as* an illusion. This is the very same kind of pleasure Lacan attributes to *trompe l'oeil* in painting, which, far from deceiving, gives itself for what it is, namely, *as* a pure appearance, *as* an illusion, in short. Many will feel that this aspect is not given nearly enough emphasis in Metz's analysis. So much is this the case that one writer (Copjec 1989: 58–59) has observed that Metz has contributed to the confusion in film theory between Foucault's panoptical subject, deluded by an all-too-powerful identification with what passes on the screen (the screen being made the equivalent of a mirror) and Lacan's theory of the subject of the gaze for whom an illusion is always perceived as an illusion (the screen is not the equivalent of a mirror).

References

Copjec, Joan (1989), 'The orthopsychic subject: Film theory and the reception of Lacan', *October*, 49 (Summer).

Freud, Sigmund (1969 [1940]), *An Outline of Psychoanalysis*, trans. James Strachey, London: The Hogarth Press.

Lechte, John (1994), 'Algirdas Julien Greimas' in *Fifty Key Contemporary Thinkers*, London and New York: Routledge.

Metz, Christian (1974), *Film Language: A Semiotics of the Cinema* (a translation of (1968) *Essai sur la signification au cinéma* (1968), Volume I), trans. Michael Taylor, New York: Oxford University Press.

—— (1983), *The Imaginary Signifier: Psychoanalysis and the Cinema*, trans. Celia Britton *et al.*, Bloomington: Indiana University Press.

See also: **Benveniste, Lacan, Jakobson, Saussure**

Metz's major writings

(1982 [1977]) *The Imaginary Signifier Psychoanalysis and the Cinema*, trans. Celia Britton, *et al.*, Bloomington: Indiana University Press.

(1977) *Essais sémiotiques*, Paris: Klincksieck.

(1976 [1973]) *Essai sur la signification au cinéma*, Volume II, Paris: Klincksieck.

(1974a) *Film Language: A Semiotics of the Cinema*, trans. Michael Taylor, New York: Oxford University Press.

(1974b [1971 and 1977]) *Film Language and Cinema*, trans. J. Donna Uniker-Sebeok, Berlin: Mouton.

Further reading

Agis Cozyris, George (1980), *Christian Metz and the Reality of Film*, New York: Arno Press.

Block de Behae, L., ed. and Intro. (1996), 'Special Issue in Honour of Christian Metz', *Semiotica*, 112, 1–2. See Odin, R., 'Christian Metz and Fiction'; Sanjines, J., 'The Screen of Our Dreams: Christian Metz and the Horizons of the Imaginary', and Bellour, R., 'Cinema and Christian Metz on Words and Images'.

Copjec, Joan (1989), 'Orthopsychic subject: Film theory and the reception of Lacan', *October*, 49 (Summer).

Henderson, Brian (n.d.), *Classical Film Theory: Eisenstein, Bazin, Godard, and Metz*, Michigan: Ann Arbor, University Microfilms International.

Rushton, Richard (2002), 'Cinema's Double: Some Reflections on Metz', *Screen*, 43, 2.

POST-STRUCTURALIST THOUGHT

Often associated with the work of Jacques Derrida, post-structuralist thought examines the notion of difference in all its facets and discovers that Saussure had left intact certain (metaphysical) presuppositions about subjectivity and language (for example, the privileging of speech over writing) – vestiges of the historicist framework with which Saussure himself was dissatisfied. Post-structuralist thought examines writing as the paradoxical source of subjectivity and culture, whereas once it was thought to be secondary. Most importantly, post-structuralism is an investigation as to how this is so.

A further aspect of post-structural thought involves a radical questioning of otherness (Levinas), and of the subject–object relation.

A factor in understanding the evolution of post-structuralist thought is the influence of Heidegger, and to a lesser extent Husserl, for inspiring the questions which it addresses, questions, for example, relating to art, community, ancient Greek thought, language, time and history.

JACQUES DERRIDA (1930–2004)

Son of an Algerian Jewish family, Jacques Derrida was born in 1930 in El-Biar in Algeria, where he failed his baccalaureate in 1947 and dreamed of becoming a footballer. He came to France in October 1949. After a miserable period at the prestigious lycée, Louis-Le-Grand, Derrida was accepted into the École Normale Supérieure (rue d'Ulm) in Paris, where he obtained an *agrégation* in philosophy. Derrida first came to the attention of a wider public at the end of 1965 when he published two long review articles on books on the history and nature of writing, in the Parisian journal, *Critique* (Derrida 1965: 23–53 and 1966: 1016–42). These pieces formed the basis of Derrida's important and possibly best-known book, *De la Grammatologie* (1967) (Eng trans. *Of Grammatology* (1976)).

Spectre

In a later book on Marx, *Spectres de Marx* (1993), Derrida uses deconstructive philosophy to examine all the permutations of 'spectre', as well as its accompaniments, 'haunting' and 'spirit'. By analysing 'spectre', not only does it become possible to engage with essentially troubling phenomena – between death and life, neither dead nor alive – but Marx and Engels's reference to communism as a 'spectre', in the *Communist Manifesto*, opens the way to use spectre as an analytical device for investigating Marx's later works, such as *Capital*. For example, the *spectre* of the commodity haunts every object used as use-value. Moreover, the very existence of the commodity is spectral: it is neither thing nor object, but it is something, not nothing. It is unreal and real at the same time. This is what adds to its mystifying status. *Capital* – the book – is thus *haunted* by a notion that is supposedly pre-*Capital*. Contemporarily, if a spectral reality haunts Marx's *Capital*, the same can be proposed for the capitalist, globalised and neo-Liberal world of post-industrialism. To be sure, the contemporary world is not going to notice – precisely because, for it, Marxism, like Marx himself, is dead. Also, for this world, there is only one kind of reality: what exists, what is concrete and empirical, what is reinforced by an epistemology based in a correspondence theory of truth, or of the true.

Spectres, then, both recalls Derrida's long established capacity – since his work on Husserl in the 1960s – to show that the present is not identical with itself (it is both same and different). 'Spectre', or the 'spectral', then, is not identical with itself: it both is and is not; it is between life and death; it exemplifies the working of *différance*, a term we will later explicate in more detail, for it is crucial to Derrida's philosophical arsenal. In addition *Spectres* continues Derrida's preoccupation with death and mourning that is also articulated explicitly in texts such as: *The Gift of Death* (1995) and *The Work of Mourning* (2001), which contains the text of Derrida's eulogies. It is a preoccupation that carries over into Derrida's work on the themes of: hospitality; donation/giving; friendship; responsibility; testimony/ witnessing; the law, justice and violence (see Derrida 1994); memory and the archive, secrecy and religion – themes particularly developed in works of the 1990s. These run in parallel with the more specifically deconstructive themes of: purity, identity and borders.

The Logic of Identity and its Deconstruction

A number of important tendencies underlie Derrida's approach to philosophy. Broadly, these include a concern to reflect upon and undermine philosophy's dependence on the logic of identity, which is also a logic of purity and the maintaining of borders. It includes, too, asking why certain questions (such as those relating to writing and literature) have not been part of philosophy's traditional field of inquiry. More specifically, Husserl (Derrida visited the Husserl archive in Louvain in the 1950s) and Heidegger provide an abiding point of engagement throughout Derrida's career. Heidegger's term '*Destruktion*' is the source of the Derridian, 'deconstruction', which initially concerned uncovering everything that covers up being. In Derrida's hands, it is a strategy used to uncover the paradoxes of identity.

The logic of identity derives particularly from Aristotle and in Bertrand Russell's words, comprises the following key features:

(1) *The law of identity*: 'Whatever is, is.'
(2) *The law of contradiction*: 'Nothing can both be and not be.'
(3) *The law of excluded middle*: 'Everything must either be or not be' (Russell 1973: 40).

These 'laws' of thought not only presuppose logical coherence, they also allude to something equally profound and characteristic of tradition in question, namely, that there is an essential reality – an origin – to which these laws refer. To sustain logical coherence, this origin must be 'simple' (i.e. free of contradiction), homogeneous (of the same substance, or order), present to or the same as itself (i.e. separate and distinct from any mediation, conscious of itself without any gap between the origin and consciousness). Clearly these 'laws' imply the exclusion on of certain features, to wit: complexity, mediation and difference – in short, features evoking 'impurity', or complexity. This process of exclusion takes place at a general, metaphysical level, one, moreover, at which a whole system of concepts (sensible–intelligible; ideal–real; internal–external; fiction–truth; nature–culture; speech–writing; activity–passivity; etc.) governing the operation of thought in the West, come to be instituted.

Through the approach called 'deconstruction', Derrida has begun a fundamental investigation into the nature of the Western metaphysical tradition and its basis in the law of identity. Superficially, the results of this investigation seem to reveal a tradition riddled with paradox and logical aporias – such as the following one from Rousseau's philosophy.

Rousseau argues at one point that the voice of nature alone should be listened to. This nature is identical to itself, a plenitude to which nothing can be added or subtracted. But he also draws our attention to the fact that nature is in truth sometimes lacking – such as when a mother cannot produce enough milk for the infant at her breast. Lack now comes to be seen as common in nature, if it is not one of its most significant characteristics. Thus self-sufficient nature, Derrida shows (Derrida 1976: 145), is, according to Rousseau, *also* lacking. Lack in fact endangers nature's self-sufficiency – that is, its identity, or, as Derrida prefers, its self-presence. Nature's self-sufficiency can only be maintained if the lack is supplemented. However, in keeping with the logic of identity, if nature requires a supplement it cannot also be self-sufficient (identical with itself); for self-sufficiency and lack are opposites: one or other can be the basis of an identity, but not both if contradiction is to be avoided. This example is not an exception. The impurity of this identity, or the undermining of self-presence, is in fact inescapable. For more generally, every apparently 'simple' origin has, as its very condition of possibility, a non-origin. Human beings require the mediation of consciousness, or the mirror of language, in order to know themselves and the world; but this mediation or mirror (these impurities) have to be excluded from the process of knowledge; they make knowledge possible, and yet are not included in the knowledge process. Or if they are, as in the philosophy of the phenomenologists, they themselves (consciousness, subjectivity, language) become equivalent to a kind of self-identical presence.

The process of 'deconstruction' does not aim to remove these paradoxes or these contradictions; nor does it claim to be able to escape the exigencies of tradition and set up a system on its own account. Rather, it recognises that it is forced to use the very concepts it sees as unsustainable in terms of the claims made for them. In short, it, too, must (at least provisionally) sustain these claims.

Différance

Différance is a neologism Derrida coined in 1968 in light of his researches into the Saussurian and structuralist theory of language. While Saussure had gone to great pains to show that language in its most general form could be understood as a system of differences, 'without positive terms', Derrida noted that the full implications of such a conception were not appreciated by either latter-day structuralists, or Saussure himself. The idea of difference without positive terms is, strictly speaking, unconceptualisable. Difference becomes the proto-type of what remains outside the scope of Western metaphysical thought because it is the latter's very precondition. Of course, in everyday life people readily speak about difference and differences. We say, for instance, that 'x' (having a specific quality) is different from 'y' (which has another specific quality), and we usually mean that it is possible to enumerate the qualities which make up this difference. This, however, is to give difference *positive* terms – implying that it can have a phenomenal form – so it cannot be the difference Saussure announced, one that is effectively unconceptualisable. The first reason for Derrida's neologism thus becomes apparent: he wants to distinguish the conceptualisable difference of common sense from a difference that is not brought back into the order of the same and, through a concept, given an identity. Difference is not an identity; nor is it the difference between two identities. Difference is differ-ence deferred (in French the same verb, *différer*, means both 'to differ' and 'to defer'). *Différance* alerts us to a series of terms given promi-nence in Derrida's early work whose structure is inexorably double: pharmakon (both poison and antidote); supplement (both surplus and necessary addition); hymen (both inside and outside).

Writing

Another justification for Derrida's neologism also derives from Saus-sure's theory of language. Writing, Saussure had said, is secondary to the speech *spoken* by the members of the linguistic community. Writing for Saussure is even a deformation of language in the sense that it is (through grammar) taken to be a true representation of it, whereas, in fact, the essence of language is only contained, Saussure claimed, in *living* speech, which is always changing. Derrida interrogates this distinction. As with difference, he notices that both Saussure and the structuralists (cf. Lévi-Strauss) operate with a colloquial notion of writing, one that attempts to evacuate all complexities. Thus writing is assumed to be purely graphic, an aid to memory perhaps, but secondary to speech; it is deemed to be fundamentally phonetic, and so represents the sounds of language. Speech, for its part, is assumed to be closer to thought, and thus to the emotions, ideas and intentions of the speaker. Speech as primary and more original thus contrasts with the secondary, representative status of writing. As grammatologist (theorist of writing), Derrida endeavours to show that this distinction is unsustainable. The very term, *différance*, for example, has an irreducibly graphic element which cannot be detected at the level of the voice. In addition, the claim that phonetic writing is entirely phonetic, or that speech is entirely auditory, becomes suspect as soon as the exclusively graphic nature of punctuation becomes apparent, together with the unpresentable silences (spaces) of speech.

One way or another, the whole of Derrida's *oeuvre* is an exploration of the nature of *différance*, of which writing, and, by extension, technics, is an incarnation. To the extent that writing always includes pictographic, ideographic and phonetic elements, it is not identical with itself. Writing, then, is always impure and, as such, challenges the notion of identity, and ultimately the notion of the origin as 'simple'. It is neither entirely present nor absent, but is the trace resulting from its own erasure in the drive towards transparency. More than this, writing is in a sense more 'original' than the phenomenal forms it supposedly evokes. Writing as trace, mark, grapheme becomes the precondition of all phenomenal forms. This is the sense implicit in the chapter in *Of Grammatology* entitled 'The end of the book and the beginning of writing'. Writing in the strictest sense, this chapter shows, is virtual, not phenomenal; it is not what is produced, but what makes production possible. It evokes the whole field of cybernetics, theoretical mathematics and information theory (Derrida 1976: 9).

Meditations on themes from literature, art and psychoanalysis, as well as from the history of philosophy, are part of Derrida's strategy to make visible the 'impurity' of any identity. That is to say, Derrida often demonstrates what he is attempting to confirm philosophically by employing rhetorical, graphic and poetic strategies (as, for example, in *Glas*, *The Post Card*, *The Politics of Friendship*, or *Monolingualism of the Other*) so that the reader might be alerted to the blurring of boundaries between disciplines (such as philosophy and literature), and subject-matter (as with writing/philosophy and autobiography), so that, 'the thing signified is no longer easily separable from the signifier' (Derrida in Wood and Bernasconi 1988: 88).

Art and Grammatology

Derrida's work has inspired artists, showing that grammatology has *practical* effects. A case in point is Derrida's influence on the architectural work of Bernard Tschumi and Peter Eisenman, as exemplified in *Choral Works*, relating to plans for the parc de la Villette in Paris (see Derrida and Eisenman 1997). 'Choral works', designs for a science park, plays, amongst other things, on the multiple meanings of 'Folie'.

Art and creativity also give rise to the improper. The name of the French poet, F. Ponge (which, in a well-known essay, Derrida makes into *éponge* (sponge)), provides an admirable source of creative philosophical and critical writing, in English, one only need think of *Words*worth and the 'joy' in Joyce for a whole series of 'improper' associations to begin. Through pun, anagram, etymology or any number of diacritical features (recall the 'joy' of Joyce), a proper name can be connected to one or more different systems of concepts, ideas or words (including those of other languages). Derrida has in fact also connected the proper name to varying series of images and sounds so that, from one point of view, the reference text appears to have a very tangential relationship to the critical text (see the treatment of the work of Jean Genet in *Glas*; or the essay, *Signéponge* 'on' the work of Francis Ponge). Indeed, whereas the traditional literary critic might tend to search for the truth (whether semantic, poetic or ideological) of the literary text written by another, and then adopt a respectful, secondary role before the 'primacy' of this text, Derrida turns the 'primary' text into a source of new inspiration and creativity. Now the critic/reader no longer simply interprets (which was never entirely the case anyway), but becomes a writer in his or her own right.

The Obsession

Derrida's philosophical *oeuvre* is extremely difficult to evaluate. In no small part this is due to its technical vocabulary; but it is also due to the fact that we are dealing with an essentially open-ended enterprise.

For everything can be endlessly analysed – analysed to infinity: these are almost Derrida's exact words. Indeed, this analytic drive, especially evident in the works of the last decade of Derrida's life, is clearly an obsession. Conference papers and lectures expand to become substantial books. *Spectres of Marx* is a case in point. Footnotes go on for pages and there is a blow-out on preliminaries: *Archive Fever* (1996) contains introductory pages, an Exergue, a Preamble and a Foreword before coming to the theses. The whole was based on a lecture. Derrida's determination to speak/write on any theme, to speak on any occasion, also exemplifies this drive to analyse. One can always ask: What? One can always question. The point is that, because of its obsessive nature, Derrida's analytical paraphernalia often exceeds scholarly requirements. The writing is often inaccessible for this reason, and not only because of the difficulty of the subject matter. This all gets caught up in Derrida's refusal to simplify, and to sustain complexity – to infinity? (see on this point, Derrida and Spire 2002: 38–42).

It is also true, of course, that one obsessive attracts another, and that those who have been Derrida's strongest critics are often those who have become obsessed with protecting the status quo with regard to thinking, right down to 'correct' punctuation. Whatever the case, the phenomenon that is, and was, Derrida, has had an impact on culture that is almost unmatched in the current era.

References

Derrida, Jacques (2001), *The Work of Mourning*, ed. Pascale-Anne Brault and Michael Naas, Chicago: University of Chicago Press.

—— (1995), *The Gift of Death*, trans. David Wills, Chicago: University of Chicago Press.

—— (1994), *Force de loi*, Paris: Galilée.

—— (1993), *Spectres of Marx*, Paris: Galilée.

—— (1976), *Of Grammatology*, trans. Gayatri Chakravorty Spivak, Baltimore and London: Johns Hopkins University Press.

—— (1966), 'De la grammatologie (II)', *Critique*, 224 (January).

—— (1965), 'De la grammatologie (I)', *Critique*, 223 (December).

Derrida, Jacques and Eisenman, Peter (1997), *Choral Works*, ed. Jeffrey Kipins and Thomas Leeser, New York: The Monacelli Press.

Derrida, Jacques and Spire, Antoine (2002), *Au-delà des apparences*, Latresne, France: Le Bord de l'eau.

Russell, Bertrand (1973), *The Problems of Philosophy*, London and New York: Oxford University Press.

Wood, David and Bernasconi, Robert (1988), eds, *Derrida and 'Différance'* Evanston, Illinois: Northwestern University Press.

See also: **Bataille, Heidegger, Husserl, Joyce, Saussure**

Derrida's major writings

(2005 [2000]) *On Touching, Jean-Luc Nancy*, trans. Christine Irizarry, Stanford: Stanford University Press.

(2004 [2001]) *For What Tomorrow: A Dialogue with Elizabeth Roudinesco*, trans. Jeff Fort, Stanford: Stanford University Press.

(2003a) *Voyous: Deux essais sur la raison*, Paris: Seuil.

(2003b [1990]) *The Problem of Genesis in Husserl's Philosophy*, trans. Marion Hobson, Chicago: University of Chicago Press.

(2002) *Without Alibi*, trans. Peggy Kamuf, Stanford: Stanford University Press.

(2001 [1997]) *On Cosmopolitanism and Forgiveness*, London: Routledge.

(1998a) *Psyché: inventions de l'autre*, tome I (new and augmented edition), Paris: Galilée.

(1998b [1996]) *Resistances to Psychoanalysis*, trans. Peggy Kamuf, Pascale-Anne Brault and Michael Naas, Stanford: Stanford University Press.

(1996) *Archive Fever*, trans. Eric Prenowitz, Chicago and London: University of Chicago Press.

(1994 [1993]) *Spectres of Marx the State of Debt, the work of mourning, and the New International*, trans. Peggy Kamuf, New York: Routledge.

(1992a) 'Force of Law: The Mystical Foundation of Authority', trans. Mary Quaintance in Drucilla Cornell, Michel Rosenfeld and David Gray Carlson, eds, *Deconstruction and the Possibility of Justice*, New York and London: Routledge.

(1992b [1991]) *The Other Heading: Reflections on Today's Europe*, trans. Pascale-Anne Brault and Michael B. Naas, Bloomington: Indiana University Press.

(1989 [1987]) *Of Spirit: Heidegger and the Question*, trans. Geoffrey Bennington and Rachel Bowlby, Chicago: Chicago University Press.

(1987a [1980]) *The Post Card: From Socrates to Freud and Beyond*, trans. Alan Bas, Chicago: University of Chicago Press.

(1987b [1978]) *The Truth in Painting*, trans. Geoff Bennington and Ian McLeod, Chicago: Chicago University Press.

(1986 [1974]) *Glas*, trans. John P. Leavy Jr and Richard Rand, Lincoln: University of Nebraska Press.

(1984) *Signéponge = Signsponge* (English and French), trans. Richard Rand, New York: Columbia University Press.

(1982a [1972]) *Positions*, trans. Alan Bass, Chicago: Chicago University Press, Phoenix Edition.

(1982b [1972]) *Margins of Philosophy*, trans. Alan Bass, Chicago: Chicago University Press.

(1981 [1972]) *Dissemination*, trans. Barbara Johnson, Chicago: Chicago University Press.

(1979 [1978]) *Spurs: Nietzsche's Styles = Eperons, Les styles de Nietzsche* (English and French), trans. Barbara Harlow, Chicago: University of Chicago Press.

(1978 [1967]) *Writing and Difference*, trans. Alan Bass, Chicago: University of Chicago Press.

(1976 [1967]) *Of Grammatology*, trans. Gayatri Chakravorty Spivak, Baltimore and London: Johns Hopkins University Press.

(1973 [1967]) *Speech and Phenomena and Other Essays on Husserl's Theory of Signs*, trans. David B. Allison, Evanston, Illinois: Northwestern University Press.

Further reading

Bennington, Geoffrey, with Jacques Derrida, (1991), *Jacques Derrida*, Chicago: Chicago University Press.

Deutscher, Penelope (2006), *How to Read Derrida*, New York: Norton.

Kates, Joshua (2005), *Essential History: Jacques Derrida and the Development of Deconstruction*, Evanston, Illinois: Northwestern University Press.

Rapaport, Herman (2003), *Later Derrida: Reading the Recent Work*, London: Routledge.

MICHEL FOUCAULT (1926–1984)

Born in Poitiers in 1926, Michel Foucault was awarded his *agrégation* at the age of 25, and in 1952 obtained a diploma in psychology. During the 1950s, he worked in a psychiatric hospital, and in 1955 taught at the University of Uppsala in Sweden. His first major book, *Folie et déraison: Histoire de la folie à l'âge classique* (1972a) (Madness and Unreason: History of Madness in the Classical Age) was published in 1961 after having been presented as a *doctorat d'état*, supervised by Georges Canguilhem, in 1959. He died from an AIDS-related illness in 1984.

Discursive Practices

In April 1970, Foucault was elected to the chair of 'history of systems of thought' at the Collège de France. The résumé of his first course, called 'The will to truth' – professed there during 1970–71 – speaks of 'discursive practices', and says, *inter alia*:

> Now these groups of regularities [in discursive practices] do not coincide with individual works. Even if they appear through them, even if they happen to become evident for the first time in one of them, they extend substantially beyond them and often unite a considerable number. But they do not necessarily coincide

either with what we habitually call sciences or disciplines, although their boundaries can sometimes be provisionally the same.

(Foucault 1989: 10)

Foucault's explanation illustrates the innovative and often strikingly individual character of his work. Thus in the passage quoted, he alludes to the thesis presented in *The Archaeology of Knowledge* (that we cannot reduce 'discursive practices' to the familiar categories of individual *oeuvre*, or academic discipline). Rather, a discursive practice is the regularity emerging in the very fact of its articulation: it is not prior to this articulation. The systematicity of discursive practices is neither of a logical nor linguistic type. The regularity of discourse is unconscious and occurs at the level of Saussure's *parole*, and not at the level of a pre-existing *langue*.

Rather than study movements in thought in the manner of the History of Ideas – where ideas are prior to the material being studied – or the way ideologies or theories *express* material conditions, Foucault analyses 'regimes of practices'. Or, because the line between saying and doing – as between seeing and speaking – is always unstable (the division itself always changing), 'regimes of practices' cannot be reduced to an a-historical form of doing, or practice, any more than saying can be reduced to the realm of theory. Put another way, Foucault's histories, inspired by Nietzsche's anti-idealism, endeavour to avoid 'projecting "meaning" into history' (see Nietzsche 1968: 523). And in this regard, even the notion of cause is suspect – like the actor behind the act. Rather, order is the writing of history itself. A new map is drawn up: practices become modes of thought with 'their logic, their strategy, their evidence, their reason'.

Nevertheless, because *The Order of Things* (1973), like its companion piece, *The Archaeology of Knowledge* (1972b), is clearly ensconced in the tradition of epistemological studies, the question arises as to how a certain knowing subject is not already presupposed. Heidegger even makes the difference between ontology and epistemology a key distinction precisely because epistemology is inscribed within an a priori, subject–object framework, and, for this reason, is designated as giving rise to modern subjectivism. Subjectivism presupposes a subject prior to any given historical formation, which is just the opposite of what Foucault aspires to. This is possibly one of the reasons as to why, despite the innovative ring of 'archaeology', the knowledge field was vacated by Foucault in the 1970s.

Before giving a brief review of some of Foucault's major works, it is important, for a fuller appreciation of Foucault's originality, to clarify five interconnected, key terms. These are: the present, genealogy, epistemology, discontinuity and technology (technique).

Key Terms

The Present

Because, as Nietzsche showed, there is no intrinsically important area or problem in history, but only areas of material interest, the historian is always taken up by what is of interest at the present moment, at a given conjuncture. History, therefore, is always written from the perspective of the present; history fulfils a need of the present. The present offers up problems to be studied historically – the rise of structuralism in the 1960s, or the disturbances in prisons in the early 1970s, are cases in point, and gave rise, respectively, to *The Order of Things*, originally published in 1966, and *Discipline and Punish: The Birth of the Prison*, first published in 1975.

If the present determines the historian's themes of interest, will there not be a danger of the past becoming a more or less inevitable lead up to the present? Foucault's response is that this is a danger exacerbated by idealism. History is only a lead up to the present if the notion of cause is allowed to predominate over (material) effect, and if continuity is allowed to override the discontinuities revealed at the level of practices. In addition, however, the fact that the present is always in a process of transformation means that the past must be continually re-evaluated; to write a history of the past is to see it anew, just as the analysand sees anew events of his or her individual biography in light of the experience of psychoanalysis. The past, in short, takes on new meanings in light of new events. This precludes the possibility of any simple relationship of causality being proposed between past and present. The danger of historicism recedes when it is realised that no past era can be understood purely in its own terms, given that history is, in a sense, always a history of the present.

Genealogy

Closely connected to the notion of the present and the continual re-evaluation of the past is the notion of genealogy. Genealogy is the history written in light of current concerns. Genealogy is history written in accordance with a commitment to the issues of the present moment, and as such it intervenes in the present moment. Genealogy, in short, is 'effective history' (Nietzsche) written as a current intervention.

Epistemology and Discontinuity

Inspired by Bachelard, Canguilhem and Cavaillès – epistemologists and philosophers of science – Foucault recognises that if history is always genealogy and an intervention, frameworks of knowledge and modes of understanding are themselves always changing. Epistemology studies these as 'discontinuities' (there is no essential development) in the 'grammar' of knowledge production, as revealed by the practice of science, philosophy, art and literature. Epistemology is also a way of connecting material events to thought or ideas. That a particular practice embodies an idea is not self-evident; the connection has to be made evident within the practice of epistemology. Even in Foucault's later work this remains important, as the following passage from his history of sexuality demonstrates:

> Thought, ... is not, then, to be sought only in theoretical formulations such as those of philosophy or science; it can and must be analysed in every manner of speaking, doing, or behaving in which the individual appears and acts as subject of learning, as ethical or juridical subject, as subject conscious of himself and others.
>
> (Foucault 1984: 334–35[1])

Technologies

Foucault, in his analyses of power in particular, is concerned to reveal the unacknowledged regularity of actions which is the mark of a technique. And, towards the end of his life, he moved on to talk about the 'technologies of the self'. As a technology, techniques can be transferred across different sets of practices, as forms of bodily discipline demonstrate. Let us now turn to a review of some of Foucault's most important texts.

Madness

The title of Foucault's major thesis, *Folie et déraison: Histoire de la folie à l'âge classique*, defended in May 1961, is a reminder that the Classical Age – the age of Descartes – is also the Age of Reason. For his part, Foucault endeavours to show how Descartes, in the 'First Meditation', excludes madness from hyperbolic doubt: Descartes can doubt everything except his own sanity. Foucault wants to find out what madness and unreason could be in the age of Descartes, and why the difference between them was such an issue. Or, as a much later formulation would have it, he wanted to study the way the division between madness and reason is established. Reason and madness are thus presented as the outcome of historical processes; they do not exist as universally objective categories. For some, such an approach appears too relativistic. By the same token, it also provides the opportunity to come to grips with a much more complex and subtle approach to historical events.

More specifically, Foucault proceeds to map the way that the mad person, who was not confined in any institution before 1600, comes to assume, by the middle of the seventeenth century, the status of excluded person *par excellence* – the position previously occupied by the leper. In the fifteenth century mad people were wanderers, as immortalized in Sébastian Brant's poem, *Stulifera navis* ('Ship of Fools', 1497) and in Hieronymous Bosch's painting of the same name inspired by Brant's poem. Moreover, the theme of madness emerged generally in literature and iconography because the mad person was seen as a source of truth, wisdom and criticism of the existing political situation. In the Renaissance, madness occupies a grand place: it is 'an experience in the field of language, an experience where man was confronted with his moral truth, with the rules proper to his nature and his truth' (Foucault 1972a: 39). Madness here has its own form of reason and is seen as a general characteristic of human beings. Unreasonable reason, and reasonable unreason could exist side by side.

With the Classical Age (the seventeenth and eighteenth centuries), madness is reduced to silence; or rather, it has no voice of its own but exists confusedly in supposedly anti-social figures such as the libertine, the homosexual, the debauched person, the dissipater or the magician. These are the people confined in hospitals, workhouses and prisons. Similarly, seventeenth- and eighteenth-century thought defines fury – which includes both criminal and insane behaviour – as 'unreason'. Not only does the figure of madness change between the Renaissance and the Classical Age, but so too do society's strategies for dealing with it. We are still a long way from anything like a medical conception of madness. Until the nineteenth century, madness, or insanity, was more a police matter than a medical matter. Mad people were not judged to be ill. Thus there is no basis, Foucault argues, for researching the antecedents of the treatment of the mentally ill in the history of psychiatry or, more generally, in the history of medicine.

Rather, historical discontinuities are revealed – first, between the Renaissance view of madness and the view of the Classical Age, which reduced it to unreason and so to silence; and, second, between the Classical Age and the nineteenth-century medicalisation of madness as mental illness. Discontinuity (between eras) thus predominates in the history of madness.

Although mad people were confined from the beginning of the seventeenth century (the formation of the *Hôpital général* in 1656 being a key event here), and although medicine in the modern era gradually moved into the asylum to treat the mentally ill, the asylum had fundamentally changed by the time Tuke and Pinel came to carry out their reforms at the end of the eighteenth century. Medicine and internment thus came closer to each other, not because of some great medical discovery, but because of two indirectly related factors: a greater concern for individual rights in the wake of the French Revolution, and the transformation of the asylum into a space of therapeutic practices, instead of being a uniquely punitive institution.

Power

As the wave of structuralist enthusiasm began to subside in the 1970s, discourse began to figure less prominently in Foucault's work and 'technology' in relation to power and the body began to take its place. Two aspects of Foucault's theory of power become evident in his two major books of the 1970s. These are: power as it relates to knowledge and the body in punishment and sexuality, and power understood as being distinct from the philosophico-juridical framework of the Enlightenment, and its emphasis on representative government. Briefly: power ceases to have any substantive content; rather than being possessed and centralised, it comes to be seen as a technology.

Discipline and Punish presents two images of the body of the condemned: the tortured and publicly mutilated body of the would-be regicide, Damiens, and the disciplined body of the prisoner in his cell, a prisoner secretly under the threat of constant surveillance. As with the history of madness, Foucault argues that it is not possible to separate the birth of the prison as the main form of legal punishment in the nineteenth century, from the history of a range of institutions – such as the army, the factory and the school – which emphasised the disciplining of the body through techniques of real or perceived surveillance. Not the good will and humanity of reformers and changes to the criminal law, but the emergence of a disciplinary society and a consequent new articulation of power gave rise to the prison.

The figure which most accurately captures the structure of the post-eighteenth-century articulation of power is, says Foucault, Jeremy Bentham's Panoptican. It allows for the invisible surveillance of a large number of people by a relatively small number. Like madness, legal punishment has a varied and unstable history which depends not only on perceptions of the criminal, but also on the changes engendered by the emergence of institutions dealing with the formation of a knowledge of individuals. Knowledge is thus linked to power, and the prison becomes a tool of knowledge.

More theoretically, perhaps, the first volume of the history of sexuality again analyses the link between power and knowledge. There, the juridico-philosophical conception – which sees power as essentially repressive, and thus as essentially negative and to be avoided – is presented as belonging to the era of the Enlightenment. Now, says Foucault, power is dispersed throughout society (it is not possessed by anyone) and it has positive effects. The persistence of the juridical definition of power as centralised and possessed, means that the king's head is still to be cut off. Just as power has no substantive content, sex has not been repressed. Instead, historical research shows that there has been a veritable explosion in discourses about sexuality and sexual activity. Thus, theories claiming to explain historical events are to be distinguished from actual events. Again, a meticulous genealogical approach discovers that theories – rather than explaining practices – are themselves part of practices situated in a specific historical era.

Sexuality

Foucault's last works on the history of sexuality turned to Ancient Greece and the way that sexuality there was part of a whole network of practices (moral, political, economic) fundamental to the production, government and care of the self. Here, the history of subjectivity is Foucault's explicit concern; but the approach adopted – the meticulous analysis of texts – recalls *The Order of Things* where subjectivity is the outcome of discursive practices. *The Use of Pleasure* shows how pleasure (sexual and other), although a legitimate part of the Greek social system, is, nevertheless, a source of tension – especially in the play of social relations between superiors and inferiors. The greatest amount of pleasure derives from the full realisation of one's social position in sexuality; pleasure is thus not the outcome of transgression, or illicit conduct, as it was to become in Christianity, but is realisable in marriage.

The Greeks also linked pleasure and individual freedom to the control over the self in one's regulated relations with others. In *The Care of the Self*, Foucault analyses the notion of self-control and outlines the way that the Greeks devoted much effort to developing various systems of rules to be applied to a great variety of conducts – not the least of these being sexual conduct. Without carrying out work upon the self – leading to ever greater self-control – access to both pleasure and truth become quite limited. For a life dominated by the care of the self, excess, rather than deviance, is the danger; not sex outside marriage, but too much inside it, is the problem.

Foucault's history thus presents another face of pleasure: pleasure through regulation and self-discipline instead of through libertine, or permissive conduct. With regard to sexuality, the Greek world is now discontinuous with the Christian world, and another received idea is shattered.

Subject as Enacted

Foucault's clear aspiration, as Judith Butler and others have noted, was to present the subject as enacted within an historical frame. No subject would exist prior to its enactment. This is both the strength and the possible weakness in Foucault's stance. It is a strength because it brings into a tight amalgam material history and a conceptual frame. There is no concept without material (that is, historical) incarnation. Consequently, dogmatic materialism and idealism would both seem to be thwarted.

On the other hand, Foucault's approach is open to the criticism that it is founded on the perverse thesis, exemplified in the notion that the Law produces the criminal, that sexual pleasures are enhanced by being forbidden; this is even exemplified in the idea that power is productive. As a number of commentators have remarked, under such circumstances, the possibilities of resistance are greatly diminished; for to resist, too, would be to play into the hands of the Law, given what counts as resistance must pass through it.

More positively, however, it is Foucault's inauguration of the field of bio-politics – dealing as it does with bare, physical life – which can alert us, as Agamben shows, to the true basis of contemporary politics based on practices of inclusion and exclusion.

Note

1 This is part of a translation of an earlier version of what would become the Introduction to *The History of Sexuality*, Vol. 2 (1984).

References

Foucault, Michel (1972a), *Histoire de la folie à l'âge classique*, Paris: Gallimard, TEL.
—— (1972b), *The Archaeology of Knowledge*, trans. A. M. Sheridan-Smith, London: Tavistock.
—— (1973), *The Order of Things: An Archaeology of the Human Sciences*, trans. from the French, New York: Vintage Books.
—— (1984), *Preface to The History of Sexuality*, Vol. 2, trans. William Smock in Paul Rabinow ed., *Foucault Reader*, New York: Pantheon Books.
—— (1989), *Résumé des cours, 1970–1982*, Paris: Julliard.
Nietzsche, Friedrich (1968), *The Will to Power*, trans. Walter Kaufmann, New York: Vintage Books.

See also: **Bachelard, Butler, Mauss, Nietzsche**

Foucault's major writings

(2005) *The Hermeneutics of the Subject: Lectures at the* Collège de France, *1981–1982*, ed. Fréderic Gros, trans. Graham Burchell, New York: Palgrave Macmillan.
(2003 [1997]) *Society Must be Defended: Lectures at the* Collège de France, *1975–1976* ed. Mauro Bertani and Alessandro Fontana; trans. David Macey, New York: Picador.
(1997–2000) *The Essential Works of Foucault, 1954–1984*, trans. Robert Hurley, New York: New Press.
(1986 [1984]) *The History of Sexuality, Volume 3: The Care of the Self*, trans. Robert Hurley, New York: Pantheon.
(1985 [1984]) *The History of Sexuality, Volume 2: The Use of Pleasure*, trans. Robert Hurley, New York: Pantheon.
(1979 [1976]) *The History of Sexuality, Volume 1: An Introduction*, trans. Robert Hurley, London: Allen Lane.
(1977 [1975]) *Discipline and Punish: The Birth of the Prison*, trans. Alan Sheridan, London: Allen Lane.
(1976 [1954 and 1962]) *Mental Illness and Psychology*, trans. Alan Sheridan, New York: Harper & Row.
(1975 [1963]) *The Birth of the Clinic: An Archaeology of Medical Perception*, trans. A. M. Sheridan-Smith, New York: Vintage Books.
(1974 [1969]) *The Archaeology of Knowledge*, trans. A. M. Sheridan-Smith, London: Tavistock.
(1973a [1966]) *The Order of Things: An Archaeology of the Human Sciences*, trans. from the French, New York: Vintage.

(1973b [1961]) *Madness and Civilization: A History of Insanity in the Age of Reason* (abridged), trans. Richard Howard, New York: Vintage/Random House.

(1972) *Histoire de la folie à l'âge classique*, Paris: Gallimard, TEL.

(1971) 'Orders of discourse', *Social Science Information*, 10, 2 (April).

(1963) *Raymond Roussel*, Paris: Gallimard.

(1961) *Folie et déraison. Histoire de la folie à l'âge classique*, Paris: Plon.

Further reading

Danaher, Geoff, Shirato, Tony and Webb, Jen (2000) *Understanding Foucault*, London: Thousand Oaks, Sage.

Dreyfus, Hubert L. and Rabinow, Paul (1982), *Michel Foucault: Beyond Structuralism and Hermeneutics*, Brighton: Harvester Press.

Gutting, Gary (2005) *Foucault: A Very Short Introduction*, Oxford and New York: Oxford University Press.

Mills, Sara (2003) *Michel Foucault*, London and New York: Routledge.

SEMIOTICS

Semiotics is the theory and analysis of signs and significations. Semioticians see social and cultural life in terms of signification, and therefore in terms of the nonessential nature of objects. Jean Baudrillard brings home this point in his book, *The System of Objects*. Through a semiotic approach, based on a Saussurian linguistic framework, social life becomes a struggle for prestige and status; or rather, it becomes a sign of this struggle. Semiotics also studies the *way* that signs signify – in conventional literary texts and legal documents, or in advertisements and bodily conduct.

Semiotics has always had two arms: one, deriving from linguistics and Saussure's theory of the sign, which emphasised that the relation between signifier and signified was arbitrary, and another, deriving from philosophy and Peirce's systems of sign classification, which included an iconic sign that could have some of the qualities of the signified.

ROLAND BARTHES (1915–1980)

Roland Barthes was born at Cherbourg in 1915. Barely a year later, his father died in naval combat in the North Sea, so that the son was brought up by the mother and, periodically, by his grandparents. Before completing his later primary and secondary schooling in Paris,

Barthes spent his childhood at Bayonne in south-west France. Between 1934 and 1947, he suffered various bouts of tuberculosis. And it was during the periods of enforced convalescence that he read omnivorously and published his first articles on André Gide. After teaching in Romania and in Egypt, where he met A. J. Greimas, then at the École des Hautes Études en Sciences Sociales, Barthes was appointed to the Collège de France in 1977. He died in Paris in 1980, the same year as Sartre, after having been struck by a van near the Sorbonne.

Biography and Criticism

Such elementary facts of biography have often provided the psycho-critic with material for explaining underlying (unconscious) aspects of the writer's *oeuvre*. Barthes, however, takes them in hand and uses them as the raw material of his own writing, and even of his style. This is so in two books he wrote towards the end of his life: *Roland Barthes by Roland Barthes*, and *Camera Lucida: Reflections on Photography*. Here, the status of raw material is the key; for Barthes in no sense becomes a conventional autobiographer. Instead, he fictionalises his life through using the third person when (conventionally) referring to himself, as he – like Joyce – reveals the profundities of life in the 'bread' of everyday experience. He writes, for example, of a photograph of his mother in the above-cited essay on photography, that he had found his mother's face – that face he had loved – in the photograph: 'The photograph was very old. The corners were blunted from having been pasted into an album, the sepia print had faded' (Barthes 1993: 67). Eventually, he says, 'I studied the little girl and at last rediscovered my mother' (Barthes 1993: 69). Godard's disenchanting words then ring in his ears: '"Not a just image, just an image"' (Barthes 1993: 70). In his grief, Barthes wants a just image.

This 'personalised' style, characteristic of the later Barthes, confirmed the semiotician and literary critic as a writer in his own right. Barthes writes 'the novelistic without the novel', as he himself put it. Indeed, this is arguably the true basis of his originality, over and above his theories of writing and signification. Thus in *A Lover's Discourse*, Barthes says that 'we do not know who is speaking; the text speaks that is all' (Barthes 1978: 112). Today, a lover's discourse can only be one of solitude; it has no specific subject but may be invoked by 'thousands of subjects'. The lover's discourse, as the equivalent of the novelistic, becomes the discourse of the construction of a lover's discourse: a pure weaving of voices spelling out what one would say and could say were the narrative to be enacted.

Photography in Detail

Barthes's writing on photography, as based on the last book he published in his lifetime, is now being seen as his culminating achievement. We shall take a moment to elaborate and interpret the more technical aspects of *Camera Lucida*, recalling that it is Sartre and phenomenology that were the basis of Barthes's original inspiration.

The Orthographic Moment

Barthes's writing on photography shows, says the noted philosopher of technology, Bernard Stiegler, that the photograph is constitutive of the self because it is (part of) the self. It does not represent or express the self. This is an 'orthographic' moment (a moment of absolutely accurate reproduction), where part of the past is reconstituted (Stiegler 1996: 78). As analogical (and this is Barthes's frame), the photograph coincides materially (i.e. chemically and luminously) with what is photographed, so that it can be simultaneously past and present. A photograph cannot be taken after the event; it is necessarily and essentially simultaneous with the event itself. In this way photographs give access to a past that 'one has not lived', the past as the 'already-there'.

Not just death, but death as a virtual object, only accessible via the photo through intuition is at issue. That is, when we say: 'he is dead and he is going to die' (= effectively: he is living *and* he is dead), as Barthes says of Lewis Payne (Barthes 1993: 95), the image of death is a strictly virtual image, an image that is quite distinct, if not quite separate, from the physical, analogical, mechanism of photography. Although time as death cannot be denied, it can only 'be' virtually. So, while there is physical evidence of life, there is no such correlate for death. Indeed, this can be tested by asking an uninformed spectator whether the person in the photo is alive or dead. This spectator will be able confirm the life of the photographic subject but not the death, at least not immediately.

Contingency and Phenomenology

Moreover, although inspired by phenomenology, Barthes also manifests an ambivalence for the phenomenological method and terminology. Thus, he refers to a paradox regarding his approach: on the one hand, he seeks, with phenomenology, the essence of photography –

an essence established, of course, by way of the *epoché*,[1] or bracketing of the contingent, natural attitude – while, on the other hand what, for him, is essential in photography is its contingency. The latter, were it to be absolutely true, would make photography difficult, if not impossible for phenomenology of a Husserlian kind, to deal with. We need to ask, then: How contingent is photography for Barthes? Although contingency is said to be primary in photography (Barthes 1993: 40), when it comes to defining the most precious element of the photograph, he invokes the uniquely Husserlian terminology of *noema*. Given the idiosyncratic nature of this term, it could hardly have been chosen by accident. Its technical aspect and its significance should therefore be noted as follows: correlate of a *noesis*, or thought act, the *noema* is a thought object. And in both cases, we are dealing with virtual objects, not real objects. The *noema* may or may not be linked to a real object. The purpose of the *noema* is to make it possible to avoid being ensnared in the natural attitude or the contingent world. Simply put: the object of thought, or of consciousness, is not the object of the natural world. Now, it is as the latter that Stiegler has defined the object of photography. Orthography means that there is a physical relation between object and inscription, object and representation.

The Punctum

In the case of Barthes, the *noema* of photography is, as we know, the 'it has been'. The question *Camera Lucida* raises is whether the *noema* can, strictly speaking, be a contingent object, or whether it is not rather the case that the 'it has been' is the object as experienced in thought and consciousness by Roland Barthes himself. There is a tension here, acknowledged by Barthes himself. There is also the difference between actual and virtual, where the virtual opens out onto subjectivity as the *punctum* (the subjective 'sting' of the image). Ultimately, the *punctum is* the 'it has been' – it is time – and is most intensely experienced in relation to death as the play between actual image as *stadium* (the narrative aspect of the image) and virtual image as *punctum*. Thus with the image of Lewis Payne, Barthes discovers something new in the *punctum*. The latter has ceased to be reducible to a detail and has become Time itself: the 'it has been' as *noeme* becomes the *punctum* as time: 'This new *punctum*, which no longer has a form but an intensity, is Time, it is the fractured force of the noeme ("*it has been*"), its pure representation' (Barthes 1993: 148).

A Diverse Oeuvre

Myth

Roland Barthes's work embodies a significant diversity. It ranges between semiotic theory, critical literary essays, the presentation of Jules Michelet's historical writing in terms of its obsessions, a psycho-biographical study of Racine, which outraged certain sectors of the French literary establishment, as well as the more 'personalised' works on the pleasure of the text, love and photography.

The early Barthes aimed, in 1957, to analyse and criticise bourgeois culture and society. *Mythologies* (1973) is the clearest statement of this. There, the everyday images and messages of advertising, entertainment, literary and popular culture and consumer goods, are subjected to a reflexive scrutiny quite unique in its application and results. Sometimes Barthes's prose in *Mythologies* is, in its capacity to combine a sense of delicacy and carefulness with critical acuity, reminiscent of Walter Benjamin's. Unlike Benjamin, though, Barthes is neither essentially a Marxist philosopher nor a religiously-inspired cultural critic. He is, in the 1950s and 1960s, a semiotician: one who views language modelled on Saussure's theory of the sign as the basis for understanding the structure of social and cultural life.

The nascent semiotician formulates a theory of myth that serves to underpin the writings in *Mythologies*. Myth today, Barthes says, is a message – not a concept, idea or object. More specifically, myth is defined 'by the way it utters its message'; it is thus a product of 'speech' (*parole*), rather than of 'language' (*langue*). With ideology, what is said is crucial, and it hides. With myth, how it says what it says is crucial, and it distorts. In fact, myth 'is neither a lie nor a confession: it is an inflexion' (Barthes 1973: 129). Consequently, in the example of the "Negro" soldier saluting the French flag, taken by Barthes from the front cover of *Paris-Match*, the Negro becomes, for the myth reader, 'the very *presence* of French imperiality'. Barthes's claim is that because myth hides nothing its effectiveness is assured: its revelatory power is the very means of distortion. It is as though myth were the scandal occurring in the full light of day. To be a reader of myths – as opposed to a producer of myths, or a mythologist who deciphers them – is to accept the message entirely at face value. Or rather, the message of the myth is that there is no distinction between signifier (the Negro soldier saluting the French flag) and the signified (French imperiality). In short, the message of the myth is that it does not need to be deciphered, interpreted or demystified. As Barthes explains, to read the picture as a (transparent) symbol is to renounce its reality as a picture; if the ideology of the myth is obvious, then it does not work as myth. On the contrary for the myth to work as myth it must seem entirely natural.

Despite this clarification of the status of myth, the difficulties in appreciating its profundity derive from the ambitiousness of the project of distinguishing myth from both ideology and a system of signs calling for interpretation. While, on the one hand, the subtlety of giving myth a *sui generis* status of naturalised speech has often been missed by Barthes's commentators, the issue is still to know what the import of this might be, other than the insight that the successful working of myth entails its being unanalysable as myth.

Writing

The analysis and practice of writing which begins in *Writing Degree Zero* (1953) gives a further clue about the concerns implicit in *Mythologies*. These centre on the recognition that language is a relatively autonomous system, and that the literary text, instead of being the transmitter of an ideology, or the sign of a political commitment, or again, the expression of social values, or, finally, a vehicle of communication, is opaque, and not natural. For Barthes, what defines the bourgeois era, culturally speaking, is its denial of the opacity of language and the installation of an ideology centred on the notion that true art is verisimilitude. By contrast, the zero degree of writing is that form which, in its (stylistic) neutrality, ends up by drawing attention to itself. Certainly, *Nouveau Roman* writing (originally inspired by Camus) exemplifies this form; however, this neutrality of style quickly reveals itself, Barthes suggests, as a style of neutrality. That is, it serves, at a given historical moment (post-Second World War Europe), as a means of showing the dominance of style in all writing; style proves that writing is not natural, that naturalism is an ideology. Thus if myth is the mode of naturalisation *par excellence*, as *Mythologies* proposes, myth, in the end, does hide something: its ultimately ideological basis.

Semiotics

Narrative and Fashion

Barthes's influential study of narrative in 1966 (Barthes 1966: 1–27) continues the semiotician's mission of unmasking the codes of the natural, evident between the lines in the works of the 1950s. Taking a

James Bond story as the tutor text, Barthes analyses the elements which are structurally necessary (the language, function, actions, narration, of narrative) if narrative is to unfold as though it were *not* the result of codes of convention. Characteristically, bourgeois society denies the presence of the code; it wants 'signs which do not look like signs'. A structural analysis of texts, however, implies a degree of formalisation that Barthes began to reject. Unlike theorists such as Greimas, the reader is nearly always struck by the degree of freedom and informality in his writing. Although linguistic notation, diagrams and figures appear in works like *The Fashion System* (1983), Barthes was unhappy with this foray into 'scientificity' and only published his book on fashion (originally intended as a doctoral thesis) at the behest of friends and colleagues. It is in *The Fashion System*, however, that Barthes clarifies a number of aspects of the structural, or semiotic, approach to the analysis of social phenomena. Semiology, it turns out, examines collective representations rather than the reality to which these might refer, as sociology does. A structural approach, for its part, attempts to reduce the diversity of phenomena to a general function. Semiology – inspired by Saussure – is always alive to the signifying aspect of things. Indeed, it is often charged with revealing the language (*langue*) of a field such as fashion. Barthes therefore mobilises all the resources of linguistic theory – especially language as a system of differences – in order to identify the language (*langue*) of fashion in his study of fashion.

Much of *The Fashion System*, however, is a discourse on method because fashion is not equivalent to any real object which can be described and spoken about independently. Rather, fashion is implicit in objects, or in the way that these objects are described. To facilitate the analysis, Barthes narrows the field: his corpus will consist of the written signs of women's clothing fashion as these appear in two fashion magazines between June 1958 and June 1959. The compli- cation is that there, fashion is never directly written about, only connoted. For the fashion system always implies that things (clothing) are naturally, or functionally, given: thus some shoes are 'ideal for walking', whereas others are made 'for that special occasion . . .'. Fashion writing, then, refers to items of clothing, and not to fashion. If fashion writing has a signified (the item), it is now clear that this is not fashion. In fact, the language of fashion only becomes evident when the relationship between signifier and signifier is taken into account, and not the (arbitrary) relationship between signifier and signified. The signifier–signified relation constitutes the clothing sign. Barthes orients his study along a number of different axes all of which have to do with the nature of signification. After methodological considerations, he looks at the structure of the clothing code in terms of: the fashion signifier – where meaning derives from the relationship between object (e.g. cardigan), support (e.g. collar), and variant (open-necked) – and the fashion signified: the external context of the fashion object (e.g. 'tusser = summer'). The fashion sign, however, is not the simple combination of signifier and signified because fashion is always connoted and never denoted. The sign of fashion is the fashion writing itself, which, as Barthes says, 'is "tautological", since fashion is only ever the *fashionable* garment' (Barthes 1993: 220n.16).

In the third section of *The Fashion System*, Barthes examines the rhetorical system of fashion. This system captures 'the entirety of the clothing code'. As with the clothing code, so with the rhetorical system, the nature of the signifier, signified and sign are examined. The rhetoric of the signifier of the clothing code opens up a poetic dimension, since a garment described has no demonstrably productive value. The rhetoric of the signified concerns the world of fashion – a kind of imaginary 'novelistic' world. Finally, the rhetoric of the sign is equivalent to the rationalisations of fashion: the transformation of the description of the fashion garment into something necessary because it naturally fulfils its purpose (e.g. evening wear), and naturally fulfils its purpose because it is necessary.

Codes and Languages

Barthes's *S/Z*, analyses Balzac's short story 'Sarrasine', and is an attempt to make explicit the narrative codes at work in a realist text. 'Sarrasine', Barthes argues, is woven of codes of naturalisation, a process similar to that seen in the rhetoric of the fashion sign. The five codes Barthes works with here are the hermeneutic code (presentation of an enigma); the semic code (connotative meaning); the symbolic code; the proairetic code (the logic of actions); and the gnomic, or cultural code which evokes a particular body of knowledge. Barthes's reading aims less to construct a highly formal system of classification of the narrative elements, than to show that the most plausible actions, the most convincing details or the most intriguing enigmas, are the products of artifice, rather than an imitation of reality.

After analysing Sade, Fourier and Loyola as 'Logothetes' and founders of 'languages' in *Sade, Fourier, Loyola* – an exercise recalling the 'language' (*langue*) of fashion – Barthes writes about pleasure and reading in *The Pleasure of the Text*. The latter marks a foretaste of the more fragmentary, personalised and semi-fictional style of the writings to come. The pleasure of the text 'is bound up with the consistency of the self, of the subject which is confident in its values of comfort, of expansiveness, of satisfaction' (Barthes 1985: 206. Translation modified). This pleasure, which is typical of the readable text, contrasts with the text of *jouissance* (the text of enjoyment, bliss, loss of self). The text of pleasure is often of a supreme delicacy and refinement, in contrast to the often unreadable, poetic text of *jouissance*. Barthes's texts themselves, especially from 1973 onwards, can be accurately described in terms of this conception of pleasure. Thus after distilling the language (*langue*) of others, Barthes, as a writer of pleasure, then came to give vent to his own, singular language. From a point where he became a critic for fear of not being able to write (fictions in particular), Barthes not only became a great writer, he also blurred the distinction between criticism and (poetic) writing.

Note

1 On this, and other terms, such as *noema*, see the entry on Husserl.

References

Barthes, Roland (1966), 'Introduction à l'analyse structurale des récits', *Communications* 8. In English as 'Introduction to the structural analysis of narratives' in Barthes (1979) *Image-Music-Text*, trans. Stephen Heath, Glasgow: Fontana/Collins.

—— (1973), *Mythologies*, trans. Annette Lavers, St Albans, Herts: Paladin, 1973, p. 129.

—— (1978), *A Lover's Discourse*, trans. Richard Howard, New York: Hill & Wang.

—— (1983), *The Fashion System*, trans. Matthew Ward and Richard Howard, New York: Hill & Wang.

—— (1985), *The Grain of the Voice. Interviews 1962–1980*, trans. Linda Coverdale, New York: Hill & Wang.

—— (1993), *Camera Lucida: Reflections on Photography*, trans. Richard Howard, London: Vintage.

Stiegler, Bernard (1996), *La Technique et le temps 2: La Désorientation* Paris: Galilée.

See also: **Benjamin, Eco, Genette, Husserl, Saussure**

Barthes's major writings

(2005) *The Neutral: Lecture Course at the Collège de France, 1977–1978*, trans. Rosalind E. Krauss and Denis Hollier, New York: Columbia University Press.

(1987a [1966]) *Criticism and Truth* trans. Katrine Pilcher Keuneman, Minneapolis: University of Minnesota Press.

(1987b [1954]) *Michelet*, trans. Richard Howard, Oxford: Basil Blackwell.

(1986 [1970]) *The Empire of Signs* (1970), trans. Richard Howard, New York: Hill & Wang, fourth printing.

(1985a [1982]) *The Responsibility of Forms*, trans. Richard Howard, New York: Hill & Wang.

(1985b [1981]) *The Grain of the Voice: Interviews 1962–1980*, trans. Linda Coverdale, New York: Hill & Wang.

(1984 [1977]) *A Lover's Discourse: Fragments*, trans. Richard Howard, New York: Hill & Wang.

(1983a [1980]) *Camera Lucida: Reflections on Photography*, trans. Richard Howard, London: Vintage.

(1983b [1967]) *The Fashion System*, trans. Matthew Ward and Richard Howard, New York: Hill & Wang.

(1979 [1966]) 'Introduction to the structural analysis of narratives' in *Image-Music-Text*, trans. Stephen Heath, Glasgow: Fontana/Collins.

(1977a [1975]) *Roland Barthes by Roland Barthes*, trans. Richard Howard, New York: Hill & Wang.

(1977b [1964]) *Elements of Semiology*, trans. Annette Lavers and Collin Smith, New York: Hill & Wang.

(1977c [1953]) *Writing Degree Zero*, trans. Annette Lavers and Colin Smith, New York: Hill & Wang.

(1976 [1971]) *Sade, Fourier, Loyola*, trans. Richard Howard, New York: Hill & Wang.

(1975 [1973]) *The Pleasure of the Text*, trans. Richard Miller, New York: Hill & Wang.

(1974 [1970]) *S/Z*, trans. Richard Miller, New York: Hill & Wang.

(1973 [1957]) *Mythologies*, trans. Annette Lavers, St Albans, Herts: Paladin.

(1972 [1964]) *Critical Essays*, trans. Richard Howard, Evanston, Illinois: Northwestern University Press.

Further reading

Allen, Graham (2003), *Roland Barthes*, London and New York: Routledge.

Gane, Mike and Gane, Nicholas, eds, (2004), *Roland Bathes*, London and Thousand Oaks: Sage.

Knight, Diana (2000), *Critical Essays on Roland Barthes*, New York: G.K. Hall.

Rabaté, Jean-Michel (1997), *Writing the Image After Roland Barthes*, Philadelphia: University of Pennsylvania.

UMBERTO ECO (b.1932)

Umberto Eco is known to a world-wide audience for his novels, particularly, *The Name of the Rose* (1983), *Foucault's Pendulum* (1989) and *The Island of the Day Before* (1995), with its discussion of the paradoxes of time. Each work, in its own way, alludes to aspects of past and present theories of signs, as well as to a vast array of scholarly (those of the Middle Ages in particular) and other texts (Sherlock Holmes in *The Name of the Rose*, and the Corpus Hermeticum in *Foucault's Pendulum*).

Joyce and the Middle Ages

Eco was born in 1932 in Piedmont, Italy. Before becoming a semiotician, he studied philosophy specialising in the philosophical and aesthetic theories of the Middle Ages. His thesis at the University of Turin on the aesthetics of Thomas Aquinas was published in 1956 when he was 24. Three years later, Eco contributed a chapter called 'Sviluppo dell'estetica medievale' ('The development of Medieval aesthetics') to a four-volume handbook on the history of aesthetics. In 1986, the lengthy chapter came in an English translation under the title of *Art and Beauty in the Middle Ages* (1986a). This erudition, we have noted, has been put to good effect in Eco's fiction, but does it have any real connection with his work in semiotics? One can answer in the affirmative here for two reasons. First, as others have shown, the age of Thomas Aquinas is also a chapter in the history of sign theory. The Aristotle who so influenced the 'Angelic Doctor' has also left his mark, Eco recognises, on more contemporary semiotics – such as in the theory of metaphor (see Eco 1984: 91–103). Second, as a medievalist, Eco became fascinated by the writings of James Joyce where one finds liberal references to Aquinas, Aristotle, Dante, Medieval bestiaries, and rhetoric.

His interest in Joyce has to be seen in the context of Eco's 'curiosity' and 'wonder' about the modern world, and about modernity as a cultural and historical phenomenon. Joyce thus bridges a gap between Eco's scholarly passion for a time now past (although it may be returning (see Eco 1986b: 59–85)), and the empirical world of the here and now – a world of complexity and diversity: a polyphonic and open world. The two poles of Eco's intellectual field can be appreciated through the knowledge that in the year that he published his chapter on Medieval aesthetics, an article under Eco's name appeared entitled, 'L'opera in movimento e la coscienza dell'epoca'

('The poetics of the open work'), which considered the way modern music (Stockhausen, Berio, Boulez), modern writing (Mallarmé, Joyce), modern art (Calder, Pousseur) in relation to modern science (Einstein, Bohr, Heisenberg) now produce 'works in movement' and 'open works' – works whereby the addressee becomes an active element in bringing a work to provisional completion, or where the work itself brings openness to the fore. From this starting point, Eco develops that theme of his intellectual trajectory which is concerned with 'the role of the reader'.

In a statement on reading and interpretation (Eco 1992: 67–88), Eco stressed that the 'anything goes' version of post-modern criticism is not what is implied in the notion of an open work. Rather, every literary work can be said to propose a model reader corresponding to real and justifiable possibilities set by the text. For Eco, to propose that an infinite number of readings is possible for *any* text is a wholly empty gesture. This does not mean, on the other hand, that an empirical author should be able to adjudicate on the validity of interpretation in the light of his or her intentions. It is a question of pointing to evidence that could lead to a pertinent and coherent interpretation, whether or not this be in spite of the empirical author. In this regard, Eco is fond of quoting the line from *Finnegans Wake* which refers to 'that ideal reader suffering from an ideal insomnia' (*FW* 120: 13–14). The ideal reader is not so much a perfect reader as one who represents the range of possible readings justified in terms of the structure of the text itself – the reader who is *awake* to these possibilities.

Semiotics and a Theory of Codes

The other dimension constitutive of Eco's intellectual and scholarly trajectory is semiotics. Since 1975, Eco has held the chair of semiotics at the University of Bologna, and he has written in English two key books which develop his theory of signs and signification: *A Theory of Semiotics* (1976) and *Semiotics and the Philosophy of Language* (1984).

Although *A Theory of Semiotics* explicitly deals with a theory of codes and of sign production, its underlying point of departure is Peirce's notion of 'unlimited semiosis'. Unlimited semiosis refers, in Eco's hands, to the kind of middle position in relation to the position of the reader. Although unlimited semiosis is the result of the fact that signs in language always refer to other signs and that a text always offers the prospect of infinite interpretations, Eco wants to avoid the extremes of univocal meaning on the one hand opposing infinite meanings on the other. Unlimited semiosis rather corresponds to

Peirce's 'interpretant', where meaning is established with reference to conditions of possibility.

In light of unlimited semiosis, how does Eco explain the nature of a code? To speak generally, codes can be of two types: univocal, where the relation between signifier and signified is fixed, or polyvocal, where the link is open-ended. Morse code, where a given set of signals (dots and dashes) corresponds to a given set of signs (letters of the alphabet) is an example of a univocal code. A code of this type – where one system of elements is translated into another system – has extremely wide application, so that the relationship between DNA and RNA in biology can be analysed in terms of a code.

Although Eco gives a number of technical examples of this type of code, his main interest is in language as composed of *langue* (where code = grammar, syntax, system) and *parole* (language act). Here, code corresponds to the structure of the language. Or, to use Hjelmslev's terms as Eco often does: the code correlates the expression plane of language with the content plane. Eco uses the term 's-code' to designate a code used in this sense. Put another way: the s-code of language is equivalent to the specific organisation of the elements of *parole*. Without a code, the sounds/graphic marks have no meaning, and this in the most radical sense of not functioning linguistically. S-codes can be either 'denotative' (when a statement is understood literally), or connotative (when another code is detected – e.g. code of courtesy – within the same statement). None of this is really foreign to Saussure's work, but Eco wants to introduce an understanding of an s-code which is more dynamic than that found in Saussure's theory, and in much of current linguistics besides. He does this by developing what he calls, after Quillian, a 'Model Q' – a model of the code which accounts for unlimited semiosis.

First, however, Eco has to show that the meaning of a 'sign-vehicle' (e.g. a word or image) is independent of a supposedly real object. In other words, it is necessary to avoid the 'referential fallacy'. Thus the sign-vehicle /dog/ is not equivalent to any particular dog (= real object), but has to stand for all dogs, both living and dead. A clearer example perhaps is the fact that /nevertheless/ does not have a referent; rather, it is a pure product of the code.

Second, Eco recognises that codes do have a context. This context is social and cultural life. 'Cultural units', then, 'are signs that social life has put at our disposal: images interpreting books, appropriate responses interpreting ambiguous questions, words interpreting definitions and vice-versa' (Eco 1979: 71). What somebody does in response to a particular sign-vehicle (e.g., /your shout/in Australia results in someone buying all the drinks) gives us, Eco points out, 'information about the cultural unit' in question (Eco 1979: 71). As a result of taking into account the sign's status as a cultural unit, a theory of codes is able to explain how signs can take on a multiplicity of meanings, how meaning is derived from the competence of the user of language or sign system, and how, as a result, new meanings can be created. *Langue* as a code thus becomes equivalent to the competence of the language-user. This is so even with the case in which the speaker of language might use the code incompetently. For 'incompetence' (e.g. that snow is peanut butter, to cite Eco) is still semiotically interesting. Laughter is a possible response to this incompetence, laughter which has to be excluded from a notion of language viewed as a semantics based on the truth-value of propositions. Indeed, laughter, lying, tragedy are fundamental to understanding the code viewed semiotically.

Ratio Facilis and Ratio Difficilis

The semantic field is rather involved 'in multiple shiftings' which render inadequate the notion of the code as the equivalence of the elements of two systems. In fact, says Eco, every major linguistic code is 'a *complex network of subcodes*' (Eco 1979: 125, Eco's emphasis). To put it in its most succinct form: Eco's model Q 'is a model of linguistic creativity'. As he confirms: 'In effect the model Q supposes that the system can be nourished by fresh information and that further data can be inferred from incomplete data' (Eco 1979: 124). With model Q, therefore, the code is modified in accordance with the changing competencies of language users, instead of being determined by the code.

The other side of a theory of codes is a theory of sign production. In his discussion of sign production, Eco focuses again on the tension between elements that can be easily assimilated, or foreseen, by the code (cf. symbols in Peirce's terminology), and those that cannot be easily assimilated (cf. Peirce's notion of icon). Elements of the former category, Eco designates as *ratio facilis* and those of the second, *ratio difficilis* (Eco 1979: 183–84). The closer one comes to *ratio difficilis*, the more the sign of the object is 'motivated' by the nature of the object itself. Icons are the category of sign which bring this out most clearly. Eco is, however, concerned to show that even the most strongly motivated signs (e.g. image of the Virgin) have conventional elements. And even where there appears to be a clear case of an object, or behaviour, which seems to exist outside any conventionalised

format (i.e. beyond the code), such instances rapidly become conventionalised. The most telling illustrations of this are Gombrich's
examples (referred to by Eco) of what passed for realism in painting
at various points in art history (e.g. the drawings of Dürer). Even a
photograph can be shown to have conventional aspects: for instance,
the development of the negative offers the possibility of a certain
conventionalisation on the part of the photographer. Again, if a
photograph is considered from the perspective of its analogical status
(how much it looks like its object), Eco reminds us that digitalisation,
as a certain form of codification, implies new possibilities of reproduction. In summary, the key elements of Eco's typology of modes of
sign production are as follows:

1 *Physical labour*: effort required to produce the sign.
2 *Recognition*: object or event is recognised as expression of a sign
   content, as with imprints, symptoms or clues.
3 *Ostension*: an object or act is shown to be the exemplar of a class
   of objects or acts.
4 *Replica*: tends towards *ratio difficilis* in principle, but takes on features of codification through stylisation. Examples are emblems,
   musical types, mathematical signs.
5 *Invention*: the clearest case of *ratio difficilis*. Unforeseen by the
   existing code; is the basis of a new material continuum.

What Eco proposes via his model Q and via the invention of sign
production – and what conventional semiotics has tended to neglect
(Kristeva's work being a notable exception) – is the need to account
for the language system's capacity for renewal and revitalisation.
Instead of being closed and static, Eco's argues that the sign system is
open and dynamic.

Dictionary and Encyclopaedia

A comparable motivation is evident in Eco's discussion of signs and
signification in *Semiotics and the Philosophy of Language*. There, Eco
argues that a sign is not only something which stands for something
else (and therefore has a dictionary meaning), but must also be
interpreted. As we have noted above, the view of interpretation in
operation here is that of Peirce's 'interpretant', which gives rise to
unlimited semiosis.

The key theme in *Semiotics and the Philosophy of Language* (taken up
again in the later *Kant and the Platypus* (Eco 2000: 224–79)) concerns

the difference between the structure of the dictionary and the ency-clopaedia. Although he does not explain it in precisely these terms, for Eco, the dictionary, as the hierarchical 'Porphyrian tree' ('that model of definition, structured by genera, species, and differentiae' (Eco 1984: 46)), corresponds to a view of language as the static and closed system of conventional linguistics. The dictionary model of language would fail to account for unlimited semiosis. By contrast, the encyclopaedia would correspond to a network without a centre, to a labyrinth from which there is no exit, or to an infinite, infer-ential model that is open to new elements. Where the dictionary suffers from the aporia of being either meaningful but limited in its scope, or of being unlimited in scope but incapable of providing a specific meaning, the encyclopaedia corresponds to a 'rhizomatic' network of local descriptions; its structure is thus map-like, rather than tree-like and hierarchical. In fact, to function properly as a net-work of words allowing for the possibility of new meanings, a dic-tionary has to be like an encyclopaedia. It is in fact 'a disguised encyclopaedia', says Eco. Thus the encyclopaedia can become a general model of language, a way of talking about it without forcing upon it an artificial and finite globality.

Perhaps finally, then, Eco's most enduring contribution to a theory of semiotics is to show that language is like the encyclopaedia, invented by the *philosophes* in the eighteenth century. Could it be that Eco is showing us that the Enlightenment, at least in this respect, is also post-modern?

References

Eco, Umberto (1979) *A Theory of Semiotics*, Bloomington: Indiana University Press.
—— (1983) *The Name of the Rose*, trans. William Weaver, New York: Har-court Brace Jovanovich. British edition by Seeker & Warburg.
—— (1984) *Semiotics and the Philosophy of Language*, London: Macmillan.
—— (1986a) *Art and Beauty in the Middle Ages*, trans. Hugh Bredin, New Haven: Yale University Press.
—— (1986b) 'The return of the Middle Ages' in *Travels in Hyperreality*, trans. William Weaver, San Diego: Harcourt Brace Jovanovich.
—— (1989) *Foucault's Pendulum*, trans. William Weaver, London: Seeker & Warburg.
—— (1992) 'Between author and text' in Stefan Collini (ed.) with Richard Rorty, Jonathan Culler and Christine Brooke-Rose, *Interpretation and Overinterpretation*, Cambridge: Cambridge University Press.
—— (1995) *The Island of the Day Before*, trans. William Weaver, London: Seeker & Warburg.

—— (2000) *Kant and the Platypus*, trans. Alastair McEwan, New York: Harcourt Brace.

Joyce, James (1939) *Finnegans Wake*, London: Faber & Faber.

See also: **Benveniste, Greimas, Hjelmslev, Peirce**

Eco's major writings

(2005) *On Literature*, trans. Martin McLaughlin, Orlando: Harcourt.

(2001) *Experiences in Translation*, trans. Alastair McEwan, Toronto and Buffalo: University of Toronto Press.

(2000 [1997]) *Kant and the Platypus*, trans. Alastair McEwan, New York: Harcourt Brace.

(1999a) *Serendipities: Language and Lunacy*, trans. William Weaver, San Diego: Harcourt Brace.

(1999b) *University and Mass Media*, Berlin: Freie Universität Berlin.

(1995a) *The Search for the Perfect Language*, trans. James Fentress, Oxford and Cambridge, Mass.: Blackwell.

(1995b[1994]) *The Island of the Day Before*, trans. William Weaver, London: Seeker and Warburg (novel).

(1992) 'Between author and text' in Stefan Collini (ed.) with Richard Rorty, Jonathan Culler and Christine Brooke-Rose, *Interpretation and Overinterpretation*, Cambridge: Cambridge University Press.

(1989 [1988]) *Foucault's Pendulum*, trans. William Weaver, London, Seeker & Warburg.

(1986 [1959]) *Art and Beauty in the Middle Ages*, trans. Hugh Bredin, New Haven: Yale University Press.

(1984) *Semiotics and the Philosophy of Language*, London: Macmillan.

(1983 [1980]) *The Name of the Rose*, trans. William Weaver, New York: Harcourt Brace Jovanovich. British edition by Seeker & Warburg.

(1981 [1979]) *The Role of the Reader: Explorations in the Semiotics of Texts*, London: Hutchinson.

(1979 [1976]) *A Theory of Semiotics*, Bloomington: Indiana University Press.

Further reading

Bondanella, Peter (2005) *Umberto Eco and the Open Text: Semiotics, Fiction, Popular Culture*, Cambridge, UK and New York: Cambridge University Press.

Capozzi, Rocco (1997) *Reading Eco: An Anthology*, Bloomington and Indianapolis: Indiana University Press.

Gane, Mike and Gane, Nicholas, eds, (2005) *Umberto Eco*, London and Thousand Oaks: Sage.

Ross, Charlotte and Sibley, Rochelle, eds, (2004) *Illuminating Eco: On the Boundaries of Interpretation*, Aldershot, Hampshire and Burlington, VT: Ashgate.

LOUIS HJELMSLEV (1899–1965)

The Danish linguist and semiotician, Louis Hjelmslev, was born in 1899 and died on 30 May 1965. Hjelmslev, who founded the Copenhagen linguistic circle, attempted to render more rigorous and clear Saussure's general theory of language and semiotics. In particular, Hjelmslev is remembered as the inventor of *Glossematik* (glossematics) (see below), and for having given a new rigour to the notion of connotation.

Like Saussure, Hjelmslev starts from the position that language is a supra-individual institution which must be studied and analysed in its own right, rather than be viewed as the vehicle, or instrument, of knowledge, thought, emotion – or, more generally, as a means of contact with what is external to it. In short, the transcendental approach (language as a means) should give way to an immanent approach (the study of language in itself) (Hjelmslev: 1963: 4–5).[1] To this end, Hjelmslev developed what he thought of as a simple and rigorous system of concepts and terms which would both clarify, at the highest level of generality, the nature of language, and also render more proficient the study of its realisations.

Sign Function

For the Hjelmslev of the *Prolegomena to a Theory of Language* – his best-known work – language is both a sign system and a process of realisation (for Saussure, the comparable terminology is, respectively, '*langue*' and '*parole*'). Like Saussure, Hjelmslev also considers language to be a system of signs, and so it is important to be clear about the nature of the sign. First of all, we note that no sign exists by itself in isolation; rather, signs are always in a context in relation to other signs. To mark this fact, Hjelmslev speaks not about a sign as such, but about a sign function. A function he defines as 'a dependence that fulfils the conditions for an analysis' (Hjelmslev 1963: 33). Just as there is a function between a class and its components, so there is a function between a sign and its components, 'expression' and 'content'. A sign, in short, is not some mark, or gesture with intrinsic qualities (an arrow might not always be a sign), but is what functions as a sign in a given context. For a sign function to exist, then, there must be – again, in Hjelmslev's terminology – an 'expression' and a 'content'. A sign function thus exists between these 'absolutely inseparable' 'terminals'. For the terminals constituting a sign function – the 'sign-expression' and the 'sign-content' – Hjelmslev gives the technical name of 'functives'. The sign-function depends on the mutual correlation of the functives in order to be what it is. Hjelmslev's point here is that a sign is not any physical or non-physical entity that can just be assumed and taken for granted by the linguist or the semiologist. Indeed, there is no actual realisation of a sign which would be identical to the sign-function. Saussure's comparable terminology of 'sign', 'signifier' and 'signified' suggests that this could be so.

'Figurae'

To construct signs, language contains various kinds of non-signs (letters of the alphabet, for example) which make up the raw material necessary for the formation of new signs. These not-yet-signs, as it were, Hjelmslev calls 'figurae'. Figurae evoke the notion of the 'floating signifier' that Lévi-Strauss discovered in Mauss's work. They suggest that language is always an open-ended totality, and not a system as such, where the elements would constitute a self-contained whole. It must be said, however, that, like Mauss, there is no explicit acknowledgement of this implication in Hjelmslev's own analysis. Even for Hjelmslev, who is intensely absorbed with working out a rigorous, simple, and exhaustive formalisation of language, language must be seen to have a fundamental link to meaning, and/or to thought. Whether it is meaning or thought that is at stake is not quite clear; in any case, Hjelmslev prefers to say that language is linked to 'purport', which is, as he puts it in one formulation, 'the factor that is common ... to all languages', namely, 'the amorphous "thought-mass"'(Hjelmslev 1963: 52) which to a certain extent is external to language as such. As we shall see, 'purport' is the most problematical factor in the whole of Hjelmslev's theory. For the moment, we note that purport is inseparable from language – language would cease to have any *raison d'être* without it – and yet, in some sense, purport is external to language. 'In itself', Hjelmslev says, 'purport is unformed, not in itself subjected to formation but simply susceptible to formation' (Hjelmslev 1963: 76). Thus, like Saussure (Saussure 1972: 155–56), Hjelmslev says that the most distinctive feature of language in general is its being form in relation to substance (purport). On the other hand, the situation is more complicated for Hjelmslev in that for him, there is both expression-purport and content-purport – and yet, in general, purport is 'inaccessible to knowledge' in so far as knowledge is a 'formation' (Hjelmslev 1963: 76). To clarify this, it is necessary to explain what Hjelmslev means by 'expression' and 'content'.

As a preliminary to understanding the full import of 'expression' and 'content', we see first of all that Hjelmslev considers language in terms of two different, but interconnected planes: that of 'system' – which corresponds to the underlying, always already realised structure of language – and that of 'process', also called 'text', which is always virtual. Process (text) is not, as one might expect, the realisation of language (system); so while it is impossible to have a text without a language, it is possible to have a language without a text (Hjelmslev 1963: 39–40). Because Hjelmslev confuses 'virtual', 'real' and 'concrete', a clearer way of putting it would be to say that language is realised, but remains virtual, while process is concrete but is only ever partially realised. System (grammar, syntax, vocabulary), then, makes possible the production of an innumerable number of texts, while a multitude of texts will only ever imply one system, or language. The relationship between 'expression' and 'content' is thus analysed by Hjelmslev in terms of both the axes mentioned.

Expression and Content

'Expression' and 'content', we find, are also the two inseparable functives of the sign-function. Expression can occur in a variety of ways: through speech, writing, gesture (sign language) – each medium itself being realisable in numerous other media (books, television, radio, newspapers, pamphlets, telephone, Morse code, semaphore, stone tablets, inscriptions of all kinds (on walls, floors, tombstones), film, posters, art-works, everyday conversation and writing). In other words, expression takes a particular form (e.g. in the words 'I love Ron'), and it exists in a substance (e.g. the human voice, or as marks carved on a wall). Consequently, there is both an expression-form (the words), and an expression-substance (the material of the words). On the content side, too, there is both 'form' and 'substance'. Content can be defined generally as the form in which a meaning is articulated. Hjelmslev prefers the term, 'content', instead of 'meaning', because the same meaning can often be articulated by different contents – the contents of a natural language. Hjelmslev illustrates this point with the example shown in Figure 1, where the content varies in relation to the same semantic area (area of purport).

Here we see that in Danish, *trae* covers all of the German *Baum* and the French *arbre*, and partly cover the German *Holz* and less of the French, *bois*. Similarly, *skov* partly translates the German *Holz* and *Wald*, as well as most of the French, *bois*, and some of the French, *forêt*. Hjelmslev comments that this 'incongruence within one and the

Danish	German	French
trae	Baum	arbre
skov	Holz	bois
	Wald	
		forêt

Figure 1 Hjelmslev's content-meaning interchange.
Source: Hjelmslev, *Prolegomena*, p. 57.

same zone of purport turns up everywhere' (Hjelmslev 1963: 54). Illustrated in the example from the perspective of the system plane is the level of the content-form of the sign-function. It is as though language, in its different articulations, divided up the same meaning area (purport) in ways specific to these different articulations (content). The purport is thus given form by the content-form), and the meaning as such is the content-substance. One way of understanding this, according to one of Hjelmslev's interpreters, is to say that 'both forms [expression-form, and content-form] manifest themselves in a "substance"'(Siertsema 1955: 17). The key term here is not 'substance', but 'manifest' – rendered visible, revealed, perceivable, made public, etc. Philosophically of course, substance, in the thirteenth century, was equivalent to essence – precisely what was not *manifest* (Hjelmslev decries so-called non-linguistic usage of terms, and yet it seems that it is precisely a feature of language to evoke a number of different contexts simultaneously). Even in connection to the more modern form of 'substantive', the sense is less to do with what is revealed, and more to do with what is hidden. Not that this would necessarily be a problem for Hjelmslev's theory if the term 'substance' could be consistently translated as what is manifest However, when purport is also said to be substance (Hjelmslev 1963: 52 and 80), confusion can only result.

Variations in content-form (different meanings attached to the same area of purport, so that languages are not directly translatable), Hjelmslev equates with the system of content, whereas constancy in the content-form (same idea expressed in different languages, so that expressions are directly translatable), Hjelmslev equates with the process of the content. Similarly, when – to take another of Hjelmslev's examples – speakers of different languages are trying to pronounce 'Berlin' the expression-purport will vary (due to accent), while the content-purport will remain the same. Again, the same pronunciation (expression-purport) in different languages might be the same (*got*, *Gott* ('God' in German), *godt* ('well' in Danish)), while the content-purport differs. Both examples come from the plane of process, according to Hjelmslev.

Glossematics

The reason for this elaboration of the sign-function, says our author, is to demonstrate that the sign is not simply a label for a pre-existing thing. It also means avoiding the artificial divisions in linguistics between 'phonetics, morphology, syntax, lexicography and semantics'. Indeed, so concerned is Hjelmslev to get the study of language on to a new footing that he invoked the name of 'glossematics' (from the Greek *glossa*, meaning 'language') to signal the innovative nature of his approach.

Glossematics would be 'an algebra of language operating with unnamed entities' (Hjelmslev 1963: 79), a science having the 'immanent algebra of language' (Hjelmslev 1963: 80) as its object. The reason for this new approach stems from the point made at the outset to the effect that for too long, according to Hjelmslev, linguistics has studied language from a transcendent point of view, meaning that non-linguistic features have been used to explain language. Glossematics, then, endeavours to provide a rigorous, simple and exhaustive framework and terminology for explaining language reality and language usage. To this end, Hjelmslev devoted his energies to developing and refining a technical vocabulary that we shall not go into here. From a more general, semiotic perspective, however, Hjelmslev's theory of 'denotation' and 'connotation' should be explained. Denotation, as the term implies, is the area of expression which refers to a content – for example, the sentence, 'The cat sat on the mat' denotes a cat sitting on a mat. The same sentence looked at from the perspective of connotation, might evoke the context of young children, or again, a kind of 'typical' example used as an example. More formally, connotation refers to the fact that the expression and content taken together become another expression referring to another content. Diagrammatically, this may be expressed as in Figure 2.

For his part, Hjelmslev says that a denotative semiotic is 'a semiotic none of whose planes is a semiotic', whereas a connotative semiotic is a semiotic 'whose expression plane is a semiotic' (Hjelmslev 1963: 114). Not only this, however. For the content plane, too, can be a semiotic, and this Hjelmslev calls a 'metasemiotics'. Linguistics, says Hjelmslev,

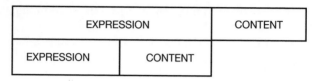

Figure 2 Expression and content in Eco's thought.
Source: 1979: 55.

is an example of a metasemiotic: the study of language which is itself
an example of language. Writers such as Barthes, Todorov and Eco
have made use of the notions of denotative and connotative semiotics, but they have been more circumspect about the viability of the
notion of metasemiotics.

Hjelmslev's theory of language and semiotics

It remains to give a brief assessment of Hjelmslev's theory of language
and semiotics. Clearly, Hjelmslev's project opens up a wide range of
issues, and the rigour introduced into semiotics reveals how easy it is
to take the notion of sign for granted, so that it becomes a simple
vehicle of meaning, regardless of the language involved. On the other
hand, Hjelmslev's own elaboration of his theory of language often
goes against the strictures of coherence and simplicity. Similarly, while
Saussure's notions of 'form' and 'substance' do indeed call for clarification,
it is precisely on this point that Hjelmslev, too, very nearly runs aground.
Indeed, a close reading of the *Prolegomena* in terms of its coherence,
leaves the reader entirely uncertain as to how 'purport' – the *inaccessible* amorphous mass outside the sign system – can be linked to
'expression' and to 'content' in the expressions, 'expression-purport'
and 'content-purport'; for in order to be implicated in either of the two
sign functives, purport has to take on a specific form, which, by
definition, it cannot have. What we have are two different purports that
are what they are in being distinguished from each other. The very
fact of its being distinguished brings purport into the semiotic sphere,
so that it ceases to be either external to language or amorphous.

There is, however, a further problem regarding purport. It is that,
even if one were to overlook Hjelmslev's inconsistent use of the term,
the author of the *Prolegomena* is forced to have recourse to an extra-
linguistic or semiotic dimension to facilitate the development of an
'immanent' linguistics. In other words, purport is Hjelmslev's inadvertent

way of giving his theory a transcendental element, the very thing he strove not to do. It is for this reason that Julia Kristeva is able to argue that Hjelmslev's theory remained rooted in the influential phenomenological framework that has dominated linguistics to this very day (Kristeva 1984: 38–40).

More positively Hjelmslev has made progress in clarifying Saussure's distinction between *langue* and *parole*. For Saussure erred in privileging the spoken word at the level of *parole*, and Hjelmslev's use of 'text', or 'process' adds to the rigour of the description. On the other hand, by defining 'system' (Saussure's *langue*) as being independent of 'text', Hjelmslev seems to be saying that language is essentially a system – for while a language without a text is 'imaginable'; a text without a language is not. The risk comes in reducing language as such to a linguistic model of it, instead of recognising that the two levels (model and usage) are inseparable from one another.

Although, as Eco acknowledges, Hjelmslev's theory often strikes the reader as being of 'apparently Byzantine complexity' (Eco 1979: 52), Hjelmslev's determination to offer a strictly 'immanent' theory of language and semiotics has provided the inspiration for others, such as Eco, Derrida (Derrida 1976: 57–60), and Deleuze and Guattari (see Deleuze and Guattari 1987) who have embarked upon a project of setting out a semiotic framework that begins to destabilise the metaphysical edifice at the heart of a transcendental theory of signs and sign systems.

Note

1 In the French translation of Hjelmslev's *Prolegomena*, 'purport' – a translation of the Danish word, *mening* – is rendered as '*sens*' (meaning).

References

Deleuze, Gilles and Guattari, Félix (1987), *A Thousand Plateaus: Capitalism and Schizophrenia*, trans. Brian Massumi, Minneapolis: University of Minnesota Press.

Derrida, Jacques (1976), *Of Grammatology*, trans. Gayatri Chakravorty Spivak, Baltimore: Johns Hopkins University Press.

Eco, Umberto (1979), *A Theory of Semiotics*, Bloomington: Indiana University.

Hjelmslev, Louis (1963), *Prolegomena to a Theory of Language*, trans. Francis J. Whitfield, Madison: University of Wisconsin Press.

Kristeva, Julia (1984), *Revolution in Poetic Language*, trans. Margaret Wailer, New York: Columbia University Press.

Saussure, F. de (1972), *Cours de linguistique générale*, Paris: Payot.

Siertsema, B. (1955), *A Study of Glossematics. A Critical Survey of its Fundamental Concepts*, The Hague and Paris: Martinus Nijhoff.

See also: **Derrida, Deleuze, Eco, Kristeva, Saussure**

Hjelmslev's major writings

(1963 [1943]) *Prolegomena to a Theory of Language*, trans. Francis J. Whitfield, Madison: University of Wisconsin Press, revised English edn, reprinted.
(1970) *Language. An Introduction*, trans. Francis J. Whitfield, Madison, University of Wisconsin Press.

Further reading

Siertsema, B. (1955), *A Study of Glossematics: Critical Survey of its Fundamental Concepts*, The Hague and Paris: Martinus Nijhoff.

CHARLES SANDERS PEIRCE (1839–1914)

Charles Sanders Peirce was born into an intellectual family in 1839 (his father, Benjamin, was a professor of mathematics at Harvard), and in the years 1859, 1862 and 1863, respectively, he received the degrees of BA, MA and BSc from Harvard. For more than thirty years (1859–60, 1861–91), Peirce did mainly astronomical and geodetic work for the United States Coast Survey. From 1879 to 1884, he was a part-time lecturer in logic at the Johns Hopkins University.

Such qualifications and experience do not really convey the classical erudition that comes through in Peirce's writings. Not only did he translate the now familiar term 'semiotic' from the Ancient Greek, he was also a scholar of both Kant and Hegel whom he read in the German, and he had a particular affinity for the philosophy of John Duns Scotus, especially Scotus's term, *haecceity*, meaning 'thisness' (Peirce 1931: vol 1. para 341. Hereafter, volume and paragraph will be specified.). *Haecceity* is also evocative of singularity.

Signs

It has often been remarked that Peirce was an original mind who, as well as being the reputed founder of pragmatism, made significant contributions in philosophical and mathematical logic, and, in particular, founded semiotics. Less often remarked upon is the fact that Peirce saw his semiotic theory – his work on signs – as being inseparable from his work on logic. In fact, according to him, logic, in its broadest sense, is 'thought always taking place by means of signs', equivalent to a 'general semeiotic [sic], treating not merely of truth, but also of the general conditions of signs being signs' (1.444[1]).

Briefly, signs are connected with logic because signs are the vehicles for thought as the articulation of logical forms. Even more pertinently, Peirce shows in a paper published in 1868, when he was 29, that: 'The only thought, then, which can possibly be cognized is thought in signs. But thought which cannot be cognized does not exist. All thought, therefore, must necessarily be in signs' (5.251). Consequently, for Peirce, philosophy in general is inseparable from the articulation and interpretation of signs. Be this as it may, our interest here is in Peirce's theory of signs; our focus will thus be on Peirce the semiotician.

Although Peirce published more than ten thousand printed pages, he never published a book-length study on any of his cherished subjects. The result is that, with regard to his work on signs, Peirce's thought has to be treated as being always in process and subject to modification and further elaboration. More than this, Peirce often gives the impression that he found it necessary to begin again at each new meditation on a question, as though, on each occasion, a new audience was envisaged (hence the repetition), and as though a previous formulation on the topic was defective (hence the alterations and elaboration). There is, in sum, no systematic and definitive Peircean document on the nature of signs; only successive reworkings which repeat as much as innovate. What, then, are the essential aspects of this material on signs?

The Interpretant and Unlimited Semiosis

Within the domain of semiotics it has often been repeated (see Eco 1979 and Kristeva 1989) that, in the most general sense, a sign, according to Peirce, is what represents something for someone (cf. 2.228). The simplicity of this formulation belies the fact that there is a sign function: sign A denotes a fact (or object) B, for an interpretant, C. A sign is thus never an isolated entity, but always has these three aspects. A sign itself, Peirce says, is an instance of Firstness, its object, an instance of Secondness, and the interpretant – the mediating element – an instance of Thirdness. Peirce, indeed, sought out ternary structures wherever they might occur. Thirdness in the context of sign production also gives rise to unlimited semiosis, in as far as an interpretant (idea), which reads the sign as a sign of something (i.e. as the representation of a meaning or a referent), can always be grasped by another interpretant. The interpretant is the indispensable element needed in order to link the sign to its object (induction, deduction and abduction (hypothesis) constitute three – again, three – important types of interpretant). A sign, to exist as a sign, must be interpreted (and so have an interpretant). The word, 'S-T-O-P' on a red background at a traffic intersection means that one must come to a halt at the intersection. The sign is /stop/; the object is 'coming to a halt', and the interpretant is the idea joining the sign to that particular object. The sign could also indicate the presence of a main road or a heavily populated area. A process of unlimited semiosis is set in train through the function of the interpretant. That is, as Eco says, the interpretant is another interpretation (Eco 1979: 68).

Icon, Index and Symbol

Like the sign function, sign-types also have a basic triadic form. The three fundamental elements of this form are icon, index and symbol. Put most simply, an iconic sign is one which is, in one or more respects, the same as the object signified. In other words, the 'significant virtue' of an icon is its quality. A portrait then is iconic to the extent that the qualities of the representation are deemed to be similar to the qualities of the subject represented. While Peirce acknowledges that icons may contain conventional elements, Eco has argued that a mirror-image is an 'absolute icon' (Eco 1984: 212). An index, for its part, is a sign physically linked to, or affected by, its object. Examples given by Peirce are a weathercock, a barometer, a sundial. Demonstrative pronouns (this, that), a cry of 'Help!' as indicative of someone in need, or a knock on the door indicating that there is someone at the door, are also examples of signs serving as indices. Unlike the icon, an index has a 'dynamical' relation to what it signifies. 'Symbol', as Peirce reminds us, originally meant something 'thrown together' making a contract or convention (2.297). In a contemporary setting, a symbol for Peirce (who differs from Saussure on this point), refers to conventional signs used, for instance, in speaking and writing. 'A genuine symbol', Peirce writes, 'is a symbol that has a general meaning' (2.293). Peirce's notion of symbol hints at Saussure's conception of the arbitrary relationship between signifier and signified. For a symbol's relation to its object is of an 'imputed' character. With the notion of symbol, the force of the notion of interpretant also becomes clearer. For no symbol, given its imputed, or unmotivated relation to its object, could be a symbol without being interpreted. Speech utterances determine corresponding signs (= interpretants) in the mind of the listener. Thus symbol and interpretant are inseparable.

Peirce continued to analyse this fundamental division of signs throughout his life. In light of these analyses he realised that the purity of his basic sign forms of icon, index and symbol was problematic. Any given instance of an icon (e.g. a portrait) could be seen to have conventional elements. And if the portrait were a photograph, both iconic and indexical features come together. Although the basic, trichotomous sign division mentioned above is his most well-known one, Peirce also distinguished signs in terms of two further trichotomies, perhaps in an effort to add a degree of suppleness to his classifications, but maybe, unconsciously, because he was driven to see things in terms of ternary structures. Whatever the case, Peirce constructed a plethora of trichotomies – to the point where, in the case of sign divisions, he produced (as in Table 1) a basic trichotomy of trichotomies.

With the first and third trichotomies, Peirce adds refinement to his division of signs, making it capable of analysing an ever greater diversity and complexity of sign production. Having this nucleus of three trichotomies as his point of departure, Peirce went even further towards constructing an analytical nomenclature for distinguishing between different signs by proposing ten classes of signs. These ten classes are made up of combinations of the founding trichotomies. To take but one example – often favoured by Peirce – that of a weathercock:

Table 1 Summary of Peirce's three trichotomies of signs

1 *Qualisign* [= a quality which is a sign.]	*Sinsign* ['sin' = 'only once': an event which is a sign.]	*Legisign* [= a law which is a sign. Every conventional sign is a legisign.]
2 *Icon* [= a sign which has the quality of the object it denotes.]	*Index* [= a sign which denotes an object by being affected by that object.]	*Symbol* [= a conventional sign.]
3 *Rheme* [= a sign of a qualitative possibility, i.e. it represents a possible object.][= a sign of the actual existence of an object.]	*Dicent sign* [= a sign of a law.]	*Argument*

it is a 'Dicent Sinsign' (a classification derived from trichotomies 1 and 3). Of such a sign, Peirce writes that it:

> is any object of direct experience, in so far as it is a sign, and, as such affords information concerning its Object. This it can only do by being really affected by its Object; so that it is necessarily an Index. The only information it can afford is of actual fact. Such a sign must involve an Iconic Sinsign to embody information and a Rhematic Indexical Sinsign to indicate the Object to which the information refers. But the mode of combination, or *Syntax*, of these two must also be significant.
>
> (2.257)

Demonstrated here is the fact that no single, material instance of a sign exactly corresponds to a given classification. Only through continually refining the nomenclature will analytical profundity be attained. By this strategy, Peirce aims to do justice to the very real complexity of sign production. In a sense, there is no Peircean theory of signs, only an ever more supple table of sign classification.

Issues

Crucial issues arise from Peirce's approach to signs. One concerns the fact that Peirce rarely moves much beyond his attempt to develop and refine a table of sign categories. Like every table of categories it is supposed to be exhaustive. One can wonder, however, as to whether a (relatively) static table does justice to the very real dynamism of sign production. Furthermore, the fact that each sign seems to have a relative autonomy *vis-à-vis* other signs only heightens the sense that, in the end, Peirce's system is rather Newtonian in character. Unlike Saussure, Peirce seemed to be much more taken with the physical aspect of material signs in themselves than in signs as elements in a system of discourse. The latter would come under Peirce's category of the symbol; and while the nature of the symbol is not neglected by Peirce, his interest is clearly centred on the essentially physical iconic and indexical signs.

While giving due recognition to Peirce's achievement in making sign distinctions, Eco has nevertheless been able to render suspect the very possibility of a truly natural property so necessary for the viability of the Peircean icon or index (Eco 1979: 191–201). According to Eco, the iconic sign is always culturally coded without being entirely arbitrary. And it would seem that it has to be if it is to exemplify

Peirce's principle of unlimited semiosis. Unlimited semiosis – perhaps Peirce's most original contribution to semiotics – implies that a sign must be translatable into other signs via an interpretant. Now, clearly, if an icon *qua* sign were to be distinguished from other signs by virtue of its having the same qualities as the object signified, the principle of unlimited semiosis would seem to be placed in jeopardy.

For Eco, a possible way out is to recognise that as far as a sign structure is concerned, so-called physical qualities are in fact embedded in a perceptual structure and are therefore coded. Because it is coded (i.e. because it is not identical with the *perceptum*) a perception can be reproduced, or translated into other signs. Eco thus proposes that 'iconic signs do not possess the "same" physical properties as their objects, but they rely on the same perceptual structure, or the same system of relations' (Eco 1979: 193). On the other hand, Eco also suggests that an iconic sign is difficult to analyse precisely because it puts the existing code in question. It is a case of *ratio difficilis* which has the potential to challenge the existing code and thereby render it more subtle.

To some extent Peirce himself anticipated the limitations that Eco and others have detected in his writings on signs. And this not only in the sense of a positivist scientist ready to cede his place in history to a new generation of researchers, but also in the sense of one who saw himself as a 'pioneer, or rather a backwoodsman' engaged in clearing and opening up' the '*semiotic*, that is, the doctrine of the essential nature and fundamental varieties of possible semiosis' (5.488). And as though anticipating Bakhtin's reading of Dostoyevsky, Peirce also argued, not only that all thinking is necessarily in signs, but that 'all thinking is dialogic in form' (6.338), even if this dialogue be only with oneself. This dynamic thread in Peirce's theory of signs makes him the father of a non-positivist semiotics.

Note

1 These figures refer to the volume and paragraph number of Peirce (1931–58).

References

Eco, Umberto (1979), *A Theory of Semiotics*, Bloomington: Indiana University Press, Midland Book edn.
—— (1984), *Semiotics and the Philosophy of Language*, London: Macmillan.

Kristeva, Julia (1989), *Language, The Unknown: An initiation into Linguistics*, trans. Anne Menke, New York: Columbia University Press.
Peirce, Charles Sanders (1931–58), *Collected Papers of Charles Sanders Peirce*, 8 vols, ed. Charles Hartshorne and Paul Weiss (vols 1–6) and Arthur Burks (vols 7–8), Cambridge Mass.: The Belknap Press of Harvard University Press.

See also: **Deleuze, Eco, Kristeva, Saussure**

Peirce's major writings

(1991) *Peirce on Signs: Writings on Semiotics by Charles Sanders Peirce*, ed. James Hope, Chapel Hill and London: University of North Carolina Press.
(1931–58) *Collected Papers of Charles Sanders Peirce*, 8 vols, ed. Charles Hartshorne and Paul Weiss (vols 1–6) and Arthur Burks (vols 7–8), Cambridge, Mass.: The Belknap Press of Harvard University Press.

Further reading

Deledalle, Gérard (2000), *Charles S. Peirce's Philosophy of Signs: Essays in Comparative Semiotics*, Bloomington, Indiana: Indiana University Press.
Fisch, Max (1986), 'Peirce's general theory of signs' in Kenneth Laine Ketner and Christian J.W. Kloesel, eds, *Peirce, Semeiotic and Pragmatism: Essays by Max H. Fisch*, Bloomington: Indiana University Press.
Misak, Cheryl, ed. (2004), *The Cambridge Companion to Peirce*, Cambridge: Cambridge University Press.
Parker, Kelly A. (1998), *The Continuity of Peirce's Thought*, Nashville and London: Vanderbilt University.
Savan, David (1988), *An Introduction to C.S. Peirce's Semiotics*, Toronto: Toronto Semiotic Circle.

FERDINAND DE SAUSSURE (1857–1913)

Before 1960, few people in academic circles or outside had heard the name of Ferdinand de Saussure. But after 1968, European intellectual life was a-buzz with references to the father of both linguistics and structuralism. That Saussure was as much a catalyst as an intellectual innovator is confirmed by the fact that the work – the *Course in General Linguistics* – for which he is now famous outside linguistics was compiled from three sets of students' lecture notes for the years of the Course in General Linguistics given at the University of Geneva in 1907, 1908–9, and 1910–11. That Saussure a linguist and, to the wider academic community and general public, an obscure specialist in Sanskrit and Indo-European languages, should become the source of intellectual innovation in the social sciences and humanities, is also cause for thought. It suggests that something quite unique occurred in the historical epoch of the twentieth century, so that a new model of language based on Saussure's structural approach emerged to become the model for theorising social and cultural life. Saussurian theory has its basis in the history of linguistics, and its implications extend to the whole of the social sciences. We thus need to consider both these aspects.

Life and Intellectual Trajectory

Saussure was born in Geneva in 1857, to one of the best-known families of the city, one famous for its scientific accomplishments. He was thus a direct contemporary of Émile Durkheim (1858–1917), Sigmund Freud (1856–1939) and Edmund Husserl (1859–1938), although there is little evidence of his ever having had contact with any of them. After an unsatisfactory year in 1875 at the University of Geneva studying physics and chemistry, Saussure went to the University of Leipzig in 1876 to study languages. Then, in the wake of eighteen months studying Sanskrit in Berlin, he published, at the age of 21, his much acclaimed *mémoire* entitled, *Mémoire sur le système primitif des voyelles dans les langues indo-européennes* (*Mémoire on the Primitive System of Vowels in Indo-European Languages*). Fifty years after Saussure's death, the renowned French linguist, Émile Benveniste, would say of this work that it presaged the whole of Saussure's future research on the nature of language inspired by the theory of the arbitrary nature of the sign.

In 1880, after defending his thesis on the absolute genitive case in Sanskrit, Saussure moved to Paris, and in 1881, at the age of 24, he was named lecturer in Gothic and Old High German at the École Pratique des Hautes Études. For just over a decade Saussure taught in Paris until he was appointed professor of Sanskrit and Indo-European languages at the University of Geneva.

Although acclaimed by his colleagues, and devoted to the study of language, Saussure's published output began to dwindle as the years wore on. As he put it, he was dissatisfied with the nature of linguistics as a discipline – with its lack of reflexiveness, as with its terminology [1] – and yet he was unable to write the book which would revamp the discipline and enable him to continue his work in philology.

The work now famous, *Course in General Linguistics*, composed from some of Saussure's lecture notes along with the notes of his students, could be seen perhaps to be a partial fulfilment of Saussure's belief that language as such needed to be re-examined if linguistics was to move on to a sounder footing.

Saussure's Approach to Language

Within the history of linguistics, Saussure's approach, as exemplified in the *Course*, is generally thought to have opposed two influential contemporary views of language. The first is that established in 1660 by the Port-Royal philosophers, Arnauld and Lancelot in their *Grammaire générale et raisonnée* (Eng. Tr., *The Port Royal Gammar* 1975), where language is seen as a mirror of thoughts and based on a universal logic. For the Port-Royal grammarians, language is fundamentally rational. The second view, is that of nineteenth-century linguistics, where the history of a particular language is deemed to explain the current state of that language. In the latter case, Sanskrit, the sacred language of ancient India, believed to be the oldest of languages, was also believed to function as the connecting link between all languages, so that, ultimately, language and its history would become one with each other. Franz Bopp's Neogrammarian (as the movement was called) thesis on the conjugation system of Sanskrit as compared with other languages (*Über das Konjugationssystem der Sanskrit-sprache* (*The Conjugation System of the Sanskrit Language*)) inaugurated historical linguistics, and Saussure's early teaching and research did not contradict the Neogrammarian position on the fundamental importance of history for understanding the nature of language. However, the aspect of the *Mémoire* highlighted by Benveniste on the fiftieth anniversary of Saussure's death – the role of arbitrariness in language – makes itself felt with a vengeance in the *Course*.

The historical approach to language and, to a lesser extent, the rationalist approach, assumes that language is essentially a naming process – attaching words to things, whether or not these are imaginary – and that there is some kind of intrinsic link between the name and its object. Why a particular name came to be attached to a particular object or idea, could, it was believed, be determined historically – or even prehistorically. The further back in history one went the closer one was supposed to comec to a coincidence between the name and its object. As Saussure put it, such a perspective assumes that language is essentially a nomenclature: a collection of names for objects and ideas.

Key Elements of the Course

What, then, are the key elements of Saussure's theory as manifest in the *Course*? To begin with, Saussure shifts the focus of study from the history of language in general, to a consideration of the present configuration of a particular natural language like English or French. Now, a history of language becomes the history of languages, without there being an a priori link between them, as nineteenth-century linguists had assumed.

To focus on the present configuration of (a) language is, automatically, to focus on the relationship between the elements of that language and not on their intrinsic value Language, Saussure says, is always organised in a specific way. It is a system, or a structure, where any individual element is meaningless outside the confines of that structure. In a strong and insistent passage in the *Course*, Saussure says: '*in language [langue] there are only differences.* Even more important a difference generally implies positive terms between which the difference is set up; but in language, there are only differences *without positive terms*' (Saussure 1976: 166 and 1993: 118). The point is not only that value, or significance, is established through the relation between one term and another in the language system – so that, in the example used by Saussure, 't' can be written in a variety of ways and still be understood – but that the very terms of the system itself are the product of difference: there are no positive terms prior to the system. This implies that a language exists as a kind of totality, or it does not exist at all. Saussure uses the image of the chess game to illustrate the differential nature of language. For in chess, not only is the present configuration of pieces on the board all that matters to the newcomer to the game (no further insight would be gained from knowing how the pieces came to be arranged in this way), but any number of items could be substituted for the pieces on the board (a button for a king, etc.) because what constitutes the game's viability is the differential relationship between the pieces, and not their intrinsic value. To see language as being like a chess game, where the position of the pieces at a given moment is what counts, is to see it from a *synchronic* perspective. To give the historical approach precedence – as the nineteenth century did – is, by contrast, to view language from a *diachronic* perspective. In the *Course*, Saussure privileges the synchronic over the diachronic aspect because it provides a clearer picture of the factors present in any state of language.

Arbitrary Relation Between Signifier and Signified

Of equal importance for grasping the distinctiveness of Saussure's theory is the principle that language is a system of signs, and that each sign is composed of two parts: a signifier (*signifiant*) (word, or sound-pattern), and a signified (*signifié*) (concept). In contrast to the tradition within which he was brought up, therefore Saussure does not accept that the essential bond in language is between word and thing. Instead, Saussure's concept of the sign points to the relative autonomy of language in relation to reality. Even more fundamentally, however, Saussure comes to enunciate what has become for a modern audience the most influential principle of his linguistic theory: that the relationship between the signifier and the signified is arbitrary. In light of this principle, the basic structure of language is no longer assumed to be revealed by etymology and philology, but can best be grasped by understanding how language states (that is, specific linguistic configurations or totalities) change. The 'nomenclaturist' position thus becomes an entirely inadequate basis for linguistics.

Langue and Parole

Perhaps the terms which have caused more conceptual difficulties and drawn more criticism of Saussure's theory than any others, are *langue* (individual natural language viewed as a structure, or system), and *parole* (individual speech acts, or acts of language as a process). This conceptual couple introduces the distinction between language as it exists as a more or less coherent structure of differences, and language as it is practised by the community of speakers. While Saussure proposed in the *Course* that a specific linguistic structure is distinct from speech, and while he argued that the basis of language, as a social fact, is to be grasped exclusively at the level of structure, it is also true that nothing enters into the realm of the linguistic structure without first becoming manifest in individual speech acts. More significantly, the very extent of the totality of the structure could only be known with certainty if the totality of speech acts were also known. In this sense, the domain of the structure always remains, for Saussure, more hypothetical than the domain of speech. However, much depends here on whether one looks at speech from an individual, psychological perspective, or whether one focuses on the whole community of speakers. In the first case, to view language through the speech of the individual *qua* individual is one thing; to view it through the speech acts of the whole community is quite another. Saussure's point is that language is fundamentally a social institution, and that, therefore, the individualist approach is inadequate for the linguist.

Language is always changing. But it does not change at the behest of individuals; it changes over time independently of the speakers' wills Indeed through a Saussurian optic, individuals are as much formed by language as it is they who form language, and the question arises as to whether such a vision might have implications for other disciplines in the social sciences. In fact, his was the case for those theorists working under the rubric of 'structuralism' in the 1960s.

Saussure and the Human Sciences

With the emergence of the Saussurian model in the human sciences, the researcher's attention was turned away from documenting historical events, or recording the facts of human behaviour, and towards the notion of human action as a system of meaning. Such was the result of emphasising, at the broader societal level, the arbitrary nature of the sign and the corresponding idea of language as a system of conventions. Whereas a search for intrinsic facts and their effects had hitherto been made (as exemplified when the historian supposed that human beings need food to survive, just as they need language to communicate with each other – *therefore* events turned out this way), now the socio-cultural system at a given moment in history, becomes the object of study. This is a system within which the researcher is also inscribed, much as the linguist is inscribed in language. A greater concern to be more reflexive thus also becomes the order of the day.

For many, like the anthropologist Claude Lévi-Strauss, the sociologist Pierre Bourdieu, or the psychoanalyst Jacques Lacan, as for Roland Barthes in literary criticism and semiotics, Saussurian insights initially paved the way for a more rigorous and systematic approach to human sciences – an approach that would genuinely attempt to take seriously the primacy of the socio-cultural domain for human beings. Just as Saussure had emphasised the importance of not studying speech acts in isolation from the system of conventions which gave them currency, so it was deemed inadequate to study social and cultural facts independently of the social or cultural system which gave *them* currency. Society or culture at a given state of development, and not discrete individual human actions in the past or present, became the focus of study. Whereas the generation before (the generation of Sartre) had sought to discover the natural (intrinsic) basis of human society in history – much as nineteenth-century linguists had sought to reveal the natural elements of language – the structuralist generation's effort was directed towards showing how the differential relations of the elements in the system – whether the latter be a series of texts, a kinship system, or the milieu of fashion photography – produced a meaning, or meanings, and thus had to be 'read' and interpreted. In other words, the study of socio-cultural life is seen to entail deciphering signs through focusing on their differential value, and not on their putative substantive value (often equated with the 'natural'), and also paying attention to the symptomatic level of signification, as well as to the explicit level.

Structure

Structure, as inspired by Saussure's theory of language, can thus refer to the 'value' of elements in a system, or context, and not to their mere physical, or natural existence. Now it has become clear that the physical existence of an entity is complicated by the effects of the linguistic and cultural milieu. Structure, then, is a reminder that nothing social or cultural (and this includes, of course, the individual) exists as a 'positive', essential element outside it in isolation from all other elements. Such an approach reverses the one taken in the political philosophy of the eighteenth and nineteenth centuries, where the biological individual is placed at the origin of social life. And just as this philosophy saw no society as existing prior to the individual, so it also denied the relative autonomy of language.

Probably the main objection that can be raised against the translation of Saussure's emphasis on structure into the study of social and cultural life, is that it does not make sufficient allowance for the role of practice and individual autonomy. Seeing human freedom as a product of social life, rather than as the origin, or cause, of social life, has made it seem, in the eyes of some observers, to be quite limited. A conservative bias, denying the possibility of change, would thus be the consequence of structure While this problem is still unresolved, it is perhaps important to recognise the difference between the freedom of the hypothetical individual (whose very *social* existence would be equivalent to a limit on freedom), and a society of free individuals, where freedom would be the result of social life understood as a structure of differences. Or, rather, we could say that perhaps researchers should begin to explore the idea that, to paraphrase Saussure: Society is a system of freedoms *without positive terms*. On this reading, there would be no *essential*, or substantial freedom – no freedom incarnate in the individual in a state of nature.

Note

1 Cf. 'I am more and more aware of the immense amount of work required to show the linguist *what he is doing*. ... The utter inadequacy of current terminology, the need to reform it and, in order to do that, to demonstrate what sort of object language is, continually spoil my pleasure in philology' (Sausssure 1964: 95, cited in Culler 1986: 24).

References

Arnauld, Antoine and Lancelot, Claude (1975), *The Port-Royal Grammar: general and rational grammar*, ed. and trans. Jacques Rieux and Bernard E. Rollin, The Hague: Mouton.

Culler, Jonathan (1986), *Ferdinand de Saussure*, Ithaca and New York: Cornell University Press.

Saussure, Ferdinand de (1976), *Cours de linguistique générale*, ed. Tullio de Mauro, Paris: Payot. In English as Saussure (1993) *Course in General Linguistics*, trans. Roy Harris, London: Duckworth.

Saussure, Ferninand de (1986), Letter of 4 January 1894, in 'Lettres de F. de Saussure à Antoine Meillet', *Cahiers Ferdinand de Saussure*, 21 (1964), 95, cited in Culler, Jonathan (1986), *Ferdinand de Saussure*, Ithaca and New York: Cornell University Press.

See also: **Barthes, Benveniste, Bourdieu, Derrida, Hjelmslev, Jakobson, Kristeva Lacan, Lévi-Strauss**

Saussure's major writings

(1993) *Course in General Linguistics*, trans Roy Harris, London: Duckworth.

(1976) *Cours de linguistique générale*, critical edn Tullio de Mauro Paris: Payot.

(1967) *Cours de linguistique générale*, 2 vols, critical edn by Rudolf Engler, Wiesbaden: O. Harrassowitz.

Further reading

Benveniste, Émile, (1971), 'Saussure after half a century' in *Problems in General Linguistics*, trans. Mary E. Meek, Miami Linguistics Series No. 8, Coral Gables, Florida: University of Miami Press.

Culler, Jonathan (1986), *Ferdinand de Saussure*, Ithaca and New York: Cornell University Press.

Gadet, Françoise (1989), *Saussure and Contemporary Culture*, trans. George Elliott, London: Hutchinson Radius.

Harris, Roy (1987), *Reading Saussure: A Critical Commentary on the Cours de linguistique générale*, London: Duckworth.

Holdcroft, David (1991), *Saussure: Signs, System and Arbitrariness*, Cambridge: Cambridge University Press.

Saunders, Carol, ed. (2004), *The Cambridge Companion to Saussure*, Cambridge: Cambridge University Press.

Strobinski, Jean (1979), *Words upon Words, the Anagrams of Ferdinand de Saussure*, trans. Olivia Emmet, New Haven and London: Yale University Press.

Thibaut, Paul (1996), *Re-reading Saussure: the Dynamics of Signs in Social Life*, London: Routledge.

SECOND-GENERATION FEMINISM

Second generation feminism questions more than the social inequalities experienced by women; it also looks at the deep-seated ideological structures which inevitably place women at a disadvantage in relation to men. It also takes language as a point of departure in formulating theories of female difference. Women are thus portrayed in language differently to men, particularly from a bodily perspective. Often inspired by the insights of Lacanian psychoanalysis, which shows that consciousness, or the ego, is not the centre of subjectivity, second generation feminism challenges the gender bias in language, law and philosophy. It argues that women should not just aim to be like men (as is often the case in the battle over social equality), but should aim to develop a new, specifically feminine, language, law and mythology.

JUDITH BUTLER (b.1956)

Judith Butler received a PhD in philosophy from Yale in 1984, with a thesis on Hegelian influences in France. She is the Maxine Elliot professor in the Departments of Rhetoric and Comparative Literature at the University of California at Berkeley.

Butler's collection of essays, *Gender Trouble: Feminism and the Subversion of Identity*, written in 1989, first published in 1990, and published with a new preface in 1999 sold over 100,000 copies world-wide and has been translated into a number of languages. Thus – almost despite itself, because of the critical edge – it gave feminist studies, and subsequently, queer theory, a massive shot in the arm. In the book, Butler critically engages with the key presuppositions of feminist theory and practice as regards gender and sexuality, arguing that these are irreducible to naturalised heterosexual categories. She sets the scene for this by invoking the idea of performative as the key to gender and sexuality as constructed. Although an adept of literary theory and philosophy, it is as feminist theorist and inaugurator of queer theory that Butler has become well known. Her work has often been characterised as post-structuralist because of its concern to oppose all essentialist claims and to emphasise that gender relations are precisely that: relations, which implies that gender and sexuality are indeed constructed. In recent studies, Butler has engaged with queer theory, political theory and ethics. Perhaps partly stunned, despite her success, by the kind of criticism Martha Nussbaum mounted against her (Nussbaum 1999), Butler seems wedded lately to intervening in more public debates (on 9/11 and censorship, for example).

Critique of Kristeva – Critique of Essentialism

Rather than beginning by providing a general account of the argument in *Gender Trouble*, we shall focus on Butler's critique of Julia Kristeva's theory of the drive-based, semiotic, for it shows in a nutshell Butler's general theoretical orientation.

For Butler, the semiotic is ultimately essentialist (and this is clearly a criticism), because of its connection to the drives – believed to be biological – and indebted, through opposition, to the socially sanctioned Symbolic: the Law of the Father, the sphere of the determination of 'normal' gender and sexuality. Kristeva thus shows herself to be ultimately Lacanian, even if she disagrees with Lacan on the role and status of the drives in Freudian theory. The semiotic is proposed by Kristeva as having subversive political implications in its capacity to disrupt the social order (language, for example), even if it cannot be the basis of a new order (for it to be so would entail a flirtation with psychosis). Before it can become truly subversive, the semiotic must be repressed by the Symbolic, so that the only way that the semiotic can find expression is 'prior' to meaning, as in the infant's holophrastic utterances, or 'after' meaning, as in psychosis, where words are no longer used to signify. Butler does not give much of a hearing to poetic language or to artistic practice in general. Problems emerge, too, in Butler's eyes, when the semiotic is equated with the organisation of the drives and the maternal body. For it seems to her that Kristeva privileges hetero- over homosexuality and, in particular, over lesbian sexuality, so that homosexuality as judged by Kristeva, according to Butler, also risks toppling over into psychosis. Moreover, Kristeva is seen to privilege the maternal body and the act of birth even as these must remain without the symbolic outlet due of the Law of the Father.

Butler's question is: how can one get an ontological purchase on the semiotic when access to it is only possible via the Symbolic itself? Surely, Butler implies, we are likely to end up, at best, without any clear knowledge of the semiotic, and at worst with the requirement that the drives of the semiotic be postulated as pre-Symbolic and existing prior to language but yet can become manifest only in and through language (the same Symbolic). Effectively, there seems to be no real outside to the Symbolic that can be accessed. Politically, Butler claims, 'all manner of things "primitive" and "Oriental" are summarily subordinated to the principle of the maternal body', which raises both the issue of Orientalism and multiplicity as a 'univocal signifier' (Butler 1999: 114).

Foucault and the Performative

In Foucault's work, on the other hand, the notion of sex is constituted through the discourse of sexuality. Quite rightly, in Butler's view, Foucault does not attempt to project anything beyond discourse. For him, there might as well not be any pre-discursive reality. Such a position would avoid the problem Kristeva faces with the semiotic as a challenge to, yet dependent upon, the Symbolic. Foucault also meets with Butler's approval because, unlike the purely negative function of the Law, and thus of power, Foucault sees power as positive, in the sense that it is a productive force that brings things into being. It is not simply a mechanism of repression, or prohibition, for example.

Inspired by Foucault, Butler employs the notion of performative to emphasise that the gendered body is enacted. And she adds, in a key passage:

> That the gendered body is performative suggests that it has no ontological status apart from the various acts which constitute its reality. This also suggests that if that reality is fabricated as an interior essence, that very interiority is an effect and function of decidedly public and social discourse, the public regulation of fantasy through the surface politics of the body, the gender border control that differentiates inner from outer, and so institutes the 'integrity' of the subject.
>
> (Butler 1999: 173)

In contrast to the approach which inserts the gendered body into pre-existing categories (such as heterosexual) linked to an ontology based on origins, 'performative' suggests that gender and subjectivity are radically contingent and subject to change. Indeed, this approach suggests that gender relations can be changed. And for Butler, writing in 1989, things needed to be changed; for heterosexually gendered bodies were hegemonic, while gay and lesbian bodies were designated as pathological. Butler considers that despite all her theoretical sophistication, Kristeva participates in the maintenance of hegemonic heterosexuality. According to Butler, even though feminism had been engaged in achieving rights for women, it had not really questioned the hegemonic characteristics of a male who identifies with being male and who *therefore* seeks out a female sexual partner, or of a female who therefore identifies with being female and seeks out a male partner. The Freudian principle at work here is embodied in the notion that one cannot desire the sex with which one identifies, so that if one identifies oneself as a woman, one cannot (normally) desire another woman. Butler seeks, above all, to challenge this theoretically by saying that, through 'subversive bodily acts', the gender bodily relations need not be beholden to such a framework. As opposed to a naturalist view, which says gender relations are imposed by nature and therefore cannot be changed in any fundamental way, the performative principle precisely enables the subversion of fixed notions of identity.

Austin's Performative

In her book, *Excitable Speech* (1997a), Butler invokes J.L. Austin's idea of performative (also called a 'speech act') to investigate the ways people can claim to have been injured by language. For Austin, it is possible to 'do' things with words (see Austin 1980). Thus for Austin, language is not only a medium of communication, or a tool for describing the world. Events such as promising, marrying, giving advice, opening a meeting, naming and launching a ship, ordering someone to do something, Austin called 'performatives' because uttering the words of these events in the correct context is to perform an act. Through the words alone the act is performed. Thus, in contrast to the sense of the proverb, 'words are only words', Austin effectively argued that words are not just words, but can be acts. These kinds of performative utterances, Austin calls 'illocutionary acts'. In addition, 'perlocutionary acts' may be defined as using words to get (persuade, seduce, cajole) someone to do something. Through the uttering of words alone perlocutionary acts take place.

Along with Foucault on sexuality and Althusser on interpellating people as subjects through the uttering of words, Butler uses the notion of performative as illocutionary and perlocutionary to analyse notions, such as 'hate speech', 'contagious words' and censorship. She finds that such events are as much or more constitutive of the subject of the utterance than they are constituted. In other words, Butler invokes her earlier use of performative as 'subject formation'. To this she adds, in her appropriation of Austin, that such subject formation takes place within a milieu of 'ongoing political contestation and reformulation of the subject as well' (Butler 1997a: 160).

Power and Resistance

Generally, Butler has been concerned with the issue of resistance to power and the place in society of gay rights and queer politics. However, critics such as Žižek have asked whether perversion can lead to subversion of the existing order (see Žižek 1999: 248). The issue is not perversion as unnatural practices, but of that, for example, of the order of the Law creating the criminal, the prohibition inciting the transgression, as seen in Foucault's work on power. A perverse theory of power, then, sees power as having an 'interest' in resistance, whereas a progressive view argues that resistance generated by power undermines the existing form of power, or even power itself.

Hegel, in his theory of Lordship and Bondage, a key reference for Butler in the *Psychic Life of Power* (1997b), shows a disavowal of the body similar to that in the relation between man and woman in patriarchal society. The misconception of feminine autonomy here is more restricting than the notion that woman is a symptom of man.

Through Althusserian interpellation, where 'the subject is constituted by being hailed' (Butler 1997b: 95), Butler's performative means, as we have shown, that subjectivity is established in the act, and does not exist as some a priori essential element. Can such absolute contingency be sustained? This is a question arising from Butler's approach.

Butler's criticism of Lacan centres on the idea that resistance depends on the symbolic structure which is to be resisted. But here two meanings of resistance need to be specified: social-political and psychic. Although the two domains relate and interpenetrate, they are not reducible to each other. Butler often risks doing precisely this. Psychic resistance to power, where issues of sexual identity might be at stake, is often reduced to the social-political articulation of power where one might want to resist the law that declares that no same sex marriages are permitted. Often, Butler gives the impression that for her, the social-political sphere determines the nature of psychic space.

Butler, then, favours Foucault over Lacan and rejects the Lacanian Symbolic as the sphere which sets the coordinates of our existence in advance. However, if, as Butler says, Foucault shows that resistance to power is at the same time an effect of power (the perverse thesis), this seems to be a no win, because there is no exit, situation.

Sexuality and the Masquerade

In her earlier work, Butler argues that the masquerade, where heterosexuality is a play of appearances, becomes central for Lacan: a man fears becoming a woman because this reveals an unconscious desire to be loved by another man, a desire for sameness, not difference. Thus Butler counters Lacan's claim that female homosexuality is a disappointed heterosexuality by claiming that female heterosexuality might be a disappointed homosexuality (Butler 1999: 63).

As Butler's critique of Kristeva shows, her key argument is that the Symbolic sets up gender identities in advance and that, in contrast to Lacan's view, gender identities can be viewed as instituted within and by a given cultural and social matrix (another name for performative) that can be subverted.

The Production of Subjectivity, Identity and Desire

In her work, *Giving an Account of Oneself* (2005), Butler returns to a consideration, opened up in *The Psychic Life of Power*, of Foucault's theory of identity formation. The latter is seen to be formed according 'to certain requirements of the liberal state' and its juridical apparatus (Butler 1997b: 100). Individuals are effectively produced by this set of arrangements and made into 'subject of the state' (1997b: 100). In the later work, Butler discusses Foucault on the subject of power, as this is effected within a 'régime of truth' (Butler 2005: 22). In *The Psychic Life of Power*, she focuses instead on his call to create new forms of subjectivity, forms which refuse those offered by the State and the existing power structure, and which have been imposed on people for 'several centuries' (Foucault, cited by Butler, 1997b: 101). Rather than follow Foucault to the letter here, Butler notes the change in Foucault from a position in *Discipline and Punish* (1977 [1975]), which argued that no resistance to power was possible, to one in 1982 where it is possible.

Butler not only notes this discrepancy, but also reflects upon the possibilities such a position might, or might not, open up. And she points out that identity, being a fundamental attachment for the subject, cannot simply be thrown off at will. Unlike Foucault, she also wants to make a space for a psychoanalytic interpretation of the Law, which says that there is no desire without the Law that, in fact, prohibition eroticises the Law. For Foucault, in Butler's reading, the Law is always external to desire, and thus an impediment which must be overcome. A certain place is thus secured for psychoanalysis as any opposition to subjection will first have to take subjection itself as a resource.

This suggests an attempt by Butler to refine the voluntarism of the performative in her earlier stance in *Gender Trouble*. By the time of her book, *Giving an Account of Oneself* (2005), which has a clear ethical focus, Butler, although referring to Foucault in order to pose key questions, nevertheless raises the prospect of an opacity in the self that remains, and which, if not inaccessible, is at least only accessible after a great deal of reflexive labour. The point is that although an ideological, and therefore relatively transparent, relation to oneself is possible, the real material bases of identity, including, if one likes, 'a régime of truth' (Butler 2005: 22), are much more difficult to ascertain. Indeed, how does one refuse what one is (the Foucauldian proposition), if it is unclear as to exactly what one is? More pointedly: the question that Butler still needs to answer is: How can performativity work as a principle of resistance (to stereotypes, etc), when a certain opacity is at the heart of every identity?

References

Austin, J.L. (1980 [1962]). *How to Do Things with Words*, Oxford, New York, Toronto and Melbourne: Oxford University Press.

Butler, Judith (2005), *Giving an Account of Oneself*, New York: Fordham University Press.

—— (1999), *Gender Trouble: Feminism and the Subversion of Identity*, New York and London: Routledge.

—— (1997a), *Excitable Speech: A Politics of the Performative*, New York and London: Routledge.

—— (1997b), *The Psychic Life of Power: Theories in Subjection*, Stanford: Stanford University Press.

Foucault, Michel (1977 [1975]), *Discipline and Punish: The Birth of the Prison*, trans. Alan Sheridan, London: Allen Lane.

Nussbaum, Martha (1999), 'The Professor of Parody', *The New Republic,* 2 February, accessible via 'The New Republic Online' at <http://www.tnr. com/index.mhtml>.

Žižek, Slavoj (1999), *The Ticklish Subject: The Absent Centre of Political Ontology,* London and New York: Verso. Cambridge, Mass. and London: MIT Press.

See also: **Foucault, Lacan, Žižek**

Butler's major writings

(2005) *Giving an Account of Oneself,* New York: Fordham University Press.

(2004a) *Undoing Gender,* New York and London: Routledge.

(2004b) *Precarious Life: The Powers of Mourning and Violence,* London and New York: Verso.

(2003) *The Judith Butler Reader,* ed., Sara Salih, with Judith Butler, Malden, Mass.: Blackwell.

(2000a) *Antigone's Claim: Kinship Between Life and Death,* New York: Columbia University Press.

(2000b) *Contingency, Hegemony, Universality: Contemporary Dialogues on the Left* (with Ernesto Laclau and Slovoj Žižek), London and New York: Verso.

(1997a) *The Psychic Life of Power: Theories in Subjection,* Stanford, Cal.: Stanford University Press.

(1997b) *Excitable Speech: A Politics of the Performative,* New York and London: Routledge.

(1993) *Bodies That Matter: on the Discursive Limits of "Sex",* London and New York: Routledge.

(1990 and 1999) *Gender Trouble: Feminism and the Subversion of Identity,* New York and London: Routledge.

(1987) *Subjects of Desire: Hegelian Reflections in Twentieth-Century France,* New York: Columbia University Press.

Further Reading

Bell, Vicki (1999), 'Interview with Judith Butler', *Theory, Culture and Society,* 16 (April).

Kirby, Vicki (2005), *Judith Butler: Live Theory,* London and New York: Continuum.

LUCE IRIGARAY (b.1930)

Luce Irigaray was trained as a linguist and Lacanian analyst. Her early publications explored the language of those suffering from dementia.

In her researches, Irigaray discovered that the language of the schizophrenic tends to be a private language, or an ideolect. But above all, she proposed that what was often taken to be incomprehensible delirium (*délire*) was in fact subject to rules of linguistic structure, even if these rules were continually broken, As Irigaray has subsequently become involved in constructing feminine forms of symbolisation and language – forms based on aspects of female experience deemed to be outside conventional modes of expression (like the ideolect of the schizophrenic) – we should keep this early work in mind in considering her endeavours as one of the leading exponents of philosophical feminism.

The Female/Feminine Lot

In 1974, Irigaray published *Speculum of the Other Woman*, which, in re-examining the notion of femininity – including the mother–daughter relationship – in Freud and psychoanalysis, sought to develop a specifically feminine writing (*écriture feminine*) – a writing that would subvert the hegemony of a male imaginary which condemns women to silence as women.

Although in fierce opposition to many of its aspects, Irigaray's philosophy of the feminine begins with the Lacanian theory of the Real, the Symbolic and the Imaginary – the Real as the place of the mother and death, the Symbolic as the domain of law founded on the Name-of-the-Father, and the imaginary as the effect of the Symbolic in consciousness and imagination. As Irigaray reads the situation, Lacan's symbolic order – the condition of language – is fundamentally masculine and patriarchal; it speaks the imaginary of men and is organised according to the law of the symbolic order which subtends it. Anything outside the domain of the symbolic order effectively has to be translated into its terms; in other words, its other as symbolised is really the same as itself. Or else, the other (like death, or the feminine) is so radically different that no symbolic means are available for it to be communicated. This is especially evident in the field of sexuality. And sexuality, as Freud showed, affects almost every sphere of intellectual and cultural life. At the moment, the supposedly neutral subject of science, or the neutral subject in language (the third person) are, for Irigaray, both gendered male. To put it in a nutshell: Irigaray's critique of the institutions of psychoanalysis, language and culture is radical in that she sees even ostensibly egalitarian gestures as being compromised from the start; for they will inevitably presuppose that women are on the deficit side of the ledger, that they 'lack' something (whether in social or sexual terms) which men have and which women, in all justice, deserve too (social status, a public life, autonomy and independence, a separate identity).

Sexually, the egalitarian gesture which attributes to the vagina a status equal to the penis unwittingly gives in to Freud's notion of penis envy. For the penis is still the benchmark. Why should it be, Irigaray leads us to ask? When Lacan seems to go even further than Freud in saying that the whole of the symbolic order is phallic (that the phallus is the signifier of all signification, that the subject is a signifier) and that it is via the symbolic order that the drama of sexual difference of fullness (the masculine) and lack (the feminine) is played out – Irigaray calls on women to note that this is a masculine view of things. In effect, 'Female sexuality has always been conceptualised on the basis of masculine parameters' (Irigaray 1988: 23). Again, a woman's lot, Irigaray confirms 'is that of "lack", "atrophy" (of the sexual organ), and "penis envy", the penis being the only organ of recognized value' (Irigaray 1988: 23). Here, Freud's theory of castration is at issue. He is seen to argue that the presence or absence of the penis is what is crucial to the sexual development of both sexes. As there is no immediate access to the real body, the presence or absence of the penis is understood by Lacan as the presence or absence of the phallus which signifies sexual difference. For Irigaray, on the other hand, the phallus symbolises lack in the woman as other because a woman is effectively a castrated man.

Language

If language (for Lacan) is irreducibly phallic, the only way women can speak or communicate at all is by appropriating the masculine instrument. One way or another, the woman has to 'have' the phallus she lacks; the deficit has to be made up. In order to speak clearly, to communicate and to forge links with others – to be social – the woman must speak like a man. Not to do so is to risk psychosis: a falling back into an ideolect, and the putting asunder of the social bond. Lacan's version (which he calls the *père-version*) of language is, for Irigaray, repeated in most psychoanalytic theories of language and sexuality. If women are to have an identity of their own, the phallic version of the symbolic to which they have been subjected for so long must be subverted. For the symbolic has been the source of women's oppression.

As Irigaray presents it, then, women have a disturbing and oppressively paradoxical status as (non) subjects; for in order to speak, they must speak like men; in order to know their sexuality at all they must compare it to the male version: they must 'be' the lack of a penis. While men can readily invoke the symbolic order (mediation) in knowing and loving themselves, and therefore in representing themselves to others in the social world, women, by contrast, are in a position of what Irigaray calls a condition of 'dereliction' (Irigaray 1984: 70) – that is, of not being able to know or to love themselves, because mediation (the symbolic order) is foreign to them. 'Women lack mediation for the work of sublimation', she says (Irigaray 1984: 70). As a result they cannot objectify themselves – or at least they find objectification difficult. Men, on the other hand, not only pose themselves as objects, but are able to objectify women as well. Correlatively, women are refused access to society and culture in direct proportion that men are of society and culture. Effectively, women's condition here is, for Irigaray, reminiscent of Marx's view of the proletariat: the proletariat, Marx said, are *in* society, but they are not *of* society. Socially speaking, women – at least from a traditional perspective – must be attached to a man in order to have a social persona; a woman thus does not have her own identity. For her part, Irigaray argues that to have an identity which is not one's own – to be a 'sex which is not one' (i.e. which is not whole because it is lacking – is not unified in itself, but dependent) – is to be excluded from the fullness of being: it is to be left precisely in a condition of 'dereliction'.

Mother–Daughter

Women *as* women are therefore excluded from the social contract. And an important contributing factor here is the difficulty (read: present impossibility) of symbolising the mother–daughter relationship. While psychoanalysis has made much, in talking of the entry of the human into the realm of language, of the separation of the child from its mother, less has been made of the fact that this child has been understood as the son. The son, then, has to separate himself from the mother via the intervention of language, or the Name-of-the-Father. The son is not only a potential father; he is also a subject: a man. The daughter, by contrast, is only a potential mother. Her womanhood thus has to be gleaned from the experience of motherhood.

The son's first lesson, so to speak, is to be able to obj[...]
mother through the symbolic order so as to comply with t[...]
diction against incest. The daughter, however, is largely [...]
means for achieving this separation, due to her impoveris[...]
tionship to the symbolic. She thus runs a greater risk of psych[...]
melancholia – or rather, her language will tend to be domin[...]
the drives, as Irigaray found in her studies of delirium. Perh[...]
garay ponders, delirium has the potential for providing the b[...]
woman's language – of providing a way that might enable wo[...]
communicate among themselves, just as men have commu[...]
among themselves.

Irigaray has worked continuously since the mid-1970s to [...]
the symbolic means equivalent to the mother–daughter relatio[...]
This work has led her to investigate those hitherto represse[...]
excluded aspects of Western culture which have been partic[...]
related to the condition of the feminine in society: the divine [...]
nine, witchcraft, and sorcery – to cite some examples. As Mar[...]
Whitford has pointed out (Whitford 1991: 84–85), the logic of Iriga[...]
project here is not to valorise an incommunicable mystical state, o[...]
essential woman, but to overcome the deficit of woman unsym[...]
lised as woman. Not mysticism, then, but bringing woman into [...]
symbolic order on her own terms is the aim. Women need to be a[...]
to represent themselves to themselves (but in a way quite differ[...]
from men) in order to constitute themselves as truly social bei[...]
who can form positive relationships with each other.

Style and a Female God

All of this has led to experimentation with different linguistic strate
gies in Irigaray's own writing, and in the evocation of experience[...]
and cultural figures which have been excluded from social and cultural life because they have been so closely associated with what was
thought to be essentially feminine. Regarding style, Elizabeth Grosz
has written of Irigaray that: 'Her writing, her "styles", involve new
forms of discourse, new ways of speaking, a "poetry" which is
necessarily innovative and evocative of new conceptions of women
and femininity' (Grosz 1989: 101). Exemplary experiments of style
in this sense are: *Marine Lover of Friedrich Nietzsche*, *Elemental Passions*, and *Forgetting of Air in Martin Heidegger*. In these readings of
figures in the history of philosophy, Irigaray is attentive to the
repressed elements which are passed over in silence – elements of

pertinence to feminists, such as the body, and the elements: water, earth, fire, air.

Similarly, Irigaray has reflected on the theological tradition in order to find in it a positive notion of the divine (the infinite) appropriate to women. Because the God of Christianity, as the exemplar of the masculine imaginary, excludes women's experience as a point of reference, Irigaray believes it is necessary to find a figure able to exemplify the feminine imaginary. The feminine god would be one to give form to multiplicity, difference, becoming, flows, rhythms, and to 'the splendor of the body' – in other words, to those things which cannot receive a viable image within a patriarchal religious experience. 'A *feminine* god', Irigaray admits, 'is yet to come' (Irigaray 1986: 8). And no doubt this is the point: the 'yet to come' of the feminine god is the god of becoming – the god of fluidity and transient boundaries, of the amorphous elements of fire, air, earth and water. 'How could our [women's] God be imagined?' Irigaray asks. 'Or our god?', she continues. 'Is there a quality pertaining to us which could reverse the order and put the predicate in subject position' (Irigaray 1986: 8)?

The search for a god that is distinctively feminine is a search for a position – a reference point – that nevertheless would not replicate the positionality of patriarchy. In current terms, such a position would have to be one which in some sense elides all positionality. For the logic of identity this is an untenable position. And the question remains as to whether it is at all sustainable. Clearly, Irigaray is convinced of the necessity and the viability of the project; but what if she were wrong? Women themselves are beginning to ask this question.

Levinas and Alterity

Irigaray's philosophical project also concerns the investigation of ethics in light of Emmanuel Levinas's notion of ethical obligation. Like Irigaray in relation to women, Levinas has been concerned to lay bare the repressed elements of the Judaic tradition within Christianity. For Levinas, the moral imperative is focused, not on the status of the self – where the other would only have relevance for confirming the self's own moral worth – but on the other as an exteriority or alterity which calls to the self, and which, in a sense, the self becomes. In short, the other is not reducible to a representation indebted, as all representations are, to the order of the Same. What attracts Irigaray to Levinas, is the emphasis he places on the material encounter in his theory of alterity. Indeed only at a

material, corporeal level is real alterity articulated; only the truly material encounter with the other can be surprising and astonishing. For Irigaray, then, the feminine is the prototype of this alterity.

Difficulties

Given the care Irigaray has brought to articulate a new vision of the feminine, it seems surprising that some basic difficulties remain, of which three in particular call for attention. In the first place, there is a debt to Lacanian psychoanalysis. Here – Levinas not withstanding – it is difficult to avoid the sense that Irigaray's work is another anti-Oedipus project, and that, as a result, it is governed by the logic it seeks to subvert. In effect, the Lacanian Real, Symbolic and Imaginary enables Irigaray to point to the inadequacy of both 'egalitarian feminism', and feminism that defines the feminine in terms of lack, and unrepresentable otherness.

A second, and more troubling point, is the way the terms, 'woman' and 'women', 'man' and 'men' are used to designate apparently homogeneous realities: that is, men must be men and women must be women. Politically, this has led to the proposition that a man (e.g. Derrida) cannot be a feminist.[1] It would seem, however, that the view that men cannot be feminist can only be maintained if the very homogeneous categories of identity (man, woman) which Irigaray intends to subvert are maintained. That is, without the logic of identity in dominance, women would not necessarily be women; the feminine would not necessarily be feminist. The risk – the very grave risk – is a possible form of racism based on an insidious mode of classification from which no one can escape.

The third point concerns elements of the feminine (female god, the elements of fire, air, earth, and water, female language and festivals), rendered visible by Irigaray's work. On one level, this approach touches on the most creative aspect of her style of feminism. Boundaries have been shaken and new ways of imagining have been opened up. However, there is a strong impression coming through that such imaginings require devotees if the desired political effect is to be achieved. The question that needs to be asked now is whether an individual could be truly feminist in Irigaray's terms and *not* subscribe to her version of the feminine. Irigaray felt a great joy – as a woman – upon seeing a female Jesus in a museum on Torcello island (Irigaray 1993: 25). But what if one were *not* moved, either as a woman, or as an individual – or as both – by such a scene? An affirmative answer would seem to render problematic the very link

Irigaray is trying to make between an iconography of the feminine and a sense of becoming a female subject.

A final difficulty concerns Irigaray's championing, supported by the Italian feminist movement, of formal rights based on sexual difference. These are advocated in *Democracy Begins Between Two* and her 'Report on Citizenship of the Union', co-authored with her Italian colleague, Renzo Imbeni, and presented to the European Parliament. Given that Irigaray initially stood for the futility of women fighting for equal rights (as First Generation feminists had done) until women had become subjects at a deeper psychological level (hence the strategies relating to language and style), people are now wondering how the later work can be reconciled with the early Irigaray and whether it really matters. The debate continues.

Note

1 For a more complete and subtle account of why this is so within the economy of Irigaray's philosophy as regards a figure like Derrida, see Whitford (1991: 123–47).

References

Grosz, Elizabeth (1989), *Sexual Subversions. Three French Feminists: Julia Kristeva, Luce Irigaray, Michèle Le Doeuff*, Sydney: Allen & Unwin.

Irigaray, Luce (1984), *Ethique de la différence sexuelle*, Paris: Minuit.

—— (1986), *Divine Women*, trans. Stephen Muecke, Sydney: Local Consumption.

—— (1988), *This Sex Which is Not One*, trans. Catherine Porter with Carolyn Burke, Ithaca and New York: Cornell University Press.

—— (1993), *Je, tu, nous. Toward a Culture of Difference*, trans. Alison Martin, New York and London: Routledge.

Whitford, Margaret (1991), *Luce Irigaray: Philosophy in the Feminine*, London and New York: Routledge.

See also: **Freud, Kristeva, Lacan, Le Doeuff, Levinas**

Irigaray's major writings

(2007 [1990]) *Je, tu, nous. Toward a Culture of Difference*, with a personal note by the author, trans. Alison Martin, New York and London: Routledge.

(2002 [1999]) *Between East and West: from Singularity to Community*, trans. Stephen Pluháček, New York: Columbia University Press.

(2001 [1994]) *Democracy Begins Between Two*, trans. Kirsteen Anderson, New York: Routledge.

(1999 [1983]) *The Forgetting of Air in Martin Heidegger*, trans. Mary Beth Mader, Austin: University of Texas Press.

(1996 [1992]) *I Love You: Sketch of a Possible Felicity in History*, trans. Alison Martin, New York: Routledge.

(1993 [1984]) *An Ethics of Sexual Difference*, trans. Carolyn Burke and Gillian C. Gill, New York: Cornell University Press.

(1992 [1982]) *Elemental Passions*, ed. Joanne Collier and Judith Still, New York: Routledge.

(1991 [1980]) *Marine Lover of Friedrich Nietzsche*, trans. Gillian C. Gill, New York: Columbia University Press.

(1988 [1977]) *This Sex Which is Not One*, trans. Catherine Porter with Carolyn Burke, Ithaca and New York: Cornell University Press.

(1986) *Divine Women*, trans. Stephen Muecke, Sydney: Local Consumption.

(1985 [1974]) *Speculum of the Other Woman*, trans. Gillian C. Gill, New York: Cornell.

(1973) *Le Langage des déments*, The Hague: Mouton, Approaches to Semiotics.

Further reading

Cimifile, Maria C. and Miller, Elaine P. (2006), *Returning to Irigarary: Feminist Philosophy, Politics and the Question of Unity*, Albany: State University of New York.

Deutcher, Penelope (2002), *A Politics of Impossible Difference: the Later Work of Luce Irigaray*, Ithaca and New York: Cornell University Press.

Krier, Theresa and Harvey, Elizabeth D., eds (2004), *Luce Irigaray and Premodern Culture: Thresholds of History*, London and New York: Routledge

Whitford, Margaret (1991), *Luce Irigaray: Philosophy in the Feminine*, London and New York: Routledge

MICHÈLE LE DOEUFF (b. 1948)

Michèle Le Doeuff is Director of Research at the Centre Nationale de Recherche Scientifique in Paris. She became interested in philosophy not through reading the great thinkers, but through identifying with the Fool in Shakespeare's plays. For the Fool is given to subversive speech, a vocation Le Doeuff initially found to be intrinsic to philosophy, which, unlike the Fool, exists in real life.

The Philosophical Imaginary

In her book, *Hipparchia's Choice*, Michèle Le Doeuff explains that she found it possible to begin her own philosophical project by proving 'that there is in philosophy an imaginary level which has not been imported from elsewhere but is specific to philosophy and sets the conditions of what can be constructed as rationality within it' (Le Doeuff 1989a: 23). Such is the way that Le Doeuff describes the trajectory for the book for which she has become best known outside France, *The Philosophical Imaginary* (Le Doeuff 1989b). There, the author shows, *inter alia*, that Kant, in the first paragraph of the section of the *Critique of Pure Reason* dealing with the distinction between phenomena and noumena, refers to the understanding as a 'territory' that the preceding section of the book has 'explored'. There is more than this image of a territory, however; for Kant goes on to say that the 'domain' of the understanding

> is an island, enclosed by nature itself within unalterable limits. It is the land of truth – enchanting name! – surrounded by a wide and stormy ocean, the native home of illusion, where many a fog bank and many a swiftly melting iceberg give the deceptive appearance of farther shores, deluding the adventurous seafarer ever anew with empty hopes, and engaging him in enterprises which he can never hope to abandon and yet is unable to carry to completion.
>
> (Kant 1970: 257)

For Le Doeuff, such images (island, fog, iceberg, stormy sea, etc.) in a philosophical text cannot simply be interpreted metaphorically. Rather, their effect is to close the text off from further scrutiny – to make it self-contained, much as the understanding as an 'island' of truth is self-contained.

More generally, Le Doeuff says that images in philosophy have been explained within philosophy's meta-discourse about itself in two ways: either they have been seen as a mark of the resurgence of a more primitive, or childlike form of thought; or, they have been seen as possessing an intuitive, and self-evident clarity, as though the image could speak directly the thought the philosopher desired to communicate. The latter quality would make images an efficacious way of transmitting thought to an uncultivated, or an untrained interlocutor. In Le Doeuff's eyes, both explanations only serve to hide the real effect of the image in philosophy. Through images, 'every philosophy can engage in a straightforward dogmatization, and decree a "that's the way it is" without fear of counter-argument, since it is understood that a good reader will by-pass such "illustrations'" (Le Doeuff 1989b: 12). Images, therefore, are a means whereby philosophy can be unphilosophical by closing off the image from scrutiny and discussion. For Le Doeuff, closing the image off from scrutiny is equivalent to the closure of philosophy itself.

Le Doeuff and Feminism

Le Doeuff's work in philosophy has often been linked to that of the feminists, Luce Irigaray and Hélène Cixous, and, to a lesser extent, Julia Kristeva. Unlike Irigaray and other 'difference feminists' who treat the language of philosophy with great suspicion because of its masculinist, rationalist and patriarchal status – a status which deprives women of their own voice – Le Doeuff argues that reason and rationality are not essentially masculine. The fact that there is a plurality of rationalities alone tends to belie the notion of a hegemonic, masculine reason. Neither, Le Doeuff adds in her influential book on knowledge and science, is scientific method essentially masculine or male. Nor, she contends, do women succeed in science in the so-called female domain of cooperation, while men go for competition. Rather cooperation is essential in science whoever practices it. Le Doeuff is against the confusion of science or philosophy with those who manage them (see Le Doeuff 2003).

Le Doeuff shows that there have always been women in philosophy and in science throughout their history – although, it is true, without the same advantages as men – so that it becomes counterproductive to repeatedly ask why there have been few women in philosophy or science. Le Doeuff pushes this point even further by saying that today, in contrast to the past, 'Nothing prevents a young woman from studying philosophy and then producing philosophical works.' And so she asks, 'What is the point, therefore, in going over and over an outdated question and talking about what happened the day before yesterday?' (Le Doeuff 1989a: 5). Or, Le Doeuff similarly ponders, there is no point saying that science is inherently masculine. Francis Bacon's strictures on method do not essentially exclude women. Science does not exclude women from science; men do (see Le Doeuff 2003: 162).

The Practice of Philosophy and Science

On the other hand, the way philosophy has been practised has undoubtedly tended to make it more difficult for women to be professional philosophers, just as it is also true that the way women have been characterised almost exclusively by their sex constitutes another largely unacknowledged element (like the image) of non-philosophy within the history of philosophy. There is a fundamental sexism in philosophy, as there is in science; but to combat it Le Doeuff calls upon the resources of philosophy and science themselves (concern for openness and method, and its effort to reflect upon its own presuppositions and empirical testing), even, it must also be admitted, that philosophy and science dream of being their founding principle and means of legitimation, and as philosophy dreams of being the basis and founding principle of all other disciplines. Philosophy's dream of its own omnipotence and autonomy is one of its most powerful myths. When all is said and done, however, Le Doeuff opposes the sexism of philosophy in the name of philosophy and the sexism of science in the name of science. Not philosophy or science *per se*, then, but the historical practice of philosophy and science is what is at stake. These practices have misrecognised the effect of images; have emphasised abstraction and universalisation at the expense of pertinence; have refused the idea of the 'wandering' of thought; have seen 'women' (Roussel 1845) as their other; have been inflexible regarding style so that the place of enunciation has, in principle, remained invisible. All these aspects of philosophical and scientific practice have contributed to women's alienation.

Devotees

Similarly, women have often been positioned as devotees and disciples of great male philosophers rather than – as has been the rule for creative work – thinking on their own account. In effect, what marks a man as a philosopher above all, is being an independent and a creative thinker to whom others defer. Those men who have not quite made it have often had a woman there to satisfy the male philosopher's 'ontological lack'. Indeed, despite his success, Sartre tended to depend on de Beauvoir in just such a way. In a detailed treatment of the de Beauvoir – Sartre relation in *Hipparchia's Choice*, Le Doeuff analyses the use de Beauvoir makes of Sartre's existential philosophy (i.e. discipleship) in *The Second Sex* in order that she (de Beauvoir) might, surreptitiously, turn the stick in the other direction. The sexism of Sartre's philosophy is not directly challenged by de Beauvoir. Rather, says Le Doeuff, Sartre's categories 'are remodelled "in the heat of the moment"'(Le Doeuff 1989a: 88). De Beauvoir takes the framework of existentialism as given (she herself is not constructing a philosophical system) and uses it in order to present a 'point of view', a perspective on the here and now. She refers to concrete examples and cites ethnographic data not in order to demonstrate a philosophical framework, but because they exist as examples of the way people live. In addition, de Beauvoir does not take a 'collection of "theoretical positions"' from existentialism, but a set of values. 'So Simone de Beauvoir's choice is first and foremost one of morality' (Le Doeuff 1989a: 90). As a result, although Le Doeuff still finds much that is problematic in *The Second Sex*, she has not, unlike other feminists, built her feminism on a complete rejection of de Beauvoir. And Le Doeuff, in the end, finds de Beauvoir significant precisely because the Sartrian 'phantasmagoria' – which rejected the idea that exteriority (the other) was in any way philosophically or morally determinate – disappears when 'de Beauvoir takes up the same philosophy'. When all is said and done, as it were, Le Doeuff finds de Beauvoir attractive because, although beginning with existentialism, she comes to speak in her own voice. In short, she ceases to be a devotee.

Enlightenment Allegiance and Critics

Her view of philosophy as a potentially liberating practice has led some to see in Le Doeuff's approach an implicit reverence for the eighteenth-century *philosophes*. Feminist critics like Elizabeth Grosz have suggested that because of this reverence and propriety in her readings it is 'almost as if she were to claim' that if philosophy is misogynist, this can be confined to those imaginary elements she has been concerned to reveal' (Grosz 1989: 212). According to Meaghan Morris, Le Doeuff's acceptance of philosophy as a globally positive force as far as women are concerned might merely be 'a salvage operation to rescue philosophy from the more damaging charges of feminist critics' (Morris 1981/2: 77 cited in Grosz 1989: 212).

Why Women Should be Philosophers and Scientists

While acknowledging that the situation is complex, Le Doeuff's response to such a criticism is to say that, whether we like it or not, philosophy – and science – offers the model of autonomy and independence of thought that women as feminists can well aspire to. Maybe this does amount to a salvage operation of sorts; but it is one that seeks to salvage philosophy from the closure it has been subject to in the hands of men. If, historically, men have limited philosophy, this does not mean that philosophy is limited in itself.

Even if one were to argue that the possibility of independence of thought offered by philosophy is illusory, it is hard to see how one can escape thinking philosophically in arriving at such a conclusion. For Le Doeuff, however, the historical limitations of philosophy can be turned to account when we recognise that, through such limitations, paradoxical as it might seem, philosophy demonstrates its pertinence. Although this link must be thought through carefully to avoid sounding glib, it is philosophy's failure to be universal, and the reality of its historical limits which makes it pertinent. In other words, historical limits mean being tied up with issues of the day.

A similar case can be made in relation to science. Women's lack of access to, and subordination in, science, throughout history, does not make science itself discriminatory. In fact, the rigorous use of science can be brought to bear in the fight against discrimination.

A final, but nevertheless fundamental, reason as to why women should not eschew philosophy or science is that it is, historically, through being designated as unphilosophical and unscientific that women have been defined as women. This has resulted in the prejudice that the man is philosophical and scientific (i.e. not determined by his sex) and the woman is only her sex. In her chapter, 'Pierre Roussel's Chiasmus', in *The Philosophical Imaginary*, Le Doeuff is able to give an example of the lengths to which scientists have gone in order to reduce women to their sex. As if inspired by Book V of Rousseau's *Émile* (where Rousseau says that abstract truths are not for women), Pierre Roussel, in his treatise of 1777 on woman (Roussel 1845), says, in effect, that women are not suited to theorising because their first impulse, in their natural roles as wives and mothers, is to be practical, to have an overactive imagination which does not allow them to retain ideas, but which enables them to identify with the suffering of others because of their own weakness. Among other things, Le Doeuff makes two general points about a Rousselesque image of woman. The first is that ideas which explain women's capacities by their sex, and, what is more, which see this sex as constant over time and in space, are still prevalent today in certain areas of biology, psychoanalysis and philosophy. The second point is that the argument which presents such views is so specious, so ideological in the end, that its very existence in a supposedly philosophical environment constitutes a limit to philosophy, as images constitute a limit.

Utopia

One of the abiding images that Le Doeuff analyses in *The Philosophical Imaginary* and elsewhere is Utopia. Thus in an article published in English in 1982 (Le Doeuff 1982: 441–66), she discusses the way Utopia, in the famous works of More, Bacon and Campanella, amounts to 'a defense and illustration of socialized intellectual life' (Le Doeuff 1982: 446). True, Utopia is a reverie of a land of the good life; but because it is also a critique of life in the here and now, it implies both a specific quality of life, and a specific means of obtaining it. Inevitably, the good life is one produced through pedagogical reforms; it requires philosophers to imagine it and educators to teach the uninformed majority about its virtues. Thus, because Utopias are brought about by way of the school, they are specific to societies based on the ideas of scholars for the school. Where Bachelard had seen a scholarly Utopia as being one form of Utopia, Le Doeuff argues that Utopia is essentially scholarly, essentially a society existing for the school. This scenario is given a contemporary twist when Le Doeuff argues that the modern critique of the power of the intellectual master – as proposed by the New Philosophers – presupposes that an intellectualist Utopia were already realised. These 'ideologues', are, says Le Doeuff, 'actually following the dreams of the first utopias' (Le Doeuff 1982: 462). Through the image of Utopia, the fantasy of the philosopher would produce a world where the intellectual master already has absolute power. The real Utopia, then, is announced by the fantasy that society is already for the school.

Through a style that evokes the place of enunciation, through a philosophy that shows that 'there is no thinking which does not wander', that does not proceed by digressions, and through a sense of engagement that is supple and reflexive, Michèle Le Doeuff has begun to give philosophy a new face. What would give her work even greater interest, perhaps, is if she engaged more fully with the hidden face (the images, etc.) of the philosophy canon. For although the work of a Pierre Roussel is no doubt significant in gauging how science has defined 'woman', Roussel would hardly qualify as a philosopher: certainly not substantively, because so many of his notions are unexamined, nor formally, for he was an eighteenth-century doctor. Le Doeuff has already shown the way in her commentaries on Descartes, Kant, Rousseau and Sartre where she has opened up new terrain. The point is to go further – much further – if philosophy is to remain open.

References

Grosz, Elizabeth (1989), *Sexual Subversions. Three French Feminists: Julia Kristeva, Luce Irigaray, Michèle Le Doeuff*, Sydney: Allen & Unwin.

Kant, Immanuel (1970), *Critique of Pure Reason*, trans. Norman Kemp-Smith, London and Basingstoke: Macmillan.

Le Doeuff, Michèle (1982), 'Utopias: Scholarly', trans. Susan Rotenstreich, *Social Research*, 49, 2.

—— (1989a), *Hipparchia's Choice. An Essay Concerning Women, Philosophy, etc.*, trans. Trista Selous, Oxford: Basil Blackwell.

—— (1989b), *The Philosophical Imaginary*, trans. Colin Gordon, Stanford: Stanford University Press.

—— (2003), *The Sex of Knowing*, trans. Kathryn Hamer and Lorraine Code, New York and London: Routledge.

Morris, Meaghan (1981/2), 'Operative reasoning: Michèle Le Doeuff, philosophy and feminism', *Ideology and Consciousness*, 9.

Roussel, Pierre (1845 [1777]) *Système physique et moral de la femme*, Paris: Charpentier.

See also: **Bachelard, Irigaray, Kristeva**

Le Doeuff's major writings

(2003) *The Sex of Knowing*, trans. Kathryn Hamer and Lorraine Code, New York and London: Routledge.

(1989a) *Hipparchia's Choice. An Essay Concerning Women, Philosophy, etc.*, trans. Trista Selous, Oxford: Basil Blackwell.

(1989b) *The Philosophical Imaginary*, trans. Colin Gordon, Stanford: Stanford University Press.

(1982) 'Utopias: Scholarly', trans. Susan Rotenstreich, *Social Research*, 49, 2.

(1977) 'Women and philosophy', *Radical Philosophy*, 17.

Further reading

Deutscher, Max, ed. (2000), *Michèle Le Doeuff: Operative Philosophy and Imaginary Practice*, Amherst and New York: Humanity Press.

Grosz, Elizabeth (1989), *Sexual Subversions. Three French Feminists: Julia Kristeva, Luce Irigaray, Michèle Le Doeuff*, Sydney: Allen & Unwin, Ch. 6.

POST-MARXISM

Post-Marxism questions the reductive, and anti-democratic nature of Marxism, and of any political movement which explains changes in history in terms of the role of a specific class, or privileged agency. Post-Marxism accepts the inspiration deriving from Marx's political involvement, but denies the Marxist emphasis on the economy as determinate, or on the idea that there is a universal class – the proletariat – which will usher in the era of socialism. Post-Marxists now often argue for radical democracy. In Hannah Arendt's work, the theme of democracy is explored in relation to freedom, community and human rights. Badiou, despite his mathematical leaning, still identifies with the revolutionary tradition.

GIORGIO AGAMBEN (b.1942)

Giorgio Agamben is a philosopher of Italian origin who, since the World Trade Centre attacks in September 2001, has challenged the wide use of emergency measures for people control. Indeed, while en route to give lectures at New York University in January 2004, Agamben became personally involved when, at New York airport, he refused to conform to the US requirement that visitors provide bio-metric information to confirm their identity. As a result, Agamben was unable to enter the United States and had to return to Italy.

Agamben has taught at the universities of Verona and Venice in Italy, and has been a visiting professor at the Collège de philosophie in Paris, as well as at a number of American universities, such as the University of California at Irvine. His contributions to political phi-losophy on the subjects of life (particularly bare life), sovereignty, power, the law and the exception have now been recognised as opening up a new era in thinking about politics. Agamben is, how-ever, also a noted theorist of art and aesthetics, particularly in the fields of poetry and language. Although a new ontology, based in ethics, also underpins his thought, the emphasis here will be on Agamben's ideas on life, art and biopolitics.

During the 1960s, Agamben wrote a thesis on the political thought of Simone Weil at the University of Rome and, in 1966 and 1968, attended Martin Heidegger's Le Thor seminars in Provence, France, on Heraclitus and on Hegel. During the 1970s he established his interdisciplinary orientation working on issues in the fields of lin-guistics, philology, poetics and mediaeval history. His book, *Stanzas* (1977), came out of a fellowship at the Warburg Institute in London in 1974–75. During the 1980s, Agamben edited the Italian edition of Walter Benjamin's works, and it is Benjamin's essay, 'Critique of Violence', which has greatly influenced Agamben's analyses of sovereignty. Always in touch with developments in artistic life, Agamben played the part of Philip in Pasolini's film, *The Gospel According to St. Matthew* (1964).

Zoē, Bios *and Biopolitics*

A key distinction maintained as a continual source of reflection by Agamben in his work – one stemming from Aristotle and classical Greek political thought – is that between *zoē* and *bios* as descriptors of life. *Zoē* refers to life as bare physical survival, including biological reproduction and domestic labour (of the household: *oikos*), as well as all the labour required to sustain biological life – the labour that was largely done by slaves. *Zoē* is thus the level of necessity and of means, not that of ends. The latter is the province of *bios*. Thus, for classical Greek culture, to remain immured in bare life was to remain at the animal level of necessity, rather than to achieve a fulfilling *way* of life as *bios*: life as freedom and ends.

Bios is the sphere of politics proper – of the polis – the sphere of freedom and the creation of a form of life. It is the sphere from which slaves, women and children were excluded, as they were part of life as *zoē*. They could not arise to the level of freedom. Hannah Arendt (a key influence on Agamben) even goes so far as to equate the social domain in its essence with necessity (with means), which implies that purely social activity would be excluded from the polis (see Arendt 1958: 38–49). Agamben is particularly interested today in the mode of exclusion of such a category of activity or existence – of *zoē* – as the being/activity of bare life.

In addition, Agamben is interested in the focus on bare life that emerges in Foucault's theory of 'biopolitics'. First mentioned as early as 1976 in the last chapter of the first volume of the *Histoire de la sexualité* (Foucault 1976: 183), the term was further elaborated in lectures Foucault gave in Paris at the Collège de France in the academic year, 1978–79. Like the theme of governmentality, biopolitics has become an important aspect of Foucault's thought, even though it was never the subject of a full-length book, and is quite different to the approach Foucault later takes to the history of sexuality, where the individual subject assumes centre stage.

For Foucault, biopolitics arises in the eighteenth century, and is defined as 'the way attempts were made to rationalise the problems raised for governmental practice by phenomena proper to a collection of living beings constituted as a population: health, hygiene, natality, longevity, races' (Foucault 1989: 109). Agamben sees this as the emergence, in the political domain, of bare life, after so many centuries of its being excluded. Biopolitics brings the domain of power and government out of a strictly juridical framework, where, in particular, Liberalism had placed it, and into the domain of life as the health – in the broadest sense – of populations.

Homo sacer *and Sovereignty*

'Exclusion' also needs explanation. For what is excluded is invariably included in some way – if we are dealing with the domain of politics. Biopolitics brings with it the echo of Roman Law, where *homo sacer* is the one who cannot be sacrificed (cannot have a definite legal or moral status), yet is the one who can be killed by anyone – because of this entity's bare life status. *Homo sacer* is thus the point of exception that gives the law its capacity to function according to the normal case. The law needs an outside, external element so as to constitute its internal order. *Homo sacer* is thus included in the legal system only by being excluded (in this sense it evokes the membership of set theory, as discussed by Badiou, where belonging does not entail membership. *Homo sacer* belongs to the polity without being a member).

The '*sacer*' in *homo sacer* evokes the sacred, but not as sacrifice. Sacrifice entails purification and consecration prior to the act of killing (the sacrifice). A passage – frequently paraphrased by Agamben, from Émile Beneveniste's *Indo-European Language and Society* (1973), explains exactly what is at stake: 'A man who is called *sacer* is stained with a real pollution which puts him outside human society: contact with him must be shunned. If someone kills him, this does not count as homicide' (Benveniste 1973: 453).

Homo sacer, then, is the outcast who can be killed, but not sacrificed. Sacrifice is a ritualised activity and thus has a quasi-legal status as it is enacted according to forms of the law (Agamben 1998: 102). *Homo sacer* is never subjected to 'sanctioned forms of execution' (Agamben 1998: 103) Thus, '*sacer*', in the sense that Agamben wants to emphasise is 'bare life', is '*zoē*, in the Greek sense, the fact of being alive and nothing more, the fact of life exposed to death. According to our author, 'the production of bare life is the originary activity of sovereignty' (Agamben 1998: 83). The point is that the sacredness of life is currently claimed to be opposed to power, whereas *homo sacer* implies that sacredness is constitutive of power. A symmetry exists between the two. Sacredness (inclusive exclusion) becomes the original mode of the inclusion (as that which is excluded) of bare life in the juridical order. Life is sacred only to the extent that it is 'taken into the sovereign exception' (Agamben 1998: 85).

Many questions arise about the nature of the relationship between *homo sacer*, the law and sovereignty in the complicated history of human, and particularly European, societies, and Agamben addresses a number of these. He considers, for example, the relationship between religious sentiment and the sacred, the nature of the sovereign's body, the connection between Roman law and modern legal forms, the basis, in the foundation of democracy, of *Habeas corpus* as a presentation of the (natural) body (Agamben 1998: 124). He also addresses these questions in his quest to show that sovereignty and bare life are inextricably linked, that *vita* is not a juridical concept in Roman law, but is excluded. In answer to the criticism that he is on thin ice when it comes to legal history, Agamben has claimed in an interview that he is working with paradigms, not taking an historical or sociological approach (Raulff 2004: 609).[1]

State of Exception

Quite pointedly (for it touches upon post 9/11 politics), a state of exception, which is *homo sacer*, gives force to sovereignty: after Carl Schmitt, whose work is also analysed in his more recent work, *State of Exception* (2005), Agamben says that the one is sovereign who can determine the state of exception. The paradox of sovereignty is that the sovereign, like *homo sacer*, is both 'outside and inside the juridical order' (Agamben 1998: 15). According to Schmitt, Liberalism is unable to understand the true nature of politics because it assumes that, on the whole, the juridical system will incorporate political events, will anticipate them and so make legal relations the dominant form of political relations. One should think here of constitutions setting the ground rules of political conduct and the court system as ensuring that constitutions are adhered to by all parties. Were such circumstances to be the norm, there would not be any issue of establishing the nature of sovereignty. However, Schmitt argues, political life is subject as much to the contingent and the unpredictable as it is to any normality anticipated by the law. The contingent and the unpredictable form the basis of the state of exception. The sovereign must, first of all, decide when a state of exception exists and, second, decide upon strategies – including the suspension of normal legal processes – to deal with it. These include, above all, calling a state of emergency. There is thus a correlation between the sovereign and the exception. The exception has no power as such (for the exception is determined by the sovereign); however, without the exception, it would be impossible for sovereignty to be and to maintain itself. Following Jean-Luc Nancy, Agamben invokes the old German term 'ban' to describe this situation (Agamben 1998: 28–29). He who is banned by the law is not simply set outside the law, but is '*abandoned* by it, that is, exposed and threatened on the threshold in which life and law, outside and inside, become indistinguishable. It is literally not possible to say whether the one who has been banned is outside or inside the juridical order' (Agamben 1998: 28–29, Agamben's emphasis). Thus, the law both posits the sovereign and makes the sovereign the one who is also outside the law. This is the paradox of sovereignty.

Violence

The issue arising for contemporary societies with their juridical systems, and in particular, for Western style liberal democracies, concerns the extent to which the empty space beyond (and within) the law is taken up by violence. For, with the law (legally) suspended, the will of the sovereign becomes supreme. This 'will' can be imposed on a situation with any means chosen by the sovereign, and these might well include violence. Indeed, the sovereign in Hobbes is precisely the extent to which the State of Nature 'survives in the person of the sovereign' (Agamben 1998: 35), and we know that this state is one where, famously, people live in fear of violent death (Hobbes 1962: 100). In the state of war, 'nothing is unjust' (Hobbes 1962: 101).

Here then is the worry behind the paradox of sovereignty: the risk that a sovereign might resort to violence in an irresponsible way. Agamben points, for example, to the suspension of law (including the suspension of the Geneva conventions on the conduct of war) in the 'war on terrorism' with respect to those interned by America at Guantanamo Bay in Cuba. There, prisoners have no legal identity and recall the plight of stateless people between the wars referred to by Hannah Arendt (see Arendt 1951: 292). Agamben also cites the arbitrary policies involving the suspension of the law being employed to deal with asylum seekers. Increasingly, asylum seekers are purposely processed and their claims assessed outside the boundaries of any state, in international territory. They thus have no legal status and thus cannot appeal to any authority if their human rights are violated. They are non-persons.

Agamben's further point is that the condition of the asylum seeker seems to be the general condition on the horizon, as ever larger numbers of people find that conditions have become impossible within the state of origin. Increasingly, too, therefore, the political entity of the nation-state is unequal to meeting the challenge of this new political reality. It is unable, for example, to guarantee human rights by virtue of a person's humanity, founded as the state is on essentially legal principles.

Law can be in force without significance, as illustrated by Kafka's *The Trial* (1968), and as demonstrated to be the normal case by deconstruction. Moreover, the 'force of law', is the phrase used when the sovereign rules by decree, the latter being said to have the 'force of law'. 'Force of law' thus implies that what would normally be outside the law (arbitrary will) is brought inside. Indeed, decrees founded on violence (sovereign violence) mean that a zone of indistinction is introduced between law and nature, outside and inside.

Human Rights and Bare Life

What is the connection between human rights and the nation state? Natural, or bare life is the subject of the French Declaration of 1789, not the free self-conscious individual. Also, the Declaration separates active rights of the citizen from passive rights acquired by virtue of one's humanity. Can passive rights (those acquired simply by virtue of being human) be sustained and defended? The record is not good when it comes to supporting refugees and stateless people.

Refugees put sovereignty in question because they cannot be classified in terms of 'blood and soil', 'nativity and nationality' (cf. the German 'blood and soil' and the juridical *ius soli* and *ius sanguinis*, from Roman law), but only in terms of passive human rights (Agamben 1998: 131). The problem is that human rights are linked to the rights of the citizen. Bare life has no rights.

> What is essential is that, every time refugees represent not individual cases but – as happens more and more often today – a mass phenomenon, both these organisations [Bureau Nansen (1922) and the UN High Commission for Refugees (1951)] and individual states prove themselves, despite their solemn invocations of the 'sacred and inalienable' rights of man, absolutely incapable of resolving the problem and even of confronting it adequately.
>
> (Agamben 1998: 133)

The problem concerns the separation of the rights of man from the rights of the citizen. Rwanda is an example where human life, as sacred, could be killed but not sacrificed.

As Hannah Arendt said, human rights are connected to the fate of the nation-state, and that when the latter declines, so does the defence of human rights. The implication is that globalisation impacts negatively on human rights.

The Camps

A key element of politics for Agamben is that it is a big mistake to see the Holocaust as sacrifice. Rather, the Jew becomes *homo sacer* (can be killed by anyone, but not sacrificed). 'The dimension in which the extermination took place is neither religion nor law, but biopolitics' (Agamben 1998: 114). The work of both Foucault and Arendt is limited, however, to the extent that it does not include a consideration of the camps.

The Nazi concentration camp is the exemplar of the space of the state of exception, created under the *Schutzhaft* (protective custody), which allowed for imprisonment without trial, and had no need for a juridical foundation in existing institutions.

The camp is included in the political system through its own exclusion. 'Whoever entered the camp moved in a zone of indistinction between outside and inside, exception and rule, licit and illicit, in which the very concepts of subjective right and juridical protection no longer made any sense' (Agamben 1998: 170). Unlike previous uses of 'states of emergency' based on a factual situation, the camp is the 'most absolute biopolitical space ever to have been realized' (Agamben 1998: 170) in order to confirm the power of the sovereign. No act committed against the inmates of the camps could count as a crime. How was this possible?

Without the camps, without refugees, without limit cases of life and death – that is, without factual situations – Agamben's thesis would have no meaning. In other words, it is not a matter of searching for the essence of the Western juridico-political system in the interest of a new political philosophy, but of understanding how, in light of the existing juridical imperatives, the most horrific political events of our era – from Nazi concentration camps to Guantanamo – could come about.

Auschwitz

In a separate book, which elaborates on the nature of the camps, *Remnants of Auschwitz: The Witness and the Archive* (2002) Agamben investigates how witnessing and thus testimony are possible in relation to the Nazi concentration camps, particularly Auschwitz. How is testimony possible? Agamben's view is that it is possible and that to deny this is, unconsciously, to accept the Nazi view that no one would believe the survivors of the camps when they described what happened. The camps are thus an inexpressible mystical realm. It is also important to link the camps to law, even if many (including Eichmann) wanted to put them beyond the law.

Using Émile Benveniste's theory of *énonciation*, (enunciating act) which sees subjectivity established in the act of language, Agamben analyses the category of the *Muselmann* (Moslem), described particularly poignantly in Primo Levi's writings. The *Muselmann* is a person in the last stages of survival, on the edge of death, a person whose status consists of nothing other than being 'bare life'. Testimony takes place in the space between the sayable and the unsayable which captures the position of the *Muselmann*. Testimony takes place even though the subject (as in the *énonciation*) is constitutively fractured.

In sum, Agamben argues for the possibility of 'speaking Auschwitz', or bearing witness, against the notion (asserted by the Nazis), that the event is too monstrous ever to be 'sayable'. Agamben is for the idea that Auschwitz is sayable, that there can be a witness: 'The witness attests to the fact that there can be testimony because there is an inseparable division and non-coincidence between the inhuman and the human, the living being and the speaking being, the *Muselmann* and the survivor' (Agamben 2002: 157). Again: '*The authority of the witness consists in his capacity to speak solely in the name of an incapacity to speak – that is, in his or her being a subject*' (Agamben 2002: 158, Agamben's emphasis). It is a matter of establishing a monument to the impossibility of fixing the truth in relation to real events, or to memory. Testimony occurs where there is an impossibility of speaking.

What we have witnessed, then, is the depth of insight that Agamben's theory has achieved in addressing the question of the camps.

Note

1 For critiques of Agamben on this issue, see Fitzpatrick (2005: 51–53) and Van der Walt (2005: 279 n. 5). Both critiques, in their own way, dispute the validity of the category of 'bare life'. Both tend to make law, or sacrifice entirely primary, so that there is no domain exterior to the law (Fitzpatrick), or one exterior to sacrifice (Van der Walt).

References

Agamben, Giorgio (1998), *Homo Sacer: Sovereign Power and Bare Life*, trans. Daniel Heller-Roazen, Stanford: Stanford University Press.

—— (2002), *Remnants of Auschwitz: The Witness and the Archive*, trans. Daniel Heller-Roazen, New York: Zone Books.

—— (2005), *State of Exception*, trans. Kevin Attell, Chicago and London: University of Chicago Press.

Arendt, Hannah (1951), *The Origins of Totalitarianism*, New York: Harcourt Brace and World..

—— (1958), *The Human Condition*, Chicago: The University of Chicago Press.

Benveniste, Émile (1973), *Indo-European Language and Society*, trans. Elizabeth Palmer, London: Faber & Faber.

Fitzpatrick, Peter (2005), 'Bare Sovereignty: *Homo Sacer* and the Insistence of Law' in Andrew Norris, ed., *Politics, Metaphysics, and Death. Essays on Giorgio Agamben's* Homo Sacer, Durham and London: Duke University Press.

Foucault, Michel (1976), *Histoire de la sexualité 1. : La volonté de savoir*, Paris: Gallimard.

Foucault, Michel (1989), *Résumé des cours, 1979–1982*, Paris: Julliard.

Hobbes, Thomas (1962), *Leviathan*, ed. Michael Oakeshot, New York and London: Collier, Collier-Macmillan.

Kafka, Franz (1968 [1925]), *The Trial*, trans. Willa and Edwin Muir, New York: Schocken Books.

Raulff, Ulrich (2004), 'An Interview with Giorgio Agamben', *German Law Journal*, 5, 5, 609–614.

Van der Walt, Johan (2005), 'Interrupting the Myth of the *Partage*: Reflections on Sovereignty and Sacrifice in the Work of Nancy, Agamben and Derrida', *Law and Critique*, 16, 277–299.

See also: **Arendt, Badiou, Benjamin, Foucault, Kafka**

Agamben's major writings

(2005a [2003]) *State of Exception*, trans. Kevin Attell, Chicago and London: University of Chicago Press.

(2005b [2000]) *The Time that Remains: A Commentary on the Letter to the Romans*, trans. Patricia Dailey, Stanford: Stanford University Press.

(2004 [2002]) *The Open: Man and Animal*, trans. Kevin Attell Stanford: Stanford University Press.

(2002 [1998]) *Remnants of Auschwitz: The Witness and the Archive*, trans. Daniel Heller-Roazen, New York: Zone Books.

(2000 [1996]) *Means without End: Notes on Politics*, trans. Vincenzo Binetti and Cesare Casarino, Minneapolis and London: University of Minnesota Press.

(1999a [1970]) *The Man without Content*, trans. Georgia Albert, Stanford: Stanford University Press.

(1999b) *Potentialities: Collected Essays in Philosophy* ed. and trans. Daniel Heller-Roazen, Stanford: Stanford University Press.

(1999c [1996]) *The End of the Poem: Studies in Poetics* trans. Daniel Heller-Roazen, Stanford: Stanford University Press.

(1998 [1995]) *Homo Sacer: Sovereign Power and Bare Life*, trans. Daniel Heller-Roazen, Stanford: Stanford University Press.

(1995 [1985]) *Idea of Prose*, trans. Michael Sullivan, Albany: State University of New York Press.

(1993a [1990]) *The Coming Community*, trans. Michael Hardt, Minneapolis: University of Minnesota Press.

(1993b [1978]) *Infancy and History: The Destruction of Experience*, trans. Liz Heron, London and New York: Verso.

(1993c [1977]) *Stanzas: Word and Phantasm in Western Culture*, trans. Ronald L. Martinez, Minneapolis: University of Minnesota Press.

Further Reading

Franchi, Stefano (2004), 'Passive Politics', *Contre Temps*, 5, (online journal).

McQuillan, Colin (2005), 'The Political Life in Giorgio Agamben', *Kritikos*, Vol. 2 July.

Mills, Catherine (2004), 'Agamben's Messianic Politics: Biopolitics, Abaondonment and Happy Life', *Contre Temps*, 5, (online journal).

Wall, Carl Thomas (1999), *Radical Passivity: Levinas, Blanchot, and Agamben*, New York: State University of New York Press.

THEODOR ADORNO (1903–1969)

Adorno was born Theodor Wiesengrund Adorno in 1903. According to Martin Jay he may have dropped the Wiesengrund when he joined the Institute for Social Research in New York in 1938 because of its sounding Jewish. Between 1918 and 1919, at the age of 15, Adorno studied under Siegfried Kracauer. After completing his Gymnasium period, he attended the University of Frankfurt where he studied philosophy, sociology, psychology and music. He received a doctorate in philosophy in 1924. In 1925, Adorno went to Vienna to study composition under Alban Berg, and at the same time he began to publish articles on music, especially on the work of Schönberg. After becoming disillusioned with the 'irrationalism' of the Vienna circle, he returned to Frankfurt in 1926 and began a *Habilitationschrift* on Kant and Freud, entitled 'The concept of the unconscious in the transcendental theory of mind'. This thesis was rejected, but in 1931, he completed another: *Kierkegaard: The Construction of the Aesthetic*, which was published in 1933 on the day of Hitler's rise to power. Once his thesis was accepted, Adorno joined the Frankfurt Institute for Social Research after Max Horkheimer became director. To escape from Nazism, the Institute moved to Zürich in 1934, and Adorno moved to England.

In 1938, Adorno rejoined the Institute, which was now located in New York, and worked on the Princeton Radio Research Project, headed by Paul Larzarsfeld. While in America he worked on a number of different projects, including one with Thomas Mann on *Doktor Faustus*. With Max Horkheimer, Adorno sounded a pessimistic note about Enlightenment reason in the *Dialectic of Enlightenment*, which was first published in 1947. In 1953, at the age of 50, Adorno left the United States and returned to Frankfurt to take up a position with the Institute, and in 1959 he became its director following Horkheimer's retirement. By the end of the following decade Adorno became embroiled in a conflict with the students who occupied the Institute's offices. Adorno died in 1969 in Switzerland while writing what many believe to be his most important work, *Aesthetic Theory* (1997).

Music

Adorno was an accomplished musician and composer who championed the cause of Schönberg and twentieth century music, while at the same time giving reinterpretations of classical composers such as Beethoven. He had a close relationship with Alban Berg, with whom he conducted a voluminous correspondence (see Adorno and Berg (2005)), and he wrote widely on the relationship between music and society, although this came with difficulty in relation to popular music.

Post-modern Thinker?

Debate on Adorno's work has, in part, centred on the extent to which he anticipates aspects of post-modern and post-structuralist thought. Particular attention is often given here to Adorno's critique of 'identity-thinking' in his *Negative Dialectics* (Adorno 1990). While it is necessary to understand what Adorno means here, we should also bear in mind a number of points which clearly separate his project from those inspired by nominally French thought.

Let us begin with science. While Julia Kristeva has said that structuralist-inspired semiotics must take its cue from developments in quantum physics, and while Jacques Derrida cited Gödel directly in formulating his philosophical notion of 'undecidability' (Derrida 1981: 219) – that is, while semiotics and post-structuralism in France forged bonds between the natural and the human sciences – Adorno, like other members of the Frankfurt School, saw modern science as inherently positivist. As Adorno aimed to produce a dialectical thought which did not 'positivise' in any way, science in general was treated with the greatest suspicion, if not contempt. Science in Adorno's philosophy would even be the form of thought he most opposed given that, like positivism in general, it is seen to be absolutely dependent on the logic of identity. Philosophy has allowed itself to be terrorised by science, Adorno claims (Adorno 1990: 109). But philosophical truth does not equal scientific truth, and philosophy should not shy away from this. In sum, 'Philosophy is neither a science nor the "cogitative poetry" to which positivists would degrade it in a stupid oxymoron' (Adorno 1990: 109). Second, Adorno retains – albeit in his works of cultural criticism rather than his philosophy – the distinction between 'essence' and 'appearance' (a distinction questioned by French thought of post-structuralist inspiration) in order roundly to reject the superficial nature of appearance in modern capitalist society. For Adorno, the world of appearance, as for Plato before him, is a world of images and mere semblances, a world of relativism and, most of all, of reification. On this reading, reification and commodities in the capitalist world are almost identical; commodities take on a life of their own independently of the conditions of their production. Commodities hide the truth of their illusory nature. They serve to titillate 'the reified consciousness' which is 'a moment in the totality of the reified world' (Adorno 1990: 95).

Appearance and Essence

Moreover, by contrast with post-1968 French thought, ideology still plays an important part in Adorno's analyses of social conditions, even if, as he shows in *Prisms* (Adorno 1981: 30-34), the analysis of ideology can no longer rely on the 'transcendent' method, where the critic claims to be detached from the milieu being analysed. The difference between essence and appearance entails the ideological effect of reification. For behind the reified appearances, lies the truth of the 'phantasmagoria' of commodity production.

This truth is that human beings, despite what they might think, are unfree; they have restrictive forms of thought and action imposed upon them by the existing social conditions of capitalist production; they live in 'the open-air prison which the world is becoming' (Adorno 1981: 34). People adapt to these conditions rather than oppose them. Consequently, the freedom that Simmel talks about in the same context is a myth. 'In a state of unfreedom', says Adorno, 'no one, of course, has a liberated consciousness' (Adorno 1990: 95).

Finally, Adorno places far more weight on the role of consciousness than is the case with comparable French thinkers such as Lacan or Foucault. Although he spent time developing ways of escaping a reductive view of the individual as 'socialised', and although his position here is in other respects complex, Adorno's view of the unconscious is extremely simple. First of all, the unconscious (like Freud's work in general) receives little elaboration in Adorno's philosophy. On one of the rare occasions in which he actually refers explicitly to the unconscious in *Negative Dialectics*, he says:

> When the doctrine of the unconscious reduces the individual to a small number of recurring constants and conflicts it does reveal a misanthropic disinterest in the concretely unfolded ego; and yet it reminds the ego of the shakiness of its definitions compared with those of the id, and thus of its tenuous and ephemeral nature.
>
> (Adorno 1990: 352)

Even if 'shakiness', 'tenuous', and 'ephemeral' suggest a movement away from the primacy of consciousness, there is little evidence that the unconscious poses a real obstacle to philosophy or to thought.

Identity/nonidentity

In other words, Adorno still seems to be far more beholden to a logic of identity than some of his more recent readers suggest. On the other hand, it is also true that his aspirations are in the direction of a thought that is not wholly and solely indebted to the logic of identity. Thus when he begins to rethink the nature of philosophy in *Negative Dialectics*, Adorno makes two key points: first, that philosophy 'lives on' after the Marxist attempt to discredit it for being too idealist had failed; and, second, that philosophy needs a sense of its own impotence before the materiality of the world in order that it might remain creative and open to the new. The materiality of the world is philosophy's inexpressible side. The essential character of philosophy thus consists in being only too well aware of the limitedness of the concepts with which it works. 'Disenchantment of the concept is the antidote of philosophy' (Adorno 1990: 13). In effect, a truly creative philosophy – which, for Adorno *is* philosophy – seeks out those things which are a challenge to thought itself. These things can be generally designated by the terms 'heterogeneity', or more pointedly, by 'nonidentity'.

Negative Dialectics

Unlike Hegel's system in which the heterogeneous element would be reclaimed dialectically through the principle of the 'negation of the negation', Adorno announces the principle of 'negative dialectics', a principle which refuses any kind of affirmation, or positivity, a principle of thorough-going negativity. Thus negative dialectics is nonidentity. This key element in Adorno's thought has a number of synonyms in addition to the ones we have given above – for instance: 'contradiction', 'dissonance', 'freedom', 'the divergent' and 'the inexpressible'. Despite the importance of nonidentity, Adorno also says that no thought can in fact express nonidentity: for 'to think is to identify'. Identity thinking can only think contradiction as pure, that is, as another identity. Where, and how, then, does nonidentity thinking actually leave its mark on thought? In short, what is the material basis of negative dialectics in thought?

To begin with, the material aspect is not philosophy as poetry, or as art. For philosophy as art is equivalent of the erasure of philosophy. Nor is philosophy permitted, according to Adorno, to give in to an aesthetic impulse. This does not of course preclude experimenting in the presentation of new concepts, a process which may lead to poetry, just as the most avant-garde art might be an immanent conceptualisation. Nevertheless, philosophy must 'void its aestheticism'. 'Its affinity to art does not entitle it to borrow from art,' and here Adorno continues the point in a tone for which he has become notorious '. . . least of all by virtue of the intuitions which barbarians take for the prerogatives of art' (Adorno 1990: 15). All that philosophy can do in such circumstances is continue as philosophy. To give up in light of the impossibility of expressing nonidentity would imply that philosophy had misunderstood the heterogeneous, dissonant nature of nonidentity; in other words, to give up 'this sense is to misunderstand that nonidentity is impure – not even a pure contradiction. Thoughts intended to think the inexpressible by abandoning thought falsify the inexpressible' (Adorno 1990: 110). Nonidentity is possibly philosophy's hidden, negative *telos*. It was thus Marx's mistake to think of the end of philosophy in precisely these terms.

The other sense in which philosophy might come to an end is if it took the form (as in Hegel) of Absolute knowledge. Then every problem confronting philosophy – especially its relationship with the material world – would be resolved through the affirmative principle of the negation which produces an affirmation.

By a surprising series of reversals, Adorno turns philosophy's potential limitations into a philosophical gesture whose implications are perhaps now only beginning to be appreciated. 'In principle', Adorno confirms, 'philosophy can always go astray, which is the sole reason why it can go forward' (Adorno: 1990: 14). Philosophy, therefore, is a negative dialectics in the strongest sense; it is itself the very nonidentity it seeks to conceptualise. In this, the role of language becomes crucial because language is equivalent to the presentation of philosophy's 'unfreedom' as equivalent, to the impossibility of conceptualising nonidentity. Were language to cease to be important in philosophy, the latter would 'resemble science'.

Adorno's declarative statements in *Negative Dialectics* need to be read in conjunction with his work in aesthetics and literary criticism. In this regard, *Minima Moralia: Reflections on a Damaged Life*, written during the Second World War in an aphoristic style counters, like Kierkegaard (on whom Adorno also wrote), Hegel's dialectical theory which 'abhorring anything isolated, cannot admit aphorisms as such' (Adorno 1985: 155). In his reflections on a diversity of topics, Adorno seeks – practically, we may assume – to make a philosophical statement, one that takes up the place of the heterogeneity of human experience.

Art and Society

Similarly, Adorno's attraction to avant-garde music and art, particularly the music of Schönberg, Webern, and Berg, was strongly motivated by a desire to see avant-garde works defy the homogenising effects of the commercialisation (read: reification) of art, where art objects would be reduced to exchange-value. Subjectivity is reduced to the status of a 'mere object' by exchange-value. There is thus a desire in Adorno to preserve the sanctity, as it were, of subjectivity embodied in the art object, against the onslaught of the market where value is equated with price. Through a paratactic style (juxtaposition of statement with the link between them being made explicit), and other devices, Adorno's presentation of his theory of aesthetics in *Aesthetic Theory* participates in an effort to by-pass the reduction of art and thought to the culture industry. One way it does this is at the level of presentation itself. Although still awaiting final revision at the time of Adono's death in 1969, the manuscript, and subsequent new translation into English, does not have the usual formal separation into chapters, but has the appearance of a seamless text, with the transition from one theme to another taking place without being signalled. Paragraphs often continue for pages and topics are not dealt with sequentially or systematically – which would emphasise logical progression – but follow Adorno's principle of 'constellation', where elements only adhere tangentially to a central theme. The work itself, therefore, defies the easy acceptance required by commodification.

At least two important principles emerge in *Aesthetic Theory* in relation to a theory of the artwork. The first is the principle of tension between the autonomy of the artwork and its being a *fait social* (see, for example, Adorno 1997: 225). Thus, the 'serious' artwork must be recognised as being unique and a source of resistance to the existing state of society, to the point where resistance keeps it alive (Adorno 1997: 226), and yet it cannot be thought or experienced outside its social context.

The second principle is that every artwork, including the most radical, contains a conservative element to the extent that it is a vehicle for helping to 'secure the spheres of the spirit and culture' (Adorno 1997: 234). Spirit becomes the point of opposition to the totalising tendencies of society. While avant-garde strategy is a point of reference, it is clear that Adorno's key reference points are Classical and Romantic rather than hypermodern or post-modern.

High and Low Art and Culture

Some (e.g. Lyotard) came to see Adorno's approach as a last-ditch attempt to maintain a boundary between high art and popular culture just at a time when the logic and social basis of such a boundary was becoming untenable in the name of the very political values (e.g. opposition to conventional Marxism) to which Adorno himself subscribed.

Furthermore, in light of Bataille's work, it is clear that exchange-value can be subverted as much by the very 'low' elements (obscenity) in social life, as by the highest and most spiritually charged products of the avant-garde. Both can entail the distancing necessary to counter the ephemeral immediacy of consumer pleasure. Perhaps the 'low' even more than the 'high'; for ultimately 'high' art depends on the judgement of criticism as to its nature and quality; it is thereby incorporated into the play of concepts. In other words, avant-garde art and philosophy become interdependent and all the more so – if an analogy with *Negative Dialectics* holds – to the extent that the art object becomes inseparable from its materiality (nonidentity). Grasping the force and significance of avant-garde art requires the use of concepts which can never do a work justice; for the materiality of the work constitutes its uniqueness, and this defies conceptualisation. As Peter Osborne has remarked, 'It is out of this critique of identity-thinking that Adorno's basic conception of aesthetic experience, as the experience of the "non-identical", arises' (Osborne 1991: 28).

Overall, Adorno's *Aesthetic Theory* struggles to reach an accommodation between avant-garde art that risks being 'normalised' and reified in capitalist society, and the essentially radical autonomy of art objects which *qua* art objects are singularly out of harmony with the social conditions (including criticism) which enable them to speak at all. There is another aspect to the question, however, one that perhaps Adorno forgets. It is that the conceptualising facility itself could become impoverished through a continual rejection of its worth and efficacy. While the detail of art which defies the system because it defies conceptualisation is no doubt fundamental, conceptualisation might well be also. In other words, what Adorno does not readily acknowledge is that a certain degree of identity philosophy is as essential as material nonidentity.

References

Adorno, T.W. (1981), *Prisms*, trans. Samuel Weber, Cambridge, Mass.: MIT Press.
—— (1985), *Minima Moralia*, trans. E.F.N. Jephcott, London: Verso.
—— (1990), *Negative Dialectics*, trans. E.B. Ashton, London: Routledge.
—— (1997), *Aesthetic Theory*, trans. Robert Hullot-Kentor, Minneapolis: University of Minnesota Press.
Adorno, T.W. and Berg, Alban (2005), *Correspondence, 1925–1935*, trans. Wieland Hoban, Cambridge and Malden, Mass.: Polity.
Derrida, Jacques (1981), *Dissemination*, trans. Barbara Johnson, Chicago: University of Chicago Press.

Osborne, Peter (1991), 'Adorno and the metaphysics of modernism: The problem of a "postmodern" art' in Andrew Benjamin ed., *The Problems of Modernity: Adorno and Benjamin*, London: Routledge.

See also: **Benjamin, Derrida, Habermas**

Adorno's major writings

(2005) *In Search of Wagner*, trans. Rodney Livingston, London and New York: Verso.

(2001) *Metaphysics: Concept and Problems*, trans. Edmund Jephcott, Stanford: Stanford University Press.

(2000) *The Adorno Reader*, Brian O'Connor ed., Oxford and Malden, Mass.: Blackwell.

(1998) *Beethoven: the Philosophy of Music: Fragments and Texts*, trans. Edmund Jephcott, Stanford: Stanford University Press.

(1997 [1970]) *Aesthetic Theory*, trans. Robert Hullot-Kentor, Minneapolis: University of Minnesota Press.

(1992 [1963]) *Quasi una Fantasia: Essays on Modern Music*, trans. Rodney Livingston, London: Verso.

(1991a) *The Culture Industry. Selected Essays on Mass Culture*, London: Routledge.

(1991b [1958, 1961]) *Notes to Literature* 2 vols, trans. Shierry Weber Nicholsen, New York: Columbia University Press.

(1990 [1966]) *Negative Dialectics*, trans. E.B. Ashton, London: Routledge.

(1989a [1962]) *Kierkegaard: The Construction of the Aesthetic*, trans. Robert Hullot-Kentor, Minneapolis: University of Minnesota Press.

(1989b [1962]) *Introduction to the Sociology of Music*, trans. E.B. Ashton, New York: Continuum.

(1986 [1964]) *The Jargon of Authenticity*, trans. Knut Tarnowski, London and Henley: Routledge & Kegan Paul.

(1981 [1987]) *Prisms*, trans. Samuel and Shierry Weber, Cambridge, Mass.: MIT Press.

(1978 [1951]) *Minima Moralia, Reflections on a Damaged Life*, trans. E.F.N. Jephcott, London: Verso.

(1973) *The Philosophy of Modern Music*, trans. A. Mitchell and W. Blomster, New York: Seabury Press.

(1972 [1947]) with Max Horkheimer, *The Dialectic of Enlightenment*, trans. John Cumming, New York: Continuum.

(1969 [1950]) with Else Frenkel-Brunswik, Daniel J. Levinson and R. Nevitt Sanford in collaboration with Betty Aron, Maria Hertz Levinson and William Morrow, *The Authoritarian Personality*, New York: Norton.

Further reading

Buck-Morss, Susan (1977), *The Origins of Negative Dialectics*, Sussex: Harvester Press.

DeNora, Tia (2003), *After Adorno: Rethinking Music Sociology*, Cambridge and New York: Cambridge University Press.

Witkin, Robert W. (1998), *Adorno on Music*, London and New York: Routledge.

HANNAH ARENDT (1906–1975)

Hannah Arendt was an intensely controversial political theorist who showed great courage and intelligence. She was passionately concerned to analyse the nature of politics and society in the 'modern age' in light of key events in the 'modern world' – the world of space travel, the theory of uncertainty, the world of the Holocaust and Stalinist death camps. By 'modern age' Arendt means the era of great geographic and scientific discovery – beginning with Columbus and Copernicus – and the period of the twentieth century, which brought the modern age to a close. At the beginning of her great work, *The Human Condition*, Arendt writes that, 'politically, the modern world, in which we live today, was born with the first atomic explosions' (Arendt 1958: 6). While Arendt hardly remained true in her political writings to her claim to focus more on the modern age than on the modern world, it is true that her most systematic and revered works – *The Origins of Totalitarianism*, *The Human Condition* and *On Revolution* – all include important historical references to the period, 1600–1900, as well as to Classical Greece and Rome. As we shall see, two themes in particular are present in Arendt's *oeuvre* to an almost obsessive degree: those of freedom and necessity, and the relationship of the exception to the norm. The profound twist Arendt manages to give to these time-honoured themes makes her work compelling reading in a post-modern age where all idealisms (all considerations of ends) have been put on notice.

Life and Career

Hannah Arendt was born in 1906 in Hanover. At the age of three, her parents returned to the quiet Baltic town of their childhood, Königsberg (where Kant was also born). When Hannah was seven, her father died of a syphilitic condition apparently contracted before his marriage. In the same year, 1913, her paternal grandfather, who had been like a second father to her, also died. Through her mother, Hannah became familiar with the political developments of the day, including the fortunes of the Sparticist faction of the Social

Democratic Party and its leaders, Rosa Luxemburg and Karl Liebknecht – both murdered after the Spartacist inspired workers' uprising of 1919.

In 1924, Arendt went to the University of Marburg to study philosophy under Martin Heidegger, with whom she had an affair. Heidegger's influence in Arendt's work can be seen not only in her valorisation of the Greeks, but also in the etymological method she often employs to establish the exact meaning of key concepts – like 'labour', for example. After the break-up of her relationship with Heidegger in 1925, Arendt became a student of the *Existenz* philosopher, Karl Jaspers. Under Jaspers's supervision, Arendt, in 1929, completed her doctorate, 'The Concept of Love in Augustine'. In the same year, she married Gunther Stern in Paris, and later, in 1932, began writing a biography of a nineteenth-century Jewish woman, and well-known Berlin figure, Rahel Varnhagen. With the rise of Nazism in 1933, Arendt and her husband were forced to flee to Paris, where they had met up with Walter Benjamin and other German Jewish emigrés. With the fall of France in 1940, Arendt managed to escape to America and to establish herself in New York where she taught (mainly at the New School for Social Research) and wrote until her death in 1975.

Totalitarianism

Arendt's first important book after the publication of her thesis – the one which made her famous and established her reputation as an important scholar and intellectual – was *The Origins of Totalitarianism*, published in 1951. Clearly inspired by the terrible events of the Holocaust, only the last third of the first edition directly analyses the rise of Nazism and Stalinism. The first two-thirds of the work outline what Arendt sees as the historical precedents to the totalitarian mode of political behaviour, especially as these apply to the Jewish people as an historical pariah caste. In the second section of the book, Arendt analyses the way that imperialism introduced an administrative structure in which efficiency alone – independently of the ends to be achieved – became the most important element – more important, certainly, than the lives and welfare of the colonised peoples. The horrific mix of racism and administrative massacre come together in aspects of imperialism.

Stateless People: the 'Calamity of the Rightless'

Stateless people, Arendt shows, posed insuperable problems for the nation-state in the period between the wars. Once deprived of citizenship, and thus of a legal identity, stateless people become potential victims of arbitrary police action, action which is outside the rule of the law. Order, rather than law becomes the goal. Here, Arendt begins to show that an essential feature of what she will define as totalitarianism is its concerted effort to deprive its victims of every semblance of identity, both civil and psychological. Thus more important than glorifying the rights of people within a legally constituted state, Arendt suggests, is the fight to save people from being legal anomalies, together with the fight against the wielding of arbitrary power that this often solicits. In effect, although the law is not good in itself, to be deprived of it is such an unspeakable indignity that the status of a criminal is often preferable because it does constitute a legal status, however minimal. The loss of human rights as a stateless person is thus equivalent to the loss of legality – 'of *all* rights' (Arendt 1951: 292).

Another consequence of the deprivation of a civil status is less the loss of freedom and the right to think, than the loss of the right to action and to opinion, and this, because action and opinion are essentially public engagements requiring the recognition of fellow human beings as the *condition sine qua non* of their realisation. This point foreshadows the long discussion and analysis of action as essentially political in Arendt's next book, *The Human Condition* (1958).

In sum, what Arendt calls the 'calamity of the rightless', entails not just a loss of specific human rights (the right to liberty, to equality, to happiness, to life, etc.) – for these have meaning only within a specific community willing to guarantee them; but the loss of law *per se*, of community *per se* (Arendt 1951: 294). Thus abstract human rights, Arendt acknowledges with Edmund Burke, rights deemed to exist independently of any community, are in fact no rights at all.

With the Holocaust and the Stalinist death camps as quintessential instances of the totalitarian form of politics, Arendt thus points to the way that whole communities of people – but particularly the Jews – were systematically deprived of their human rights; were systematically deprived of their humanity, in short. Of course, the question that is there, woven into the fabric of all that she is saying is: What was it that happened? The unbridgeable gap between the horror of genocide and its representation is indeed at issue. The horror of genocide is no doubt made all the more acute by the fact that the observers who come after it, and the victims who survived it might be forced to concede that it was the result of a totally evil human project. An intimation almost as dark as the evil itself now descends: the two genocides in question might just be understandable as the ultimate in evildoing, powered by a kind of heroism, however perverted, but heroism, nevertheless: the heroism of those who will not stop at the worst excesses, and who undeniably mark themselves out in some way as a result. Thus, not only can we not remember the victims, but we cannot *forget* Hitler.

How Totalitarianism Works

Arendt tries to meet this enormous difficulty head-on. And so, rather than making judgements about Nazism or Stalinism, she begins to analyse, systematically, the way that totalitarianism works. Totalitarianism is not, then, equivalent to despotism, where the ruler tries to force the community to conform to his own image: in that case, the despot is the one who makes everyone else into a real or potential enemy. Totalitarianism does not have enemies, it has victims: totally innocent people who, like the Jews, are often perfectly integrated community members. Only the innocent, Arendt points out, can have their juridical status expunged so completely; the true enemy of the state is always someone with at least a semblance of a legal status. Again, the totalitarian regime perpetrates terror against a 'completely subdued population'; but most of all, it murders the moral and psychological person, so that death becomes anonymous. The totalitarian state is like a 'secret society in broad daylight', Arendt says; it uses the state and the secret police in its normal operations; it is not founded on anything but the myth that it produces of itself. The totalitarian state is essentially founded on propaganda and is quite impervious to material reality. Through propaganda the very difference between crime and virtue, persecutor and persecuted, reality and fantasy is erased. The Jews, Arendt points out, were forced into complicity with those in charge of the death camps.

The Banality of Evil

Numerous commentators have remarked that the *coup de grâce* of *The Origins of Totalitarianism* is not to be found in that work, but rather in articles on the trial of Adolf Eichmann, that Arendt wrote for the *New Yorker* in February and March 1963, subsequently published as *Eichmann in Jerusalem*. What struck Arendt most at the trial was the difference between the image of Eichmann the monster, and Jew-hater, and the real, innocuous individual, a man without spirit and without emotion, a mere cog in the Nazi machine and too limited in imagination to be anything but absolutely content with his unexceptional status. Eichmann's demeanour and the facts about what he had done in sending vast numbers of Jews to their deaths confirmed for Arendt that Nazi genocide resulted from the most banal, most systematic, efficient, and bureaucratically inspired motives: 'the banality of evil', is Arendt's famous phrase. In light of her effort to demystify totalitarianism, Eichmann became indispensable; for he was the embodiment of the shallowness and ordinariness of the Nazi enterprise. The latter could now clearly be seen as the outcome of unquestioning obedience, regardless of the ends to be achieved regardless of the cost in human life. Whether Eichmann, and the regime in general aimed to improve the rail services or exterminate millions of human beings made no difference; the point was to devise the most efficient and effective means for achieving the end and to follow orders. The real horror of totalitarianism, then, is in the banality and utter servility of its agents, not in any deep psychological explanation, or in any vertiginous political will. This is the real basis of its truly abject status.

Freedom and Necessity in Politics Today

If Arendt's study of totalitarianism is derived from the need to come to terms with the most terrible events of the twentieth century, her book, *The Human Condition*, seeks to develop a theory of politics very much alive in Classical Greece, but since lost in the modern age. The motivating factor for her inquiry is the perception that politics as the sphere of freedom – of action – among equals no longer exists in a general sense in the modern world, since the social sphere (or what is equivalent to the household (*oikia*) in Classical Greece – the sphere of necessity (housekeeping)) and the satisfaction of needs has all but completely dominated what is nevertheless still called political life. For Arendt, this is equivalent to the banalisation of politics (the evocation of totalitarianism is no doubt not accidental), where utilitarianism reigns and action, having ceased to be creative and an end in itself, has become a mere means to action. Conformity and necessity have squeezed the political dimension out of human life, and an essential aspect of the human condition is thereby stunted: the aspect of creativity. Schematically, Arendt in fact makes a general distinction between the *vita activa* – which is comprised of labour, work and action – and the *vita contempletiva*, the realm of thought, or more precisely, the realm of the contemplation of the eternal. While the main focus of Arendt's analysis here is on the *vita activa*, she argues that there is complete equality between the two realms.

Both labour and work in the *vita activa* – the one concerned directly with necessity and the satisfaction of immediate biological needs, the other concerned with utility and the world of durable objects – are activities of means; they are not essentially ends in themselves. A person's life should not only consist of labour and work – the tragedy of modern democratic societies being that so many lives are indeed so limited. The realm of action is where individuals act in complete equality with others – freedom only being realisable in association with others. In general, the social has come to dominate what was once the dichotomy between the private realm of necessity and the public, political realm of politics. And the most influential political thinkers such as Locke and Marx only confirm the importance of necessity. Marx's position is acutely paradoxical here. For while on the one hand he extols labour power (and not work) as the creator of all wealth and the 'essence' of man, he also says that with the communist society and the 'withering away of the state', no one will be forced to labour out of necessity, each having the freedom to be a hunter in the morning and a critic at night, without anyone being essentially a hunter or a critic. This conception of labour approaches what Arendt is alluding to with the realm of politics as pure creativity, the realm of the beautiful deed.

The human condition (which is never fixed) can have the realm of freedom restored to it, now, in the modern world, says Arendt, because developments in technology have rendered the 'social question' (about needs and how to satisfy them) redundant.

Revolution

Arendt returns to the 'social question' in her study of the French and American revolutions in her book, *On Revolution* (1963). There, she argues that while the first, Girondist, part of the French Revolution emphasised human rights and so was an important event in political history, the Jacobin terror of 1793 reduced the potential freedom of the Revolution to a concern with necessity. The urgency of solving the 'social question' and ameliorating suffering led to a disregard for 'the Rights of Man' inaugurated by 1789. The Revolution thus turned decidedly inward, and failed to realise its universalist potential. The American Revolution, by contrast, saw a flurry of constitution-making after independence from Britain had been won. Through this gesture the Americans placed rights and freedom above the 'social question' and (although this is rarely acknowledged) they thereby presented a more progressive revolution to the world. For Arendt, the Americans thus came closer than the French to instituting the realm of politics and freedom.

Perhaps, predictably, Arendt's distinction between action and labour and work, has often been sharply criticised. In particular, critics have not failed to ask how Arendt can claim (as she does) that action which contributes to ameliorating social conditions, or which is based on a choice of helping others, can be considered a lesser form of life.

Arendt's Influence: Bare Life and a Way of Life, or Zoē and Bios

Both Julia Kristeva and Giorgio Agamben have been inspired by Arendt's thought. For Kristeva, Arendt shows that it is crucial, in moving from a state of 'bare life', or *zoē*, to life as active and creative – as a way of life, or *bios* – that there be a narrativisation of life to bring it into the sphere of culture, as it were (see Kristeva 2001). Event and act coincide in Aristotle, and from this Arendt derives the necessity to tell the story of one's life: *bios* takes precedence over *zoē*. The necessity to tell is a kind of destiny of man in the public sphere. The man – the hero – assumes his destiny in the public sphere through acts – memorable acts, as Kristeva notes. And for Arendt, the telos of the act is the act itself. Potentially (for more is needed than just action), the act is an event in the public sphere. As an act, it is a potential nullity; or better: it is *nullius* – an act that belongs to no one, that cannot be attributed to anyone.

But the act that cannot be attributed to anyone is also typical of the instrumental act that remains in the dark, in the *oikos*. This is the act that has not been disclosed as such which, for Arendt, perhaps should never be disclosed, its disclosure being the equivalent of the emergence of the social, the sphere of decidedly unmemorable acts, which are all too often remembered. The social is the bastard form of the act: the private which should remain in the shadows but which does not do so – which now even refuses to so – to the detriment of the nobility, and thus heroic quality, of all truly public acts. Acts (also events) also disclose the *who* and bring it into unconcealment. This mode of the unconcealment in the act of the *who* – which is not the *what* – is freedom. The emergence of the social as a force is the emergence of what should remain hidden: it is, in a word, necessity.

For his part, Agamben shows that Arendt's appropriation of the Greek distinction between *zoē* and *bios*, reminds us of the extent to which *zoē*, as bare life, goes to the heart of the problem of sovereignty, in that sovereignty is concerned with inclusion and exclusion from the polity, and *zoē* is the excluded element that is included in order that the Law can be constituted. Even more: for Agamben, Arendt's theses about the fragility of human rights, has opened the way for deepening insights today into the dilemma of asylum seekers and refugees, people for whom basic human rights often do not apply due to statelessness (see Agamben 1998: 126–35).

Through Kristeva and Agamben, we thus see that the richness of Arendt's political thought is still to be tapped in its full profundity.

References

Agamben, Giorgio (1998), *Homo Sacer: Sovereign Power and Bare Life*, trans. Daniel Heller-Roazen, Stanford: Stanford University Press.

Arendt, Hannah (1951), *The Origins of Totalitarianism*, New York: Harcourt Brace and World.

—— (1958), *The Human Condition*, Chicago: University of Chicago Press.

Kristeva, Julia (2001), *Hannah Arendt*, trans. Ross Guberman, New York: Columbia University Press.

See also: **Agamben, Kristeva**

Arendt's major writings

(2006a) *Between Past and Future: Eight Exercises in Political Thought*, New York: Penguin.

(2006b) *Eichmann and the Holocaust*, New York: Penguin.

(2005) *Essays in Understanding, 1930–1954: Formation, Exile, and Totalitarianism*, ed. Jerome Kohn, New York: Schocken Books.

(1996) *Love and Saint Augustine*, ed. Joanna Vecchiarelli Scott and Judith Chelius Stark, Chicago: University of Chicago Press.

(1982) *Lectures on Kant's Political Philosophy*, London: Harvester Press.

(1978) *The Life of the Mind*, New York: Harcourt Brace and World.

(1970) *On Violence*, New York: Harcourt Brace and World.

(1963a) *On Revolution*, New York: Viking Press; London: Faber & Faber.

(1963b) *Eichmann in Jerusalem: A Report on the Banality of Evil*, New York: Viking; London: Faber & Faber.

(1958a) *The Human Condition*, Chicago: University of Chicago Press.

(1958b) *Rahel Varnhagen: The Life of a Jewish Woman*, London: East and West Library.

(1951) *The Origins of Totalitarianism*, New York: Harcourt Brace and World.

Further reading

Birmingham, Peg (2006), *Hannah Arendt and Human Rights: The Predicament of Common Responsibility*, Bloomington: Indiana University Press.

Canovan, Margaret (1992), *Hannah Arendt: A Reinterpretation of her Political Thought*, Cambridge: Cambridge University Press.

Johnson, Patricia Alternbernd (2001), *On Arendt*, Belmont, Cal.: Wadsworth/Thomson Learning.

Villa, Dana (2000), *Cambridge Companion to Hannah Arendt*, Cambridge and New York: Cambridge University Press.

—— (1999), *Politics, Philosophy, Terror: Essays on the Thought of Hannah Arendt*, Princeton, N.J.: Princeton University Press.

Williams, Garrath, ed. (2005), *Hanna Arrendt: Critical Assessments of Leading Political Philosophers*, New York: Routledge, 4 vols.

ALAIN BADIOU (b. 1937)

Alain Badiou was born in Rabat, Morocco. With a father an agrégé, like himself, in philosophy, and a mother agrégée in French, Badiou is also a product of the École Normale Supérieure (ENS) (rue d'Ulm). It was at the École in the 1950s that he came under the influence of Louis Althusser. From Althusser, Badiou came to appreciate that philosophy has no object and is not a discourse about the whole, or totality, but is a specific discourse amongst others. Badiou's other 'masters' (the term is Badiou's) are: Jean-Paul Sartre, from whom he learnt the importance of existence as the domain of choice and decision-making, and Jacques Lacan who, in Badiou's eyes, demonstrated that the subject is axiomatic (a product of truth, not of interpretation). In the 1960s at the École, Badiou was in fact a member of the famous Lacanian study group based around the journal, *Cahiers pour l'Analyse*, and published articles there on mathematical topics. He taught at the University of Paris VIII (Vincennes-Saint Denis) from 1969 until 1999, when he returned to ENS as the *Chaire* of the philosophy department. He continues to teach a popular seminar at the Collège International de Philosophie.

Always the political activist (influenced by his parents) much of Badiou's life has been shaped by his dedication to the consequences of the May 1968 revolt in Paris. Not only the student revolt of May

1968, but also the Algerian war and the 1960s general strike in Belgium shaped Badiou's political orientation. Arriving in Paris in 1956, Badiou experienced at first hand the violent methods used by the French police to quell the demonstrations against the war. Later, Badiou was sent to Belgium as a journalist to cover the strike and talk with miners and others, experiencing at first hand the plight of the workers. Since those days, he has refused to give up, like so many others, on the struggle to change society, and argues that the central maxim of philosophy is that equality should prevail. Just what Badiou means by equality is another matter.

Knowledge and Truth

Badiou's central proposition is that knowledge does not give access to truth. Truth is a 'hole' in knowledge, even if being and knowledge go together. Truth here is the truth of the event as that which changes the basic parameters of how the world is known and understood. In addition, the approach Badiou uses to reveal his notions of being, truth and event are as much, or even more, mathematical than philosophical.

The collection of his essays, *Infinite Thought* (2003a), sets out, in schematic form, a number of the key themes of Badiou's philosophical stance, a stance that re-joins Jean-Paul Sartre's *philosophie engagée*: a philosophy of commitment, or more literally: a philosophy engaged with the world. For Badiou, the flaw in contemporary philosophy, in its tripartite orientations of Hermeneutics, Analytical and Postmodern philosophy, is that the 'axioms' it follows – truth is impossible; language is the site of philosophical thinking – are inadequate for dealing with philosophy's historical mission to be concerned with the universal, revolt, logic and risk. A concern for truth is implicit within this mission. Without it, philosophy cannot meaningfully intervene in world affairs and so contribute to changing the world, a world 'subordinated to the merchandising of money and information' (Badiou 2003a: 48). In effect, Badiou is worried about the actual political impotence of contemporary philosophy in its three orientations, and, at the same time, about it failing in its mission to be universally transmissible (2003a: 51). Moreover, in light of the speed at which things happen in the contemporary world (also highlighted by Virilio), philosophy must act as a force for retardation: philosophical thought is leisurely; revolt today must as a consequence be leisurely.

In contrast to the human sciences, which are primarily concerned with statistical averages, philosophy is concerned with singularity. It is also concerned with rationality – not the rationality of the past, but with a revised rationality that is concerned with consolidating intellectual strength to counter fundamentalist passions. The violence of the contemporary world and, more broadly, what happens in it, means that philosophy must also be a philosophy of the event. Philosophy must be able to confront and intervene in world events as 'the singularity of what happens'. Truth, as something new, is to be distinguished from knowledge, which is the knowledge of being. Justice and equality are not the result of true definitions, nor are they empirically demonstrable; they are rather part of thought itself – are a way of thinking.

The Multiple, the Event, Fidelity, Mathematics

In his overall trajectory, Badiou agrees with Lacanian psychoanalysis, which argues that truth and knowledge are quite distinct and that truth is founded on the void (Badiou 2003a: 86). However, Badiou's view of this void is mathematical. The presentation of it can no longer be left to the province of intuition. Badiou's fullest elaboration of the mathematics of set theory that underpins is given in his magnum opus, *L'Être et événement* (1988).

Badiou's fundamental theses are also oriented towards mathematics in another, more general way. Going back to Plato, Badiou observes that Plato relates mathematics favourably to philosophy because it breaks with *doxa* (opinion). Even if mathematics here means geometry and arithmetic, and refers to a set of objects, it is more insightful than the Romantic conception, as found in Hegel, which evaluates mathematics in terms of the way it presents its main concept, namely, the infinite. Because of this, Hegel sees mathematics as philosophy's rival. He thus had to prove that the Romantic, philosophical concept of the infinite was superior to the mathematical one. So, whereas Plato sees mathematics as an ally of philosophy, Hegel sees the need to assert the superiority of the philosophical concept of the infinite over that of mathematics because the latter has no concept. In the Romantic view, then, mathematics must rely upon philosophy to provide the concepts of what it is doing; in itself, it is conceptually blind.

Romanticism separates philosophy from mathematics because, effectively, it could claim that philosophy ultimately dealt with the same thing (the infinite) as mathematics, but dealt with it more profoundly. To Romantic philosophy, mathematics would be naïve, while, in Badiou's view, it is necessary to break with Romanticism so that mathematics can claim its rights as a type of thinking. Badiou thus works, as he says to 're-entangle' mathematics and philosophy primarily for the reasons given above concerning the ontological status of infinite multiplicities. Not only does Badiou want to turn the tables on Romantic philosophy à la Hegel and 're-entangle' mathematics and philosophy, he wants to suggest, on the question of Being, that mathematics might have priority, that 'mathematics *is* ontology' (Badiou 2004: 38, emphasis added).

As Badiou sees Deleuze as the other philosopher for whom multiplicities are fundamental, he proposed to Deleuze that set theory maybe a better way of getting at notions like: 'fold', 'interval', 'enlacement', 'serration', 'fractal' or 'chaos' (Badiou 2000: 46). However, the author of *The Fold* was not persuaded, thus indicating a certain allegiance to the Romantic tradition. Badiou's philosophical difference with Deleuze centres on the latter's privileging, without argument, a set of key terms that then form the basis of a 'norm': movement, life, time, affirmation, multiplicity, difference.

Trained as a mathematician, Badiou realises that being, as a 'multiple multiplicity' (without unity), can only be presented as a kind of unity by mathematics – or, more bluntly, can only be presented at all by mathematics. The latter thus becomes the site of the elaboration of Badiou's ontology. Consequently, mathematics has a higher mission than to be the handmaiden of applied science. It, and not traditional philosophy, truly addresses being because the absolute de-substantialisation of being, that much of post-modern thought has striven for, is essentially mathematical. And the mode of mathematics that Badiou considers to be fundamental in the task of presenting being as a kind of unity, is set theory. Mathematics also addresses the void – for the primordial opposition of unity and void (or One (Being) and Nothingness (which also has a being) cannot be sidestepped). However, to avoid the elemental unity simply sliding back into the unity of the time-honoured One, the 'unity' of the non-unity of multiplicities must be composed of further multiplicities, so that a single concept of multiplicity is avoided.

Set theory becomes appropriate for engaging with the multiple because there is no 'set of all sets'; therefore no element in the theory implies an initial a priori global unity. Moreover, there is no definition of a set in set theory, but rather a relation of belonging 'as well as a series of variables and logical operators, and nine axioms stating how they may be used together' (Badiou 2003a: 15).

The void, or nothingness, is the other dimension upon which Badiou's thought is focused. Here, the question concerns the status of the void in relation to being. Is there a being of nothingness, for instance? Can nothingness, for the mathematician, count for 'something'? The answer is that both nothing and something constitute a situation (multiple of the multiple), but are not presented in it. In set theory, the void corresponds to the 'null set', the empty set that must be posited in order that sets in general can be presented. It is the 'primitive name of being' (Badiou 2004: 57) Against Heidegger, Badiou proposes that mathematics becomes the thinking of being *qua* being, not philosophy.

The Set, Event and Being

In *Être et événement* (1988), Badiou addresses in detail the difference between 'belonging' ($\in$) and 'inclusion' ($\subset$) in relation to the void. A sub-set can belong to a set, but only the set itself can be included (see Badiou 1988: 95). Everything that is included belongs, but not everything that belongs to a set is included in it. Only the void is included in the void (Badiou 1988: 103). This evokes Agamben's discussion of the exception in politics (*Homo sacer*), which belongs to politics but is not included (see entry on Agamben in this volume). The void is, Badiou concludes, the being of the multiple (Badiou 1988: 109). Singular multiples of a situation are presented in it, but are not represented. They belong to the situation, but are not included. Normal multiples are both represented and included. To change a situation radically, the aim is to have what belongs to it (singularity) included in it. As an example, we could say that early twentieth-century, avant-garde, music (Schoenberg) initially belonged to music, but was not included in it, whereas, latterly, this music is now included in music. The singular multiplicity is what Badiou calls an event, the key term in his philosophy (Badiou 1988: 195). In relation to this, 'fidelity', for Badiou, enables the discernment of singular multiples in a situation. It is the belief, if one likes, that at the beginning of the twentieth century Schoenberg's music, as atonal, was music.

Being and the void become being and the event, and Badiou is concerned, theoretically and philosophically, with the gap between them – between something and nothing. This compares to the gap in Heidegger's ontology between being and beings. Because he wants to avoid any hint of substantialisation, Badiou chooses the term, 'situation' to convey the nature of the multiple within which an event arises. Situation accommodates anything that is, regardless of its mode of being. A situation, then, is a 'multiple multiplicity'. The aim is to arrive at the most elementary point of thought in relation to Being as de-substantialised, or de-essentialised. This point is that of the 'multiple multiplicity', which is even less substantial than 'formlessness' because matter as such has to be stripped away in order to get at the elemental point of thought: its 'real', as Badiou says, thus invoking Lacan.

An event challenges being (and therefore challenges mathematical and philosophical thought). And this challenge can occur at any time but not in just any place; an event will generally be located close to the edge of whatever qualifies as the 'void' or as what is indistinguishable in the situation. The material of an event is a site. As Badiou says: 'an event is nothing other than a set, or a multiple, whose form is that of a site' (Badiou 2004: 100). An event is also an unfounded multiple. It has no foundation outside itself (unlike being). Truth also has this quality. Again, unlike being, an event is not One. It has no determinable or perceptible unity. Truth is a multiplicity and is also something which disappears in its appearance.

Truth

A truth then can be of four types: scientific, artistic, political and amorous (Badiou 2004: 110). It is always a novelty, like the event. The axiom of truth is: "'this took place, which I can neither calculate nor demonstrate'" (Badiou 2004: 112). It is in no sense an a priori, static thing, but is an act, something which brings something into being. Truth operates in a situation (as a multiplicity), within experience, not outside it. It is immanent in experience. Truth is not therefore given, nor is it a given point of departure, but has its origin in the very disappearance of givenness. And to this, Badiou adds: 'I call "event" this originary disappearance supplementing the situation for the duration of a lightening flash' (Badiou 2004: 122). Events can range from the French Revolution and atonal music to love. Love is an event because it is totally contingent; it cannot be anticipated or predicted. Genius, too, is an event and as such gives rise to truth.

To all this, Badiou adds the supplementary requirement of faith: an event (truth) entails faith that it has occurred in order that it be thought, for it is outside all regular and existing laws. Faith is the basis of a new way of being and acting in a situation. In relation to this, the subject is the bearer of faith, a bearer whose existence does not precede the event, but who is constituted – or is induced –

by it. The subject is not psychological, reflexive nor transcendental. Thus, the subject in a love situation did not exist prior to the event of love. Such a subject has no 'natural' pre-existence (Badiou 2003b: 64). 'The lovers enter as such into the composition of *a* subject of love, which *exceeds* both of them' (Badiou 2003b: 64, Badiou's emphasis).

Love, then, is one of the four domains of truth (science, politics and art, as well as love). These are four domains of subjectivation within which a genuine subject may appear because it is constituted by the domain itself. In each domain, the truth of the event gives rise to a subject, as we have seen already in the case of love: politics, giving rise to a revolution, gives rise to its subject; science, giving rise to totally new discoveries, similarly gives rise to its subject; art, in bringing forth that which is original and unanticipated, also gives rise to the subject of art. This notion subjectivation linked to the event may be contrasted with the abstract, formal, empty space for a subject supported by Žižek's psychoanalytic approach. For Badiou, by contrast, nothing, the void, the empty space pre-exists a subject; it is not equivalent to a subject.

From another angle, truth and the event are mathematical following Cantor's non-denumerable, transfinite numbers, which constitute the infinite. Thus truth is the realm of the infinite; it is not a finitude, as knowledge often proposes. Consequently, the event, too, participates in the infinite. With knowledge, a particular entity or phenomenal form is presented as truth. This cannot be; for truth as the infinite is universal not particular. Another implication drawn from this by Badiou is that truth has nothing to do with hermeneutics or interpretation. The latter is always concerned with finitude, never with the infinite. Meaning (finitude) and truth are thus at odds with each other, even in psychoanalysis, in relation to which Badiou still maintains his view that analysis is about truth more than it is about interpretation. As Marx, said, interpretation changes nothing.

An Original Thought with Difficulties

Badiou's philosophy is certainly original in its use of mathematics and the idea of truth and the event as separate from knowledge and being. In addition, the idea of subjectivation that Badiou works with, coupled with the notion of faith provides a refreshing counter to cynicism and nihilism. On the other hand, difficulties arise when it comes to evaluating events that have taken place and forms of subjectivation that have come into being. These would include: Nazism, Stalinism, and aspects of the Chinese Cultural Revolution, or even art as pure narcissism. These may well be events, but what is the truth they convey? Partly, at least, that it would have been better had they not taken place. In effect, Badiou spends so much time using sophisticated mathematical axioms demonstrating what an event is and how it is imbued with truth – always a term to capture attention – that *what* is happening – today, as well as in the past – very much takes second place. Thus another dimension to Badiou's philosophy is required: a strategy for evaluating events and their related forms of subjectivation, in order that we can, as well as grasp the nature of an event, also stand against certain events. The extent to which such evaluation would also involve interpretation (not in the realm of truth for Badiou) remains an open question.

References

Badiou, Alain (2000), *Deleuze: The Clamor of Being*, trans. Louise Burchill, Minneapolis and London: University of Minnesota Press.
—— (2003a), *Infinite Thought: Truth and the Return to Philosophy*, trans. Oliver Feltham and Justin Clemens, London and New York: Continuum.
—— (2003b), *L'Éthique: essai sur la conscience du mal*, Caen, France: Nous.
—— (2004), *Theoretical Writings*, trans. Ray Brassier and Alberto Toscano, London and New York: Continuum.
—— (2005), *Being and Event*, trans. Oliver Feltham, London and New York: Continuum.

See also: **Agamben, Heidegger, Lacan, Virilio, Žižek**

Badiou's major writings

(2005a [1988]) *Being and Event*, trans. Oliver Feltham, London and New York: Continuum.
(2005b [1998]) *Briefings on Existence: A Short Treatise on Transitory Ontology*, trans. Norman Madarasz, Albany: State University of New York Press.
(2005c [1998]) *Metapolitics*, trans. Jason Baker, New York: Verso.
(2005d) *Le Siècle*, Paris: Seuil.
(2004a) *Theoretical Writings*, trans. Ray Brassier and Alberto Toscano, London and New York: Continuum.
(2004b [1998]) *Handbook of Inaesthetics*, trans. Alberto Toscano, Stanford: Stanford University Press.
(2003a) *Infinite Thought: Truth and the Return to Philosophy*, trans. Oliver Feltham and Justin Clemens, London and New York: Continuum.
(2003b [1997]) *Saint Paul: The Foundation of Universalism*, trans. Ray Brassier, Stanford: Stanford University Press.
(2003c [1995]) *On Beckett*, trans. Alberto Tascano, London: Clinaman Press.

(2003d) *L'Éthique: essai sur la conscience du mal*, Caen, France: Nous, in English as: *Ethics: An Essay on the Understanding of Evil*, trans. Peter Hallward, New York: Verso.

(2000 [1997]) *Deleuze: The Clamor of Being*, trans. Louise Burchill, Minneapolis and London: University of Minnesota Press.

(1999 [1992]) *Manifesto for Philosophy*, trans. Norman Madarasz, Albany: SUNY Press.

(1992) *Conditions*, Paris: Seuil.

(1990) *Le Nombre et les nombres*, Paris: Seuil.

(1988) *L'Être et l'événement,* Paris: Seuil.

(1985) *Peut-on Penser la politique?* Paris: Seuil.

(1982) *Théorie du sujet*, Paris: Seuil.

(1976) with François Barmès *De l'idéologie*, Paris: Maspero.

(1975) *Théorie de la contradiction*, Paris: Maspero.

Further reading

Barker, Jason (2002), *Alain Badiou: Strong Thought*, London: Pluto Press.

Hallwood, Peter (2003), *Badiou: A Subject to Truth*, New York: Continuum.

Hallwood, Peter (2004), *Think Again: Alain Badiou and the Future of Philosophy*, London: Continuum.

Wilkens, Matthew, issue editor (2005), 'The Philosophy of Alain Badiou', *Polygraph* 17, Durham: Duke University.

JÜRGEN HABERMAS (b. 1929)

Jürgen Habermas is the most renowned member of the second generation of the Frankfurt School of Social Research. Born in 1929 in Düsseldorf, Habermas wrote his PhD dissertation (published in 1954) on the conflict between the Absolute and history in Schelling's thought. Between 1956 and 1959, he was assistant to Theodor Adorno in Frankfurt. He has subsequently been professor of philosophy and the director of the Max Planck Institute in Starberg.

Like other members of the Frankfurt School, Habermas has been strongly influenced by the writings of Hegel and Marx, as well as American pragmatism (Dewey) and systems theory (Parsons and Luhmann).

Unlike Adorno and Horkheimer, Habermas rejects Marx's theory of value, as well as the cultural pessimism of the first generation of the School. As with Weber, Habermas also believes that the first generation of the Frankfurt School erred in confusing 'system rationality' and 'action rationality', a confusion which parallels another: the 'uncoupling of system and life world' (Habermas 1987a: 333. For a general discussion of this, see Habermas 1987a: 153–97). The result, says Habermas, is that the system (e.g. the economy) is seen to dominate the whole of society at the expense of what Habermas, after Husserl and Schutz, calls the 'lifeworld', which is the immediate milieu of the individual social actor.

On the other hand, like the early Frankfurt School, Habermas's writing also bears the marks of Hegel's abiding influence. Thus, in the mid-1980s, he began his lectures on modernity by arguing that, philosophically at least, modernity begins with Hegel: 'Hegel was the first philosopher to develop a clear concept of modernity,' Habermas claims (Habermas 1987b: 4[1]). Although these lectures subsequently treat the work of thinkers like Bataille, Derrida and Foucault – that is, thinkers whose work has posed questions for Marx and Hegel's social theory – the theorist of communicative action shows his allegiance to the tradition that he has always held dear by using it to point out the inadequacies of the so-called 'radical critique of reason' found in the thought of 'postmodern' thinkers, the point where the 'irrational', supposedly dominant in Bataille's thought, begins to hold sway. Such claims, with regard to deconstruction, led, in the 1980s, to an acrimonious dispute with Jacques Derrida, subsequently put in limited abeyance in a show of solidarity in the aftermath of 9/11.

Anti-Positivism

Characteristic of Habermas's work in the 1960s was its anti-positivism. In particular, he rejected the positivism of Marx's later writings and sought to turn the early work into a more effective springboard of an immanent critique of capitalist society by emphasising Marx's hermeneutic aspect. This critique had the following features. First of all, Habermas argued that science, and even aspects of philosophy, had ceased to have a critical role in determining the worth of the ends to be pursued, and had instead become the slave of 'instrumental', or 'purposive' rationality (Weber's *zweckrationalität*). Science thus contributed to the technical rationality which enabled capitalism to develop more diverse and complex commodity forms, as well as sophisticated weaponry; it was, however, incapable of producing a creditable justification of the capitalist system itself. In short, the technical understanding of science was positivistic, and therefore ultimately ideological. For it denied the hermeneutic component in science as it was practised. As a result, Habermas saw science and rationality in the capitalist era being turned against human beings – impoverishing their cultural lives, and exacerbating pathological forms – instead of being used for them. Critical theory was needed to combat this negative form of positivistic science and turn it into an emancipatory activity concerned with political and social reform.

In contrast to Adorno and Horkheimer's pessimistic account of reason in the *Dialectic of Enlightenment*, Habermas seeks to turn the tide against such a negative conception and works to 'complete the project of modernity' begun in the Enlightenment. Again, this goal necessitates a critique of the purely instrumentalist view of science dominant in post-war capitalism.

The State and Critique

Habermas's early work also aimed to show how the modern state was an outcome of, and contributed to, capitalism's very survival. At one point in the 1970s, Habermas argued – in light of the work of certain political economists – that the state would not be able to cushion people from the worst excesses of the crises in the capitalist economy because its capacity to collect the revenue necessary to support welfare programmes was limited. This, according to Habermas, entailed a limit to the state's legitimacy. For the more it became incapable of protecting people from economic crises, the less its legitimacy could be guaranteed.

In keeping with the German idealist tradition, Habermas uses Marx to develop a strategy of critique which would be, as he sees it, essentially emancipatory. Thus while Marx emphasised the self-formative role of practical labour, Habermas, with a nod to Hegel, sees labour as critique – one particularly aimed against the numbing force of instrumental reason. By showing what had been achieved in a practical sense by the German hermeneutic tradition – in which Habermas includes Freud – the way is opened for a much greater emphasis to be placed on symbolic forms of interaction than Marx had ever envisaged.

Theory of Communication

In this vein, the early 1970s sees Habermas formulating the first elements of a theory of language, communication and the evolution of society intended to provide the basis of a normative framework within which an emancipatory interest could be realised. This work culminated in the massive volumes of *The Theory of Communicative Action*, first published in Germany in 1981. From this we can note that while Habermas never gives up the impetus for emancipation found in Marx, he is not prepared to accept either a revolutionary or a positivistic means of achieving it. Capitalism ushers in a class society, Habermas agrees, and bureaucratic, or purposive rationality has an ever-increasing hold over individual lives, but it is important not to equate the 'self-regulating system whose imperatives override the consciousness of the members integrated into them' (Habermas 1987a: 333) with the 'lifeworld': the world of consciousness and communicative action. The greater part of Habermas's later work centres around an exploration of the structures (particularly language and communicative action, and moral consciousness) of the lifeworld. The lifeworld is founded on an interest in emancipation; only a distorted use of reason and language makes this difficult to appreciate. In effect, emancipation is the very basis of social (thus human) life. The task is, therefore, to provide a theory which will make universal lucidity possible on this point.

Lifeworld and Communicative Action

Specifically, Habermas begins a discussion of the notion of lifeworld in the early 1980s by returning to Durkheim and the phenomenological sociology of Mead and Schutz. For Schutz, the lifeworld was the world of everyday life, the total sphere of an individual's previous experiences; it is the biographically determined situation into which the individual is inserted, willy-nilly. This is 'the world as taken for granted' in which individuals seek to realise pragmatic objectives. For Habermas, the lifeworld is a horizon of consciousness which includes both the public and private spheres. It is the sphere of identity formation and communicative action. By the latter, Habermas means action which 'relies on a cooperative process of interpretation in which participants relate simultaneously to something in the objective, the social, and the subjective worlds, even when they *thematically stress only one* of the three components in their utterances' (Habermas 1987a: 120, Habermas's emphasis). Communication is, for Habermas, the most important aspect of all the activities in the lifeworld because it is here that, ideally, individuals can gain recognition for the validity of their utterances, as it is here also in which the structures of the lifeworld in general can be modified. These modifications are supposed to react back on to the broader social system, thereby stemming the growth of instrumental rationality.

Concomitant with his investigation of the lifeworld in light of Talcott Parsons's theory of society as a social system, Habermas engages to write a theory of both the evolution of society and of the evolution of the individual within it, particularly as these emerge within specific norms and symbolic forms. Relying on the work of

Kolberg and Piaget to develop a theory of moral competence, and on the work of Chomsky for a theory of linguistic competence, Habermas endeavours to show that there must be a normative element dominant in human interaction, as well as a purely instrumental one concerned with the satisfaction of needs. Mistaken, according to Habermas, are those who argue with Weber that a purposive, technical science of action alone is possible, with issues of morals and even true understanding being a matter of personal choice. Norms and values have to be the object of rigorous critical reflection, if only because the very distinction between 'technical' and 'normative' itself depends on a prior distinction of a normative kind. Thus even an ostensibly technical, or strategic, interest cannot be seen in isolation from an interest in an ethically-informed set of universal principles.

Intersubjective Recognition

As a result it becomes crucially important to know what the basic needs of human beings are, just as the nature of undistorted and free communication must be revealed. Always on the look-out for immanent features of the social situation which will give force to his interest in the normative aspects of society, Habermas finds that the very nature of language as communication means that both the speaker and the hearer of speech have an a priori interest in understanding each other. Understanding means participants reach agreement; agreement entails the 'intersubjective recognition' of the validity of the other's utterance. In this process each participant will be drawn into reflecting upon their own position in the communicative process. For Habermas, this means that the structure of language is fundamentally hermeneutic: it calls for participants to engage in interpretation at all levels, thus heightening the degree of each person's self-understanding as this derives from his or her interaction with others. This, Habermas believes, is the very telos of language. Consequently, language must be understood according to a consensus model of rules. One way or another, the proper function of language is to allow communication to take place; where communication fails systematically, there is a pathological form of language use.

Moral Consciousness

With regard to 'moral consciousness', Habermas seeks to ground what he accepts (from Kohlberg, Piaget, Mead and others) as moral stages in a 'logic of development'. He aims to show how the moral point of view is grounded in an original element in the structure of human life experience. 'What moral *theory* can do and should be trusted to do is to clarify the universal core of our moral intuitions and thereby refute value scepticism' (Habermas 1990: 211). Although Habermas denies that this means laying claim to any moral truth, it is difficult to see how 'value scepticism' can escape a substantive claim about what constitutes a moral issue.

Even more problematic than the claim that a substantive moral position is derived from a 'universal core' of morality is Habermas's concern to pick out the pathologies and disequilibria in modern capitalism. The cultural impoverishment brought about by an excessive emphasis on technical, purposive rationality at the level of the system would thus be an example of a pathological social form. Generally speaking, a pathological situation emerges for Habermas when a disequilibrium – i.e. a fundamental disturbance – occurs in society. Modernity, as a socio-cultural, as well as an economic, form runs the risk of degenerating into a totally pathological state. Correctives found in the modern tradition itself – correctives going back to the use of reason inaugurated by the Enlightenment – must be brought into play if serious consequences are to be avoided. Because correctives are needed, it is imperative that the normative basis of the lifeworld be revealed with all possible clarity. Habermas sees himself as engaged in this process; while others have wondered how Habermas's rather turgid style has contributed to the clarity he seeks to achieve.

Discourse of Modernity

From another angle, Habermas analyses what he calls the 'philosophical discourse of modernity' by examining how various thinkers – recalcitrant to the tradition of modernity, as Habermas outlines it – exact 'a high price for taking leave of modernity'. What bothers Habermas about Adorno, Bataille, Foucault and Derrida in particular is their apparent refusal to accept that reason must have its rights, and that, in any case, to mount a radical critique of reason, as Habermas believes is the case, is, without knowing it, still to be beholden to reason. Most of all, Habermas claims, the critics of modernity 'blunt' the distinction between alienation and emancipation; they refuse, in short, to tell us (we, who must be told!) where the road to freedom lies. Here, Habermas is particularly upset by claims – echoing those of Adorno and Horkheimer – that modern reason and enlightenment have participated in political repression of the very worst kind.

Clearly, we are dealing here with an extremely contentious point. And much has been written about the way Habermas's views have been rejected or ignored by key French thinkers. Whatever one thinks about the merits of one side of the debate or the other, a number of basic differences between Habermas and thought inspired by post-structuralism need elaboration. Some of these differences are described in the following section.

Difficulties with Habermas's Approach

First, few can accept in isolation, as Habermas seems to, the totalising effect of Hegel's philosophical system, or the idea that modernity begins with Hegel rather than with other claimants for the mantle, such as Rousseau, Descartes – or Columbus, for that matter. Similarly, Marx's claims about labour and revolution are, in isolation, becoming more redundant by the hour. As the core of Habermas's thought seems to rely on these two thinkers, even though, it is true, he claims to have introduced fundamental modifications to their philosophies, it is to be wondered how a concern for the universal can be reconciled with the maintenance of what is rapidly becoming an idiosyncratic intellectual baggage.

Second, Habermas has an outdated view of modern science which fails to see that – after Einstein, Heisenberg and Gödel – science is no longer easily reduced to a purely technical interest, one justified in positivist terms. Given his concern with norms and the pathological, Habermas could have profited from a reading of works like Georges Canguilhem's *On the Normal and the Pathological* (1978). There, we see how the history of science can be concerned with the normative dimension of human life.

Third, despite his efforts to constitute a general theory of linguistic competence and undistorted communication at the level of the lifeworld, his approach to language is based on a number of presuppositions that have been exhaustively questioned in linguistics and semiotics. While a number of commentators have pointed out that poetic language is excluded from Habermas's theory, the more striking thing is that, in his own terms, Habermas insists on giving what amounts to an instrumental interpretation of language by reducing it to a means of communication. And even if he were to reply that this is an unintended result of his theory and can, in principle, be incorporated into it, the difficulty is that Habermas analyses language by way of an ideal model based on a hypothetical sender and receiver of a message. For instance, in *The Theory of Communicative Action*, Habermas speaks of 'what it means for a speaker, in performing one of the *standard* speech acts, to take up a pragmatic relation' to something in the objective, social or subjective 'actor-worlds' (Habermas 1987a: 120, emphasis added). Habermas works with a model of an ideal speaker and hearer of language so that the speaker–hearer couple is effectively prior to language, whereas this couple (if it be only a couple and not a triad) is arguably constituted by language itself. Language thus speaks *in* its users as much as they speak language. Unlike Julia Kristeva's notion of the subject-in-process, the ideal model based on a standard speech is – even if not fully realised – static, and potentially closed. The point is to work for the openness that 'process' implies.

Hence, even though communication does break down, transparency, for Habermas, is nevertheless language's telos. Clearly, one can note that literary and fictional works of all kinds are also embodiments of language in action; they are rarely entirely transparent in principle – *Finnegans Wake* being a case in point – but are part of language for all that. Opaque works are often instances of language in the process of formation – or deformation in the case of *Finnegans Wake*.

Finally, one of the major difficulties in accepting much of what Habermas writes stems from his insistence on assuming that there can be a relatively fixed universal subject, identical with itself. The existence of this subject is confirmed by the emphasis Habermas – after phenomenology – places on consciousness in the lifeworld to the exclusion of the unconscious and symptomatic conduct. This is not only a philosophical objection: it arises as a specific problem in some kinds of statements. Thus in speaking of modernity, largely under the influence of Hegel, Habermas writes: 'Modernity sees itself cast back upon itself without any possibility of escape. This explains the sensitiveness of its self-understanding, the dynamism of the attempt, carried forward incessantly down to our time, to "pin itself down"' (Habermas 1987b: 7). Here, the whole of modernity is psychologised as though it were a homogeneous, perfectly lucid identity. In this regard, it is not a question of insisting that Habermas accept the notion of the radically de-centred subject he opposes, but rather one of suggesting that to rid modernity – or language, or science, or the subject – of the complexity of its mode of unity is surely inadequate.

From a more directly political perspective, Habermas's laudable call for a revival of the public sphere suffers from being based on a very modernist and thus slightly antiquated model of politics as an endless discussion of ideas. As has been frequently said, the development and subsequent domination of a mediatised 'society of the spectacle' has entirely transformed the nature and relation between public and private in the twenty-first century. There is no public sphere any more in the eighteenth-century Enlightenment sense.

In the end, then, Habermas raises pertinent questions regarding politics and society, but these cannot be answered within the philosophical and epistemological framework to which he subscribes.

Note

1 The lectures on the philosophical underpinnings of modernity were given in Paris, Frankfurt, New York and Boston in 1983–84.

References

Canguilhem, Georges (1978 [1943, 1966]), *On The Normal and the Pathological*, trans. Carolyn R. Fawcett, Dordrecht, Holland: Reidel Publishing Company.

Habermas, Jürgen (1987a), *The Theory of Communicative Action Volume 2. Lifeworld and System: A Critique of Functionalist Reason*, trans. Thomas McCarthy, Boston: Beacon Press.

—— (1987b), *The Philosophical Discourse of Modernity*, trans. Frederick Lawrence, Cambridge: Polity Press in association with Basil Blackwell.

—— (1990), *Moral Consciousness and Communicative Action*, trans. Christian Lenhardt and Shierry Weber Nicholsen, Cambridge: Polity Press in association with Basil Blackwell.

See also: **Adorno, Benjamin, Derrida**

Habermas's major writings

(1989 [1962]) *The Structural Transformation of the Public Sphere: An Inquiry into a Category of Bourgeois Society*, trans. Thomas Burger with the assistance of Frederick Lawrence, Cambridge: Polity Press.

(1988 [1970]) *On the Logic of the Social Sciences*, trans. Shierry W. Nicholsen and Jerry Stark, Cambridge, Mass.: MIT Press.

(1987 [1981]) *The Theory of Communicative Action Volume 2. Lifeworld and System: A Critique of Functionalist Reason*, trans. Thomas McCarthy, Boston: Beacon Press.

(1985 [1987]) *The Philosophical Discourse of Modernity*, trans. Frederick Lawrence, Cambridge: Polity Press.

(1981 [1984]) *The Theory of Communicative Action. Volume 1. Reason and Rationalization on Society*, trans. Thomas McCarthy, Boston: Beacon Press.

(1979 [1976]) *Communication and the Evolution of Society*, trans. Thomas McCarthy, London: Heinemann.

(1975 [1973]) *Legitimation Crisis*, trans. Thomas McCarthy, Boston: Beacon Press.

(1973 [1963]) *Theory and Practice*, trans. John Viertel, Boston: Beacon Press.

(1971 [1968]) *Knowledge and Human Interests*, trans. Jeremy J. Shapiro, Boston: Beacon Press.

(1970 [1968–69]) *Toward a Rational Society: Student Protest, Science and Politics*, trans. Jeremy J. Shapiro, Boston: Beacon Press.

Further reading

Aboulatia, Mitchell; Bookman, Myra and Kemp, Cathy, eds (2002), *Habermas and Pragmatism*, London and New York: Routledge.

Edgar, Andrew (2006), *Habermas: The Key Concepts*, London and New York: Routledge.

Finlayson, James Gordon (2005), *Habermas: A Very Short Introduction*, Oxford: Oxford University Press.

Johnson, Pauline (2006), *Habermas: Rescuing the Public Sphere*, London and, New York: Routledge.

Rasmussen, David; Swindal, James, eds (2002), *Jürgen Habermas*, London and Thousand Oaks: Sage.

SLAVOJ ŽIŽEK (b. 1949)

Slavoj Žižek uses the principles of Jacques Lacan's psychoanalytic theory and, secondarily, German Idealist philosophy (Kant, Hegel, Schelling), to illuminate political action and theory, economic rationality, high and popular culture, sexuality and love, technology, society, history and Christianity. Possibly, no other thinker has been so successful in bringing Lacan to life in the current climate of globalisation and political centralism. Briefly, if we were to ask, 'what can we do now, politically speaking?', Žižek's answer is that we can engage in political and philosophical debate invoking the work of Jacques Lacan. Such reverence for, and commitment to, Lacan does risk alienating certain liberal sensibilities. Where is Žižek's scientific and philosophical objectivity or neutrality? – one might lament. Such a question leads in part to one of Žižek's key points about the current, globalised, post-modern present, which is that the lack of commitment to intellectual, political or religious figures taps into a larger issue: that of the death of the spirit, of the soul, and a simple concern to avoid for as long a possible so-called physical death. Indeed, Žižek sees Lacan's interpretation of Freud's death drive as being more about the death of the soul, than about physical death (death of the flesh).

Background and Theoretical Orientation and Concerns

Žižek, the only child of middle-class bureaucrats, was born in 1949 in Ljubljana, the capital of Slovenia and, at that time, part of Yugoslavia. Yugoslavia, then under the rule of Marshal Tito (1892–1980), was one of the more 'liberal' communist countries in the Eastern Bloc. However, the freedoms the régime granted its subjects were rather ambivalent, inducing in the population, according to the philosopher, a form of pernicious self-regulation (does not Foucault actually apply here, despite Žižek's critique of him?). One aspect of state control that did have a positive effect, however, was the law which required film companies to submit to local university archives a copy of every film they wished to distribute. Žižek was, therefore, able to watch many American and European releases and establish a firm grasp of the traditions of Hollywood, a grasp which has served him so well since, providing insights into Lacanian theory as well as into issues in contemporary society and politics.

Žižek quite trenchantly opposes post-modern thought (seen as ultimately relativist), and the bland, 'radical' centrist politics accompanying it. Such politics gives free rein to a totally de-politicised view of the market and its globalising tendencies. A key aim of Žižek's work, then, is to revitalise Marxist political action in order to take over the radical ground now occupied by the extreme Right. To some, therefore, Žižek's political views are going to seem very old fashioned. He is quite aware of this, and even makes it a focus of his analyses: classifying certain kinds of Left wing political aspiration as old fashioned is just part of conservative post-modernism's strategy.

More philosophically – and Žižek would say, more psychoanalytically – this master of Lacanian interpretation supports a Cartesian conception of the subject, which he defends against post-modern attack: not the subject as psychological content, as ego, but the subject (implicitly specified by the cogito) as empty, one capable of taking on a variety of contents. Moreover, it is claimed, the subject of democracy is Cartesian; it is not an individual, but an empty punctuality, 'a pure singularity, emptied of all content' (Žižek 1991: 164).

This subject is also defended against post-structuralism, which sees the idea of the subject as prior to any substantive content as a metaphysical gesture linked ultimately to an original 'self-presence'.

Still in a philosophical vein, Žižek points out in *The Ticklish Subject* (1999a: 13) that he began as a Heideggerian and published his first book on Heidegger. This, in no small measure, was to counter the Yugoslav official communist philosophers. Ultimately, the problem with Heidegger centres on his distinction between 'ontic' (scientific) thought and ontological (philosophical) thought. The notion of 'being-in-the-world' (immersed in the world) and engaged in scientific thought allows no real scope for the necessary distancing of ontological thought (which addresses being) to operate. Politically, this led Heidegger astray in a very practical sense in his relation to Nazism, for he mistook the movement as having 'inner greatness' and ontological authenticity, while in fact it was anything but truly great. The political implications of Heidegger's thought are of particular concern to the analyst. To escape from the problem raised by total immersion in the world, the Cartesian version of subjectivity, as elaborated by Lacan, is necessary. It is as though detachment and abstraction were a virtue rather than a problem.

As Žižek is so indebted to Lacan, it is well to revise some of the analyst's key concepts. We shall limit ourselves to explaining four of these: the Imaginary, the Symbolic and the Real, as well as *jouissance*.

Real, Symbolic, Imaginary

The *Real*, as Lacan says, is impossible (it cannot be symbolised) and relates to the unconscious, whereas reality is perfectly possible (it can be symbolised) and relates to consciousness. Reality has a void at its heart, and the Real is the counterpoint to this. One of Žižek's most intriguing treatments of the Real is to be found in his reading of Hitchcock's films where the real equates with some element, often a traumatic stain, or remainder, that cannot be integrated into the main narrative or diegesis of the film (see Žižek 1991: 93–97 and 1992: 248–49).

Looked at from a structuralist perspective of oppositions, such as 'presence–absence', the Real is beyond absence and is a complete fullness, from which nothing can be added or subtracted. As Lacan put it in his seminar on Poe's 'The Purloined Letter': the Real is what is never 'missing from its place': there is no lack, whereas in the Symbolic, lack is primary (Lacan 2006: 6–48). As Žižek emphasises, the Real is both the foundation of symbolisation and at the same time a 'remainder, leftover, scraps of this process of symbolization, the remnants, the excess which escapes symbolization and is as such produced by the symbolization itself' (Žižek 1989: 168). In Freud's terms, the primary process (Real), cannot actually be symbolised by the secondary process (the Symbolic), but must be presupposed by it.

The *Symbolic*, the realm of subjectivity, is the dimension that pertains to the signifier, where elements have no positive existence but are, in structuralist terms, constituted by virtue of their mutual differences. This register is determinant of subjectivity, in the sense that the 'signifier represents the subject for another signifier'. It is also the realm of the 'big Other', source of all processes and resources of symbolisation and of the Law, which regulates desire and the Oedipus complex. The unconscious is the discourse of the Other and thus belongs to the symbolic order. The Symbolic is both the 'pleasure principle' that regulates the distance from *das Ding* (the Thing), and the 'death drive', which goes beyond the pleasure principle by means of repetition: 'the death drive is only the mask of the symbolic order' (Žižek 1989: 132). Thus, for Žižek, this drive is not to be understood only in terms of physical death ('the way of all flesh'), but as the realm in which a certain life continues (that of the 'undead') in the Symbolic after the death of the flesh. The Lacanian notion of language as being founded in the Name-of-the-(dead). Father, derives from this. Only after physical death can one live on in the Symbolic

The basis of the *Imaginary* is the formation of the ego in the 'mirror stage'. When the baby recognises, between six and eighteen months, its image in the mirror at the point of the acquisition of articulate language, it is still lacking motor coordination. This image has both a symbolic and imaginary aspect. From the point of view of the Imaginary – also the point of view of identification – the image 'is' the child. From the point of view of the Symbolic, the image is only an image. Recognition (Imaginary) of itself in the mirror is also the child's misrecognition (*méconnaisance*) (Symbolic).

For Žižek, the Imaginary is most significant as the basis of fantasy and, in particular, of the subject's structuring fantasy. If the satisfaction of desire is continually thwarted because of the impossibility of an object ever objectively giving complete satisfaction (every object only ever approximates it), fantasy fills the gap. More schematically, fantasy bridges the gap between the Symbolic and the Real. It 'sustains the subject's sense of reality' (Žižek 1999a: 51). Fantasy is the substitute for the hard-core of identity; the latter is an illusion but, nevertheless, we have to believe in it. There is no sexual relationship in the Lacanian frame, and yet it is necessary to proceed as if there were. Such a belief, or structuring fantasy, is a formation of the Imaginary.

Jouissance, Sinthome *and the Subject*

The subject is, as a Cartesian void, available to be 'pathologised' – that is, to assume a unique content/character. Part of this assumption is in terms of an enjoyment which transcends the subject's reflexive capabilities: it is the subject as more than the subject itself knows.

With *jouissance* (in French, it has the sense of 'bliss' beyond pleasure, but is often translated as enjoyment), Žižek focuses on the command to enjoy (= surplus of pleasure) coming from the Superego, with the result that enjoyment becomes pain, as well as the striving for *jouissance* coming from the (impossible) satisfaction of desire. Thus there is always too much or too little *jouissance*. To the extent that it is realised *jouissance* is essentially drive-based. The symptom, as the realisation of *jouissance* is, in the Lacanian terminology used by Žižek, called, *sinthome*, and is best illustrated by the enjoyment in puns (especially homophony) found in James Joyce's *Finnegans Wake*. A symptom is a coded message, whereas the *sinthome* (derived by Lacan from the name, Saint Thomas Aquinas). Enjoyment of the symptom is a *sinthome*: a *jouis-sens* (enjoyment in sense). The ethic of psychoanalysis is connected to *jouissance* in the sense that it involves pursuing what gives enjoyment, no matter what the cost. Thus, in the example invoked by Žižek, Don Giovanni, when given the chance by the Commander at the moment of judgement to recant all his sins, refuses. This is what constitutes Don Giovanni as a subject 'more than himself', as a *sinthome* on the verge of madness, as we all are as unique beings.

The Psychoanalytic (Kantian) Ethic Against Perversion

Not to compromise on one's desire (*ne pas céder sur son désir*) is the psychoanalytic ethic, and this is what Don Giovanni demonstrates in his final confrontation with the Commander. Here, as Žižek interprets it, desire is not a transgression against the Law, but is raised to the level of ethical duty, 'so that "*ne pas céder sur son désir*" is ultimately another way of saying "Do your duty"' (Žižek 1999a: 153). Such a notion of desire is to be distinguished from 'perverse' desire generated by the Law, so, as St Paul saw, the commandment makes sin flare up ('For without the law *sin* was dead', Epistle to the Romans, Chapter 7). The Law becomes the very instigator of the behaviour it forbids. Indeed, as Foucault later noted with regard to sexuality, the Law even marks out and elicits the behaviour it forbids. This 'morbid' and 'perverse' form of the Law, Žižek tells us, is to be distinguished from Lacan's psychoanalytic approach, which sees the determination to follow one's desire (to sin) to the end – like Don Giovanni – as a form of ethical imperative.

Perverse desire leads to nothing but pleasure (and thus to deca-dence). It is where contemporary market-based society is headed because it pays so little attention to spirituality and the soul – those elements beyond the flesh and the pleasure based on it. Consequently, it is in the organisation of enjoyment that key ethical questions are raised.

In a more orthodox vein, for Lacan, Kant is not a sadian version of moralism: Sade is a Kantian version of reason (Sade is a closet Kantian). As Žižek sees it, the point is to show that Kant's ethic of fol-lowing the moral law is also part of the 'crucial antecedent' to psychoanalytical ethics. Rather than this ethic being caught up in abstraction and thus unable to deliberate on concrete situations, the moral Law is based in a radical indeterminacy: it does not say what one should do; it simply says that one should fulfil one's moral duty. It is thus the ethical subject's own responsibility to translate the moral Law. Duty in Kant is not following the Moral Law literally, but of taking responsibility for one's interpretation of it. Indeed, there is no escape from this responsibility.

In a more contemporary vein, Žižek considers the way that mod-ernist ethics – where the subject would, at all times, refrain from doing wrong, from sinning – has given way to post-modern ethics, where one 'sins' for a noble reason, or cause. Thus, in Lars von Trier's film, *Breaking the Waves*, the heroine, Bess, gives herself to sexual promiscuity in order to tell her experiences to her paralysed husband, injured on an oil rig. Despite the ostracism of the local village for her actions, Bess believes that by following her husband's request to experience sex by proxy, he may get better. The highest sacrifice thus comes to be sinning and we enter the era of 'post-classical tragedy', where, instead of suffering from repressing the desire to act in a sinful way, one acts in a sinful way for altruistic reasons. As an additional point, Žižek claims that subjectivity in post-modernity takes the form of feature film.

Sexual gratification, for its part, is beyond egoism, beyond the plea-sure principle, so that following one's desire overlaps with doing one's duty (cf. Don Giovanni and the woman who sins for good reason).

Hegel on Conditions; Speech and Evil

As a supplement to his Lacanian framework, Žižek uses Hegel. In particular, Hegel is read as not having an appearance/reality episte-mology, as tradition has often asserted, but is a philosopher who puts depth (ground) and surface (conditions) on the same level. Thus, against the view that violence in society is the outcome of some deep-seated, natural human tendency, a Hegelian reading would place ground (source of violence) and conditions (provoking vio-lence) on the same level.

Thus, Žižek is against the idea that circumstances bring out latent forces ('psychic dispositions'): 'what counts as ground and what counts as conditions are ultimately contingent and exchangeable' (Žižek 1999b: 232). Conditions indeed become 'ground'.

The notion of the origin of language as a wound in the subject provides Žižek with a pretext to revisit Lacan's notion of 'full' (communicative speech) and 'empty' speech. The latter operates like a password, that is, as a gesture of recognition. Emptiness, then, does not mean being empty of meaning or significance.

With '"radical Evil" there opens up a space for Good in precisely the same way empty speech (recognition) opens up the space for full speech' (Žižek 1999c: 272)

Radical evil ontologically precedes the Good (cf. Don Giovanni and the Commander), where evil is another name for the death drive: 'the fixation on some Thing that derails our life circuit' (Žižek 1999c: 273). Thus Hegel speaks about man's 'fall' into sin (as what precedes the Good).

Post-modern Issues: From Ideology to Cyberspace and Liberal Politics

Rather than dispense with the notion of ideology, as post-modern thought has done, Žižek points out that ideology is not defined by the dichotomy of true–false. Politically, true facts can be called upon but used in an ideological way. In particular, ideology works as an invisible frame on the world, resolving all essential antagonisms, such as that between man and woman (of sexual difference), or between the market and social responsibility. Indeed, at its purest, ideology is the effect of depth, giving onto naturalism. In this sense, the market system as a natural way of distributing wealth is ideological. The problem arises, of course, in defining the position from which ideology can be denounced. This place, Žižek says, must always remain empty, never be given a material content, for all such content is contingent and will in the end become ideological in its turn.

The key issue with regard to cyberspace is whether Oedipus is present, or whether there is a risk of falling into psychosis. Žižek concludes that cyberspace is still a form of mediation and that, therefore, Oedipus is still present. In particular, cyberspace cannot destroy, and even depends on, the sphere of fantasy; 'the frame that guarantees our access to reality our "sense of reality" (Žižek 1999d: 122)

Žižek illustrates the passive-interactive dynamics of cyberspace by invoking the Japanese electronic toy, the *tamogochi*, a toy which has to be looked after as though it were alive, and can 'die' from neglect. The point here is that passivity still has to be externalised, enacted. So that even within the most passive behaviour, there is active behaviour. The *tamogochi*, then, can allow you to 'love your neighbour' without having a troublesome neighbour to worry about. This is the ultimate point of Left-Liberal politics (of which Žižek is particularly scathing): being able to support causes without having to deal with the real world consequences. Multiculturalism throws up this dilemma in an acute way. For while Liberals might support multiculturalism from a distance, they are less willing to live multiculturally (i.e. live according to the strictures of certain non-European cultural norms).

Žižek's Strengths and Weaknesses

As a thinker in the Lacanian style, Žižek has been able to extend and deepen our understanding of contemporary politics and society, including the concept of the subject that is embedded in it. He has also provided an insight into how domains like that of the market have become de-politicised, while actually being ideological. Moreover, Žižek, more than any other contemporary thinker, perhaps, has been willing to engage with features of popular culture that others have shunned. In this vein, his exposition of Lacan by way of cinema and popular literature has given a real fillip to Lacanian scholarship. Žižek has genuinely extended the audience for Lacanian psychoanalytic theory. These, then, are Žižek's undoubted strengths.

On the other hand, he often seems to embody the very notion of post-modern paradox that he rails against. For, his expositions are often carried out at top speed: that is, he pours out the insights often without taking time to complete the elaboration necessary to convince his audience. In relation to politics, this is most evident in the claim that the market and the accompanying trend towards globalisation are ideological, not natural, and are at the heart of capitalism, and that to oppose one (the market) is to oppose the other. Not only is this claim not new, it requires a whole additional dimension of analysis regarding the processes of commodification in order to give it plausibility. The short, the question is: to what extent can one fight against the market and commodification when opposition is itself marketed and commodified?

Similarly, the speed at which Lacan is brought to bear in popular culture (specifically, in cinema) often covers over the complexities relating to representation, mediation and the image. How, for example, does the image *qua* image relate to the Imaginary? It is not just through fantasy because the image is the material incarnation of the fantasy.

These, then, are a few of the issues that seem in need of attention in relation to Žižek's undeniably stimulating work.

References

Lacan, Jacques (2006), 'Seminar on "The Purloined Letter"', in *Ecrits: The First Complete Edition in English*, trans. Bruce Fink, New York: Norton.
Žižek, Slavoj (1989), *The Sublime Object of Ideology*, London: Verso.
—— (1991), *Looking Awry: An Introduction to Jacques Lacan through Popular Culture*, Cambridge, Mass. and London: MIT Press.
—— (1992), ' "In His Bold Gaze My Ruin is Writ Large"' in Slavoj Žižek, ed., *Everything You Always Wanted to Know about Lacan (But Were Afraid to Ask Hitchcock)*, London and New York: Verso.
—— (1999a), *The Ticklish Subject: The Absent Centre of Political Ontology*, London and New York: Verso. Cambridge, Mass. and London: MIT Press.
—— (1999b), 'Hegel's "Logic of Essence" as a Theory of Ideology' in Elizabeth Wright and Edmund Wright, eds, *The Žižek Reader*, Oxford and Malden, Mass.: Blackwell.
—— (1999c), 'A Hair of the Dog that Bit You' in Elizabeth Wright and Edmund Wright, eds, *The Žižek Reader*, Oxford and Malden, Mass.: Blackwell.
—— (1999d), 'Is it Possible to Traverse the Fantasy in Cyberspace?' in Elizabeth Wright and Edmund Wright, eds, *The Žižek Reader*, Oxford and Malden, Mass.: Blackwell.

See also: **Butler, Deleuze, Freud, Heidegger, Kristeva, Lacan, Saussure**

Žižek's major writings

(2006) *The Parallax View*, Cambridge, Mass.: MIT Press.
(2005a) *The Universal Exception* New York: Continuum.
(2005b) *Interrogating the Real: Selected Writings*, New York: Continuum.
(2004) *Organs Without Bodies: On Deleuze and Consequences*, New York and London: Routledge.

(2003) *The Puppet and the Dwarf: The Perverse Core of Christianity*, Cambridge, Mass: MIT Press.

(2002) *Welcome to the Desert of the Real*, New York: The Wooster Press.

(2001a) *Did Somebody Say Totalitarianism? Five Essays in the (Mis)Use of a Notion*, London and New York: Verso.

(2001b) *On Belief*, London: Routledge.

(2000a) *The Fragile Absolute, Or Why the Christian Legacy is Worth Fighting For* London and New York: Verso.

(2000b) *The Art of the Ridiculous Sublime, On David Lynch's Lost Highway* Walter Chapin Center for the Humanities: University of Washington.

(2000c) with Judith Butler and Ernesto Laclau, *Contingency, Hegemony, Universality: Contemporary Dialogues on the Left*, London and New York: Verso.

(2000d [1992]) *Enjoy Your Symptom! Jacques Lacan In Hollywood and Out* New York: Routledge. Second expanded edition.

(1999a) *The Ticklish Subject: The Absent Centre of Political Ontology*, London and New York: Verso. Cambridge, Mass. and London: MIT Press.

(1999b) Elizabeth Wright and Edmund Wright, eds, *The Žižek Reader*, Oxford and Malden, Mass.: Blackwell.

(1997a) with F.W.J. von Schelling, *The Abyss Of Freedom – Ages Of The World*, Ann Arbor: University of Michigan Press.

(1997b) *The Plague Of Fantasies (Wo Es War)*, London and New York: Verso.

(1996) *The Indivisible Remainder: An Essay On Schelling And Related Matters* London and New York: Verso.

(1994a) *The Metastases Of Enjoyment: Six Essays On Woman And Causality (Wo Es War)*, London and New York: Verso.

(1994b), ed. *Mapping Ideology*, London and New York: Verso.

(1993) *Tarrying With The Negative: Kant, Hegel And The Critique Of Ideology* Durham: Duke University Press.

(1992) ed. *Everything You Always Wanted to Know about Lacan (But Were Afraid to Ask Hitchcock)*, London and New York: Verso.

(1991a) *Looking Awry: An Introduction to Jacques Lacan through Popular Culture*, Cambridge, Mass. and London: MIT Press.

(1991b) *For They Know Not What They Do: Enjoyment As A Political Factor* London and New York: Verso.

(1989) *The Sublime Object of Ideology*, London: Verso.

Further reading

Butler, Rex (2004), *Slavoj Žižek: Live Theory*, London: Continuum.

Kay, Sarah (2003), *Žižek: A Critical Introduction*, London: Polity.

Myers, Tony (2003), *Slavoj Žižek*: London: Routledge (Routledge Critical Thinkers).

Parker, Ian (2004), *Slavoj Žižek: A Critical Introduction*, London: Pluto Press.

MODERNITY/MODERNISM

Modernity/Modernism can refer to industrialisation, but more frequently refers to the Enlightenment aspect of industrialisation, which focuses on knowledge freed from religious influence, and the artistic aspect captured by modernism, that include and emphasise the role of avant-garde practices. Thinkers became fascinated by the very real changes that modernity/modernism ushered in, and particularly with regard to changes in consciousness. In fact, modernity/modernism could in large part be understood as the valorisation and recognition of consciousness as a force in its own right. Baudelaire's dictum that modernity is the 'transitory, the fleeting and the contingent' could be understood in this sense. Joyce is an author who seriously attempts to work through the consequences of this for the art of writing (the novel).

WALTER BENJAMIN (1892–1940)

As scholars of the work of Walter Benjamin have begun to make clear, 'any attempt to establish a unity from a series of texts as clearly diverse as Benjamin's will always be thwarted from the start' (A. Benjamin 1991: 143). Similarly, Benjamin's *oeuvre* resists any unified theoretical position (A. Benjamin 2005: 2; McCole 1993: 10–21). Not only did Benjamin invoke various theoretical frameworks and write on an extraordinarily wide range of topics – from German tragic drama, Romanticism, history, language and translation, to film, Paris, Baudelaire, Marxism, storytelling and violence – but he also moved stylistically between prose, fragment, aphorism and citation, often placing himself between the genres of storytelling, literary criticism, historiography, and philosophy. Influenced variously by Judaism, Marxism, and by what he saw as the progressive aspects of modernity, Benjamin stands at the threshold of a new intellectual era. And yet he lived his own life steeped in the accoutrements of the private scholar – a form of existence which, like the storyteller Benjamin himself described so well, was on the point of disappearing – perhaps for ever.

Walter Benjamin was born in Berlin in 1892, the son of a Jewish art dealer. After his schooling at a humanistic gymnasium he studied philosophy and literature in Freiburg as well as Berlin. While at university, he became leader of the Jewish radical students and, like his friend Gershom Scholem, came under the influences of Jewish messianic and Kabbalistic thinking.[1] Scholem's brand of Zionism mixed with anarchistic political sympathies exerted a strong influence on Benjamin. While studying Hebrew in Munich, Benjamin met the Utopian philosopher Ernst Bloch, and contemplated going with Scholem to Palestine in 1924, but his marriage to the Latvian actress and committed communist, Asja Lacis intervened.

For most of the 1920s Benjamin lived the precarious life of a private scholar, supported mainly by his father, with whom he had difficult relations, yet he managed to travel and take holidays, and these trips provided materials for his writing. To ameliorate his financial situation, he set to work to obtain a university post – a fearfully difficult operation at the time – and in 1925 submitted a *Habilitationsschrift*, 'The Origin of German Tragic Drama'. The thesis was rejected by the University of Frankfurt because of its unconventional, and often lyrical, personal style. *The Origin of German Tragic Drama* was Benjamin's only completed book, the rest of his writings being in the form of essays, articles (both academic and journalistic), translations, and fragments, many published posthumously. Through this literary activity, which included translations of Proust and Baudelaire, Benjamin managed to earn some money for himself and his family. With the Nazi rise to power in 1933, Benjamin went to Paris, where he met Hannah Arendt. There, he lived off a modest scholarship awarded to him by the Institute for Social Research.

Once in Paris, Benjamin associated with the surrealists, and to a lesser extent, with members of the College of Sociology, run by Georges Bataille, and embarked on an enormous study of Baudelaire and the nineteenth century in The Arcades Project (see Buck-Morss 1991). At the outbreak of war, with the Arcades Project unfinished, Horkheimer and Adorno persuaded Benjamin to come to America via Spain. When he reached the border at Port-Bou, however, he was refused a pass, and, apparently unable to face the thought of being caught by the Gestapo, committed suicide on the night of 25 September 1940. The next morning, the border guards, upon whom Benjamin's death had made an impression, allowed the group he was with to pass through into Spain. 'Suicide', Benjamin had written in his study of Baudelaire, 'is the achievement of modernity in the field of passions.'

The Work of Art and its Reproduction

Although the whole of Benjamin's *oeuvre* resonates with inspired ideas about modernity in all its aspects, possibly no work has drawn more attention, particularly in the debate over post-modernity, than his essay – of which there are three versions – 'The Work of Art in the Age of its Mechanical Reproducibility' (see Benjamin 2002: 101–33). Although written ostensibly in the tenor of a political analysis of the reproduction of the work of art, particularly in the age of film and photography and mass access to these, Benjamin in fact offers an astute analysis of a fundamental change in the aesthetic quality of the work of art. Once, by being reproducible, the work of art's aura of authenticity has withered away, sense perception changes along with humanity's entire mode of existence. The technique of reproduction brings art objects closer to a mass audience. Even more: a certain reversibility develops and the work of art as reproduced leads to the work of art being designed for reproducibility. As always with Benjamin's analyses, there is never a unilateral movement between positions or situations, but a movement to and fro between them.

Thus, despite the title to his piece, Benjamin sees more than the mere reproduction of works of art in the modern age (late-nineteenth and twentieth centuries) as being significant. Indeed it is the process of reproduction as such which is revolutionary: the fact, for instance, that the photographic negative enables a veritable multiplication of 'originals'. With the photograph, the spectre of the simulacrum emerges, although Benjamin never names it as such. Not simulacra, but *technik* (German for technique; the term also connotes technology) is the focus of Benjamin's interest.

Photography, Photographs and Aura

Keeping photography as our example, we note that technique in photography is not an incidental, but an essential part of the art. The photographic work of art might not have the aura of an original classical painting consecrated by tradition, but it is not a simple negation of aura either. This is not to deny that Benjamin also lauds the democratic potential of the reproduction of classical art objects; but it is to suggest that of greater interest to him are the new aesthetic possibilities brought to bear in the wake of *technik*. Reversibility (the effect on the type of art work produced), along with a new conception of 'originality' are just two of the issues opened up by Benjamin's discussion.

Two additional elements stand out. The first is that with the possibility of reproduction a work of art can receive meaning from a diversity of different contexts.

Although Benjamin has been often been thought of exclusively as the theorist of the technology of art, we should also note Benjamin's relation to specific photographs from the early years of photography in the nineteenth century.

The concept of 'aura' was used by Benjamin for the first time in his 'Little History of Photography' published in 1931, before the 'Work of Art' essay (see Benjamin 1999: 507–30). There, the author seems to foreshadow Barthes's discerning the 'magic' of a photograph (not photography in general). Thus, the production of the photograph is both a physical, technical procedure and is the precondition of the realisation of the photograph as image, so that the physical side (light hitting a photo-sensitive surface) is embodied in the image as image, without the image being reducible to this. In this sense, the photograph is not a copy of the real, but an emanation of it, as Barthes says (Barthes 1993: 88). It is as an emanation that the photographic image has such power to fascinate. Benjamin, on at least one occasion, seems to recognise this power of the photographic image. He is entranced by particular photographic images. One such is a work by the now little known English painter, David Octavius Hill (who painted portraits from photos) and is called, 'New Haven Fishwife'. Here, for Benjamin, there is something beyond the image, 'beyond testimony' (Benjamin 1999: 510) that 'fills you with an unruly desire to know what her name was, the woman who was alive there, who even now is still real and will never consent to be wholly absorbed in "art"' (1999: 510). The image is completely transparent, so that no technology intervenes in Benjamin's relation to this woman, 'her eyes cast down in such indolent, seductive modesty' (1999: 510). These eyes are, after Barthes, the *punctum* for Benjamin. Or, again foreshadowing Barthes, the true *punctum* is 'the woman who is dead and who is going to die', the one who was alive at that moment, and could be still living for Benjamin, thus echoing a version of the 'He is dead and he is going to die', the caption Barthes attaches to the image of condemned Lewis Payne, 1865 (see Barthes 1993: 95), a caption that could apply to any photograph as a freezing of the moment. Whatever the case, Benjamin experiences this woman as alive, as present, through the photograph, through the image as virtual, yet she is dead. This is to say that the image is transparent for him: the woman is *immediately* present (and yet is no longer alive); he does not 'read' the image; he does not interpret it. He breaks with hermeneutics. This experience of the *immediately* present is an experience of time itself.

As has been recognised (see Costello 2005: 165), Benjamin's attitude to aura should thus not be limited to the 'Work of Art' essay, but is, like so much of Benjamin's terminology, an ambiguous term. The question is: Does photography connect with the aura of tradition, or does it break with it? Such is the question that Benjamin has left for us.

The second element of Benjamin's essay worthy of note is his characterisation of film. While some of the early commentators on film had attempted to compare it with Egyptian hieroglyphics or classical painting, Benjamin's approach is once again to see film as a new *technik* of art, one where, unlike the theatre (where the audience identifies with the actor), the film audience occupies the same position as the camera. This implies two things. First: contrary to expectations, the audience may have quite an active role in the viewing of a film, and, second: film can change 'our field of perception'. Thus, just as Freud and psychoanalysis have sensitised people to the fact of slips of the tongue and to the unconscious generally – although these clearly existed prior to Freud, but went unnoticed – so the camera sensitises people (with the close-up, for example) to aspects of the environment that were hitherto unnoticed.

Theorist of Tradition

Even though Benjamin was clearly enthralled by modernity – as the Arcades Project, as well as his other writings indicate – he has also been seen as a theorist of tradition, which, on the face of it was supposed to be what modernity swept away. Without, at this point, seeking a Jewish motive for this interest, it is possible to suggest that the connecting point between tradition and modernity in Benjamin's work is the notion of reproduction. It emerges in a number of different guises in Benjamin's writing: in the image of the storyteller, in the conception of translation, in the valorisation of Proust's *mémoire involontaire*, in the lyrical aspect of Baudelaire's poetry, and in the notion of cultural transmission in the Arcades Project. Very briefly, let us look at each of these in turn.

In the earliest text, 'The Task of the Translator' (1923), Benjamin begins by saying that the translator's task is not illuminated if it is looked at from the point of view of the audience. Rather, one has to assume that '[n]o poem is intended for the reader, no picture for the beholder, no symphony for the listener' (Benjamin 1979a: 69). Instead it is the text which must be the centre of attention. In this regard, the difference, in principle, between the 'original' and the translation has to be taken into account. And here Benjamin makes a quite singular move. He says that an 'original' should not be understood to be essentially hermetically sealed off from subsequent translations by a quality of purity. Were this the case, no text (and even an interpretation is a translation) would survive the time of its immediate production. The text, or art object, thus has an 'afterlife' which propels it into history via tradition – via translation, we should rather say. To take the concrete case with which Benjamin is dealing, it is a question of how Baudelaire's originally French poetry can be faithfully translated into German. Not by attempting a literal translation, but by 'touch[ing] the original lightly' is the response. A literal translation 'demolishes the theory of the *reproduction* of meaning and is a direct threat to comprehensibility' (Benjamin 1979a: 78, emphasis added). The 'reproduction of meaning' is the translation of the poetic element of the work, and it is this which calls for translation. It is part of the work. Reproduction is part of the work. This is Benjamin's most salient argument. To illustrate the point he says that just as the broken fragments of a vessel differ between themselves and yet constitute the same vessel, so the different, non-literal fragments of a translation can reproduce the whole of the original. The principle of the reproduction of significance (not the literal meaning) is in the word itself. 'In the beginning was the word', Benjamin reiterates after the New Testament. The principle of translation – the principle of reproduction – is original, therefore, not the object reproduced.

In 'The storyteller' (1936), a similar structure is in evidence. What allows the story told by the storyteller to be reproduced is not the content of what is told – not the information, as Benjamin puts it – for it would not survive the moment of its initial telling. Rather, it is the story in the memory which is important. A story is what allows the content to be retained in the memory. Story and memory are thus homologous with news and oblivion. Story is the element of transmission – also called tradition by Benjamin – and transmission is fundamentally the story of a life after death. The story, in effect, is the 'afterlife' of people, just as translation is the afterlife of the poem. The story, which always presupposes a community, is what turns a listener into a storyteller: 'The cardinal point for the unaffected listener is to assure himself of the possibility of reproducing the story' (Benjamin 1979b: 97). Here we see that as a principle of reproduction, the story also contains a principle of reversibility, with the listener becoming the storyteller.

Memory and the Arcades Project

Again, with Baudelaire's lyric poetry, as with Proust's *mémoire involontaire*, the difference between 'remembrance' and 'memory' is proposed. Remembrance derives from an experience of memory which was not first of all conscious. Like the Freudian unconscious, remembrance gives rise to experience (Proust's *madeleine*), but is not itself an experience. The same pertains to the lyrical in Baudelaire's poetry: as a traumatic shock, lyricism becomes the principle of poetry's transmission as a kind of aftershock, just as the *mémoire involontaire* carries a life forward, despite the fact that the events at issue may have been forgotten by consciousness. The subject may have forgotten the basis of the lyricism, or the memory, but these have not forgotten the subject. Once again, in the act of reproducing the experience, reversibility is in evidence

With regard to the Arcades Project, the situation is much more complex. Scholars are only now beginning to work their way into its labyrinthine structure, a structure which Adorno claimed only Benjamin himself could fully explain. Let us simply note two important aspects of this project: the first is that Benjamin based it on the revolution in architecture that the use of iron and glass had made. Here commentators have noted in particular that Benjamin was fascinated by the new spatial relationships between interior and exterior that the use of glass made possible: the street could be brought inside, and this inside was opened up to the outside. The difference between private and public was thus becoming problematic.

Second, although Benjamin was engaged in working out a philosophy of history, and/or a social and cultural history, as Buck-Morss and McCole have suggested, the question arises concerning the mechanism by which Benjamin saw modernity – as the ephemeral incarnate in Baudelaire's terms – could reproduce itself. How, in short, would the theorist and writer of tradition understand modernity in its ever-changing capitalist variant? Opinion seems to be agreed on the fact that in the most general sense, Benjamin tried to reconcile a version of Marxism with a version of Jewish theology, the Marxist element providing a clinical analysis of the reality of capitalism, and Jewish theology providing an explanation of how a tradition was embodied in this most disembodied of cultural formations. The key, no doubt, is to understand how, for Benjamin, history is embedded in modernity, not separate from it – how the 'original' thing, produced in a moment of time, contains the possibility of its reproduction within it. History, or rather historical understanding, might be the 'afterlife' of modernity (see McCole 1993: 248n).

For her part, Buck-Morss illustrates the issue exactly when she refers to Benjamin's fascination with a female wax figure adjusting her garter in the Musée Gravin. Buck-Morss comments: 'Her ephemeral act is frozen in time. She is unchanged, defying organic decay' (Buck-Morss 1991: 369). What remains to be understood is how the wax figure – or its aesthetic equivalent perceptible throughout the labyrinth of society – can become the 'afterlife' – the embodiment – of history. To answer this question is to begin to unlock the sphere of Benjamin's most enigmatic writing.

Critique of Violence

With increasing interest in the notion of sovereignty and bio-politics (see Agamben), Benjamin's essay, 'Critique of Violence' (Benjamin 1996: 236–52), is of growing interest. Jacques Derrida's controversial paper, 'Force of Law', is ostensibly a reading of this essay which focuses on the tension between the formal essence of the law, enshrined in myth and the problematic nature of its application (Derrida 1992: 3–67). There is no application of the law which is equivalent to its essence, only particular acts and decrees which have the force of law.

In his article, Benjamin, points out that violence cannot easily be separated into legitimate, legal violence, and natural 'illegal' violence. For legal violence weakens the law, rather than strengthens it.

Moreover, law is the result of a prior, mythic violence, violence committed in the interest of creating a particular form of life, rather than preserving pure existence, or 'mere life'. From this ancient tradition of myth comes the idea that to live is, constantly, to create new forms of the social world, ultimately through violence, not through the law. For to the extent that the law itself is founded in violence, in the sense that the very presence of the law means that violence has already taken place, it is thus already immanent in the law. Because, in Benjamin's view, humanity cannot be said to coincide with mere life, the prospect of violence is always present. Indeed, Benjamin goes further and suggests that it is even 'ignominious' for humanity to protect existence for its own sake. The sacred thus does not emerge here in the 'sacredness of life' for its own sake, but rather in the violent act that creates a new form of life. Such is the view many moderns find so unpalatable.

Moreover, Benjamin shows that violence cannot easily be separated into legitimate, legal violence, and natural 'illegal' violence. For legal violence weakens the law, rather than strengthens it.

Note

1 On the intellectual implications of Benjamin's Jewish experience, see McCole (1993: 1–10), and Irving Wohlfarth (1991: 157–215).

References

Barthes, Roland (1993) *Camera Lucida*, trans. Richard Howard, London: Vintage.

Benjamin, Andrew (1991), *Art, Mimesis and the Avant-garde*, London and New York: Routledge.

—— (2005), 'Introduction' in Andrew Benjamin, ed., *Walter Benjamin and Art*, London and New York: Continuum.

Benjamin, Walter (1979a) 'The task of the translator' in *Illuminations*, trans. Harry Zohn, Glasgow: Fontana/Collins.

—— (1979b), 'The storyteller' in *Illuminations*, trans. Harry Zohn, Glasgow: Fontana/Collins.

—— (1996) 'Critique of Violence', trans. Edmund Jephcott in Marcus Bullock and Michael W. Jennings, eds, *Walter Benjamin: Selected Writings, Vol 1, 1927–1934*, Cambridge, Mass. and London: The Belknap Press of Harvard University Press.

—— (1999 [1931]) 'Little History of Photography', trans. Edmund Jephcott and Kingsley Shorter in Michael W. Jenning, Howard Eiland and Gary Smith, eds, *Walter Benjamin: Selected Writings, Vol 2, 1927–1934*, Cambridge, Mass. and London: The Belknap Press of Harvard University Press.

—— (2002 [1935–36]) 'The Work of Art in the Age of its Technological Reproducibility' trans. Edmund Jephcott and Harry Zohn in, Howard Eiland and Michael W. Jennings, eds, *Walter Benjamin: Selected Writings, Vol 3,* Cambridge, Mass. and London: The Belknap Press of Harvard University Press.

Buck-Morss, Susan (1991) *The Dialectics of Seeing: Walter Benjamin and the Arcades Project*, Cambridge, Mass. and London: MIT Press.

Costello, Diarmuid (2005), 'Aura, Face, Photography' in Andrew Benjamin, ed., *Walter Benjamin and Art*, London and New York: Continuum.

Derrida, Jacques (1992), 'Force of Law: The Mystical Foundation of Authority', trans. Mary Quaintance in Drucilla Cornell, Michel Rosenfeld and David Gray Carlson, eds, *Deconstruction and the Possibility of Justice*, New York, London: Routledge.

McCole, John (1993), *Walter Benjamin and the Antinomies of Tradition*, New York: Cornell University Press.

Wohlfarth, Irving (1991) 'On some Jewish motifs in Benjamin' in Andrew Benjamin, ed., T*he Problems of Modernity: Adorno and Benjamin*, London and New York: Routledge, 'Warwick Studies in Philosophy and Literature'.

See also: **Adorno, Barthes, Baudrillard, Habermas**

Benjamin's major writings

(1996–2003) *Walter Benjamin: Selected Writings, Vol 1: 1927–1934, Vol 2: 1927–1934, Vol 3, 1935–1940*, ed. Marcus Bullock and Michael W. Jennings, Cambridge, Mass., London: The Belknap Press of Harvard University Press.

(1989) *The Correspondence of Walter Benjamin and Gershom Scholem, 1932–1940*, trans. Gary Smith and André Lefevere, New York: Schocken Books.

(1986 [1955]) *Reflections. Essays, Aphorisms, Autobiographical Writings*, trans. Edmund Jephcott, New York: Schocken Books.

(1985a) *One Way Street and Other Writings*, trans. Edmund Jephcott and Kingsley Shorter, London: Verso.

(1985b [1963]) *The Origin of German Tragic Drama*, trans. John Osborne, London and New York: Verso.

(1973a) *Understanding Brecht*, trans. Anna Bostock, London: NLB.

(1973b) *Charles Baudelaire: A Lyric Poet in the Era of High Capitalism*, trans. Harry Zohn, London: NLB.

(1973c [1955]) *Illuminations*, trans. Harry Zohn, Glasgow: Fontana.

Further reading

Benjamin, Andrew, ed. (2005), *Walter Benjamin and Art*, London and New York: Continuum.

Benjamin, Andrew and Hanssen, Beatrice, eds (2002), *Walter Benjamin and Romanticism*, London and New York: Continuum.

Ferris, David S, ed. (2004), *The Cambridge Companion to Walter Benjamin*, New York: Cambridge University Press.

McCole, John (1993), *Walter Benjamin and the Antinomies of Tradition*, New York: Cornell University Press.

Osborne, Peter, ed. (2004), *Walter Benjamin: Critical Evaluations in Cultural Theory*, New York: Routledge.

MAURICE BLANCHOT (1907–2003)

In the 1983 edition of the *Fontana Dictionary of Modern Thinkers* there are entries for Francois Mitterand and Michel Foucault (as well as for Marilyn Monroe), but no entry for Maurice Blanchot, one of France's foremost post-war writers and critics, and a thinker who has exerted a powerful influence on Foucault and many others. From his critical writings we can deduce that this fact would not trouble Blanchot at all; in fact, because he sees writing as autonomous, and the outcome of a profound solitude, a biography, or a *curriculum vitae*, is of little relevance for assisting a reader in coming to grips with the enigmas of a truly literary work. In fact, Blanchot's silence on matters biographical constitutes an important part of his literary project. For him the literary object is at one and the same time irreducible (to psychological or sociological explanations) and indeterminate (it is never possible to recover all of the meaning and significance of a literary text). Whether this amounts to a continuation of Romanticism is perhaps one of the key issues pertaining to an understanding of Blanchot's *oeuvre*.

Enigmatic Writing

Blanchot met Emmanuel Levinas (who died in 1995) in Strasbourg in the 1930s, and they became close friends. Despite some stiff competition, Blanchot – who was born in 1907 – acquired a reputation for writing some of the most enigmatic prose in modern French. Considering that he himself indirectly clarified some of the motivations for his literary work in his critical writings (most notably in Blanchot 1982, 1992 and 2003), this claim is no doubt extreme. On the other hand, as a certain force drives writing towards an unknowable centre of attraction – one that is only dimly perceptible to the one who is writing – a degree of obscurity seems to be built into Blanchot's project. While there are good reasons for refusing the epithet of Romanticism in Blanchot's case (Blanchot's refusal of the notion of the author as origin being one of them), there is a much stronger case for saying that Blanchot is a lucid proponent of artistic modernism. This does not imply an acceptance of a particular version of the principle of original creativity. Blanchot has indeed heeded the warning represented by the Hegelian dialectic, where, in the end, everything will be recuperated within the framework of Absolute Knowledge. Eventually, Hegel argues, history will come to an end; the goal of the system will be united in the process of arriving at it. All of Blanchot's *oeuvre* could be seen as a refusal to accept the basis of Hegel's philosophy of the inevitability of the homogenity implied in the end of history.

Readable but Obscure

Unlike Joyce, Blanchot does not write 'unreadable' prose; neither does he compose explicitly musical texts, like Mallarmé – although the author of *Un Coup de dés* is an important point of reference for him. On the contrary, the immediate limpidity of Blanchot's fictional writing leads the reader to expect that its meaning will be correspondingly accessible. The opening sentence of *L'Arrêt de mort* (*Death*

Sentence), is exemplary. 'These things happened to me in 1938' (Blanchot 1978: 1). Gradually this limpidity of style and meaning gives way to a profound obscurity. Names are erased à la Kafka; the place where events occur seems to be Paris, but full addresses are never given; 'J' is a woman with a terminal illness who seems to die of her own accord, and who, later, seems to be helped to die by the narrator who administers a lethal cocktail of morphine and sedative. The events appear to take place at the time of the Munich crisis, but the narrator also gives the impression that the 'events' concerned are those pertaining to the writing as such of the story – a writing which the narrator continually refuses to assume. In effect, the time of writing is ambiguous. An initial draft of the narrative was destroyed, and this propels the writing into the distant past, while at the point after J's death, the narrator says that the events being narrated have not yet happened. These kinds of features in Blanchot's *oeuvre* have prompted the description of them as swirling in indeterminacy. And in fact Blanchot's own literary theory offers some grounds for this.

Reading the Text's Singularity

From his critical writings of the 1950s, it is clear that Blanchot is opposed to any easy appropriation of the authentically literary text. This frequently happens, however, with few critics actually reading what they claim to have read. Rather, they prefer to write their commentaries on the basis of readings which set new works in pre-existing categories; when the critic does happen to see that a work cannot be thus interpreted, it is too late for reading; for the critic is already an author and thus unable to become a reader. True reading, Blanchot implies, is one that respects the literary work's singularity. True reading, in effect, is a crisis in reading. Such would be the modernist and avant-garde impetus in Blanchot's approach in the 1950s. A number of other features that still figure largely in Blanchot's later work accompany it. First of all, against any easy labelling of Blanchot as a Romantic, we note that any truly literary or artistic work is for him anonymous. This does not mean that the author is simply trying to hide in the work, but rather that the creative force of the work itself effaces the presence of the author. To be totally aware of the work is to be totally unaware of the author of it. Indeed while an author can be consciously linked to a book or to a painting, his or her true artistic merit is only perceptible at the level of a range of works – at level of the *oeuvre*, in short. Given changes in creative orientation over time, however, the exact nature of an *oeuvre* is never present to any author of it. To understand a work in its singularity it is necessary to grasp the movement that produced it. Thus, to understand writing, one must understand the conditions of possibility of writing. This means, almost inevitably, that the nature of the determination of any singular work is never immediately present.

No Institution Exists Prior to the Literary Work

With regard to the literary work in particular, the nature of determination takes another turn, one that seems to be an important element in Blanchot's own writing practice. It is that, 'the essence of literature is to escape any essential determination, or any affirmation which stabilises or even realises it: it is never already there; it is always to be found or to be reinvented' (Blanchot 2003: 293–94). In other words, Blanchot's modernist impulse entails that it is far from certain that there is any such thing as an art institution – a mechanism would be waiting to receive the new work within a framework which would pre-exist it. To give priority to the institution of art over the singularity of the work of art is, effectively, to efface that singularity by turning each work – however different from others it might be – into a repetition of the institution. This is why Blanchot argues that nothing exists prior to the work, every work being a reinvention of the practice of writing. From the point of view of the institution of literature, therefore, every singular work is characterised by its non-literary quality.

Solitude

Given the singularity of the literary work, we can see why, earlier in his career, Blanchot had spoken of the significance of the writer's solitude. Solitude refers to the way a literary work and the process giving rise to it is cut off from all others – even if, as is often the case, it alludes to other works. Solitude means that whoever reads the work in question will experience its uniqueness. Solitude is the way in which the work speaks – a speaking which is also the form of the author's silence. Playing on this, Blanchot speaks about the work as being the way that the writer's silence takes shape. In accordance with Blanchot's penchant for the rhetorical figure of the oxymoron, silence becomes the form of the author's speaking. Because the writer is within an *oeuvre*, partially produced in light of his or her unconscious desire, the discovery of the form of the *oeuvre* is of interest to both writer and reader. The *oeuvre* is a source of the writer's fascination precisely because it is not consciously determined. Only the specific work is. Fascination is the look of solitude in the *oeuvre*. The source of fascination *par excellence* is the image; and, interestingly, Blanchot does not automatically accept that the image is an unproblematic reflection of the object. The image, which is essentially visual, is in fact a way of grasping the object through distancing, or objectifying.

The Look and the Image

Many of Blanchot's fictional works play on the paradoxical status of the image as it is conveyed by the look. The image is a closeness brought about by a distancing. Solitude, fascination, image and the look thus form a fundamental series of notions which inform Blanchot's writing practice. This practice gives rise to indeterminacy. Whoever is fascinated does not see a real object or figure, 'for what is seen does not belong to the world of reality, but to the *indeterminant milieu of fascination*' (Blanchot 1982: 26, emphasis added). In a characteristically enigmatic move, Blanchot also separates the image from meaning, and relates it instead to ecstasy. Many would argue that such a notion hardly comes through in the somewhat melancholic event of Blanchot's fiction.

Waiting, Death, Chance and Indeterminacy

While it is impossible to claim to be able to plumb all the depths of Blanchot's modernist project, it is clear that death, forgetting, waiting and finality constitute another important series of concepts underpinning much of his writing. Death, Blanchot has famously said, cannot be experienced. Rather than attempting to make death the subject of an imaginary projection, or attempting a phenomenological reconstruction of dying, Blanchot writes the experience of the impossibility of the experience of death. No doubt this is the sense behind J's coming back to life in *L'Arrêt de mort*. *L'Attente l'oubli* (*Waiting, Forgetting*) and *Au moment voulu* (English translation *When the Time Comes*) as both explore the complexities of waiting and forgetting. Waiting is a kind of event that arrives, becomes impossible, while forgetting is caught between the given moment and the wanted moment; forgetting is always a kind of remembering in this sense.

In view of Blanchot's inclination for pointing out ways in which finality does not occur, or at least cannot be experienced, we note that the last man in the book of the same name is, in fact, like all other men; it is as though the last man – one who should be completely singular – is, in fact, everyman. Similarly, the 'last word' is a play on 'there is', which is not itself a word, but that which hints at the being of the word in general. The last word suggests what is given. The last word also calls for explanation, thus for more words.

Around the time of Blanchot's middle to late writings (1960s onwards), chance assumes a more obvious presence. Death only assumes its full significance in relation to chance. In *Le Pas au-delà*, Blanchot refers to the unpredictability of death and of dying (Blanchot 1973: 133). But his most systematic elaboration of chance is found in an essay on André Breton and Surrealism (Blanchot 1967: 283–308). There, Blanchot proposes chance as a particular kind of experience, one in which the prevailing system of thought is given a shake. Chance is what existing thought leaves out of account; it is what passes it by, without, on that account, having any less of an effect. Death occurs, then, but exactly when it will occur is a matter of chance. To the extent that chance is not taken into account, therefore, death does not occur; rather, it floats in indeterminacy. In this very specific sense which interested the Surrealists, death escapes a cause and effect logic because causality is the mark of determinacy. Blanchot thus proceeds in his writing according to the principle that chance gives rise to uncertainty and indeterminacy. Implied here is a connection between determinacy, and the reversibility of time, and indeterminacy, which corresponds to irreversible time. Many of Blanchot's fictional texts raise the question as to whether or not something has really taken place – the death of 'J' in *L'Arrêt de mort*, for example. Or again, through chance, a moment comes to pass. At a certain moment in *Au moment voulu*, Claudia seems to stop and look at the narrator, as though invited 'by chance' to do so. A short time later, chance and the moment are once more at issue: 'at such a moment' the narrator sees Claudia's face 'by chance'. 'At such a moment?' the narrator asks, 'and from when dated this moment?' Doubt exists as to whether anything has really happened. The scene is one of indeterminacy. Chance cannot be seen simply as an isolated and discrete occurrence; rather, it spreads its mantle over the whole, like the ink of an octopus.

If the true event is chance, writing the event, clearly, will be equivalent to exploring indeterminacy. Blanchot in fact raises the prospect that writing itself is an event and so is subject to indeterminacy. Already we have seen that this possibility was prepared by the idea of the *oeuvre* as a product of the writer's unconscious desire. There is a sense in which the writer does not go where his writing is going. The writer writes into the void: the white page, in Mallarmé's terms. Thus, largely in terms of an exploration of chance, Blanchot's writing presupposes that nothing exists prior to it; this is the deepest sense of the notion of the solitude and the autonomy of writing.

The Fragment and Community

In his later work, the elementary and fragmentary form of narrative (*récit*) gives way to a series of marked fragments, as though the order could be reconstituted if the reader so desired. Here, Blanchot is effectively writing in order to give as great a reign as possible to indeterminacy. From the reader's point of view this implies giving reign to the greatest range of meaning possible. It would be out of keeping with the logic of Blanchot's enterprise to claim to be able to explain its innermost workings. Instead it is preferable to remain circumspect, and in so doing perhaps move closer to genuine insight.

Briefly, and to conclude, reference should be made to Blanchot's interest in the notion of community. His views here can be compared to those of his friend, Georges Bataille. The point, then, that Blanchot wants to make is that a true community has no other end than its own existence. To this extent, it is indeterminate – impossible to represent or to symbolise. The nature of the community is thus incommunicable. For the writer, this community is the audience of unknown readers with no definable identity without whom the writer could not exist. For Blanchot, then – as for Bataille – the indeterminate, unknown reader constitutes the void into which every writer must venture.

References

Blanchot, Maurice (1967), 'Le demain joueur (sur l'avenir du surréalisme)' in *La Nouvelle Revue Française*, 172 (April).
—— (1973), *Le Pas au-delà*, Paris: Gallimard.
—— (1978), *L'Arrêt de mort/Death Sentence*, trans. Lydia Davis, New York: Station Hill.
—— (1982), *The Space of Literature*, trans. Ann Smock, Lincoln: University of Nebraska.
—— (1992), *The Infinite Conversation*, trans. Susan Hanson, Minneapolis: University of Minnesota Press.
—— (2003), *The Book to Come*, trans. Charlotte Mandell, Stanford: Stanford University Press.

See also: **Bataille, Derrida, Levinas**

Blanchot's major writings

(2007 [1992]) *Voice from Elsewhere*, trans. Charlotte Mandell, Albany: State University of New York Press.

(2004 [1963]) *Lautréamont and Sade*, trans. Stuart Kendall and Michelle Kendall, Stanford: Stanford University Press.

(2003 [1959]) *The Book to Come*, trans. Charlotte Mandell, Stanford: Stanford University Press.

(1997) *Awaiting Oblivion (L'attente l'oubli)*, trans. John Gregg, Lincoln: University of Nebraska Press.

(1997) *Friendship*, trans. Elizabeth Rottenberg, Stanford: Stanford University Press.

(1996) *The Most High* (translation of *Le très-haut*), trans. Allan Stoekl, Lincoln: University of Nebraska Press.

(1995a) *The Blanchot Reader*, Oxford and Cambridge, Mass.: Blackwell.

(1995b [1949]) *Work of Fire*, trans. Charlotte Mandell, Stanford: Stanford University Press.

(1992a [1973]) *The Step Not Beyond*, trans. Lycette Nelson, Albany: State University of New York.

(1992b [1969]) *The Infinite Conversation*, trans. Susan Hanson, Minneapolis: University of Minnesota Press.

(1989 [1953]) *The One Who was Standing Apart from Me*, trans. Lydia Davis, New York: Station Hill.

(1988a [1983]) *The Unavowable Community*, trans. Pierre Joris, New York: Station Hill.

(1988b [1950]) *Thomas the Obscure* (new version), trans. Robert Lemerton, New York: Station Hill.

(1987 [1957]) *The Last Man*, trans. Lydia Davis, New York: Columbia University Press.

(1986 [1980]) *The Writing of the Disaster*, trans. Ann Smock, Lincoln, University of Nebraska.

(1985a) *Vicious Circles*, trans. Paul Auster, New York: Station Hill.

(1985b [1951]) *When the Time Comes* (translation of *Au moment voulu*), trans. Lydia Davis, New York: Station Hill.

(1982a) *The Sirens' Song: Selected Essays*, ed. Gabriel Josipovici, trans. Sacha Rabinovitch, Bloomington: Indiana University Press and Brighton: Harvester Press.

(1982b [1955]) *The Space of Literature*, trans. Ann Smock, Lincoln: University of Nebraska.

(1981a) *The Gaze of Orpheus and Other Literary Essays*, ed. P. Adams Sitney, trans. Lydia Davis, New York: Station Hill.

(1981b [1973]) *The Madness of the Day* (translation of *La folie du Jour*), trans. Lydia Davis, New York: Station Hill,.

(1978 [1948]) *L'Arrêt de mort/Death Sentence*, trans. Lydia Davis, New York: Station Hill.

(1962) *L'Attente l'oubli* (translation of *Waiting, Forgetting*), Paris: Gallimard.

(1942) *Aminadab*, Paris: Gallimard.

(1941) *Thomas l'Obscur*, Paris: Gallimard.

Further reading

Gill, Carolyn Bailey (1996), *Maurice Blanchot: The Demand of Writing*, London and New York: Routledge.

Hart, Kevin (2004), *The Dark Gaze: Maurice Blanchot and the Sacred*, Chicago: Chicago University Press.

Hart, Kevin and Hartman, Geoffrey (2004), *The Power of Contestation: Perspectives on Maurice Blanchot*, Baltimore: Johns Hopkins University Press.

Hill, Leslie (1997), *Blanchot, Extreme Contemporary*, London and New York: Routledge.

Hill, Leslie, Nelson, Brian and Vardoulakis, Dimitri, eds (2006), *After Blanchot: Literature, Criticism, Philosophy*, Newark, NJ: University of Delaware Press.

FRIEDRICH NIETZSCHE (1844–1900)

In terms of the number of books and articles produced in English, French and German – thus in purely quantitative terms – no philosopher surpasses the influence today of Friedrich Nietzsche.

Nietzsche's philosophy has been seminal for contemporary thought, and especially for that thought – exemplified in the work of Michel Foucault – which has refused to take the ego/subject as the key point of reference in the study of history, society, politics and culture. That so singular and opaque a thinker could have such an impact becomes all the more surprising when we recall that Nietzsche's biography and supposed influence on Nazism have further complicated the task of interpreting his texts. Despite this, Nietzsche has been the focal point in recent times of a new departure in thought, one which refuses to accept the necessity of a relatively stable subject–object relation.

Life and Intellectual Trajectory

Friedrich Nietzsche was born in 1844 in Saxony, Prussia, he was the son of a Lutheran minister, Ludwig, who died in 1849 at the young age of 36, after having gone insane a year earlier. The son, who always suffered from poor health, thought that he was destined to die at 36. As Walter Kaufmann's classic study tells us (Kaufmann 1968: 22), from the age of six years, following the death of his younger brother in 1850, Nietzsche was brought up by his mother in an entirely female household. From 1858, he attended the old boarding school of Pforta, and excelled in religion, German literature and the classics, but was poor in maths and drawing (Kaufmann 1968: 22). It was at this time that the young scholar first suffered from the migraine headaches that were to be with him for most of his adult life.

After graduating from Pforta in 1864, Nietzsche went to the University of Bonn and studied theology and classical philology. In 1865, he gave up theology and went to Leipzig where he came under the influence of the Schopenhauer of *The World as Will and Idea*. And he was thought to be a brilliant student, the University of Basel called him to the chair of classical philology at the age of 24, even though he had not received his doctorate. Arrangements were hastily made for the doctorate to be awarded after his appointment, and Nietzsche taught at Basel from 1869 to 1879 when he was forced to retire due to ill-health. His productive life continued until January 1889, when he collapsed in Turin with his arms around the neck of a horse that had been cruelly whipped by its coachman. He never regained his sanity, and died in 1900.

Between 1872 and 1888, Nietzsche published nine books, and prepared four others for publication. His magnum opus, *The Will to Power*, based on notes from his notebooks of the 1880s, and first published posthumously in 1901, provides the strongest confirmation of Nietzsche's radically anti-idealist stance. It is this stance in particular which has attracted the attention of post-modern and post-structuralist thinkers alike.[1] Such a thorough-going anti-idealism is what allows us to designate Nietzsche as a radically horizontal thinker. Before proceeding further it is necessary to explain Nietzsche's relation to what we have designated as 'horizontal' thought.

Intuitively, one might think that to invoke the horizontal axis is to place thought on a single level, and that therefore Nietzsche is perhaps proposing a certain equality of thought. Might not horizontal thought be precisely democratic thought? The answer is that horizontal thought has nothing to do with the notion of equality or of democracy. Indeed horizontality does not refer at all to any kind of isomorphism, but to the exact opposite. Horizontal thought, in effect, is incomparable; it cannot be put on a scale; for horizontal thought is the thought of difference, not of identity. On many occasions throughout his work, Nietzsche refers to the conventional idea of equality as the exemplar of the order of the Same. For example, Nietzsche argues that the ideal equality of democracy or Christianity is a fundamentally homogenising equality of a 'herd-animal morality'. Similarly, Nietzsche claims that the idealist[2] principle, often put forward (as he says) by 'physiologists', that all human life is ultimately reducible to the 'drive to self-preservation' is an unwarranted, homogenising teleology. Human life, rather, is a venting of life, which is at the same time a 'will to power' (see Nietzsche 1973: 26). What undermines the credibility of the principle of self-preservation are the facts (violence, sacrifice, unhealthy living, etc.) which contradict it. Any essentialism or teleology, as versions of idealism, have to deny one or more aspects of life in order to be coherent. This is why Nietzsche says that idealism is life-denying – to the point, in the modern era, of producing pathological consequences. Life is always irreducible; it is a totality of differences, not an identity. An identity can be represented and put on a scale with a common measure. Horizontality, by contrast, refers to the impossibility of ever finding a scale that is adequate to difference. Horizontality opens up the 'ideolectal' (private language) end of the communicative process. And this raises issues regarding Nietzsche's whole project that we shall return to.

Dionysus vs. Apollo

The above explanation of idealism and the will to power is closer to the point of arrival of Nietzsche's thought than to its point of departure. In his first book, *The Birth of Tragedy*, published in 1872 when he was 28, Nietzsche introduces two principles which would be present in his writing to the end: the Dionysian principle – the principle of chaos, dream and intoxication – and the Apollonian principle – the principle of order and form-giving. Both these principles are associated with an aesthetic disposition – of life as a work of art, in effect. Thus, in the first Preface to the work written in 1871, Nietzsche says: 'art represents the highest task and the truly metaphysical activity of this life' (Nietzsche 1967: 31–32). Within this perspective, the Greeks showed how art – as a kind of will to illusion composed of the principles of form-giving and intoxication – could function as the true vantage point of life. Art thus becomes equivalent to a recognition that life is unknowable in terms of any ultimate truth, as implied by an idealist metaphysic. This is life seen as tragedy. Art becomes then a way of not having to deny life. Life as tragic is played out in particular in the spirit of music as the embodiment of the Dionysian principle (the first edition of Nietzsche's book was in fact called, *The Birth of Tragedy Out of the Spirit of Music*). For this reason, Nietzsche focuses on the strategic role of the Chorus in pre-Socratic, Greek drama. Far from being equivalent to the audience (who could hardly mistake the drama for life) as Schlegel had proposed, the Chorus sees the action on the stage as real, and responds to life through rhythmic intoxication. As such, the Chorus gives form to the Dionysian impulse. Apollo, as god of plastic powers and sooth-saying, gives rise to the visual, objectifying aspect of the drama. Nietzsche notices, however, that the rise of Platonism destroyed Greek tragic drama from within: Platonism, as high idealism, led to a denial of the tragic tenor of life, and so to a denial of the need for an intoxicating element. Modern philosophy – and certain aspects of modern science – as the heir of Platonism, thus denies life it blots out the spirit of music – the recognition of the tragic element So much is knowledge dominant in modern culture, that people have ceased to be able to act. 'Knowledge kills action', Nietzsche says in *The Birth of Tragedy*, 'action requires the veils of illusion' (Nietzsche 1967: 60).

Christianity and Reactive Thought as Ressentiment

While philosophy has become life-denying in the sphere of knowl-edge, Christianity is so in the sphere of morality. Here Nietzsche relentlessly homes in on the role of Christian guilt. This theme allows us to touch on another: the relationship between active and reactive dispositions. Christian morality proposes a fundamental principle of equality between human individuals. The difficulty is, Nietzsche points out, that life shows that there are differences – differences between: the strong and the weak, the rich and the poor, the gifted and the mediocre, man and woman; in fact there is in life every variety of difference imaginable. However, to maintain the illusion of (i.e. the ideal of) equality, Christianity invented guilt, or 'had conscience' which those who judged themselves to be different in a positive sense would be obliged to turn upon themselves. For with their difference (especially as a sense of superiority) they would be found to be responsible for the suffering of others.

Within the Nietzschean schema, guilt is the mark of reactive thought – the thought of the weak, not necessarily the weak in a strictly physical sense, but in the sense of those who cannot accept life as it is, who are governed by *ressentiment*, and who have to invent ideals in order to cover up their weakness. Guilt, in sum, is the weapon the less endowed use against free and original spirits who often reach new heights. Rather than attempting to raise themselves up to new heights in order to maintain equality, they deny that these heights exist. In his most poetic and famous work, *Thus Spoke Zar-athustra*, Nietzsche has Zarathustra – the exemplar of the 'higher man' – come down from the mountain to speak to the people in the market-place. Because the people in the market-place only understand the language of utility (the language of exchange value and calculability), they fail to understand Zarathustra, and take him for a madman. Dominated by the ethic of equality and the attachment to utility which goes with it, the people of the marketplace all want the same thing. 'No herdsman and one herd. Everyone wants the same thing, everyone is the same: whoever thinks otherwise goes voluntarily into the madhouse' (Nietzsche 1969: 46). As inexorably reactive, the herd cannot think of any other end than to be happy. This is the happiness deemed to come with equality and utility. The crowd calls on Zarathustra to bring them the Ultimate Man who invented happiness. Zarathustra stands for the higher man, who, as the overcoming of all idealism in favour of life, is the overcoming of man as well; for man, too, is an ideal that does not correspond to anything in reality. Reactive thought, however, wants happiness, not the risks and suffering which often accompany creativeness and originality. The Ultimate Man (equivalent to man in general) is reactive man; the higher man, or Superman, is the active individual with the determination to be creative and to avoid his life being submerged in the calculating ethic of equality. As an exemplar of the higher man, Zarathustra cannot – almost by definition – be understood, for he embodies horizontal thought; as a result, his language can only rarely be translated into common parlance. The thought of the higher man, is, in short, poetic.

Will to Power

The figure of the higher man reaches its apogee in the posthumously published *The Will to Power*. Interestingly, Nietzsche characterised himself as being a quintessentially posthumous thinker – a thinker out of tune with the times. Despite its posthumous status, *The Will to Power* is the most sustained articulation of a number of key aspects of Nietzsche's thought. These include: the will to power; the eternal recurrence; nihilism; anti-idealism; and a revaluation of all values. We will elaborate here on the first two aspects in particular, as they have recently assumed enormous importance in contemporary thought.

As explained earlier, the will to power is to be understood as the basis of Nietzsche's anti-idealist stance. It is the embodiment of the principle of the affirmation of life. The will to power is, in a sense, equivalent to everything that actually happens in life, making Nietzsche, in the eyes of some, a radically realist thinker. The will to power is the 'world', as our author says; and he continues: '*This world is the will to power – and nothing besides!* And you yourselves are also this will to power – and nothing besides!' (Nietzsche 1968: 550, Nietzsche's emphasis). There is no willing subject behind power, no reality behind the play of forces, no division into will and its other, or into being and nothingness, or into subject and object – for the division itself is part of the will to power. The will to power is a plurality of forces, from which identities have to be constructed, not an underlying unity behind appearance. The revaluation of values is equivalent to the making of values within the play of forces of the will to power. Values always have to be affirmed; they do not exist 'in themselves', as Kant thought.

Again, the will to power has no origin or purpose, no beginning or end – for these, too, are idealist and hence metaphysical categories. Or at least, the world has no origin other than the one given to it by a genealogy. Under these circumstances, Nietzsche forges his controversial notion of the 'eternal recurrence', the doctrine of the play of difference and uncertainty. In other words the form taken by the will to power is essentially unpredictable. It is: 'the enjoyment of all kinds of uncertainty, experimentalism, as a counterweight to this extreme fatalism; abolition of the concept of necessity; abolition of the 'will'; abolition of 'knowledge-in-itself' (Nietzsche 1968: 546). As the world has no goal, it is in continual, 'aimless' flux of transformation. Everything recurs; the world is not, Nietzsche says, a world of infinite novelty. The system is not in equilibrium, but nor is it infinitely open. It is rather like a game (of dice) played an infinite number of times, so that eventually the outcomes are repeated. The principle of the eternal recurrence is the most enigmatic of this entire philosophy. At times Nietzsche seems to want to link it to the nineteenth-century theory of thermodynamics (hence references to a constant amount of energy, and to the disequilibrium of the system); at other times, the issue seems to be centred on the will to power and a preparedness not to deny any aspect of life – even its most horrific events – such as occurs, Nietzsche says, when life is divided into an acknowledged good side, and a denied evil side; here, the will to power is the will of the eternal return of every event, whatever it might be. *Amor fati* – love of fate – is the phrase used which best evokes this approach.

Nietzsche's Project

Clearly, Nietzsche's project is nothing if not exorbitant. But it is not mad, or irrational; it has its own very definite and coherent logic, and this makes it communicable and amenable to being pressed into serving the ends of a *fin-de-siècle* anti-idealism. What then are its difficulties?

To begin with if the will to power is all there is why is Nietzsche moved to explain it? Perhaps he might have responded by claiming that he is not explaining it but, through the style of his philosophising, is providing an instance of it. However, no one reading his work can fail to see that there is a message accompanying the style. Nietzsche is unique as a thinker, of this there can be no doubt; but he also says as much himself. He does not write pure poetry. His theories therefore have to be seen as moves in the game of philosophy; to deny this is to deny an important dimension of Nietzsche's thought. To admit it, on the other hand, is to render suspect the possibility of a radically heterogeneous thinker.

Second, Nietzsche's anti-idealism would appear to stand or fall on the possibility that an event can be reduced to a description of it; such a claim is clearly questionable if metaphor is at the very heart of language as thinkers like Kristeva have argued.

Finally, if Nietzsche is to avoid being a 'denier' of life himself, does he not have to accept that life partly entails the denial of life? – that a will to illusion may not only take the form of art, but might also take the form of a will to happiness?

Notes

1 See, for example, the work of Bataille, Blanchot, Deleuze, Derrida, Foucault, Lyotard, and Irigaray, as being particularly influenced by Nietzsche.
2 For Nietzsche, any principle which is proposed as an underlying and coherent truth for the diverse facts of appearance is idealist. In all probability, any form of reductionism (whether in the form of an essence or teleology – purpose) would be idealist according to Nietzsche's scheme of things.

References

Kaufmann, Walter (1967), *The Birth of Tragedy* in *The Birth of Tragedy and The Case of Wagner*, trans. Walter Kaufmann, New York: Vintage Books.
—— (1968), *Nietzsche*, New York: Vintage Books, third edn.
Nietzsche, Friedrich (1968), *The Will to Power*, trans. Walter Kaufmann and R.J. Hollingdale, New York: Vintage Books.
—— (1969), *Thus Spoke Zarathustra*, trans. R.J. Hollingdale, Harmondsworth: Penguin.
—— (1973), *Beyond Good and Evil*, trans. R.J. Hollingdale, Harmondsworth: Penguin.

See also: **Bataille, Deleuze, Foucault**

Nietzsche's major writings

(2006) *The Nietzsche Reader*, ed. Keith Ansell Pearson and Duncan Large, Malden, Mass. and Oxford: Blackwell.

(2005) *Why I am So Wise*, trans. R.J. Hollingdale, New York: Penguin.

(1989a [1908]) *Ecce Homo* (prepared for publication), trans. Walter Kaufmann, New York: Vintage Books.

(1989b [1887]) *On the Genealogy of Morals*, trans. Walter Kaufmann and R.J. Hollingdale, New York: Vintage Books.

(1986) *Human All Too Human*. trans. R.J. Hollingdale, Cambridge: Cambridge University Press, includes:.

Volume One [1878].

Volume Two. First Section: Assorted Opinions and Sayings [1879].

Volume Two. Second Section: The Wanderer and His Shadow [1880].

(1983) *Untimely Meditations*, trans. R.J. Hollingdale, Cambridge: Cambridge University Press, includes:.

First Part: David Strauss, the Writer and the Confessor [1873].

Second Part: On the Use and Disadvantage of History for Life [1874].

Third Part: Schopenhauer as Educator [1874].

Fourth Part. Richard Wagner in Bayreuth [1876].

(1982 [1881]) *Daybreak: Thoughts on the Prejudices of Morality*, trans. R.J. Hollingdale, Cambridge: Cambridge University Press.

(1976 [1895]) *Nietzsche contra Wagner* (prepared for publication, 1888), trans. Walter Kaufmann (selection) in Walter Kaufmann, ed., *The Portable Nietzsche*, Harmondsworth: Penguin.

(1974 [1882]) *The Gay Science: With a Prelude in Rhymes and an Appendix of Songs*, trans. Walter Kaufmann, New York: Vintage Books.

(1968a [1895]) *The Antichrist* (prepared for publication, 1888), trans. R.J. Hollingdale, Harmondsworth: Penguin.

(1968b [1889]) *The Twilight of the Idols* (prepared for publication, 1888), trans. R.J. Hollingdale, Harmondsworth: Penguin.

(1967a [1888]) *The Case of Wagner*, trans. Walter Kaufmann, New York: Vintage.

(1967b [1872, 1874, 1886]) *The Birth of Tragedy*, trans. Walter Kaufmann, New York: Vintage Books.

(1966a [1886]) *Beyond Good and Evil*, trans. Walter Kaufmann, New York: Vintage Books, 1966; edition used (1973), trans. R.J. Hollingdale, Harmondsworth: Penguin.

(1966b [1883, 1884, 1885]) *Thus Spoke Zarathustra*, trans. Walter Kaufmann, New York: Viking 1966; edition used (1969), trans. R.J. Hollingdale, Harmondsworth: Penguin.

Not published by Nietzsche

(1968c [1901 and 1906]) *The Will to Power* (selections of excerpts from Nietzsche's notebooks of the 1880s), trans. Walter Kaufmann and R.J. Hollingdale, New York: Vintage Books.

Further reading

Abbey, Ruth (2000), *Nietzsche's Middle Period*, Oxford and New York: Oxford University Press.

Ansell Pearson, Keith, ed. (2006), *A Companion to Nietzsche*, Malden, Mass. and Oxford: Blackwell.

Kaufmann, Walter (1968), *Nietzsche: Philosopher, Psychologist, Antichrist*, New York: Vintage.

Magnus, Bernd and Higgins, Kathleen M., eds (1996), *The Cambridge Companion to Nietzsche*, Cambridge and New York: Cambridge University Press.

JAMES JOYCE (1882–1941)

In his book on *Ulysses* and *Finnegans Wake* (Derrida 1987[1]) Jacques Derrida relates how Joyce was present in his very first book, the *Introduction to Husserl's Origin of Geometry* (1962), and present again in a key essay, 'Plato's pharmacy', first published in 1968 (see Derrida 1981: 67–171). Derrida further confirms the importance of Joyce for the understanding of his works, *Glas* (1974) and *The Postcard* (1980). As opposed to Husserl's univocity of meaning, Derrida poses Joyce's 'generalised equivocity' (Derrida 1987: 28). 'Plato's pharmacy', for its part, refers to Thoth (present in *Finnegans Wake*), the Egyptian god of writing, said by Plato to be the inventor of a false memory: memory as mnemonics (as opposed to lived memory). Thoth would be present as the inspiration of Joyce's mnemonic procedure where links may be forged between the most unlikely elements. For such a procedure, the point is not to produce the thing itself in the memory, but to produce a procedure which would make recall possible. Plato, in the *Phaedrus*, calls mnemonics defective memory without seeming to recognise that it would not be necessary if memory were not already defective. Mnemonics, therefore, is a confirmation of the arbitrary nature of the sign as proposed by Saussure. *Glas*, says Derrida, is also a kind of wake, this time, in the sense of mourning. Finally, Derrida claims that *The Postcard* is 'haunted by Joyce': '[I]t is above all the Babelian motif, which obsesses the *Envois* (Derrida 1984: 151) – in the sense, among other things of: meaning as a multiplicity of voices, meaning as always open.

Reference to Derrida reminds us that as well as being a fundamental influence in literature and literary criticism in the English-speaking world and elsewhere, Joyce has also been the inspiration for new ideas – a focus, in the twentieth century, for a new understanding of writing: a force that has brought about a re-evaluation of the relationship between art and reality. Again, reference to Derrida reminds us that there are few philosophers or writers in the latter part of the twentieth century who – either consciously or unconsciously – have not been touched by Joyce. Although Joyce wrote a number of important works – such as *Dubliners* and *A Portrait of the Artist as a Young Man* – in addition to *Ulysses* and *Finnegans Wake*, the focus here will primarily be on the latter two texts, as it is these which have had the greatest impact on thought and writing.

Life and Intellectual Trajectory

James Joyce was born in Dublin in 1882. He attended Clongowes School and Belvedere College in Dublin before completing a degree in modern languages at University College, Dublin. Upon graduation in 1902, Joyce was fluent in Italian, French, German and literary Norwegian, as well as Latin. To his chagrin, Joyce never studied Ancient Greek, even though he was fascinated by Greek myths. Determined to make a name for himself, he left Dublin for Paris soon after graduation in order to study medicine at the Sorbonne.

In 1904, Joyce lived in the Martellow Tower made famous by his novel, *Ulysses*, and began to write *Stephen Hero*, the forerunner to *A Portrait of the Artist as a Young Man*, first serialised in the *Egoist* in 1914. The latter work was published while Joyce was living in Trieste with his wife, Nora Barnacle, with whom he had eloped in 1904. Also published in 1914, after much difficulty with the censor, was *Dubliners*, a collection of short stories each introducing a particular aspect of the 'paralysis' (Joyce) of Dublin life. As one critic put it, '*Dubliners* is, in a sense, justification for Joyce's exile' (Arnold 1969: 26). After spending the remainder of the War in Zürich, Joyce and his family arrived in Paris in 1920. It was there that Sylvia Beach published Joyce's *Ulysses* in 1922 in an edition of 1,000 copies, and it was there, too, that Joyce wrote *Finnegans Wake* from 1923 to 1938. In May 1939, *Finnegans Wake* was finally published by T.S. Eliot's publishing house, Faber & Faber, an advance copy being sent to Joyce in time for his fifty-seventh birthday on 2 February.

One year after the war had begun, Joyce was still undecided about what to do. He had the opportunity to go to America, but elected to apply for Swiss visas for himself and his family, and in December of 1940, the Joyces arrived in Zürich where Joyce had sat out the First World War. Suspected of having a stomach ulcer, Joyce's health progressively deteriorated. In January 1941 he died of a perforated duodenal ulcer and was buried in the Fluntern cemetery in Zürich.

Ulysses

Ulysses is ostensibly a day (16 June 1902) in the life of Molly and Leopold Bloom, presented within the framework of the popular, romanised version of Homer's poem and containing, in displaced form, biographical elements as well as many details deriving from the history of Dublin and the history of English literature (e.g. Shakespeare). While it is true that Homer's poem and Joyce's biography provide the reader with relatively fixed reference points in relation to which many of the novel's details may be understood, contingency is also a key aspect here. Contingency fascinated Baudelaire, we should recall, and gave him a clue to the nature of a truly modern experience centred on consciousness. 'To be away from home and yet to feel at home' – this, according to Baudelaire distinguished modern experience from all other (Baudelaire 1972: 399–400). Here, to be away from home means being opened up to the new and the ephemeral, the fleeting and the transient. Prior to modernity, experience could be 'homely' – i.e. predictable and familiar. Modern experience, then, is confronted with, if it does not actively search it out (as did Baudelaire), the unpredictable, the unfamiliar, change and novelty. To be at home, by contrast, is to exist in a closed system, where equilibrium and repetition (of the familiar) always prevails and the new is excluded or repressed.

How can a Baudelairian framework be applied to Joyce's *Ulysses* when, in speaking of the novel, we have just pointed to Homer and biography as two stable – and quite 'homely' – points of reference? An attempt to answer this question should give a deeper grasp of Joyce's project here.

While Homer's *Odyssey* – as well as Catholicism – provides a kind of anchorage for the text, this is only of the most provisional kind. What is notable and relevant in Homer *vis à vis* Joyce, is that the hero of the *Odyssey* leaves home, wanders about, takes undetermined trajectories, even if, in the end, he also struggles to return. So it is with Leopold Bloom. He leaves 7 Eccles Street returning only at the end of the novel, a return which is in no sense predictable. Indeed, apart from the title (what Genette would call the 'paratext') and structure, no other explicit evocation of Homer is visible – Joyce having erased the Homeric chapter titles in the definitive version of the novel. Much of *Ulysses*, then, is 'coincidence of meeting, discussion, dance, row, old salt of the here today and gone tomorrow type, night loafers, the whole galaxy of events' (Joyce 1986: 528), events which serve to make 'up a miniature cameo of the world we live in' (Joyce 1986:

528). Chance thus plays a role. Joyce's writing is effectively situated at the point where chance – or contingency – and structure coincide. This is his great contribution to literature in the twentieth century – and certainly to the English language version of it.

The problem of writing evident in a text like *Ulysses* is that of how to give a literary – written – form to chance and contingency; in other words, to the events of the here and now. Kristeva has called this aspect of Joyce's writing a 'revelation' – by which she means that the text is a writing of what cannot be predicted by a (symbolic) structure, or framework. This might seem to be an odd thing to say, given that Joyce's writing seems to deal with the very banality of existence, that is, with those things which seem to be as far away as possible from the exotic or the heroic. The kind of passage which brings the issue into sharp focus would be one like the following, from the opening of Chapter 5:

> By lorries along Sir John Rogerson's quay Mr Bloom walked soberly, past Windmill Lane, Leask's the linseed crusher, the postal telegraph office. Could have given that address too. And past the sailor's home. He turned from the morning noises of the quayside and walked through Lime Street. By Brady's cottages a boy for the skins lolled, his bucket of offal linked, smoking a chewed fagbutt. A smaller girl with scars of eczema on her fore-head eyed him, listlessly holding her battered caskhoop. Tell him if he smokes he won't grow. O let him! His life isn't such a bed of roses.
>
> (Joyce 1986: 58)

Bloom's walk is, in almost surrealist fashion, a series of chance encounters. It is a walk of almost pure contingency. 'Almost' – because the text has to be written down. The insignificant unpredictable detail has to be turned into a sign in order that it might then give up part of its ephemeral status and be communicated, that is become part of Joyce's novel itself. To avoid denotation in passages such as the one cited above from remaining a pure inventory, two strategies emerge: (1) the development of a minimal narrative structure; and (2) the development of a definite style. For Joyce, style makes words – or specific units of writing, like phrases – count for themselves in their relation to other words. Poetry is the ultimate presentation of a style in this sense. If Homer forms a structural, or narrative, backdrop to *Ulysses*, this is to be understood as an open structure which can accommodate an almost infinite series of contents. And few commentators have failed to remark on the poetic quality of Joyce's writing – Molly Bloom's monologue in the last chapter being cited as a prime example. Fewer, however, have been able to link Joyce's style to the problem of writing that he was grappling with. Style is Joyce's answer to the problem of how contingency can appear in the novel. Thus while nineteenth-century realist writers worked to make contingent details appear necessary to the whole of the novel's narrative fabric, Joyce's strategy, by contrast, is to place the very possibility of narrative at risk by making the contingent detail relatively autonomous, subordinate to nothing other than its own (poetic) existence.

For a nineteenth-century sensibility, Joyce does the impossible: he founds his novels on contingency and indeterminacy. Indeterminacy arises precisely because a complete narrative structure, founded on a logic of causality, is only ever partially visible. Events that occur by chance, contingently, unpredictably, have no discernible origin. Joyce develops the spoken, active side of language, rather than the side, in Saussure's terminology, of *langue*, or fixed system. As chance, speech–act events are, in principle, unique. They defy the logic of causality. This is what makes them indeterminable. The classical nineteenth-century narrative follows the principle of causality as verisimilitude to the letter. Everything has a reason and there is a reason for everything. If Joyce, too, partially subscribes to verisimilitude in *Ulysses*, the greater part of the novel – its most innovative aspect – defies it. Any doubt as to Joyce's position here is swept away in *Finnegans Wake*.

Finnegans Wake

Ulysses, as Joyce continually proclaimed is the 'story' of the day. By this he did not simply mean that the events of the novel take place during the day. Nor did he only mean that seeing is the dominant sense used in the work. He also tried to make it known that, in terms of its syntax, grammar, vocabulary, and sentence structure, *Ulysses* is perfectly readable. At an immediate level, in other words, *Ulysses* communicates with the reader. To gain a better grasp of what is at stake in *Finnegans Wake* we first of all return to a key passage in *Ulysses*. In it, Stephen Dedalus ponders a theme that is also important in Homer, namely, the nature of fatherhood, 'Paternity' Stephen says, 'may be a legal fiction. Who is the father of any son that any son should love him or he any son?' (Joyce 1986: 170). Stephen is leading up to the idea that fatherhood is clouded in uncertainty – if only, to begin with, that no one can be absolutely certain as to who their father is. If, second, it is through the father principle that a name is given, the aforementioned uncertainty becomes an uncertainty with regard to one's very identity.

As psychoanalysis has emphasised, the father principle – the Name-of-the-Farther – is crucial to the communicative function of language. The father principle, then, is the principle of determinacy, meaning and causality. Joyce challenges this principle in *Finnegans Wake* by rendering meaning entirely fluid. The scene which enables him to do this is the night – the world of dreams. One technique he uses is agglutination: running words and phrases together so as to make them ambiguous. Possible meanings are multiplied – as with 'meanderthalltale' (Joyce 1939: 19), 'automutativeness' (Joyce 1939: 112), 'chaosmos' (Joyce 1939: 118), and 'continuarration' (Joyce 1939: 205) – what could be called, following *Finnegans Wake*, a 'polygluttural' technique (Joyce 1939: 117). In addition, we find what contributes to the distorting, or 'warping process' (Joyce 1939: 497) (= a work in progress): a writing which uses rhythms, intonations and modulations to render fluid all fixed communicative forms. However, to render meanings fluid is not to render the text meaningless. It is, though, to be made aware of the repressed semiotic (Kristeva) level of language. Once immersed in the text, the reader often finds that it takes over, that criticism of the usual kind – where the critic comments *on* the text – becomes extremely difficult, if it is not made impossible. In short, it becomes difficult to objectify *Finnegans Wake*, the very thing for which the 'father principle' would be the pre-condition.

Questions, then, as to what happens in the novel, who the main protagonists are, who the actual dreamer who dreams is, are impossible to answer with certainty, although many have tried. Joyce himself forecast that, with *Finnegans Wake*, he had set critics a task which would last for three hundred years. Such a claim is misleading – at least in one sense – for it suppresses the possibility that, in the end, *Finnegans Wake* is an indeterminate text, which, as such, has no final meaning, or meanings. Rather, its poetic function renders meaning indeterminate; it definitively challenges the father. It is an analogue of the principle that there is no essential core to language – only a system of differences.

Note

1 The second half of this book is in English as 'Two words for Joyce' (Derrida 1984: 145–59).

References

Arnold, Armin (1969), *James Joyce*, New York: Frederick Ungar.
Baudelaire,Charles (1972), *The Painter of Modern Life: Selected Writings on Art and Artists*, trans. P.E. Charvet, Harmondsworth: Penguin.
Derrida, Jacques (1981), 'Plato's Pharmacy' trans. Barbara Johnson, in *Dissemination*, Chicago: Chicago University Press.
—— (1984), 'Two Words for Joyce', trans. Geoff Bennington, in Derek Attridge and Daniel Ferrer (eds), *Post-Structuralist Joyce*, Cambridge: Cambridge University Press.
—— (1987), *Ulysses, gramophone. Deux mots pour Joyce*, Paris: Galilée.
Joyce, James (1939), *Finnegans Wake*, London: Faber & Faber.
—— (1986), *Ulysses* (The Corrected Text), London: The Bodley Head.

See also: **Derrida, Kafka, Kristeva, Saussure**

Joyce's major works

(2004 [1914]) *The Dead*, Hoboken, N.J.: Melville House Publications.
(1986) *Ulysses* (The Corrected Text), London: The Bodley Head.
(1963 [1944]) *Stephen Hero*, London: Jonathan Cape; Norfolk, Conn.: New Directions, Revised edn.
(1939) *Finnegans Wake*, London: Faber & Faber; New York: Viking Press.
(1922) *Ulysses*, Paris: Shakespeare & Co.
(1918) *Exiles*, London: Grant Richards.
(1916) *A Portrait of the Artist as a Young Man*, New York: B.W Huebsch.
(1914) *Dubliners*, London: Grant Richards.
(1907) *Chamber Music*, London: Elkin Mathews.

Further reading

Attridge, Derek and Ferrer, Daniel (1984), *Post-Structuralist Joyce*, Cambridge: Cambridge University Press.
Benstock, Barnard (1988), *The Augmented Ninth, Proceedings of the Ninth International James Joyce Symposium, Frankfurt 1984*, Syracuse: Syracuse University Press (See pieces by Kristeva and Derrida).
Bulson, Eric (2006). *The Cambridge Introduction to James Joyce*, Cambridge: Cambridge University Press.
Connolly, Thomas E. (1997), *James Joyce's Books, Portraits, Manuscripts, Notebooks, Typescripts, Page proofs, Together with Critical Essays about Some of his Works*, Lewiston, N.J.: Edwin Mellen Press.
Ellmann, Richard (1982), *James Joyce*, New York: Oxford University Press.
Ellmann, Richard (1984), *Ulysses on the Liffey*, London and Boston: Faber & Faber.
Hart, Clive and Hayman, David (1977), *James Joyce's 'Ulysses': Critical Essays*, Berkeley, Los Angeles: University of California Press.
Lernout, Geert (1990), *The French Joyce*, Ann Arbor: University of Michigan Press.

Litz, A. Walton (1964), *The Art of James Joyce. Method and Design in Ulysses and Finnegans Wake*, London: Oxford University Press.

O'Neill, Patrick (2005), *Polyglot Joyce: Fictions of Translation*, Toronto and London: University of Toronto Press.

PHILIPPE SOLLERS (b.1936)

Just as Georges Bataille used biographical fragments to develop his writing of transposition, so Philippe Sollers (admirer of Bataille) uses his biography to develop a writing of the act of writing: analogical writing, as Philippe Forest says in his scholarly study of Sollers's *oeuvre* (Forest 1992: 59–611). One of the obstacles to grasping the specificity and uniqueness of Sollers's project relates to the emphasis the world of criticism has always placed on the apparently spectacular and perverse changes in Sollers's public persona, rather than on the content of his literary, theoretical and critical writing – a state of affairs for which Sollers is not entirely blameless. From the *Nouveau Roman* (which saw the conventional, nineteenth-century model of the novel as severely limiting) and a critique of literature *engagé*, passing by Maoism and Catholicism, to a return to French eighteenth-century classicism (Voltaire, Crébillon-fils) and to 'meaning', Sollers has always provided media critics with what they needed: a figure who can be both despised and loved (the writer people 'love to hate' is a phrase that pleases Sollers) because he also plays their game of mirrors – and plays it well.

Regardless of the position taken regarding his writing or persona, however, there is little doubt that Sollers's founding (with others) of the literary journal *Tel Quel* in 1960, and the publication in it of important works by Foucault, Barthes, Derrida and Kristeva – among others – transformed the literary environment in France. *Tel Quel*, for many, was the French literary avant-garde. Again, with the foundation of *L'Infini* in 1983 in the wake of *Tel Quel*, the change from the idea of avant-garde writing as concerned with an absence of meaning to the idea of avant-garde writing as the 'return of meaning', would hardly have been marked.

The Life of a Literary Entrepreneur

Philippe Sollers was born Philippe Joyaux in 1936 in Bordeaux where the family owned a factory. His parents were Anglophiles – a tendency accentuated by the Occupation. As a result, the young

Philippe became a fervent devotee, first of all of jazz, and later of James Joyce. Educated by the Jesuits at the École Sainte-Geneviève at Versailles, Sollers was also expelled from the school for indiscipline. He was thus forced to educate himself in the history of literature and philosophy, a notable embarrassment in a culture where formal learning is prized so highly. Opposition to discipline and to all forms of militarism led to Sollers feigning schizophrenia at the time of his military call-up during the Algerian War in 1962. By that time, however, he had already won literary awards, first, for his short work, *Le Défi* (*The Challenge*), published in 1957, and then for *Le Parc* (*The Park*), published in 1961. His first real novel, *Une curieuse solitude* (*A Strange Solitude*) published in 1958 was praised by Louis Aragon, just as the conservative writer, François Mauriac, had praised *Le Défi*.

During his adolescence and youth, Sollers was influenced by Baudelaire, Poe, Proust, Lautréamont and Surrealism. Later, in 1960, the poet Francis Ponge assumed great importance, with Sollers at the age of 24 giving a lecture on Ponge at the Sorbonne. In 1965, Sollers would point out that Francis Ponge was one of the rare writers to treat language as a milieu providing body and soul for the human being, rather than as a vehicle for an ideology (Sollers 1968: 198–205). By 1972 Sollers argued that Surrealism had been responsible for the censoring of Joyce who, together with Artaud, represented 'the greatest revolution in language in the twentieth century' (Sollers 1972: 12). After supporting some of the aspirations of the *Nouveau Roman*, Sollers, in 1964, distanced himself from it and its originator, Alain Robbe-Grillet. Although critics had detected the imprint of Robbe-Grillet's project in *Le Parc*, for Sollers, the *Nouveau Roman* had become too academic, that is, it had become sterile. From another angle, although Robbe-Grillet's writing confronts a void in reality which cannot be written (it can only be implied), Sollers aims to speak – write – the void as such. For Sollers, that is, writing is an analogue of the void; just as surrealist writing would be an analogue of *délire* (*delirium*), rather than being a theory of it (see Roudinesco 1990: 26).

Analogical Writing

All analogical writing aspires in some sense to be a practice of writing: it neither seeks to be transparent in a realist sense (a window on the world), nor, on the other hand, does it fall back on being pure poetry in which the opacity of the word would predominate. Although writing is never entirely opaque, this does not mean – far from it – that rhythm is absent. Thus in speaking of his early 1970s novel, *Lois* (Laws), Sollers remarks on the decasyllabic rhythm of the work – a rhythm, however, which issues from the unconscious and evokes the songs of gesture. The rhythm of *Lois* is initially unconscious; gradually, however, its effects can be controlled so that in the unpunctuated novel, *Paradis*, the decasyllabic rhythm is consciously developed as the basis of the force of the writing.

Between 1961 – with the publication of *Le Parc* – and the publication of *Paradis* in 1981, Sollers's writing, at the most general level, moves through the stages of a brief accommodation to certain stylistic strategies of the *Nouveau Roman*, to the highly formalised structure of *Drame*, *Nombres*, *H* and *Lois* – written between 1965 and 1972 – to the unpunctuated and lyrical avant-garde texts reminiscent of Joyce and Mallarmé of the early 1980s.

The Literary Ear

Sollers has emphasised that he writes to the rhythm of music – inspiration coming in particular from Purcell, Monteverdi, Schönberg, and Webern, and from jazz greats such as Parker, Konitz and Braxton. The ear, he has said, is the first priority. It is the first priority, but is not the only priority. While Sollers's literary works are far removed from a literature *engagé à la* Sartre, hardly any are not at least indirectly linked to events in the author's biography or to events occurring in the social milieu in which Sollers has always been an active participant. As Forest notes, the biographical element becomes a particularly notable feature of the novels (beginning with *Femmes* (*Women*)) of the 1983–93 decade. As a scarcely veiled protagonist in his own later works, Sollers explores, through writing, his relationship to the *fin de siècle* society of the spectacle where sex is obligatory and a rejection of meaning is now the norm. Overall, then, the Sollersian project aspires to produce a writing that is simultaneously poetic (fiction) and descriptive – which is a transcription of the act of writing, and at the same time an intervention as revelatory of the censorship in place to curb the writing of 'exceptions'.

Exception

'Exception' is a key term in Sollers's theory of writing, and so it is worthwhile spending a moment to clarify its significance. Like Nietzsche in philosophy, Sollers argues that the writer who is truly immersed in writing as a vocation is inevitably an exception. For Sollers, exception 'is the rule in art and literature' because to be a writer in the fullest sense, the form and the protocols of writing must be transformed, leaving the writing subject in an often unbearable solitude. As a result, the true writer does not write *within* the already existing conventions of his or her art, but remodels them, or at least is the catalyst of a remodeling. Because writing conventions are always social conventions, the effect of such writing (Joyce is an example) is to shake – and perhaps remake – the social milieu in question. Writing, and perhaps art in general, cannot simply be explained sociologically: rather, it has to be grasped in the sense of set theory where the part is often greater than the power of the whole. Journalistic writing, which often embodies the socially accepted norms of writing (the writing *doxa*), is in its own sphere a legitimate form of writing: the problem arises for Sollers when writing in the fullest sense ('great' writing) is equated with journalism. Although there is clearly no model with which it can he or she can be equalled, the true writer's art is always an avant-garde art – always an exception. The writer, as exception, then, cannot be easily located on an existing scale or table of categories. In relation to society's norms, he or she is always other and is only ever integrated into social life with difficulty, if at all. Here, the risk that writing (art) might degenerate into a self-indulgent narcissism is very real. However, what distinguishes the narcissist from the true writer is that, in the end, the narcissist never really shakes the social milieu because his art never takes in charge the quasi-universal norms of society. The exception, by contrast, takes on the universal as a personal problem; in fact, for the exception, the universal and the exception are inseparable, for the pure narcissist, on the other hand, universality essentially does not exist.

Disagreement with such an argument sometimes centres on its alleged elitism. An elitist theory, however, inevitably proposes a clearly recognisable system of gradations based on inferiority and superiority; it is irrevocably hierarchical. Elites, in short can only exist within the given system of social relations; they do not challenge the system's competence to judge. A much more horizontal approach characterises Sollers's theory of the exception. Horizontally speaking, the writer is essentially *sui generis*: incomparable – an exception. This, of course, has a Kantian ring to it, where Kant says that the genius sets the rule rather than being the best at enacting the rule.

Singularity

A term that is for Sollers almost synonymous with 'exception', is 'singularity'. To get a better grip on this notion in the early 1980s, Sollers, along with some of his colleagues such as Jean-Houdebine, sought an elaboration of 'singularity' in Duns-Scotus's notion of 'haecceity'. Literally, haecceity is the 'thisness' of a thing. It is absolute particularity or individuality In effect, haecceitas is what cannot be accounted for by any pre-existing social convention or norm; rather the norm itself has to be modified to make way for the singularity which is haecceity. The social system inevitably censures singularity; but, like an open system in biology, singularity is also essential for maintaining the vitality of the system.

At the level of the interaction between the writer and the reader of his text, Sollers fundamentally challenges familiar norms of reading; he challenges the reader to transform his or her existing preconceptions and to expand imaginary capacities. For Sollers, a work which does not do this might be good journalism, but it cannot be great writing.

The Narrative Act

Although 'exception' and 'singularity' could be said to govern the overall economy of Sollers's enterprise, a more specific principle, or practice, governs his writing. This is the principle, first highlighted in *Drame* and *Nombres*, of 'searching for as tight a coincidence as possible between the act of writing and the narrative; the act dictating the narrative, the narrative recounting the act' (Sollers 1981:100).

Even after the 'break' with the visibly poetic writing of the 1970s, which culminated with the publication of the entirely unpunctuated novel, *Paradis* in 1981, the concern is still explicitly about producing a writing about writing. Hence in the novel *Femmes*, which marks the transition to a more recognisably conventional style, the narrative is still a narrative of the writing of the novel itself. According to the information provided by the intrigue, the character, 'Will' (an American journalist), says that *Femmes* will be published in Paris under the name of S, who has previously published an unpunctuated and 'unreadable' novel. To all appearances, S is now in the process of publishing an entirely 'readable' work – something guaranteed to raise a scandal among the critics, given S's 'avant-garde' past. As indeed the Paris critics did respond by criticising Sollers's lack of consistency and lack of loyalty to his avant-garde principles, the response was incorporated by the fictional work, thereby closing the conventional gap between fiction and non-fiction, and between the written narrative and the writing of the narrative.

As Forest points out, the gap between *Paradis* and *Femmes* is, in fact, not as great as one might have thought from the public response to the novel. Rather, *Paradis*, with all its contemporary and historical references, is an unpunctuated *Femmes*; *Femmes*, with all its literary and historical references is a punctuated version of *Paradis*. Or to put it in terms of *Femmes* itself, Will, the American journalist, and S are, as we know, really the same person (this is emphasised by the *roman à clé* aspect of the text). Even in a text as explicitly autobiographical as *Le Portrait du Joueur* (*The Portrait of the Player*), with a single narrator, the narrative becomes attracted to the play on the names, Sollers–Diamant. The identity of the narrator becomes fictive (i.e. written) to the extent that, through the name, identity is pluralised.

Secret and the Novel of 'Facts'

In 1992, Sollers published a novel called *Le Secret*. Loosely set around the attempted assassination of Pope John Paul II on 13 May 1981, the intrigue partly focuses on a lost note containing information about the attempted crime. The loss of the note leads to the effort to establish what it had to say about the motive and the mechanics of the attempted murder. Like the purloined letter in Edgar Allan Poe's short story, the absence of the letter allows for the projection of imaginary contents onto the note. The contents of the note thus remain a secret. While different aspects of a secret are explored (the secret agent, the secret/private life of the narrator, the secret in military strategy), a key point made is that the difference between fiction – in terms of strangeness, unreality – and reality is fast disappearing. Especially is this the case with regard to life and death in the context of artificial insemination and proxy parenting, and new media technology.

To write a novel today, says Sollers, is only possible if one starts with the facts. Facts are singularities; they are unpredictable, and beyond the control of a collective consciousness, as this is manifest in the mass media. 'Reality is stranger than fiction' is the principle enunciated. Sollers claims that he 'invents nothing'. The danger is that with the media's capacity for the reproduction of events, and with a medium's role in the reproduction of human life, the exception is in danger: the exception can be neither reproduced nor collectivised; in short, it cannot be codified. Sollers's great fear, then, is that post-modern society is the society of the pure spectacle, where there is no uniqueness, no surprise, no secret, in fact. The emergence of this reality is why Sollers has been, since 1988, wedded to the writing of Guy Debord who famously invented the idea of the 'society of the spectacle' in the late 1960s (Debord 1994). Through his writing, Sollers aims to constitute the exception – not through the violence of an untamed imagination, but through a respect for a reality that he says is fast disappearing. This is the reality of the multiplicity of identities assumed by both writer and secret agent.

Note

1 Although Forest is in fact referring mainly to *Le Parc* (*The Park*), the term is illuminating with regard to Sollers's work as a whole.

References

Debord, Guy (1994), *The Society of the Spectacle*, trans. Donald Nicholson-Smith, New York: Zone Books.

Forest, Philippe (1992), *Philippe Sollers*, Paris: Seuil.

Roudinesco, Elisabeth (1990), *Jacques Lacan & Co.*, trans. Jeffrey Mehlman, Chicago: Chicago University Press.

Sollers, Philippe (1968), 'La poésie, oui on non' in *Logiques*, Paris: Seuil, Coll. Tel Quel.

—— (1972), 'Philippe Sollers: "ébranler le système"' (interview), *Magazine littéraire*, 65.

—— (1981), *Vision à New York. Entretiens avec David Hayman*, Paris: Grasset.

See also: **Blanchot, Duras, Joyce, Kafka**

Sollers's major writings

(2006a) *Une vie divine*, Paris: Gallimard (novel).

(2006b) *L'évangile de Nietzsche*, Paris: Le Cherche Midi (novel).

(2005a) *Logique de la fiction et autres textes*, Nantes: C. Defaut.

(2005b) *Poker: entretiens* [interviews] *avec Ligne de risque*, Paris: Gallimard.

(2001) *Mystérieux Mozart*, Paris: Plon.

(2000a) *Passion fixe*, Paris: Gallimard (novel).

(2000b) *L'année du tigre: journal de l'année 1988*, Paris: Seuil.

(1993) *Le Secret*, Paris: Gallimard (novel).

(1992) *Le Rire de Rome*, Paris: Gallimard (novel).

(1991) *La Fête à Venise*, Paris: Gallimard (novel).

(1990 [1983]) *Women*, trans. Barbara Bray, New York: Columbia University Press (novel).

(1989) *Le Lys d'or*, Paris: Gallimard (novel).

(1988) *Les Folies françaises*, Paris: Gallimard (novel).

(1987) *Le Coeur absolu*, Paris: Gallimard (novel).

(1986a) *Théorie des exceptions*, Paris: Gallimard, Folio/Essais.

(1986b) *Paradis II*, Paris: Gallimard (novel).

(1984) *Portrait du joueur*, Paris: Gallimard (novel).

(1983 [1971]) *Writing and the Experience of Limits*, ed. David Hayman, trans. Philip Barnard with David Hayman, New York: Columbia University Press.

(1981a) *Vision à New York. Entretiens avec David Hayman*, Paris: Grasset.

(1981b) *Paradis*, Paris: Seuil, Tel Quel (novel).

(1973) *H*, Paris: Seuil, Tel Quel (novel).

(1972) *Lois*, Paris: Seuil, Tel Quel (novel).

(1968a) *Nombres*, Paris: Seuil, Tel Quel (novel).

(1968b) *Logiques*, Paris: Seuil, Tel Quel.

(1968 [1981]) *The Park: A Novel*, trans. A.M. Sheridan-Smith, London: Calder and Boyars.

(1965) *Drame*, Paris: Seuil, Tel Quel (novel).

(1963) *Francis Ponge ou la Raison à plus haut prix*, Paris: Seghers, 'Poètes d'aujourd'hui'.

(1959 [1958]) *A Strange Solitude*, trans. Richard Howard, New York: Grove Press (novel).

(1957) *Le Défi*, Paris: Seuil: 'Ecrire' (novel).

Further reading

Barthes, Roland, (1987), *Sollers Writer*, trans. Philip Thody, London and: Althone, Minneapolis: University of Minnesota Press.

Champagne, Roland A (1996), *Philippe Sollers*, Amsterdam and Atlanta: GA: Rodopi.

Clark, Hilary (1990), *The Fictional Encyclopaedia: Joyce, Pound, Sollers*, New York: Garland Publishing.

POST-MODERNITY/POST-MODERNISM

Although there are various understandings of what post-modernity is, a key notion in this book, deriving from the work of Jean-François Lyotard and Jean Baudrillard, is that post-modernity involves a questioning of a modernist epistemology based on a clear distinction between subject and object. Other things said in describing post-modernity concern the 'incredulity toward metanarratives' (Lyotard) – meaning that no global explanation of conduct is credible in an age of purposive rationality. Moreover, technology is seen to lead to a focus on reproduction, in contrast to the modernist paradigm of production. Or again, post-modern thought takes the implications of modernity absolutely seriously. For instance, if signs and language are the result of differential relations rather than an essential quality, and if, following Foucault, power has no essential quality, post-modernity follows through some of the radical implications of this.

Post-modernity also raises questions about the efficacy of the objectivity of the Enlightenment heritage, based on the idea of progress, for providing guidance in science, politics, culture and religion.

Post-modernism in art opposes the 'form follows function' of modernism and introduces decorative and retro elements.

JEAN BAUDRILLARD (1929–2007)

In a society dominated by production, Jean Baudrillard argues, the difference between use-value and exchange-value has some pertinence. Certainly, for a time, Marx was able to provide a relatively plausible explanation of the growth of capitalism using just these categories. The use-value of an object would be its utility related in Marx's terms to the satisfaction of certain needs; exchange-value, on the other hand, would refer to the market-value of a product, or object measured by its price. The object of exchange-value is what Marx called the commodity form of the object.

Starting with a re-evaluation and critique of Marx's economic theory of the object, especially as concerns the notion of 'use-value', Jean Baudrillard develops the first major phase of his work with a semiotically based theory of production and the object, one that emphasises the 'sign-value' of objects. In the second major phase of his work, Baudrillard argues that even the notion of the sign as a vehicle of meaning and signification is too reductive; rather, the Saussure of the anagrams, where words seem to emerge mysteriously, and almost magically, through the letters, is more in keeping with the way language works. Finally, from his writings of the mid-1970s onwards, starting with *Symbolic Exchange and Death*, Baudrillard has taken up the radical consequences, as he sees them, of the pervasiveness of the code in late-modern societies. The code certainly refers to computerisation, and to digitalisation, but it is also fundamental in physics, biology and other natural sciences where it enables a perfect reproduction of the object or situation; for this reason the code enables a by-passing of the real and opens up what Baudrillard has famously designated as 'hyperreality'.

Although Baudrillard preferred to be without a background (see letter in Gane 1993: 6), it is possible to ascertain that he was born in 1929 in Reims, the same town as his intellectual mentor, Georges Bataille. He died in Paris in March 2007. While his grandparents were peasants, his own family was in transition to an urban life and jobs in the civil service. The milieu was not an intellectual one, and Baudrillard worked hard at the lycée to compensate for this, becoming the first of his family to do intellectual work in a serious way. Although he attempted the *agrégation* he did not succeed, nor did he ever succeed (he has now retired) in gaining a permanent university post. Personally, Baudrillard thought of his life as one of a 'virtual state of rupture'. In 1966, Baudrillard completed a thesis in sociology at Nanterre with Henri Lefebvre, an anti-structuralist. Later, he became associated with Roland Barthes at the École des Hautes Études, and wrote an important article on the object and sign-function in the journal, *Communications*, in 1969. Baudrillard's book, *Le Système des objets* (*The Object System*) (1968), echoes Barthes's work, *The Fashion System*.

Critique of Production and the Object

Baudrillard's earliest writings on Calvino, and others published in Sartre's, *Les Temps modernes*, together with his translations of Brecht and Weiss hardly presage the explosive critique of Marx's theory of value that would emerge less than a decade later. Quite unlike Lefebvre, Baudrillard did not reject structuralism; he rather worked through it. This allowed him to use the notions of the 'sign', 'system' and 'difference' to spell out the limit of the structuralist endeavour, especially as far as the distinction between the real and imagination are concerned.

While Baudrillard's reservations regarding Marx's political economy are largely fuelled by a semiotic conception of the object in capitalism, he has also been crucially influenced by Mauss's theory of the gift and Bataille's theory of expenditure. For the latter two thinkers, no human economy can be reduced to a putative utilitarian base, with equilibrium being its normal state. By contrast, institutions such as the Kula and the potlatch show that waste in the drive for prestige was the original, non-utilitarian basis for consumption. Seen in this light, political economy's distinction between use-value and exchange-value is quite limited. An object also has to be understood to have a symbolic value which is irreducible to either use- or exchange-value. A gift (e.g. a wedding ring) is an object of this nature. The gift still exists – albeit in a reduced form – in capitalist societies; it is the obstacle to any easy theory of the economy as equilibrium.

But even if one were to accept the division between objects of use-value (objects of utility and needs), and objects of exchange-value, the question arises as to where precisely the line is to be drawn between these two forms. In his books which address this issue – *Le Système des objets* (1968), *Consumer Society* (1970), *For a Political Economy of the Sign* (1972) – Baudrillard first broadens the scope of the analysis by adding the symbolic object and the sign object to the category of the object. He then argues that it is necessary to distinguish four different logics: (1) The logic of practical operations, which corresponds to use-value; (2) The logic of equivalence, which corresponds to exchange-value; (3) The logic of ambivalence, which corresponds to symbolic exchange; and (4) the logic of difference, which corresponds to sign-value. These logics may be summarised, respectively, as those of utility, the market, the gift and status. In the logic of the first category, the object becomes an instrument, in the second, a commodity, in the third, a symbol, and in the fourth, a sign (Baudrillard 1981a: 66).

With his semiotic writings on the object, Baudrillard, now following Saussure and the structuralists, endeavours to show that no object exists in isolation from others. Instead their differential, or relational, aspect becomes crucial in understanding them. In addition, while there is a utilitarian aspect to many objects, what is essential to them is their capacity to signify a status. In this regard, even denial can be a kind of luxury – as when 'good taste' demands that a room not be overly cluttered with objects. To be emphasised here, is that objects are not simply consumed in a consumer society; they are produced less to satisfy a need than to signify a status, and this is only possible because of the differential relationship between objects. Hence, in a thorough-going consumer society, objects become signs, and the realm of necessity is left far behind – if it ever really existed.

Code

Baudrillard's aim, then, is to render the very idea of needs, or utility, problematic. Needs, he suggests, can only be sustained by an ideologically based anthropology of the subject. Often this takes a psychologistic (needs as a function of human nature), or a culturalist form (needs as a function of society). Once the work of Veblen (on conspicuous consumption), Bataille and Mauss is considered, and different social and cultural formations are brought into the equation, the notion that irreducible primary needs govern human activities becomes a myth. Subject and object are not joined, Baudrillard points out, on the basis of the eternal qualities of the subject, but – following Lévi-Strauss – are joined through the unconscious structure of social relations. In sum, human beings do not search for happiness; they do not search to realise equality; consumption does not homogenise it – differentiates through the sign system. Life-style and values – not economic need – is the basis of social life.

An important outcome of Baudrillard's analysis of consumption in terms of signs is that it undermines the validity of the distinction – used by Galbraith and the Frankfurt School alike – between true and false, artificial and real, needs. What must be avoided, says Baudrillard, is a critique of consumerism and the notion of *homo eco-nomicus* at the cost of a renewed moralism. In elaborating on this, Baudrillard sets out an idea at the end of his analysis of consumer society which will serve as a touch stone for all of his subsequent work. It is that in the discourse of consumption, there is an anti-discourse: the exalted discourse of abundance is everywhere duplicated by a critique of consumer society – even to the point where advertising often intentionally parodies advertising. Everything 'anti-', says Baudrillard, can be recuperated; this is what consigns Marx to another, by-gone era. The society of consumption is also the society of the denunciation of consumption.

On a number of occasions in his early writings, Baudrillard uses the term, 'code' when referring to the system of signs. While this term may have been there as a synonym for system, or language (Saussure's *langue*), in his most important work of the mid-1970s – *Symbolic Exchange and Death* – the notion of 'code' assumes an importance that it would be hard to overestimate. Not that Baudrillard (unlike Eco) spends much time in defining the nature and subtleties of the notion of code. Indeed, we can note in passing that he rarely defines his key terms in anything like an exhaustive fashion, the sense largely being derived from the context, and from the view that Baudrillard accepts the developments in semiotics and other fields as given. Here, though, we can say that the meaning of 'code' is quite straightforward: the code is the binary code of computer technology; it is the DNA code in biology, or the digital code in television and in sound recording, as it is the code in information technology. The era of the code in fact supersedes the era of the sign. None of this is spelled out, but is clearly implied by the context. Central to Baudrillard's concerns is the connection between code and reproduction – reproduction which is itself 'original'. The code entails that the object produced – tissue in biology, for example – is not a copy in the accepted sense of the term, where the copy is the copy of an original, natural object. Rather, the difference between copy and original is now redundant. How redundant? This is a key question. Baudrillard tends to say entirely redundant; but this is also in keeping with his belief that the only way to keep the social system from imploding is to take up an extreme theoretical position. Many would argue, however, that the code has not yet, and will not, assume the hegemonic proportions Baudrillard sketches out. That the code is of extreme importance, however, cannot be denied. Virtual reality, global communications, the hologram and art are just some of the areas in addition to those enumerated above where it is exemplified.

Simulacra and Simulation

In an era when the natural object is no longer credible (structuralism having been the first modern movement to challenge the credibility of the natural object), the code has raised simulation to an unprecedented importance in social life. Simulation and models are the exemplars of pure reproduction. Because the code enables reality – as it was understood in the age of production – to be bypassed, a curious potential emerges; Baudrillard calls it 'reversibility'. Reversibility entails that all finalities disappear; nothing is outside the system, which becomes a tautology. This is seen most starkly with simulation and simulacra.

With regard to simulation, Baudrillard defines three kinds: that of the counterfeit dominant in the classical era of the Renaissance, that of production in the industrial era, and, finally, simulation of the present era governed by the code. With the counterfeited object, the difference between the real, or 'natural' object is made apparent; in industrial production, the difference between the object and the labour process is made evident; in the era of simulation, not the production, but the *re*production of objects becomes crucial. And, as we have seen, the principle of reproduction is contained in the code. With regard to reproduction, it is clear that labour power, or the worker, is also reproduced. Reproduction, therefore, includes what would have been both sides of the equation in the era of industrialism. Now, the origin of things is not an original thing, or being, but formulae, coded signals, and numbers. Given that the origin in reproduction is the principle of generation, and not the object generated, complete reversibility is possible: the last 'original' produced can be perfectly reproduced. The difference between the real and its representation is erased, and the age of simulacra emerges. In its extreme form, therefore, even death can be integrated into the system: or rather, the principle of reversibility implies that death does not really happen.

If, as Foucault's work sought to demonstrate, power no longer has a substantive content – is no longer something possessed and centralised – the continued operation of the institutions of centralised power would become a simulation of a certain form of power relations. In short the claim that power has a content becomes a pretence. Generalised simulation thus accompanies the death of all essentialisms.

Socially speaking, Baudrillard notes that the era of the code begins to penetrate the whole of the social fabric. One of the symptoms of this is that opposites begin to collapse and 'everything becomes undecidable': the beautiful and the ugly in fashion, the left and the right in politics, the true and the false in the media, the useful and the useless at the level of objects, nature and culture – all these become interchangeable in the era of reproduction and simulation.

Baudrillard thus shows how the system is potentially a closed system which risks imploding. Hyperreality effaces the difference between the real and the imaginary. The question to be answered is that of how a political intervention which does not get recuperated by the system is possible. Baudrillard suggests a path with his elaboration of 'seduction' and 'fatal strategies'. In both cases, he argues that it is necessary to give primacy to the object over the subject, fatal theory determined by the object over banal, critical theory determined by the subject. The point is to move to extremes in order to counteract the system's equilibrium. Ecstasy, fascination, risk and vertigo before the object which seduces, takes precedence over the sober reflexivity of banal theory. Banal theory is always tautological: the beginning always equals the end; with fatal (= death and destiny), there is no 'end' in any representational or teleological sense. Seduction, then, is fatal in the sense that the subject is dominated by the unpredictable object – the object of fascination. The masses who, due to their lack of reflexivity and conformity, were the despair of revolutionary intellectuals now become the model to be followed. For they have always given precedence to ecstasy and fascination, and thus to the object; the masses thus converge towards the potential extremities of the system. In speaking of the masses' relationship to the image, Baudrillard writes: 'There is in this conformity a force of seduction in the literal sense of the word, a force of diversion, distortion, capture and ironic fascination. There is a kind of fatal strategy of conformity' (Baudrillard 1981b 15).

Forget Baudrillard?

A great deal of Baudrillard's writing has raised heated debate – no more so than when he wrote articles in the French daily, *Libération*, claiming that the 1991 Gulf War did not take place, and then, in 2001, after an article in *Le Monde* on the September 11 terrorist attacks on the World Trade Center, where he referred to the 'spirit of

terrorism'. Baudrillard was accused of denying material facts, in relation to the first Gulf War, and in justifying terrorism in the second
article. Of course, Baudrillard was in both instances misunderstood, if
one spent time unpicking the crux of the arguments. But perhaps this
is no longer the point.

What is more to the point in relation to Baudrillard's work is that
his publications from the mid-1990s onward (*The Perfect Crime* (1996
[1995]), *Impossible Exchange* (2000 [1999]), *Screened Out* (2000 [1997])),
lack the rigorous theorising of the works of the 1980s, linked as these
were to key works in Marxism, structuralism and semiotics. These
works constituted, in light of real developments in technology, particularly
digitalisation and cybernetics, a genuine engagement with history,
unlike the ironical and nihilist position Baudrillard has adopted over
recent years. Of course, Baudrillard's supporters are quick to point
out that there is a strategy here; for Baudrillard was cool (despite his
birth date) and anything but naïve. There is, then, the fatal strategy of
the object, an object that outplays the subject; the strategy of seduction, which poses itself as a foil to the society of the spectacle; the
strategy of pataphysics (from Alfred Jarry) as a science of imaginary
solutions which, in the contemporary world, would entirely super-
sede metaphysics (see Baudrillard 2002). Pataphysics is the only way
theory can outfox a virtual reality of simulation, where radical and
(under normal circumstances) unanticipated reversals occur with
increasing frequency.

However, if the virtual and symbolic, along with an accompanying
digital techno-culture, are totally dominant, then this 'reality', as
Baudrillard showed in the 1970s, is governed by the code – or by
codes. As such, the world would become the height of predictability,
not the reverse. Chance would have no role to play here. In short, it
is precisely because the world (social and cultural reality) is not as
Baudrillard says it is that crises of theory, crises of predictive science
can occur. A world of pure appearances would be easy to manage.
The truth, though, is that such a media world does not exist – even
in imagination (even in pataphysics).

References

Baudrillard, Jean (1981a), *For a Critique of the Political Economy of the Sign*,
trans. Charles Levin, St Louis: Telos Press.
—— (1981b), *The Evil Demon of Images*, trans. Paul Patton and Paul Foss,
Sydney: Power Institute.
—— (2002), *Pataphysique*, Paris: Sens et Tonka.

Gane, Mike, ed. (1993), *Baudrillard Live. Selected Interviews*, London and New York: Routledge.

See also: **Bataille, Mauss, Virilio**

Baudrillard's major writings

(2005a) *Cool Memories 5, 2000–2004*, Paris: Galilée.

(2005b [2004]) *The Intelligence of Evil or the Lucidity Pact*, trans. Chris Turner, Oxford and New York: Berg.

(2005c [1996]) *The Conspiracy of Art: manifestos Interviews, Essays*, trans. Ames Hodges, New York: Semiotext(e).

(2005d [1968]) *The System of Objects*, trans. James Benedict, London and New York: Verso.

(2004) *Mots de passe*, Paris: Librairie générale française.

(2003a) *The Spirit of Terrorism and Other Essays*, trans. Chris Turner, London and New York: Verso.

(2003b) *Mass, Identity, Architectural Writings of Jean Baudrillard*, ed., Francesco Proto, Chichester, Eng.: Wiley Academy.

(2003c [2000]) *Passwords*, trans. Chris Turner, London and New York: Verso.

(2002a) *Pataphysique*, Paris: Sens et Tonka.

(2002b [1997]) *Screened Out*, trans. Chris Turner, London and New York: Verso.

(2001a) *Uncollected Baudrillard*, ed. Gary Genosko, London and Thousand Oaks: Sage.

(2001b) *Selected Writings* (2nd edition), ed. Mark Poster, Cambridge: Polity Press.

(2001c [1999]) *Impossible Exchange*, trans. Chris Turner, London and New York: Verso.

(2000a) *Vital Illusion*, ed. Julia Witner, New York: Columbia University Press.

(2000b) *Cool memories 4, 1995–2000*, Paris: Galiée.

(1998 [1970]) *The Consumer Society: Myths and Structures*, Thousand Oaks: Sage.

(1996a [1995]) *Perfect Crime*, trans. Chris Turner, London and New York: Verso.

(1996b [1990]) *Cool Memories 2 1987–1990*, trans. Chris Turner, Durham: Duke University Press.

(1994 [1981]) *Simulacra and Simulation*, trans. Sheila Glaser, Ann Arbor: University of Michigan Press.

(1993a) *Baudrillard Live. Selected Interviews*, ed. Mike Gane, London and New York: Routledge.

(1992b [1990]) *The Transparence of Evil: Essays on Extreme Phenomena*, trans. John J. St. John, Baddeley: Routledge.

(1993 [1976]) *Symbolic Exchange and Death*, trans. Ian Grant, London: Sage.

(1990a [1987]) *Cool Memories 1* trans. Chris Turner, London: Verso.

(1990b [1983]) *Fatal Strategies. Crystal Revenge*, trans. Philip Beitchman and W.G.J. Niesluchowski, New York: Semiotext(e); London: Pluto.

(1990c [1979]) *Seduction*, trans. Brian Singer, London: Macmillan; New York: Saint Martins.

(1989 [1986]) *America*, trans. Chris Turner, London and New York: Routledge.
(1987 [1977]) *Forget Foucault*, New York: Semiotext(e).
(1981a[1972]) *For a Critique of the Political Economy of the Sign*, trans. Charles Levin, St Louis: Telos Press.
(1981b) *The Evil Demon of Images*, trans. Paul Patton and Paul Foss, Sydney: The Power Institute.
(1975 [1973]) *The Mirror of Production*, trans. Mark Poster, St Louis: Telos Press.

Further reading

Gane, Mike, ed. (2000), *Jean Baudrillard*, London and New York: Routledge.
Hegarty, Paul (2004), *Jean Baudrillard: Live Theory*, London and New York: Continuum.
Lane, Richard (2000), *Jean Baudrillard*, London and New York: Routledge.

MARGUERITE DURAS (1914–1996)

Marguerite Duras is one of France's most important and interesting intellectual figures. She excelled at being a writer, filmmaker and dramatist. After the Second World War she also worked for a number of years as a journalist for *France-Observateur*. She was often at the forefront of political movements, such as the opposition to the Algerian War, May '68 and feminism. Surprisingly, Duras supported of the sinking, by the French secret service, of the Greenpeace vessel, *The Rainbow Warrior* in 1985, her view being at the time that any impediment – which Greenpeace represented – to French nuclear testing in the Pacific only encouraged Soviet expansionism.

The Oeuvre *of Marguerite Duras*

In her extensive *oeuvre*, Duras particularly explored the emotional disequilibrium brought by love, desire, suffering and death, especially as these affect women and propel them towards the abyss of madness. In addition, Duras's writing explores the space between fusion and separation (e.g. in love and sexuality) as it breaks down the boundary between private (family) and public (political and artistic) life – between the symbolic and the imaginary, and between the time of narrative and the event recounted. Often narrative appears as a kind of distancing from the real, so that writing becomes the only reality. Subject and object thus become difficult to separate in many of Duras's key fictional texts. This is illustrated in *The Ravishing of Lol V. Stein* (Duras 1966), where the writer/narrator and what is being written about become particularly difficult to determine. For this reason, Duras has come to be seen as a post-modern writer.

Duras's own life was a crucial source of material and inspiration for her fictional writing. Few could transform everyday life fragments into artistic statements with the combination of intensity and starkness that characterises Duras's prose. Although, as Leslie Hill has pointed out (Hill 1993: 1), there is no absolutely true and unchanging set of biographical facts pertaining to Duras's life, certain points can be taken as given.[1]

A Life

Marguerite Duras was born Marguerite Donnadieu in 1914 at Gia-Dinh near Saigon in Cochinchina (now South Vietnam). Both her parents had been married previously and had met in Vietnam. Duras's father was a mathematics teacher from southwest France, while her mother came from a poor farming family in the north. Shortly after being posted to Phnom Penh in 1918, the father contracted dysentery and had to return to France, where he later died. Duras's mother was thus forced to bring up Marguerite and her two older brothers alone in various abodes in Cambodia and Vietnam. Until the age of eleven, when she completed her first school certificate, Marguerite spoke more Vietnamese than French.

In 1932–33, Duras returned permanently to France and took up the study of mathematics, but soon abandoned this to study political science and law. After her studies, she was employed in the Colonial Office as a researcher and archivist, and shortly before the outbreak of the war, she married the writer Robert Antelme. Between 1940 and 1942, Duras published her first work with Philippe Roques, *L'Empire français*, but her first novel written under the family name Donnadieu, *La Famille Tanéran*, was refused by Gallimard. Also in this period, Duras's first child was stillborn. She would subsequently have a son in 1947 with her partner, Jean Mascolo, her marriage with Robert Antelme having been dissolved in 1946.

The year 1943 proved to be a major turning point: *Les Impudents* appeared, Duras's first published novel, and the first piece of writing to appear under the pseudonym 'Duras', and Duras made friends with Georges Bataille, Maurice Merleau-Ponty, Edgar Morin and others. At the same time, she and her husband joined the French movement for prisoners of war. While active in the Resistance with François Mitterand, Duras, in 1944, joined the communist party, from which she was expelled in 1950. Robert Antelme was arrested and sent to Buchenwald and Dachau. The painful experience of waiting for his return inspired the novel, *La Douleur*, published in 1985. In 1984, Duras received the prix Goncourt for her novel, *The Lover*.

Prior to her public acclaim in 1985, however, Duras had become known to a wider public for her script for Alain Resnais's film, *Hiroshima mon amour* (1959), for her own film, *India Song* (1974) based on her novel *Le Vice-consul* (1966), and for two much-discussed novels, *Moderato Cantabile* (1958), and *The Ravishing of Lol V. Stein* (1964).

Generally speaking, Duras's writing does not focus on the elaboration of ideas or on the experimental side of art (although these were of course implicit in everything she did), but rather on emotional experiences which are barely translatable into symbolic form: silences, inarticulateness, deep sadness, sudden and inexplicable violence, loss in love, almost imperceptible – yet fundamental – changes in emotional, or bodily states, odd flights of imagination – it is these which are at the heart of her artistic effort. The focus on emotional states in particular has given Duras's *oeuvre* an allure that feminists have claimed has undermined the supposedly rationalistic and phallocentric narrative of highly regarded male writing.

Style

One can no doubt point to the unique rhythm of the articulation of the fragmentary narrative in the film *India Song* as illustrative of Duras's 'feminine' style – a style contrasting with the tightly ordered realist approach typical of much conventional cinema. Shot in black and white, *India Song* plays on a dissonance between the sound-track and the images; the dialogue is spoken off-screen rather than on, most shots are static, and there is a refusal of the shot/reverse shot technique. Clearly, the film's poetic character sharply contrasts with the diegetic emphasis of a conventional realist film.

Duras's writing style, while clearly singular, often evokes the experimental realism of the *Nouveau Roman*. Short sentences focus on small details, thus slowing the rhythm of the articulation of the intrigue. A look, a sigh, a touch, often seem to be as important in their own right as the significance they are charged with conveying – which is often a mood, or an emotional crisis, rather than an idea. Typically, the novel, *L'amour* (*Love*), does not contain a discussion of what love is; rather, it evokes and denotes love in dialogue and short sentences. As if to reinforce a minimalist, and non-Baroque style, most of Duras's novels are short by conventional standards (around

40,000 words). Such minimalism is more than a stylistic device; it is also part of an effort to focus on the *difficulty* of speaking and writing; it contains a barely suppressed silence.

Deficit of Language

The features of the Durasian *oeuvre* mentioned above have prompted Julia Kristeva to see Duras's writing as symptomatic of a world where a deficit of language and representation has emerged in light of the terrible events of the twentieth century. While it is true that Kristeva uses a psychoanalytic framework that some might find problematic to interpret features of Duras's *oeuvre*, few commentators seem to disagree about what these features are. Indeed, while Leslie Hill is critical of Kristeva's reading of *The Ravishing of Lol V. Stein*, his insight that indeterminacy is a fundamental feature of the novel in question, would only seem to confirm the problematic status of identity typical of the crisis of representation that characterised the end of the twentieth century.

For Kristeva, then, Duras's work has to be seen against a background of apocalyptic themes: Hiroshima, the Holocaust, Stalinism, Colonialism. She thus participates in the search for a symbolic means adequate to represent the horror of what has happened. Rather than focusing on a public sense of the suffering, the latter is presented in an intensely private context. People become locked in their private grief – or depression – so that their speech, rather than being a means to some kind of catharsis or coming-to-terms with the horror, is in fact a symptom of it. Because it is so intensely evocative and descriptive of sadness, rather than being an analysis of it, Duras's writing, in Kristeva's view, brings us to the verge of madness; her texts fuse with it rather than represent, or transcend it. This madness, though, is now the only way of living one's individuality, so impoverished are the public means of representation.

Leslie Hill's remark in the context of a discussion of *The Lover* confirms the thrust of Kristeva's interpretative insight: Duras's '*L'Amant* does no more than repeat episodes rather than account for them' (Hill 1993: 118). Indeed, many scenes and characters in Duras's repertoire are reworked in her novels, and none more than those related to her own autobiography.

Kristeva thus notes the importance of the mother and the theme of separation in Duras. The presence of the mother, from *The Sea Wall* (1950), *The Lover*, and further, to *The North China Lover* (1991) is not only to be seen in the figure represented in a narrative, but also in the writing itself. The mother, on this more psychoanalytic reading, is the emotion of lived experience, it is the madness that cannot be transcended. To begin to understand this one need only refer to how the narrative (such as it is) of *The Lover* stays so close to the well-known facts of Duras's life. As Duras writes in the novel, she wanted to kill her brother because her mother loved him so much. Moreover, she writes that, 'I've written a good deal about the members of my family, but then they were still alive, my mother and my brothers. And I skirted around them, skirted around all these things without really tackling them' (Duras 1986: 11). Although setting out to tackle the things concerning her life, 'The story of my life,' she says 'doesn't exist. Does not exist. There's never any centre to it. No path, no line' (Duras 1966: 11). Again, what she is doing now 'is both different and the same' (Duras 1966: 11).

Duras reworks the same material, but the question is whether she is thereby able to transcend the despair and the hatred depicted in this novel and elsewhere, or whether her writing is indeed an analogue, and thus a confirmation, of it. In other words, did Duras remember her past, and to that extent transcend it, or did she rather have a largely affective and nostalgic relationship to it? In favour of the first explanation, and against Kristeva's view perhaps, is the fact of Duras's undoubted success as a writer – and no more so than with *The Lover* which became a worldwide bestseller. Therefore, even if she could not remember for herself, Duras, it seems, remembered for others. To this extent, the work transcends despair. On the other hand, the absence of transcendence may well confirm the despair present in modem society, and it may be this which is at the heart of Duras's success. Just as it is possible to respond to suffering by suffering oneself, so readers may respond to Duras empathetically, in a fascinated rather than an analytical way. Whatever the case, it is certain that Duras prompts one to think seriously about the nature of writing.

The Ravishing of Lol V. Stein

One of the most intriguing and renowned of Duras's novels is *The Ravishing of Lol V. Stein*. Its complex narrative – or absence of a clear narrative – has given rise to numerous interpretations, one of the most famous being by Jacques Lacan (Lacan 1987: 12–129). Lacan famously sees in Duras's story an exemplification of his own psycho-analytic teaching, even though Duras, in 1964, was not in the least familiar with his theories, nor had she ever attended his seminar. For Lacan, the novel is the repeated attempt at the rememoration of the traumatic primal scene, where Lol Valerie Stein's fiancé goes off with an older woman, Anna-Maria Stretter, at the ball at T. Beach. This event is at least in part doubly filtered: first of all through the narrator, Jacques Hold – also an active protagonist in the events – and through Tatiana Karl (wife of Hold's superior at the hospital where Hold, a doctor, was employed, and also Hold's lover) who, Hold's narrative suggests, had told him what had transpired at T. Beach. What is also clear, however, is that the telling of the story of T. Beach is not separate from the events being recounted. This is reinforced by the fact that part of the narrative describes the attempted re-enactment of the fateful night.

On this night, the shock of her fiancé, Michael Richardson, departing with Anna-Marie Stretter seems to send Lol V. Stein into a state of madness. However, she seems to recover, and leaves her native town, S. Tahla, in order to marry Jean Bedford, with whom she has three children. Eventually, Lol V. Stein returns to S. Tahla after an absence of ten years, and renews her acquaintance with Tatiana, and at the same time meets Tatiana's lover, Jacques Hold. A key element of the novel concerns the ambiguous place of Lol V. Stein. Initially it appears (whether appearance is ever really transcended is a key issue) that Lol is devastated by being thrown over for another woman. A number of things complicate the situation, however, not the least of these being that, later, Lol cannot remember exactly what happened on the fateful night, and claims not to have loved her fiancé from the moment when Anne-Marie Stretter entered the dance hall. Given Lol's forgetting, Tatiana's testimony, filtered through Jacques Hold's narrative, is crucial for the reconstitution of events, that is, effectively, for the story itself. As her story is entirely in the second degree, we suspect that being unable to tell it herself is part of Lol's condition; the trauma, unable to manifest itself in a symbolic form, is continually acted out. And in fact, the last part of the text concerns Lol's return to the scene of the dramatic events, and their attempted re-enactment.

Very quickly, the reader, increasingly on the alert for new evidence that might throw light on the meaning of the story, realises that the story is less about an event than it is about how this event can be told. Lol cannot tell it, because she was too close to it; only the witness has the symbolic means to tell the story. Even this is not a simple matter, however; for in Jacques Hold's telling, Lol is placed in the mediating, third position of the symbolic when she becomes a witness to the affair between Hold and Tatiana. It is as though Lol desperately wants to be in the position which allows her to speak of what she sees instead of being the traumatised victim: the object of another's discourse.

Lol V. Stein's relation to her trauma would seem to correspond to Marguerite Duras's relation to her own family (particularly to her mother and brother). Again, the issue is not one of reconstituting the true events of one's past, but of being able to occupy the position of witness to one's own life. How to speak and write at all is at stake, not whether what one says or writes is true or false, fictional or non-fictional. Taking a pseudonym, giving up the family name, should therefore be seen as an essential, and not an accidental part of Duras's art. It is the means whereby she can begin to become a witness to her own life. It entails the separation from (and even denial of) the very real trauma of that life. In this way Duras may well have achieved something that few writers have achieved: a putting into language – however minimal this might be – of the struggle for language.

Note

1 The following biographical details about Duras come largely from Leslie Hill (1993), and Christiane Blot-Labarrère (1992).

References

Blot-Labarrère, Christiane (1992), *Marguerite Duras*, Paris: Seuil 'Les Contemporains'.
Duras, Marguerite (1966), *The Ravishing of Lol V. Stein*, trans. Richard Seaver, New York: Grove Press.
—— (1986), *The Lover*, trans. Barbara Bray, London: Collins, Fontana/Flamingo.
Hill, Leslie (1993), *Marguerite Duras: Apocalyptic Desires*, London: Routledge.
Lacan, Jacques (1987), 'Hommage to Marguerite Duras', trans. Peter Connor in *Duras on Duras*, San Francisco: City Lights Books.

See also: **Irigaray, Kristeva, Lacan**

Duras's major works

(1998 [1995]) *No More*, trans. Richard Howard, New York: Seven Stories.
(1993 [1990]) *Summer Rain*, trans. Barbara Bray, New York: Collier Books; Toronto: Maxwell Macmillan Canada; New York: Maxwell Macmillan International.
(1992 [1991]) *The North China Lover*, trans. Leigh Hafrey, New York: The New Press.
(1989 [1987]) *Emily L.*, trans. Barbara Bray, London: Collins, Fontana/Flamingo.

(1988 [1986]) *Blue Eyes, Black Hair*, trans. Barbara Bray, London: Collins, Flamingo.

(1987) [(1981 and 1984)] *Outside: Selected Writings*, trans. Arthur Gold-hammer, London: Collins, Fontana/Flamingo.

(1986a [1985]) *La Douleur* (also published as: *The War: A Memoir*), trans. Barbara Bray, London: Collins, Fontana/Flamingo.

(1986b [1982]) *The Maladie of Death*, trans. Barbara Bray, New York: Grove Press.

(1986c [1950]) *Sea Wall*, trans. Herma Briffault, London: Faber & Faber.

(1985 [1984]) *The Lover*, trans. Barbara Bray, London: Collins, Fontana/Flamingo.

(1976 [1973]) *India Song*, trans. Barbara Bray, New York: Grove Press.

(1971) *L'Amour*, Paris: Gallimard.

(1969 [1970]) *Destroy, She Said*, trans. Barbara Bray, New York: Grove Press.

(1968 [1967]) *L'Amante anglaise*, trans. Barbara Bray, London: Hamish Hamilton.

(1966a [1964]) *The Ravishing of Lol V. Stein*, trans. Richard Seaver, New York: Grove Press.

(1966b [1960 and 1966]) *Hiroshima Mon Amour and Une aussi longue absence*, trans. Richard Seaver and Barbara Wright, London: Calder & Boyars.

(1966c [1958]) *Moderato cantabile*, trans. Richard Seaver, London: John Calder.

(1944) *La Vie tranquille*, Paris: Gallimard, folio.

Further reading

Harvey, Robert and Volat, Hélène (1997), *Marguerite Duras: A Bio-bibliography*, Westport, Conn. and London: Greenwood Press.

Hill, Leslie (1993), *Marguerite Duras: Apocalyptic Desires*, London: Routledge. This book contains an exhaustive English and French bibliography of Duras's works.

Knapp, Bettina L., ed. (1998), *Critical Essays on Marguerite Duras*, New York: G.K Hall.

Williams, James S. (1997), *The Erotics of Passage: Politics and Form in the Later Work of Marguerite Duras*, Liverpool: Liverpool University Press.

Williams, James S, ed. (with the assistance of Jane Sayers) (2000), *Revisioning Duras: Film, Race, Sex*, Liverpool: Liverpool University Press.

Winston, Jane Bradley (2002), *Postcolonial Duras: Cultural Memory in Postwar France*, New York and Basingstoke: Palgrave.

FRANZ KAFKA (1883–1924)

The uniqueness of Kafka stems, in large measure, from the intersection of writing and lived experience. Born into a Jewish family in Prague in 1883, Franz Kafka was the son of a prosperous self-made businessman. Although his parents spoke Czech in their native village, they did everything they could to ensure that their son had a good education, and in particular, that he could speak and write good German – like the privileged German-speaking minority in

Prague. The father also wanted the son to know and to appreciate the Jewish side of the family history, a factor which tended to bring Kafka and his father into conflict; for Franz had a very different view of Jewishness, a point brought out in his famous letter to his father, written in November 1919.

Life and Literary Background

From 1893 to 1901, Kafka attended the German gymnasium, after which he studied jurisprudence at the Karl-Ferdinand University. In 1906, he took his doctorate in Law. In 1902, Kafka first met the critic and novelist Max Bred who introduced him to Prague literary circles. In 1907, he began work at an Italian insurance company before leaving in July 1908 to work, until his retirement in 1922 due to ill-health, for the semi-government Workers Accident Insurance Bureau. The company gave Kafka extended sick-leave, and this allowed him more time to write.

In 1909, Kafka's first story was accepted by a Prague journal and he read to Brod chapters of his novel, *Wedding Preparations in the Country*. In 1910, he began to keep his diaries and also became involved with the Yiddish theatre company. In 1912, Kafka met Felice Bauer, to whom he was twice engaged and with whom he conducted a voluminous correspondence. He also wrote letters, since published, to the Czech translator of his stories, Milena Jesenská. In 1914, Kafka read the first chapter of *The Trial* to Brod, and in 1918, a year after tuberculosis had been diagnosed, he became engaged to Julie Wohryzek. In the winter of 1920–21, while in a sanatorium for his tuberculosis, Kafka told Brod that he wished all his work to be destroyed after his death, a request subsequently confirmed in writing. After living in Berlin with a Polish Hebrew student, Dora Dymant, Kafka died of tuberculosis in 1924.

Influence

Kafka's influence has been profound from at least two points of view. In the first place, his writings – in which an enigmatic, skeletal world has apparently been created – have touched a nerve in the life as lived in modern, industrial society. The nihilism of a society without God, the hyper-rationalism of bureaucratic domination, which strangles the innocent in its web, and the end of all idealism – including perhaps, the end of the notion of causality along with all first principles – is sketched out. Here in Kafka's *oeuvre* is an allegory of a society without any particular end, but which is assuredly destined to come to an end in a material sense. Thus Joseph K cannot find out for what crime he has been arrested in *The Trial*, just as K in *The Castle* cannot enter the castle, but does not know why. At one level, then, Kafka has been taken up as the revealer of the dangers of social and psychological relations that are reduced to nothing but means. And he seems to be all the more successful in creating this world to the extent that he never describes or characterises it, but always only ever suggests or evokes it. Quite possibly, readers looking in Kafka for a message about modernity are able to find it because the suggestion of a message is one of the fundamental traits of Kafka's writing strategy. To suggest and to evoke – to work by way of enigma – rather than to state, gives things a profoundly kaleidoscopic quality. The strangeness of Kafka's writing, that few readers prior to the 1980s could have failed to notice, is to be found in this minimalist style of suggestion. The strangeness has meant that each reader can begin to find there something for him or herself, in other words, the lack of definition and specificity in Kafka's world produces the 'Kafkaesque' – the enigma, the darkness and the mystery within which everyone can find a place, however discomforting and depressing this may be.

Writing and Life

Enigma and Obscurity

The role of enigma and obscurity is by no means the unambiguous outcome of a writing strategy, but often seems to be intrinsic to the object being described. Nowhere is this better demonstrated than in the discussion of the law in *The Trial*. The law, which is supposed to illuminate the case, at the same time obscures it. The law in fact seems to have a blind spot right at its core. For it is unable to answer definitively the question as to who is inside and who is outside the law. In principle, the law is unable to admit its limits; it pretends to be all-powerful. In fact, however, there are always areas outside the law, such as the areas of enjoyment, horror and death – the very areas with which Kafka's text is obsessed.

The Writer

In the second place, Kafka and his *oeuvre* offer an insight into the mode of being a writer in the twentieth century. Kafka's life in and for writing – a life partially revealed with great force and poignancy in his *Diaries* – raises the question of what it might really mean for someone to be devoted to art in general, and to writing in particular in the twentieth century. Why is this such a difficult question to answer? Why is it not simply that some people are called to the vocation of 'writer', just as some are lawyers or doctors? A response to this question hinges on what it is that the writer *qua* writer in modern society feels called upon to do. If he or she is content to conform to the existing conventions of writing, there is really no problem; the doors of journalism and writing within well-established genres (e.g. the detective novel) are open to them. Rightly or wrongly, however, the category of literature has, since the middle of the eighteenth century, emerged in modern society. Literature, from one point of view at least, is the 'canonisation' of a truly singular writing. In Kafka's case, this entails the consecration of his most intimate inner-experience. This consecration, or the becoming-literary of writing, sets up a profound tension. For after the writer has made his play, burned his bridges, put his own being on the line, and set the scene of his challenge to the deepest conventions of the art of his day, he may not be recognised; it may all be for nothing. The possibility of the most profound failure has to be entertained. The stakes have thus been raised very high; the temptation to compromise is extremely strong.

From this angle, a writer not only lives for his writing, but more profoundly lives *in* his writing, and is even formed by it in a physical sense. This is writing as the expenditure of a certain energy without return. Certain traits of Kafka's biography confirm and illustrate what is at stake. For instance, rather than becoming a fully professional writer who lived from his work, Kafka remained working in the government insurance office during the day, and only wrote at night, or in the late afternoon. Second, as is known, Kafka told his literary executor, Max Brod, that he wanted all his extant works (with a few exceptions) burned. Just as the origin of the events in Kafka's fiction is shrouded in the mists of enigma, so, too, is this request. Why would Kafka, who was still correcting the proofs of one of his works on his death bed, have made such a request? As Max Brod refused to go along with his protégé on this crucial point, and instead set to work producing a five-volume set of Kafka's complete works, Kafka has become immortalised; his writing has become literature. He did finally, gain recognition on his own terms, but, tragically, did not live to see it.

The Practice of Writing

Although there are undoubtedly elements in Kafka's fiction which lend themselves to an allegorical reading, and thus to a political use, the main way in which Kafka's writing can be seen to have political effects is a more indirect one, achieved through the valorisation of a practice of writing. Kafka's writing is not engaged, in the manner of Sartre; for the ideal truth necessary for such a political stance is missing from Kafka's fiction. Indeed, the impossibility of such an engagement is more in keeping with Kafka's approach. The practice of writing is writing produced despite the despair and obscurity of the world, despite the absence of rational protocols that could be followed with a degree of certainty. In this sense, Kafka's is a writing of sacrifice. Its enigmas become essential to it; the effort it cost is also essential to it: Kafka exhausts himself in writing. On one now well-known occasion he wrote his story *The Judgement* in one sitting on the night of 22–23 September 1912. As he comments in his diary:

> I was hardly able to pull my legs out from under the desk, they had got so stiff from sitting. The fearful strain and joy, how the story developed before me, as if I were advancing over water. Several times during this night I heaved my own weight on my back. ... At two I looked at the clock for the last time. As the maid walked through the ante-room for the first time, I wrote the last sentence. ... The slight pains around my heart. The weariness that disappeared in the middle of the night.
>
> (Kafka 1964: 212)

Minor Writing

Although they, too, do not see the political effect of Kafka's writing as being committed in the Sartrian sense, Deleuze and Guattari argue that Kafka's fiction is political in that it constitutes a 'minor' writing within a major linguistic formation (Deleuze and Guattari 1986: 16–18). Thus as a Czech Jew — that is, a member of a minority group – writing in German, Kafka manages to make his own way in the dominant language by constructing a minor idiom in it. Kafka plays with the tonality of German; refuses metaphors; writes so as to defamiliarise (deterritorialise) the language; refuses genealogical connections and focuses on the very small things around him; produces a flood of letters rather than an overall vision. In short, Kafka changes the nature of German significantly, if imperceptibly, and makes a unique place for himself in it, one that was in no sense anticipated by the current usage of the language at the time when he was writing.

Without analysing this turn of events any further, let it suffice to say that Kafka's life brought to the fore a new way of understanding the link between writing and life. This may be summarised in the following way: Kafka showed in his writing practice that writing is a way of life, that it demands a concentration of forces (see Kafka 1964: 163); he also made visible the real stakes at play in the constitution of the literary object; finally, through the use of enigma, he set writing free from a sociological, or psychological determinism that would seek to explain writing in terms of material conditions or a writer's biography. After Kafka, writing (literature) is no longer a product of conditions, but is also constitutive of those conditions.

According to the French critic, Marthe Robert, Kafka makes use of the anonymity of his key characters like K in order to bring out their transcendent quality (Robert 1982: 5). In other words, they are freed from the environment in which they may have originated and can take root in many different environments. This character is thus an exile – like the Jews (although none of Kafka's fiction ever says this) – capable of transgressing boundaries of all kinds – moral, legal, cultural, psychological. The character is the anonymous, rootless person always in search of a community, much as many displaced persons are today in Europe in the first decade of the twenty-first century. Kafka's own life, being half Jewish, half German, also embodies this theme of exile and 'extraterritoriality'.

Absence of Transcendence

Absence of fixed boundaries can be seen as a feature of Kafka's novels from another angle. This time, the collapse of boundaries evokes an absence of transcendence. The source, or origin, is erased: the origin of the law, the origin of change, of sexuality, the cause in cause and effect all evaporate into an enigma. 'Why', in short, finds no answer. In this sense, Kafka becomes Nietzschean and radically anti-idealist. As Georges Bataille put it (Bataille 1979: 272), there is no promised land in Kafka; Moses's goal is unattainable because it is human life – the physical material world – we are dealing with, and not with any transcendent realm. No doubt Kafka tends to fit into some of the features designated as 'post-modern' in his effort to render all boundaries, and thus all identities more fluid.

The spectre of death, together with anguish and despair haunts Kafka's fiction. Faith may be excluded, but not the search for faith. As Maurice Blanchot has said, there is an uncertainty about meaning because despair and anxiety are literary equivalents of death within life (Blanchot 1981: 66). Despair arises here because existence is an exile; there is no true home where one could avoid the anxiety of modern life. To be modern is to be Jewish in a way. Few have better summarised the uniqueness of Kafka than Blanchot when he argues that Kafka's work shines forth despite itself, that is, despite its preoccupation with death: 'This is why we only understand [Kafka's *oeuvre*] in betraying it; our reading turns anxiously around a misunderstanding' (Blanchot 1981: 74).

References

Bataille, Georges (1979), 'Kafka' in *La Littérature et le mal* in *Oeuvres complètes, IX*, Paris: Gallimard.

Blanchot, Maurice (1981), *De Kafka à Kafka*, Paris: Gallimard/Idées.

Deleuze, Gilles and Guattari, Félix (1986), *Kafka: Toward a Minor Literature*, trans. Dana Polan, Minneapolis: University of Minnesota Press.

Kafka, Franz (1964), *The Diaries of Franz Kafka 1910–23*, ed. Max Brod, trans. Joseph Kresh and Martin Greenberg, Harmondsworth: Peregrine/Penguin.

Robert, Marthe (1982), *Franz Kafka's Loneliness*, trans. Ralph Manheim, London: Faber & Faber.

See also: **Bataille, Blanchot, Duras**

Kafka's major writings

(1988 [1948 and 1949]) *Diaries* (one volume), ed. Max Brod, 1910–13, trans. Joseph Kresh, 1914–23, trans. Martin Greenberg and Hannah Arendt, New York: Schocken Books.

(1978) *Wedding Preparations in the Country and Other Stories* (also includes: *Letter to His Father*; *Meditation*; *The Judgement*; and *A Country Doctor*), Harmondsworth: Penguin.

(1976a [1931]) *The Great Wall of China and Investigations of a Dog*, trans. Willa and Edwin Muir, London: Seeker & Warburg/Octopus Books.

(1976b [1919 and 1933]) *Metamorphosis and, In the Penal Settlement*, trans. Eithne Wilkins and Ernst Kaiser, London: Seeker & Warburg/Octopus Books.

(1974 [1926]) *The Castle*, trans. Willa and Edwin Muir, New York: Schocken Books.

(1973) *Letters to Felice*, ed. Erich Heller and Jürgen Born, trans. James Stern and Elisabeth Duckworth, New York: Schocken Books.

(1968 [1925]) The *Trial*, trans. Willa and Edwin Muir, New York: Schocken Books.

(1962) *Letters to Milena*, ed. Willy Haas, trans. Tania and James Stern, New York: Schocken Books.

(1962 [1927]) *America*, trans. Willa and Edwin Muir, New York: Schocken Books.
(1954) *Dearest Father* (Letter to His Father), trans. Ernst and Eithne Wilkins, New York: Schocken Books.

Further reading

Anderson, Mark, ed. (1989), *Reading Kafka: Prague, Politics and the Fin de siècle*, New York, Schocken Books.
Bataille, Georges (1973), 'Kafka' in *Literature and Evil*, trans. Alastair Hamilton, London: Calder & Boyars.
Benjamin, Walter (1979), 'Franz Kafka on the tenth anniversary of his death' in *Illuminations*, trans. Harry Zohn, Glasgow: Fontana/Collins.
Blanchot, Maurice (1981), *De Kafka à Kafka*, Paris: Gallimard/Idées.
Deleuze, Gilles and Guattari, Félix (1986), *Kafka: Toward a Minor Literature*, Minneapolis: University of Minnesota Press.
Gray, Richard T., Gross, Ruth V., Goebel, Rolf J. and Koelb, Clayton, eds (2005), *A Kafka Encyclopedia*, Westport, Conn.: Greenwood Press.
Reece, Julian, ed. (2002), *The Cambridge Companion to Kafka*, New York: Cambridge University Press.
Robertson, Richie (2004), *Kafka: A Very Short Introduction*, Oxford and New York: Oxford University Press.
Robert, Marthe (1982), *Franz Kafka's Loneliness*, trans. Ralph Manheim, London: Faber & Faber.

JEAN-FRANÇOIS LYOTARD (1924–1998)

Jean-François Lyotard was born in 1924 at Versailles and died in Paris in 1988. For ten years to 1959, he taught philosophy in secondary schools, and later became a professor of philosophy at the University of Paris VIII (Saint-Denis) – a post which he held until his retirement in 1989. From 1956 to 1966, Lyotard was on the editorial committee of the socialist journal, *Socialisme ou barbarie* and the socialist newspaper, *Pouvoir ouvrier*. As well as being an active opponent of the French government over the war in Algeria, Lyotard participated in the events of May 1968.

Libido

Although a political activist of Marxist persuasion in the 1950s and 1960s, Lyotard became the non-Marxist philosopher of post-modernity in the 1980s. Post-modernity thus marks a fundamental disengagement from the kind of totalitarian thought Marxism (but not only Marxism) represents. Before the appearance of, arguably, his most important book of philosophy – *The Differend: Phrases in Dispute* – Lyotard had already signalled this change of philosophical direction in both his doctoral thesis, *Discours, figure*, and in *Économie libidinale*. In the name of '*figure*' – of artistic experience which cannot be incorporated into signification – the former work gives a critique of the 'hyper-rationalism' of structuralism. The latter work looks to escape from the theoretical 'coldness' of Marxism by way of Freud's economy of libidinal energy and the notion of the primary process. Now, a libidinal economy becomes the basis of the political instead of a political economy. This extreme break with Marxism in *Économie libidinale* becomes much more nuanced in the philosophy of postmodernism.

Despite his prolific output, especially in the area of aesthetics, much of Lyotard's truly innovative (or experimental) thinking comes together in three key books: *Discours, figure, The Postmodern Condition*, and *The Differend*.

Discours, figure: *Lyotard's First Major Work*

Discours, figure was published in 1971, the year Lyotard successfully defended it as his *Doctorat d'état*. An extremely complex work, *Discours, figure* engages with art, structuralist psychoanalysis, semiotics and theories of language, as well as with phenomenological philosophy in the manner of Merleau-Ponty. Indeed, that Lyotard's interest would be in phenomenology, rather than structuralism, was evident in his small book published as an introduction to phenomenology in 1954 (Lyotard 1991). Given that the ascendancy of structuralism is inseparable from the ascendancy of the social and human sciences (anthropology, linguistics, psychoanalysis, literary criticism), it is precisely the foundations of the sciences (invisible to them) which it is phenomenology's task to uncover, even if this foundation is the logic of oppositions and binary principles giving rise to differential relations. Thus the notion of '*figure*' in *Discours, figure*, is linked to finding the founding principles of art, principles not reducible to rules of signification, the primary dimension of structuralism (see Lyotard 1971: 13). In addition, '*figure*', does not mean 'figurative', for it is not a form of rhetoric or representation. Furthermore, *figure* is not immediately transparent, even at the level of interpretation. An experience of the world is never entirely captured in a reading of the world, the world as represented.

The play between '*discours*' (= discourse) and '*figure*' is also incisive, although Lyotard is coy about spelling out the nature of this relation, if 'relation' is the right word (note the weight of the comma between the two terms). A structural linguistic, or semiotic take on discourse sees it as 'reading', or giving meaning to, *figure*, so that through signs *figure* can be represented. This notion of *discourse* is significant in that, without comprehending it, *figure* is its precondition; *figure* operates as that which by-passes discourse understood in a structuralist sense (system of differences). At best, *discourse* can only ever struggle to grasp *figure*, which becomes the core of the real that cannot be contained in a representation. The drive dimension of Freud's work is also of the order of *figure*, hence the lengthy treatment that Lyotard gives it in his book.

Post-modernity

The *Postmodern Condition* examines knowledge, science and technology in advanced capitalist societies. Here, the very notion of society as a unified totality (as in national identity) is judged to be loosing credibility, whether this be conceived as an organic whole (Durkheim), or as a functional system (Parsons), or again, as a fundamentally divided whole composed of two opposing classes (Marx). Indeed, Lyotard, speaking at the end of the 1970s, finds a growing 'incredulity towards' legitimating 'metanarratives'. A metanarrative provides a frame of reference in which people have faith; it is the basis of a 'credible' purpose for action, science, or society at large. At a more technical level, a science is modern if it tries to legitimate its own rules through reference to a metanarrative – that is, a narrative outside its own sphere of competence. Metanarrative provides meaning at a macro level.

The post-modern response to metanarratives is that these macro goals are now contested and, furthermore, there is no ultimate proof available for settling disputes over these goals. In the computer age where complexity is perceived to be ever increasing, the possibility of a single, or even dual, rationale for knowledge or science becomes remote. Before, faith in a narrative (e.g. religious doctrines) would have resolved the potential difficulty. Since the Second World War techniques and technologies have, as Weber anticipated, 'shifted emphasis from the ends of action to its means' (Lyotard 1984: 37). Regardless of whether the form of narrative unification is of the speculative or of the emancipatory type, the legitimation of knowledge can no longer rely on a 'grand narrative', so that science is now best understood in terms of Wittgenstein's theory of 'language game'.

Language Game and 'Performativity'

A language game signifies that no concept or theory could adequately capture language in its totality, if only because the attempt to do so itself constitutes its own particular language game. Thus, again, grand narratives no longer have credulity, for they are part of a language game which is itself part of a multiplicity of language games. Lyotard has written of speculative discourse as a language game – a game with specific rules which can be analysed in terms of the way statements should be linked to each other.

Science therefore, is a language game with the following rules:

1 Only denotative (descriptive) statements are scientific.
2 Scientific statements are quite different from those (concerned with origins) constituting the social bond.
3 Competence is only required on the part of the sender of the scientific message, not on the part of the receiver.
4 A scientific statement only exists within a series of statements which are validated by argument and by proof.
5 In light of (4), the scientific language game requires a knowledge of the existing state of scientific knowledge. Science no longer requires a narrative for its legitimation, for the rules of science are immanent in its game.

For science to 'progress' (i.e. for a new axiom, or denotative statement to be accepted), science practitioners win the approval of other scientists in the same field. And as scientific work becomes more complex, so do the forms of proof: the more complex the proof, the more complex the technology necessary to achieve generally accepted levels of validation. Technology, crucial for understanding the form of scientific knowledge in the society of the last quarter of the twentieth century, follows the principle of optimal performance: maximum output for minimum input. Lyotard calls this the principle of 'performativity', and it now dominates the scientific language game precisely because a scientific discovery requires a proof which costs money. Technology thus becomes the most efficient way of achieving scientific proof: 'an equation between wealth, efficiency, and truth is thus established' (Lyotard 1984: 45). Although 'wildcat' discoveries (where technology is very minimal) can still take place, technology tends to link science to the economy. Although inexpensive, pure research in search of truth is still possible, expensive research is becoming the norm; and this means obtaining funding assistance. To get funding, the long-term relevance of the research has to be justified; and this brings pure research under the auspices of the language game of performativity. Once performativity dominates science, truth and justice become the outcome of the best-funded research (best-funded, therefore most convincing); 'by reinforcing technology, one "reinforces" reality, and one's chances of being just and right increase accordingly' (Lyotard 1984: 47).

Lyotard also claims that systems theory is located within a modernist epistemology. For within the very terms of the system as performativity, control through knowledge lowers its performance, since uncertainty increases rather then decreases with knowledge (cf. Heisenberg). Now, according to Lyotard, a new, post-modern paradigm is coming into being, one that emphasises unpredictability, uncertainty, catastrophe (as in René Thom's work), chaos, and, most of all, paralogy, or dissensus. Dissensus challenges the existing rules of the game. Paralogy becomes impossible when recognition is withheld and legitimacy denied for new moves in the game. Silencing – or eliminating – a player from the game is equivalent to a terrorist act. The notion of being unable to present a position that is at variance with the dominant rules of argumentation and validation provides an appropriate point of transition to Lyotard's later work, *The Differend*.

Phrases in Dispute

As though having sensed the political issues at stake – especially with regard to justice – Lyotard proceeds to develop his philosophy of the differend – the real philosophical basis of the more sociological work, *The Postmodern Condition*. The differend is the name Lyotard gives to the silencing of a player in a language game. It exists when there are no agreed procedures for originality and different ideas to be presented in the current domain of discourse. This is graphically illustrated when revisionist historians refuse to recognise the existence of the Nazi gas chambers unless a victim of the gas chambers can be brought as a witness. To be a victim, one must have died in the chambers. Many historians have been justifiably outraged by this perverse use of the rules of evidence, and refer to the bad faith of the perpetrators. Lyotard, on the other hand, emphasises that the problem arises because too much has been invested in what amounts to an empiricist historiography. The latter assumes that the mere existence of the referent (e.g. the gas chambers) is sufficient for a cognitive phrase (e.g. 'the gas chambers existed') to be accepted as true. It also accepts that this principle of proof is universally valid. The proof is said to be universally valid because reality is deemed to be a universe (a totality) which can be represented, or expressed in symbolic form. However, even in physics no such universe exists which can be put fully into symbolic form. Rather, any statement which lays claim to universality can be quickly shown to be only *part* of the universe it claims to describe.

For Lyotard it is necessary to adopt a regional, rather than a universal approach to issues in history, politics, language, art, society. Instead of speaking of language games, Lyotard speaks, in *The Differend*, of 'regimes of phrases', and 'genres of discourse'. Like language games, regimes of phrases have their rules of formation, and each phrase presents a universe. There is thus no single universe, but a plurality of universes. A phrase regime presents a sentence universe, or type of phrase: prescriptive, ostensive, performative, exclamatory, interrogative, imperative, evaluative, nominative, etc. A genre of discourse, on the other hand, attempts to give a unity to a collection of sentences. A genre of discourse must be invoked to identify a phrase regime, since phrases can be cited and imitated. A cognitive (factual) phrase in a fictional work is not the same as a historian's cognitive phrase.

Because the genre of historiography has tried to conflate history and the cognitive genre, it has enabled Faurisson – a revisionist historian – to mount a case against the existence of the gas chambers. He is able to undermine the procedures of the historical genre because within this genre it has been claimed that history is only about what is knowable via a cognitive phrase. In short, cognitive phrases deal uniquely with the determinable; the unknowable and the indeterminate are beyond their ken. Just as science is inseparable from conditions of proof (it is not a simple reporting of reality), so the rules for establishing the reality of the referent determine the 'universe of cognitive phrases', 'where truth and falsity are at stake' (Lyotard 1983a: 35). True statements do not automatically result from the simple existence of the referent. This is why there will be not only disagreements as to the true nature of the referent, but also claims by those (of bad faith) who refuse to accept that the rules of proof have been adhered to, or who interpret the rules in such a way as to subvert them – by claiming, for example, that only a dead person can be a witness.

The possibility of this subversion of the cognitive gives rise to the differend. Its existence cannot be established cognitively; for it is the sign of an injustice which, *qua* injustice, cannot be given expression in cognitive terms. Whether someone is or is not a victim of an injustice cannot be validated by cognitive phrases because, as a victim, he or she is the subject of a differend. The differend marks the silence of an impossibility of phrasing an injustice.

The Sublime and the Law

In a discussion 'The Sign of History' (Lyotard 1983b: 218–60), Lyotard takes up the issue of interpreting historical events in light of Kant's notion of the sublime in *The Critique of Judgement*. For Kant, the sublime feeling does not come from the object (e.g. nature), but is an index of a unique state of mind which recognises its incapacity to find an object adequate to the sublime feeling. The sublime, like all sentiment, is a sign of this incapacity. As such the sublime becomes a sign of the differend understood *as* a pure sign. The philosopher's task now is to search out such signs of the differend. Again, because no universal – be it humanity, freedom, progress, justice, the law, beauty, society, or language – can correspond to a real object, the attempted link between the universal and a real object can only result in totalitarianism and the consequent exclusion of otherness. Kant, however, was a keen observer of the French Revolution. He looked to it as an event signalling that humanity was progressing. He had the *enthusiasm* of its many interested, external spectators. Was Kant therefore going against the logic of the sublime and confusing a strong sentiment (enthusiasm) with a concrete historical event: the Revolution? He was not because enthusiasm is a sign that the Revolution has a sublime – that is, an unpresentable – aspect; and this, precisely because it *is* a historical event. A true historical event cannot be given expression by any existing genre of discourse; it thus challenges existing genres to make way for it. In other words, the historical event is an instance of the differend.

Unlike Hegel, Kant does not try to make a speculative phrase equivalent to a cognitive phrase. Speculative phrases always relate to signs (i.e. sentiments and emotions), and Hegel was wrong to think that a speculative phrase could have a concrete realisation. Hegel in this way was tied to a philosophy of the result – of how things would turn out in a determinant way. The indeterminant – the sign, emotion, event, differend – is entirely absent from the Hegelian system.

Like Kant's critique of history, the problematic of obligation is taken up in Lyotard's book, *Just Gaming*. The search that guides Lyotard's discussion of the basis of an ethical phrase, and thus for the basis of being obligated. He concludes, perhaps paradoxically, by saying that the basis of obligation cannot be specified – first, because an obligation cannot be explained descriptively; if it could be, the obligation *qua* obligation would evaporate. One can only be obligated if – as Kant says – one is free not to accomplish the obligation. A description can only show why an obligation *cannot* be avoided. In short, 'ought' cannot be derived from 'is'.

Second, though, obligation is not the outcome of 'my' law, but of the 'other's' law: I can only be obliged if the obligation comes from outside my own world: from the world of the other. The other's law which obliges is evidence of the impossibility of ever constructing an adequate representation of it. The ethical phrase can only be a sign indicating an obligation that never has concrete form. At stake is whether Kant's categorical imperative could ever be the basis of an ethical community. Here, we see the pertinence of Levinas's philosophy which invokes Jewish theological sources in order to show the necessary primacy of the other (the 'you') at the origin of the moral law. Not only does Kant refuse to compromise by not reducing the genre of discourse of obligation to the cognitive genre, but he also offers a way of thinking about the way genres of discourse are 'connected' to each other. Each genre of discourse is analogous to an 'archipelago', while judgement is a means of passing from one archipelago to another. Unlike the homogenising drive of speculative discourse, judgement allows the necessary heterogeneity of genres to remain. Judgement, then, is the way of recognising the differend – Hegelian speculation, a way of obscuring it.

The force of Lyotard's argument is in its capacity to highlight the impossibility of making a general idea identical to a specific real instance (i.e. to the referent of a cognitive phrase). Philosophers, mathematicians and scientists now recognise the paradoxes arising when a general statement about the world is forced to take its own place of enunciation into account. Lyotard's thought in *The Differend* is a valuable antidote to the totalitarian delirium for reducing everything to a single genre, thus stifling the differend. To stifle the differend is to stifle new ways of thinking and acting.

On a more problematical note, however, Lyotard's promotion of the phrase to a privileged position in relation to the differend itself seems to risk obscuring a differend. For here there is no non-phrase. A silence, an interjection, a shrug of the shoulders are all phrases. Moreover, there is no first or last phrase because there is always a linking of phrases. To say that there is no other of the phrase surely implies that the phrase emanates from itself – that it is its own law. But this claim is in danger of becoming a restrictive totalisation which flies in the face of the principle of allowing the differend to emerge from silence. Lyotard might reply that this is to deny the (radically) heterogeneous status he has attributed to phrase regimes – a status ensuring the differend. What kind of heterogeneity can it be however, which denies otherness? To say that there is always a phrase – that there is always something rather than nothing – does not eliminate the problem of 'nothing', even if nothing is an impossibility. This problem indicates that a more intricate elaboration of the 'phrase' is necessary before Lyotard's claim that a philosophy of phrases is the way to gain an insight into the differend could be accepted.

Last Works

Towards the end of his life, in 1996, Lyotard published *Signed Malraux*, a kind of biography (or anti-biography) of André Malraux, the man of action and man of culture. Then, two books appeared posthumously, one, incomplete at the time of the philosopher's death: *The Confession of Augustine*, the other, a collection of various writings ranging from an essay on Kant's aesthestics to a memoriam in 1995 for Gilles Deleuze, collected under the title: *Misère de philosophie* (The Poverty of Philosophy) (2000).

In a text on glory and Malraux, Lyotard more or less explains the significance of 'signed' in his Malraux book. It derives from the fact that everything (all the 'evidence') collected for a biography comes from written sources; nothing is immediate and therefore nothing, as Malraux saw, comes directly from 'life'. A biography in this sense is a kind of fiction (Lyotard 2000: 242).

Another text throws more light on Lyotard's thought on aesthetics in relation to Kant's notion of beauty. Each new pleasure before beauty is like re-birth (Lyotard 2000: 38). This is because beauty is not an ideal, nor perfection. It does not pre-exist the experience of it – nor does the subject *qua* subject. For beauty is the 'making' of the subject. For Lyotard, the most appropriate analogy is a musical one: beauty is an 'internal music' (2000: 28) or 'internal euphonie' (2000: 35). As musical, beauty also locks into time. But in being entirely unanticipated (as an event), beauty also has nothing to do with the lack of desire. One does search for beauty; one finds it in possibly the most unexpected ways. Lyotard adds: 'I have said, music, because it is the art of time, of internal time, and the unison concerned is interior to the subject' (2000: 35). From this point, Lyotard argues that, 'not only is there no knowable [aesthetic] experience, there would not even be a subject' (2000: 36). And further: 'pleasure in the beautiful is not experienced by an already constituted and unified subject' (2000: 37). Thus, the subject of knowledge and of consciousness cannot be the subject of aesthetic experience. In effect, as Lyotard emphasises, the 'subject' of aesthetic experience is in time: fundamentally, *in* time, and therefore not given from the start. And Lyotard concludes his essay by affirming that: 'the feeling of beauty: it is the subject in an emergent state (à l'état naissant), the first uniting of incompatible powers' (2000: 41). Our understanding of Lyotard's thought is also in an emergent state as we continue to come to grips with its complexity.

References

Lyotard, Jean-François (1971), *Discours, figure*, Paris: Klincksieck.
—— (1983a), *Le Différend*, Paris: Minuit.
—— (1983b), 'Le signe de l'histoire' [The sign of history] in *Le Différend*.
—— (1984), *The Postmodern Condition: A Report on Knowledge*, trans. Geoffrey Bennington and Brian Massumi, Minneapolis: University of Minnesota Press.
—— (1991 [1954]) *Phenomenology*, trans. Brian Beakley, New York: State University of New York Press.
—— (2000), *Misère de la philosophie*, Paris: Galilée.

See also: **Husserl, Levinas, Nietzsche**

Lyotard's major writings

(2006) *The Lyotard Reader and Guide*, ed. Keith Chrome and James Williams, New York: Columbia University Press.
(2001 [1998]) *Soundproof Room: Malraux's Anti-Aesthetic*, trans. Robert Harvey, Stanford: Stanford University Press.
(2000 [1998]) *The Confession of Augustine*, trans. Richard Beardsworth, Stanford: Stanford University Press.
(1999 [1996]) *Signed Malraux*, trans. Robert Harvey, Minneapolis: University of Minnesota Press.
(1997a) *Jean-François Lyotard: Collected Writings on Art*, London: Academy Editions.
(1997b [1993]) *Postmodern Fables*, trans. Georges van den Abbeele, Minneapolis: University of Minnesota Press.
(1994 [1991]) *Lessons Analytic of the Sublime: Kant's Critique of Judgement*, trans. Elizabeth Rottenberg, Stanford: Stanford University Press.
(1993 [1974]) *Libidinal Economy*, trans. Iain Hamilton Grant, Bloomington: Indiana University Press.
(1992 [1988]) *The Postmodern Explained to Children: Correspondence 1982–1985*, trans. Julian Pefanis and Morgan Thomas, Sydney: Power Publications.

(1991a [1988]) *The Inhuman: Reflections on Time*, trans. Geoffrey Bennington and Rachel Bowlby, Cambridge: Polity Press.

(1991b [1954]) *Phenomenology*, trans. Brian Beakley, New York: State University of New York Press.

(1990 [1988]) *Heidegger and 'The Jews'*, trans. by Andreas Michel and Mark Roberts, Minneapolis: University of Minnesota Press.

(1988) *Peregrinations: Law, Form, Event*, New York: Columbia University Press, 'The Welleck Library Lectures'. Contains a 'checklist' of writings by and about Lyotard.

(1986a) *L'Enthusiasme: la critique kantienne de l'histoire*, Paris: Galilée.

(1986b [1983]) *The Differend: Phrases in Dispute*, trans. George van den Abbeele, Minneapolis: Minnesota University Press; Manchester: Manchester University Press.

(1984a [1979]) *The Postmodern Condition*, trans. Geoffrey Bennington and Brian Massumi, Minneapolis: Minnesota University Press; Manchester: Manchester University Press.

(1984b [1979]) with Jean-Loup Thébaud, *Just Gaming*, trans. Wlad Godzich, Minneapolis: Minnesota University Press; Manchester: Manchester University Press.

(1977) *Instructions païennes*, Paris: Galilée.

(1973a) *Des dispositifs pulsionnels*, Paris: Union générale d'éditions.

(1973b) *Dérive à partir de Marx et Freud*, Paris: Union générale d'éditions.

(1971) *Discours, figure*, Paris: Klincksieck.

Further reading

Bennington, Geoffrey (1988), *Lyotard: Writing the Event*, Manchester: Manchester University Press.

Harvey, Robert and Roberts, Mark S., eds (1998), *Towards the Postmodern*, Amherst, New York: Humanities Books.

Williams, James (1998), *Lyotard: Towards a Postmodern Philosophy*, Cambridge: Polity Press.

Williams, James (2000), *Lyotard and the Political*, London and New York: Routledge.

POST-HUMAN THOUGHT

The post-human is a category which derives from developments in cybernetics and information technology that have fuelled the quest to reproduce and reconstruct the human being. In light of such developments questions arise about the definition of the human. Whereas, previously, the human in the context of biology was seen exclusively as a product of carbon-based processes, it is now being proposed that silicon-based processes, as well as bionics, might now have to be seen as a part of the meaning of the human. It also taps into the way electronic technologies, such as the internet, have changed the nature of human relations, partly because they operate at close to the speed of light.

This category also includes a thinker like Serres, for whom both the body and humanity itself is in the process of changing so fundamentally, due largely to developments in science and technology, that it is becoming unrecognisable compared to the humanity of the past.

DONNA HARAWAY (b.1944)

Donna Haraway has been concerned with deflating the uncritical acceptance of key oppositions, which have political implications, related to the domain of science, particularly to biology: human–animal, animal–machine, mind–body, male–female, fiction–reality, nature–culture, science–society. She is famous, above all, for having given a new lease of life to the term, 'cyborg', an entity combining both cybernetic, non-organic, as well as organic qualities, and she has been involved with socialist- and eco-feminism.

The Cyborg

For Haraway, the existing system (political, social, economic, cultural) is sustained, not by essential truths discovered by science, but by the stories science tells, or constructs, for itself and the world, as well as by the stories told within the political order, stories which often serve to perpetuate the inequalities in the system. 'Cyborg' derives, she tells us, from science fiction, not initially from developments in science, even if science subsequently comes to invent a similar entity. Cyborg is the paradigm case of the 'confusion of boundaries' – and thus of boundaries as constructed – characteristic of all attempts to keep opposing fields separate. As Haraway's manifesto says: 'we are cyborgs', both machine and organism. Even more: 'The cyborg is our ontology; it gives us our politics' (Haraway 2004a: 8). It is also more female than male and thus serves as the basis of a new feminist relation with technology.

Haraway's Career

Haraway's first job after completing her PhD at Yale's Department of Biology was at the University of Hawaii from 1970 to 1974, where she taught biology and the history of science. Haraway then taught in the History of Science Department at Johns Hopkins University until she was appointed, in 1980, as one of the foundation members of the History of Consciousness program at the University of California at Santa Cruz. During her tenure there, she published *Primate Visions: Gender, Race and Nature in the World of Modern Science* (1989), her most well-received and well-known work, after *Simians, Cyborgs and Women: The Reinvention of Nature* (1991). In her own words, most reviews saw this work as being essentially about gender and science, but, says Haraway, 'I read the book to be about race, gender, nature, generation, simian doings, and primate sciences, as well as about many other things' (Haraway 2004b: 2007). The impact of *Primate Visions* and *Simians, Cyborgs and Women* cannot be overestimated, not only because of the huge number of times these have been cited, but because they transformed women's relation to the theorising and interpreting of science, particularly, biology and physical anthropology.

Confusion of Borders, and Science's 'Story Telling'

Haraway's keen interest in porous borders of all kinds, which produced the theory of the cyborg, is thus situated (a term Haraway likes) in the context of socialist feminism at a political level and within a sociology of knowledge frame, at an epistemological level. This implies that knowledge, including scientific knowledge, will be a 'situated knowledge', a knowledge inflected by the historical and social conditions of its production. Modernist Western knowledge, for example, will be dominated by a male vision set in an Enlightenment frame, which sees the other (the other culture or society) as a lesser version of itself. Thus, the Enlightenment also contributes to the colonialist mentality, which says that indigenous peoples cannot speak for themselves, they must be spoken for and represented. In effect, it fails to grasp the implications of situated-ness in its drive for objectivity and the glorification of Reason and rationality – 'its' rationality, of course. Objectivity, in Haraway's terms, is a story Enlightenment consciousness tells itself.

As part of this epistemological view, science, rather than being exclusively the source of rigour and objectivity is also socially constructed – is 'woven of social relations' (Haraway 2004c: 187): it has a class, gender, culture, species and biological context, as well as a methodological context. It is woven of layers and has no core. It is also connected to a love of knowledge bordering on erotic enjoyment. Many ideas of science about nature are the result of the stories it tells itself: at one time, nature is the untamed other in feminine guise, or it is comforting Mother Earth; at another time, it is the inscrutable object that science ceaselessly investigates in order to discover its Laws and its essence; at yet another time, nature is the colonial other of African or Pacific societies; more recently, nature is the text to be read in the code of mathematics and biomedicine. For Haraway, we will never get away from 'story-telling' in science, or from bias. So it is important for those who care about the world to invent their own stories while at the same time scrutinising those which have become part of accepted wisdom and a substitute for truth, those, in short, which are ideologically inflected, but appear as essential truths. Or, indeed, just as Edward Said in *Orientalism* (1978) had proposed that Western visions of the Orient were an implicit statement about how the West saw itself as superior, so studies of primates often imply what it means to be a superior and civilized white man. Through the 'other' (the Orient, the Primate) one establishes the coordinates of the white, 'First World "self"'.

Tropes and narratives articulate the ideas of science. This can also be seen in the notion of the cyborg. For not only is this entity fully technological, it is also part of a narrative of the new human, or the post-human, being. As Katherine Hayles has pointed out, were Haraway's figure simply the product of a narrative discourse about what might be possible, we would be dealing with science fiction. Were it an exclusively technological phenomenon, without any discursive identity, it could be consigned to the domain of bionics or medical prostheses. The cyborg thus 'partakes of the power of the imagination as well as the actuality of technology' (Hayles 1999: 115). The great strength of Haraway's approach thus pertains to embedding the practices of science and its products within a discursive formation. This is why she invokes semiotics, philosophy and literary theory in her analyses and, in particular, regularly cites Foucault, Bakhtin and Whitehead as well as feminist scientists and philosophers such as Harding, Irigaray and Fox Keller.

Embedding

The notion of 'embedding' might also be emblematic of Haraway's subtle feminist approach in analysing the practices, history and female scientists' contribution to primatology in *Primate Visions*. As well as the actual study of apes, primatology includes dioramas of stuffed animals in museum presentations, especially as these were established between the wars. Given that sexual behaviour, survival and leisure strategies and categories such as male and female, are as much a part of the study of primates as they are of human society and evolution, the boundaries between the human and the animal world become ever-more porous leaving the analyst with the challenging task of interpret-ing the work of the interpreters of primate behaviour. What Haraway discovers is that in Natural History, which studies the evolution of all living things, the ideological assumptions about female–male relations (man, the hunter, for example), which primatology seeks to confirm, are often projected back onto current human behaviour, so that one can speak of 'simian' (ape-like) behaviour in those human groups which have not reached the heights of the civilization of Western man. Primate evolution, then, was, and sometimes still is, seen as a primi-tive precursor to the human species. Representing Natural History itself (part of a larger theme of scientific principles and their repre-sentation), Haraway shows, constitutes a story in its own right. Thus a diorama in a Natural History museum might show a gorilla 'family' as the precursor to the modern nuclear family, but the quest to obtain gorilla skins in Africa, as was the mission of Carl Akeley, could allow all the aspects of male 'machismo' to play themselves out in the hunt. As Haraway puts it: 'What qualities did it take to make animal "game"? One answer is the similarity to man, the ultimate quarry, a worthy opponent. The ideal quarry is the "other", the natural self. . . . Hunter, scientist and artist all sought the gorilla for his revelation about the nature and future of manhood' (Haraway 2004c: 158–59). Ideally, the animal slain should put up a brave fight, not be cowardly, and be as close as possible to an ideal representative of its species. What Haraway shows, therefore, is that not only is there a plethora of stories implicit in the representation which is the diorama itself (in its text, as it were), but the very construction and emplacement of the diaramic elements is inscribed with another set of theoretical and ideological assumptions. Thus, 'form' (the diaramic element) does not simply give shape to a textual and image content, or to stories, but itself contains another story, or set of stories. The same can be said of the rise of Natural History museums as institutions. On one level, the contents of museums instruct and educate the public about the evo-lution of living creatures, including the human species. Often this story is politically tendentious, privileging certain aspects of evolution over others. On another level, the way this educating is done is also part of the political and social implications of Natural History: thus, it makes all the difference in the world as to whether the contents of the museum are the result of hunting safaris, or whether they are largely photographic and painterly representations.

Immanence Over Transcendence?

As a number of astute readers have noted, Haraway's writing embodies a subtle fabric of erudition, theoretical sophistication, vivid description and political astuteness. This, however, is also an author who ultimately plumbs for immanence (= immersion) over transcendence (= objective detachment). Knowledge, she argues, 'is *always* an engaged material practice and *never* a disembodied set of ideas' (Haraway 2004b: 199–200, Haraway's emphasis). Knowledge is thus always 'embedded' in a situation, rather than being external to it. This includes the fact that a passion for knowledge implies that the boundary between objective principle and subjective desire is always fluid. Of course Haraway rejects the charge, so crudely put, of relativism. Not all 'stories' (as she says) carry equal weight with regard to validity. And her success in practising feminist theory in the realm of Natural History and biology, and what has allowed a sympathetic hearing from critics who might otherwise disagree with her political stance, is her capacity in her studies to more than match the rigour of science itself.

Nevertheless, the kind of immanent transcendentalism Haraway practises cannot be sustained. For situated knowledge – where Haraway immerses herself in the stories, both personal and otherwise, of the fields she studies – is also supposed to allow the interpretation *of* and commentary *upon* that knowledge. In other words, Haraway, like certain representatives of the phenomenological tradition, refuses to acknowledge externality there where it is most evident: in the practice of analysis and interpretation, an externality seen most of all in the recognition that science itself is woven of stories (is narrativised). Consequently, Haraway must invoke a certain transcendentalism (= detachment, externality) in order to demonstrate the very insights (that science is immersed in social and ethical processes of all kinds) that she has been so successful in bringing to the fore.

Finally, the realisation of her insights owes much to the theoretical tradition (Western philosophy) that is the object, both implicitly and explicitly, of critique. Such a critique is only possible because of the very transcendence that this same tradition makes possible. The question is not whether transcendence is inevitable (it is), but whether, passion – a love of knowledge, in Haraway's terms – rules out, or is at least the binary opposite of, transcendence. We can have a passion for transcendence, as monastic life illustrated (not to be imitated, perhaps), a passion for Spartan living. With her concern to break with binaries, is it not true, then, that Haraway has one last binary to deflate: transcendence–situatedness?

References

Haraway, Donna (1989), *Primate Visions: Gender, Race and Nature in the World of Modern Science*, New York: Routledge.

—— (1991), *Simians, Cyborgs and Women: The Reinvention of Nature*, New York: Routledge.

—— (2004a), 'A Manifesto for Cyborgs: Science, Technology, and Socialist Feminism in the 1980s' in *The Haraway Reader*, New York and London: Routledge.

—— (2004b), 'Morphing in the Order: Flexible Strategies, Feminist Science Studies, and Primate Visions' in *The Haraway Reader*, New York and London: Routledge.

—— (2004c), 'Teddy Bear Patriarchy: Taxidermy in the Garden of Eden, New York City, 1908–36' in *The Haraway Reader*, New York and London: Routledge.

Hayles, N. Katherine (1999), *How We Became Posthuman: Virtual Bodies in Cybernetics, Literature, and Informatics*, Chicago and London: University of Chicago Press.

Said, Edward W. (1978), *Orientalism*, New York: Pantheon.

See also: **Maturana, Virilio**

Haraway's major writings

(2004) *The Haraway Reader*, New York and London: Routledge.

(2003) *The Companion Species Manifesto: Dogs, People, and Significant Otherness*, Chicago: Prickly Paradigm Press.

(2000) *How Like a Leaf: An Interview with Thyrza Nichols Goodeve*, New York: Routledge.

(1997) *Modest_Witness@Second Millenium: FemaleMan©_Meets_Oncomouse^{TM}: Feminisms and Technoscience*, New York: Routledge.

(1991) *Simians, Cyborgs and Women: The Reinvention of Nature*, New York: Routledge.

(1989) *Primate Visions: Gender, Race and Nature in the World of Modern Science*, New York: Routledge.

(1976) *Crystals, Fabrics, and Fields: Metaphors that Shape Embyos*, New Haven, Conn.: Yale University Press.

Further Reading

Bell, David (2006), *Cyberculture Theorists: Manuel Castells and Donna Haraway*, London and New York: Routledge.

Schneider, Joseph (2005), *Donna Haraway: Live Theory*, New York and London: Continuum.

HUMBERTO MATURANA (b.1928)

Humberto Maturana, a neurophysiologist from Chile, was a member of the second wave of cybernetics (1960–85) (Hayles 1999: 131), and has made a name for himself in developing a theory of autopoiesis, or the nature of reflexive feedback control in living systems. Maturana was also part of a research team which investigated the frog's visual system in the late-1950s. This research was able to show that the frog did not so much represent reality as construct it: the frog sees what it wants, or needs to see – small, fast-moving flies rather than large, slow-moving cows. Such a discovery served as a spring board for Maturana's investigation into epistemology and the nature of the observer's role in investigating living systems. Like the frog, the observer, Maturana and his colleague, Francisco Varela proposed, does not discover a pre-existing reality, but creates it in the act of observation. In other words, the realist epistemology that is implicitly challenged here has to take a back seat to a notion of reflexivity which turns reality into the product of the dynamic interaction between observer and the system of which he or she is a part. For living systems, such as the human, Maturana and Varela found the real, external world is in fact part of the living system itself and is not something that can be proved to be external to it. The activity of the nervous system is thus a product of the structure of the organisation of the nervous system itself, and not the result of the impact on it of external reality. Before proceeding to look in detail at the way Maturana places biological imperatives in the front line of what it means to be human, we provide a summary of key concepts that underpin all of Maturana's work. This summary is partly indebted to information available from Randall Whitaker's web site (see Whitaker <http://www.acm.org/sigois/Main.html>).

Key Concepts in Maturana's Work

Autopoiesis: This is the main concept in Maturana's research into the relation between observer and system. It derives from the Greek where 'auto-' means 'self' and 'poiesis' means 'production' or 'creation'. The point for Maturana is to highlight the self-formative aspect of living systems. The latter are unities, or wholes, made up of a variable number of elements. As a unity, a system is more than the sum of its parts. Autopoiesis, which is about the maintenance of a unity's organisation (see below), may be contrasted with *allopoiesis*, which is about realising goals other than the maintenance of organisation.

That is, allopoiesis is means oriented, while autopoiesis is ends oriented, the end being the maintenance of the system itself as a unity.

Structure: This is the particular configuration of elements in a given unity (or system). Structure can vary to a certain extent without there being a change in the system. Beyond a certain point, however, further change will endanger the integrity of the system as a particular unity.

Structural Coupling: A living system's structures are invariably situated in, and dependent on, an environment. Humans, for example, depend on the resources of the environment to continue to exist. But certain structures can also be dependent on other structures for their survival. Thus, a cell in my body is a system but is coupled to the body as a whole for its continued existence (Hayles 1999: 138).

Organisation: It is a crucial term in the debate about the way systems articulate themselves. It refers to the specific form of the relation between the elements of the system. Organisation also gives an insight into the kind of unity that a system is. It is used by Maturana and Varela to develop a definition of a 'living system'. The latter is recognisable through its 'autopoietic' organisation, not through its capacity to reproduce itself. Reproduction is not part of the organisation of living beings. The reason is that reproduction presupposes an already existing organisation as its precondition.

As Whitaker suggests on his web site – in light of the example in *The Tree of Knowledge* (1998: 73) – the difference between structure and organisation can be illustrated by the famous proto-surrealist, sixteenth-century painter, Arcimboldo. In the artist's work, the face and upper body are equivalent to organisation, while the material used to make the organisation is called structure. In other words, organisation refers to the unity (face, body) and structure refers to the material used to incarnate this unity (fruit, fish, books, flowers, bodies, etc). It is interesting to note, however, that, like surrealism à la Dalí, it is sometimes difficult to discern the unity of the picture (its form of organisation) because the structure is so dominant.

Autonomy: A system is autonomous 'if it can specify its own laws'. It is a unity which regenerates the network of interactions which produced them. That is, an autonomous system is not generated, or regenerated by a factor external to it; it generates itself. Autopoiesis is what makes living beings autonomous systems.

Domain: A domain is a field with a specific set of properties defined by the unity which constitutes it. Domains include those of: language, phenomenology, cognition, consensus, interactions, relations.

Ontogeny: This is the history of structural change in a unity without change occurring in its organisation.

Biological Processes as Epistemological and Meaning Determinants

The dissolution of a realist epistemology, exemplified in Maturana's early work on the frog's eye view, corresponds to the cybernetic notion that the boundaries of the human subject are constructed, not given. Not an objective, external reality, then, but biological processes necessary to the ongoing 'praxis of everyday life', or to life as 'perturbations', as Maturana also calls it, are at the heart of cognition and language. Cognition as a biological phenomenon is not 'about' anything: it is not a representation of the external world, for example.

As a crucial cognitive domain, language exemplifies, more than any other, how cognition and biology are intertwined in Maturana's scheme of things. By 'biology', one should understand those processes necessary for the continued life of a system. Language – or 'languaging', as Maturana prefers – is not about the communication of knowledge and information, even if an observer understands it this way. Instead, language is internal and functional to the living system that is the human being. As living systems within language humans operate in a domain of reflexivity and reciprocal, consensual everyday actions that serve to instantiate their continued existence. By languaging, in effect, human beings are able to reflect upon their conditions of living and in so doing are able to conserve these conditions. Language objects are thus not reflections of external reality, but are those objects generally accepted as such by the language community: they are thus 'consensual objects'. Prior to language there are no objects. For objects are essentially cognitive, tied ultimately to the biological imperatives of the system. This of course does prevent observers from acting as though an objective world were reflected in language. Indeed, it might be functionally necessary that this be so. Here, we have what could be called, after Lacan (see the mirror stage), a process of necessary misrecognition.

Language is also implicated in 'structural coupling'. Put simply, each human as a living system is dependent for maintaining its qualities on 'reciprocal consensual' interactions with other humans. Or, more prosaically, language is essentially social. It needs to be social in the interests of the survival of the living system, not because communication implies more than one. Language activates a triggering mechanism for structures other than those of the observer. Words, in short, have the power to induce reciprocal bodily changes. They are concentrations of meaning within structures of action. Such concentrations can initiate, or incite action. Here, we can think of words with highly charged emotional impact. Maturana goes so far as to say that languaging as structural coupling can serve to preserve the organisation of the living system; in effect, this implies preserving the life of the system. Body and language change reciprocally.

Self-consciousness and 'observing' arise only within language. For Maturana, this entails that the self and self-consciousness as self-identity only exist in language. Also, since language coordinates language consensually and is essentially social, self-consciousness is also social; it is not located in the body, but in the domain of social interaction as the coexistence of individuals.

Implications of Matura's Work

A key aspect of the 'observer theory' is that what is observed depends on the position of the observer and not, as objectivist theory would have it, on the nature of the system observed. Moreover, a living system constitutes itself recursively as an observer through interacting with the representations produced. The point is that the observer, then, is constituted reflexively through the system observed. As Maturana explains:

> We become *observers* through recursively generating representations of our interactions, and by interacting with several representations simultaneously we generate relations with the representations of which we can then interact and repeat this process recursively, thus remaining in a domain of interactions always larger than that of the representation.
>
> (cited in Hayles 1999: 144)

The insight that a realist epistemology is no longer viable when it comes to understanding the nature of living systems has implications for the practice of science. For while the realist epistemology allowed the observing scientist to take a neutral position with regard to what was being observed, the notion that the observer is inextricably involved with what is observed opens the way for science to be directly connected to ethics. If the observer contributes to the formation or construction of the observed, there ceases to be a clear-cut separation between the theory and application of science. In the case of nuclear physics, for example, there is a link between the theory and development of nuclear weaponry and the ethics surrounding its use. The use of nuclear weaponry becomes an inextricable part of the social system understood as individual members interacting in the interest of coexistence. Action can no longer be understood in isolation, as many scientists have wanted to do, and this gives all actions an ethical status.

Strengths of Maturana's Work

As well as alerting us to the ethical dimension of science, Maturana's theories have the following strengths.

Maturana's development of a non-realist epistemology based on the concept of an autopoietic system came at a time (1950–70) of the positivist ascendency in science, and the accompanying scepticism towards any framework which emphasised a constructivist approach to knowledge and subjectivity. For positivism, truth, or validity, is decidedly not to be determined by the position of an observer; truth is not relative, but is based on the correspondence between language and reality. As such, Maturana's work was a breath of fresh air, giving due weight to what might now be called the 'subjective' side of the epistemological equation, and he does this in an area of 'hard' science (neurobiology).

Furthermore, Maturana's theory attributes to language a dynamic role in the understanding of human life, rather it being a neutral system of mediation facilitating pure communication. Such a theory gives weight to the *énonciation* (statement as enacted) over the *énoncé* (statement made). In short, through being enacted – as 'languaging' – rather than in being referential, language is important for Maturana. And in this, Maturana's theory even has links with certain avant-garde poets and linguists (cf. Mallarmé and Benveniste).

Problems

Despite its strengths, Manturana's work throws up the following problems due, at least in part, to the neurobiologist's almost dogmatic determination to reject anything even hinting at a realist epistemology. Broadly speaking, as there is an almost total scepticism regarding objectivity, the very idea of externality is expunged from Maturana's version of systems theory. There is more, however.

1. Autopoietic systems are constructed as though the external environment acts only as a trigger for the system's own activity and

development. In short, there is no real 'outside' of the system. This could be described as the 'autistic' aspect of the theory (see Hayles 1999: 148).

2. Related to the above, we can see that, with the construction of perception, and with language functioning as a mechanism for the self-constitution of unity rather than as a vehicle of inter-subjective communication, there is a risk of solipsism. The latter implies that, again, there is no valid external domain, only the system's own self-representation.

3. Knowing, says autopoietic theory, occurs through doing: 'all knowing is doing and all doing is knowing' (Maturana and Varela 1998: 27). The circularity of autopoietic theory is thus reinforced by such a principle. A similar circularity is reinforced through the definition of the key concept, organisation. The implication of this circularity is that once organisation changes, the system's unity collapses. For it to exist, change in organisation – if not in structure – must be kept to a minimum. As a self-contained mode of organisation, the unity is impervious to historical contingency, including linear, evolutionary change in biology. In short, there is an in-built resistance to change in autopoietic theory itself.

The truth of the matter is that any theory that promotes its own qualities to the exclusion of all other theoretical perspectives begins to undermine its own credentials. Thus despite its innovation in challenging validation through reference to an independent objective reality, autopoiesis, in ruling out external, independent reality, perhaps goes too far in the other direction. It is almost as though, for the autopoietic system, there were no externality other than what passes as such in the interests of the continuation of the everyday life of the system. Even if Maturana says that, for the observer in a living system, the distinction between internal and external makes no sense, and that perception is functional to the living system rather than objective, what remains to be seen is exactly how the system would deal with entirely chance occurrences. Chance occurrences would qualify as those events essentially external to and outside of the current purview of the living system. Not to be able to adjust to them would amount to putting the system in jeopardy. Such is the risk that the solipsistic tone of autopoiesis brings into view. For in Maturana's general account, there is no room for such radical externality. Such a deficit is precisely what other systems theorists, such as Luhmann (1995), have endeavoured to overcome.

References

Hayles, N. Katherine (1999), *How We Became Posthuman: Virtual Bodies in Cybernetics, Literature, and Informatics*, Chicago and London: University of Chicago Press.

Luhmann, Niklas (1995), *Social Systems*, New York: Columbia University Press.

Maturana H.R. and F.G. Varela (1998 [1987]), *The Tree of Knowledge*, Boston and London: Shambhala, New Science Library, revised edition.

See also: **Haraway, Lacan, Virilio.**

Maturana's major writings

(1980) with Varela, Francisco J., *Autopoiesis and Cognition* Dordrecht: Reidel.

(1978) 'Biology of language: epistemology of reality', in G.A. Miller and Elizabeth Lenneberg, eds, *Psychology and Biology of Language and Thought,* New York: Academic Press.

(1975) 'The organization of the living: a theory of the living organization', *International. Journal of Man-Machine Studies* 7: 313–32.

(1969) 'The Neurophysiology of Cognition' in Garvin, P. ed., *Cognition: A Multiple View*, New York: Spartan Books.

(1960) with Lettvin, J., McCulloch, S. and Pitts, W., 'Anatomy and physiology of vision in the frog', *Journal of General Physiology*, 43: 129–75.

Further reading

Mingers, J. (1994), *Self-Producing Systems: Implications and Applications of Autopoiesis*, New York: Plenum Publishing.

Roth, G., and Schwegler, H., eds. (1981a), *Self-organizing Systems: An Interdisciplinary Approach*, Frankfurt and New York: Campus Verlag.

Zeleny, Milan ed. (1981b), *Autopoiesis, a Theory of Living Organizations*, New York: North Holland.

MICHEL SERRES (b.1930)

Michel Serres was born in 1930 at Agen in France, son of a bargeman. In 1949, he went to naval college and subsequently, in 1952, to the École Normale Supérieure (rue d'Ulm). In 1955, he obtained an *agrégation* in philosophy, and from 1956 to 1958 he served on a variety of ships as a marine officer for the French national maritime service. His vocation of voyaging is therefore of more than academic import. In 1968, Serres gained a *Doctorat d'état* for a thesis on Leibniz's philosophy. During the 1960s he taught with Michel Foucault at the Universities of Clermont-Ferrand and Vincennes and was later appointed to a chair in the history of science at the Sorbonne. Serres has also been a full professor at Stanford University since 1984, and he was elected to the French Academy in 1990.

The Voyager

Michel Serres is a 'voyager' between the arts and the sciences, and a thinker for whom voyaging is invention. Invention is also called 'translation', 'communication' and 'metaphor'. By way of introduction to Serres's simultaneously philosophical, scientific and poetic work, we will refer to a nodal event in the history of science: thermodynamics, and the consequent transcending of the closed system of Newtonian mechanics. To transcend the closed system is, for Serres, to fuel invention. But first, we look briefly at Serres the voyager.

In his work over the decade, 1996–2006, Serres has pursued his insight that voyaging, as the 'in-between', or 'third' element, the element of communication – and indeed, communication itself – is what renders all boundaries permeable. The third element (cf. the *Le Tiers-instruit* (Serres 1997) – *The Educated Third*) is a metaphor, but its incarnation is multiple – at one time an angel, at another, the Harlequin, at still another, the atlas of the world. Whatever it is, the in-between element facilitates communication between what can be utterly diverse elements, be these spatial, as with the example of the discovery of the North-West passage and the connection between the local and the global via an atlas, or temporal, as when Lucretius is brought forth to reveal insights about modern science, or they can be cultural, which is both spatial and temporal, as when languages are translated. In his writing on the dilemmas faced by humanity in the twenty-first century, Serres has made recourse to the idea and practice of narrative as a way of constituting a common pool of knowledge for the whole of humanity (see Serres 2006).

The Sciences

In 1824, a French army engineer, Sadi Carnot drew attention to the fact that in the steam-engine heat flowed from a high-temperature region (the boiler) to a low-temperature region (the condenser). Although Carnot incorrectly concluded that no energy was lost from the system, he did appreciate that the more efficient the system, the less the energy required for its operation, and that it was the difference in the temperature between the boiler and the condenser which produced energy. Carnot's work ended prematurely when he died at the age of 36. A number of people like Hermann Helmholtz and Rudolph Clausius in Germany, and William Thompson (Lord Kelvin), in Glasgow, further developed Carnot's work, with the result that in 1865, Clausius coined the term 'entropy' for the heat lost from any mechanical system. The era of thermodynamics had arrived. Its first and second laws are, respectively, that 'The energy of the world remains constant', and that 'The entropy of the world tends to a maximum'.[1] Entropy is also the tendency towards disorder in a system.

Of interest here with respect to Serres is the difference between a simple mechanical notion of energy, and that of thermodynamics. In Newton's mechanical model, no energy in principle is lost from the system: the mechanics of the system are reversible. There are in principle no chance effects. 'According to the second law of thermodynamics ... the unidirectional motion of [a] projectile would be continuously transformed by the frictional resistance of the air into heat, that is, into random, disorderly motions of the molecules of the air and the projectile' (Mason 1962: 496).

This randomness, or disorder – as in the unstable borders of a cloud, or in the effects of steam, or in the movement of the tides – is only now being taken in charge by chaos theory. Prior to this, stochastics – the theory of randomness – like the theory of probability developed principles aimed at explaining disorderly phenomena.

From this brief outline we note that a Newtonian mechanical system is a system of reversibility: time in it is reversible. With the thermodynamic system, contingency and chance predominate, making it a system of irreversible time. To give a sociological twist to this, we can note that Bourdieu has called the logic of practice the logic of irreversible time.

Serres is ostensibly a philosopher of science. But unlike even his mentor, Gaston Bachelard, he has never accepted that any particular science – let alone natural science – conforms to the positivist determination of a hermetic and homogeneous field of enquiry. The 'educated third element', noted above, refers to a figure of knowledge which, Serres has indicated (Serres 1997), approximates that of the Harlequin: a composite figure that always has another costume underneath the one removed. The Harlequin is a hybrid, hermaphrodite, mongrel figure, a mixture of diverse elements, a challenge to homogeneity, just as chance in thermodynamics opens up the energy system and prevents it from imploding.

Science and Communication

With the recognition of the interrelation between different sciences and different forms of knowledge, as well as between science and different artistic practices, has come Serres's effort to plot the way that different knowledge domains interpenetrate. Even more: Serres has set himself the task of being a means of communication (a medium) between the sciences and the arts – the Hermes of modern scholarship.[2] With the advent of information science, a new figure for representing science becomes possible: this is the 'model' of communication. Accordingly, we have three elements: a message, a channel for transmitting it, and the noise, or interference, that accompanies the transmission. Noise calls for decipherment; it makes a reading of the message more difficult. And yet without it, there would be no message. There is, in short, no message without resistance. What Serres initially finds intriguing about noise (rather than the message) is that it opens up such a fertile avenue of reflection. Instead of remaining pure noise, the latter becomes a means of transport. Thus in the first volume of the Hermes series noise is analysed as the third, empirical element of the message. Ideally, communication must be separated from noise. Noise is what is not communicated; it is just there as a kind of chaos, as the empirical third element of the message, the accidental part, the part of difference that is excluded. Every formalism (mathematics, for example) is founded on the exclusion of the third element of noise. Every formalism is a way of moving from one region of knowledge to another. To communicate is to move within a class of objects that have the same form. Form has to be extracted from the cacophony of noise; form (communication) is the exclusion of noise, an escape from the domain of the empirical.

In his book, *The Parasite* (1982), Serres recalls that 'parasite' also means noise (in French). A parasite is a noise in a channel. And so when describing the rats' meals in a story from the fables of La Fontaine – the meals of two parasites – Serres also refers to noise:

> The two companions scurry off when they hear a noise at the door. It was only a noise, but it was also a message, a hit of information producing panic: an interruption, a corruption, a rupture of information. Was this noise really a message? Wasn't it, rather, static, a parasite?
>
> (Serres 1982: 3)

Again, in *The Parasite*, Serres asks whether a system is a prior set of constraints, or whether, on the other hand, a system is the regularity manifest in the various attempts to constitute a system. 'Do these attempts themselves constitute the system?' Serres asks. Noise, we have seen *is* the system. 'In the system, noise and message exchange roles according to the position of the observer and the action of the actor' (Serres 1982: 66).

Noise is a joker necessary to the system. It can take on any value, and is thus unpredictable so that the system is never stable. Instead, it is non-knowledge. Systems work because they do not work. Dysfunctioning remains essential for functioning. The model, then, is free of parasites, free of static (as in mathematics), while the system is always infected with parasites which give it its irreversible character. The system is a Turner painting. With his representation of the chance effects of clouds, rain, sea and fog, Turner interprets the second law of thermodynamics – the law made possible by Carnot. Turner translates Carnot. Such is Serres's poetic insight.

Translation

Serres's interest in 'noise' as the empirical third excluded element in human existence led him to translate (*traduire*) between apparently heterogeneous domains in an effort to forge 'passages' (e.g. North-West passage) between them – passages not just of communication, but also of non-communication, and static. At one point in his intellectual trajectory, the notion of structure seemed to serve the purposes of translation – and therefore, transport – very well. Indeed, Serres characterises the structuralist method as a method in the 'etymological sense: that is to say, a mode of transfer' (Serres 1972: 145). Beginning as part of Serres's mathematical training in algebra and topology, structure is brought to the human sciences where a structural analysis, examines one or two particular models reduced to a form (or to several): a pre-established, transitive order. Then, analogically, it finds this form or structure in other domains, *et similia tam facilia*. Whence its power of comprehension, of classification and of explication: geometry, arithmetic, mechanics, method, philosophy (Serres 1969: 121).

Influenced less by Saussure than by the Bourbaki group of mathematicians, Serres finds in structural analysis a means of travelling between different domains, and even between different realities. Structural analysis inevitably leads to comparison, and this is why Serres has great respect for Georges Dumézil's work; for Dumézil was able to show, through a comparison of sets of relations, that Indo-European mythology has the same structure, despite the variety of contents. In a very precise formulation Serres says: 'with a given cultural content, whether this be God, a table or a washbasin, an analysis is structural (and is only structural) when it makes this content appear as a model' (Serres 1969: 32) – a structural model being defined as 'the formal analogon of all the concrete models that it organises'. Rather than 'structural analysis', Serres proposes the term, '*loganalyse*'.

Through its non-referential and comparativist approach to place (no single place constitutes the object of structural analysis), the structuralist place is both 'here and there' at the same time. It is a highly mobile site that is constituted through an enunciation. There is no fixed point, here and now, but a multiplicity of spaces and of times. This implies, too, that there is no punctual empirical, subject, but rather a subject as a discontinuous virtuality.

Poetry

Serres's work has also emphasised the importance to him of poetry and the effect of new technologies (such as information technology) on everyday life. Poetry, in a sense, is the noise of science. Without poetry there would be no science. Without science – or at least philosophy – there can be no poeticising and fictionalising. Serres's reading of Jules Verne and Emile Zola, and the paintings of Turner serve to confirm this point. In Verne, for example, the meaning of coming to grips with non-knowledge is demonstrated. Non-knowledge is the mystery – the noise, we could now say – necessary to the constitution of knowledge as such. Non-knowledge in Verne is the unknown that one must venture into in order to constitute knowledge. The unknown is composed of worlds for which there would be as yet no concept or language. With Zola and Turner, the principle of stochastics is illustrated by their artistic endeavour in presenting steam, smoke, water and a variety of indeterminate phenomena.

For Serres, 'the perception of stochastics replac[ing] the specification of form' is a breakthrough in linking the sciences. *For science is a system, just as poetry is a system*. Rain, sun, ice, steam, fire, turbulence – they all engender chance effects. Modern physics begins here with the realisation that turbulence prevents the implosion of systems. The 'outside' of the system is what prevents implosion.

'What exists', says Serres, 'is the most probable' (i.e. disorder, chance and the exception). The real is not rational. 'There is only science of the exception, of the rare, and of the miracle' (i.e. of law, order, rule). System in the Classical Age is an equilibrium; in the nineteenth century it is thermodynamics and meteorology becomes a metaphor for knowledge.

Hermes and the Harlequin

Two key figures, already mentioned, which inform Serres's *oeuvre* are Hermes and the Harlequin. Hermes the traveller and the medium allows for the movement in and between diverse regions of social life. The Harlequin is a multi-coloured clown standing in the place of the chaos of life. Two regions of particular interest to the voyager in knowledge are those of the natural sciences and the humanities. Should science really be opened up to poetry and art, or is this simply an idiosyncrasy on Serres's part? Is this his gimmick? The answer is that Serres firmly believes that the very viability and vitality of science depends on the degree to which it is open to its poetical other. Science only moves on if it receives an infusion of something out of the blue, something unpredictable and miraculous. The poetic impulse is the life-blood of natural science, not its nemesis. Poetry is the way of the voyager open to the unexpected and always prepared to make unexpected links between places and things. The form that these links take is of course influenced by technological developments; information technology transforms the senses, for example.

Travelling in Time

Serres's writing is a challenge for good reason. In his view, not to stimulate the reader to find the coherence in his work is to render it sterile and subject to the collapse that inevitably awaits all closed systems. In the history of physics Serres has argued that Lucretius anticipates the framework of modern physics. *De rerum natura* (*On the Nature of Things*) has conventionally been treated as a piece of poetic writing that has little relevance to modern science. But, Serres argues, clearly, turbulence of all kinds is fundamental to Lucretius's system. With the idea of the *clinamen* – of infinite variation in the course of an object's trajectory – Lucretius anticipates the theory of disorder (entropy) of modern physics. More than this, though, Serres endeavours to show that a mathematics can be produced in light of Lucretius's writings of the last century before Christ.

By extension, the history of science itself is subject to turbulence: it is subject to chance connections of all kinds being made between various domains. Against the rigid orderliness of convention, Serres proposes the relative disorder of poetry, that is, of the miracle, chance and the exception. In its own way, Serres's writing is a glimpse of this miracle of poetry in an island of order.

Being Human in the Twenty-First Century

Given his propensity to find avenues of communication between otherwise impenetrable universes, Serres's writing on humanity in the twenty-first century is instructive. Two huge gaps need to be bridged: the first is between the individual and the wider society. The other is between life as it is lived in the First compared to life in the Third World.

Previously, humanity could be attributed certain characteristics (through biology, archaeology and the social sciences) which would provide approximate markers as to what it means to be human. Now, with changes in science and the nature of life, the individual today bears little resemblance to the individual of even 70 years ago. Life, in the past was one of permanent suffering and of a shorter span (caused by disease, poverty, conflict), whereas, now, science has made it possible for humanity to choose who it is – at least in the First World. This is what Serres, in a book published in 2001, calls 'hominescence', the emergence of a new humanity (see Serres 2001). Change has been so fundamental, with developments in science, and with new technologies giving humans the possibility of a new body, that humanity, for the first time, can become its own creator. In the wake of this, other domains of life have become entirely outdated. The whole of the political realm and the current practice of politics, for example, need to be thoroughly revised.

Moreover, a new political will is needed because not only is there a new humanity fast becoming cut off from the humanity of the past, but this is also manifest in the disappearance of any form of community, or collective identity. Instead, the human is the individual as formed by his or her own singular experience, more often than not an experience and experiences recounted in auto- or biographical writing. We are, or have become, our own narrations (*récits*).

Extreme forms of individualism, however, make it difficult to address key problems facing humanity on a global scale, such as global warming and inequalities of wealth between First and Third World nations. There is just no comparison, or viable means of communication, between people in Africa, who live in a state of permanent poverty and have a life expectancy of 32, and those in the West, who are rich and can expect to live to 84.

A mechanism is needed to bridge this gap, and Serres finds it in narrating a story. Even science has need of narrative when it comes to accounting for its origins. So Serres's aspiration is that, through narrating a story, humanity can find the basis of a new distribution of knowledge, and that through this, science can be brought to bear on a tragedy of our time. Story telling can thus provide a new community, albeit one that will have the universal as its focus.

Notes

1 The information on the history of thermodynamics comes from Mason (1962).
2 See the five volumes published under the title of *Hermès*, the Greek messenger god, listed in 'Major writings' (Serres 1969, 1972, 1974, 1977, 1980).

References

Mason, Stephen (1962), *A History of the Sciences*, New York: Collier, new revised edn.
Serres, Michel (1969), *La communication*, Paris: Minuit.
—— (1972), *L'interférence*, Paris: Minuit.
—— (1982), *The Parasite*, trans. Lawrence R. Schehr, Baltimore: Johns Hopkins University Press.
—— (1997 [1991]) *The Troubadour of Knowledge* (a translation of *Le Tiers-instruit*), trans. Shiela Faria Glaser and William Paulsen, Ann Arbor: University of Michigan Press.
—— (2001), *Hominesce: essais*, Paris: Pommier.
—— (2003), *Incandescent: essais*, Paris: Pommier.
—— (2006), *Récits d'humanism*, Paris: Pommier.

See also: **Bachelard**

Serres's major writings

(2006) *Récits d'humanism*, Paris: Pommier.
(2003) *Incandescent: essais*, Paris: Pommier.
(2001) *Hominesce: essais*, Paris: Pommier.
(2000 [1977]) *The Birth of Physics*, trans. Jack Hawkes, Manchester: Clinamen.
(1997 [1991]) *The Troubadour of Knowledge* (a translation of *Le Tiers-instruit*), trans. Shiela Faria Glaser and William Paulsen, Ann Arbor: University of Michigan Press.
(1995a [1992]) with Bruno Latour, *Conversations on Science, Culture, and Time*, trans. Roxanne Lapidus, Ann Arbor: University of Michigan Press.
(1995b [1990]) *The Natural Contract*, trans. Elizabeth McArthur and William Paulson, Ann Arbor: University of Michigan Press.
(1995c [1982]) *Genesis*, trans. Genviève James and James Nielson, Ann Arbor: University of Michigan Press.

(1991 [1983]) *Rome: The Book of Foundations*, trans. Felicia McCarren, Stanford: Stanford University Press.

(1987) *Statues*, Paris: François Bourin.

(1985) *Les cinq sens*, Paris: Grasset.

(1983a [1989]) *Detachment*, trans. Genviève James and Raymond Federman, Athens: Ohio University Press.

(1983b [1969]) *Hermes: Literature, Science, Philosophy*, trans. Josve Harari and David Bell, Baltimore: Johns Hopkins University Press.

(1983c [1980]) *The Parasite*, trans. Lawrence R. Schehr, Baltimore: Johns Hopkins University Press.

(1982a [1972]) 'Turner translates Carnot', trans. Mike Shortland, *Block*, 6. This article first appeared in 1972 as a review of an exhibition of English and pre-Raphaelite paintings held at the Petit Palais in Paris and was subsequently published in Serres, Michel (1974), *Hermès III. La traduction*, Paris: Minuit, 233–42.

(1982b [1968]) *Le Système de Leibniz et ses mathématiques*, Paris: Presses Universitaires de France, in one volume.

(1980) *Hermès V. Le passage du nord-ouest*, Paris: Minuit.

(1977) *Hermès IV. La distribution*, Paris: Minuit.

(1975a) *Feux et signaux de brume. Zola*, Paris: Grasset.

(1975b) *Auguste Comte. Leçons de philosophie positive*, Vol. 1., Paris: Hermann.

(1974a) *Jouvences. Sur Jules Verne*, Paris: Minuit.

(1974b) *Hermès III. La traduction*, Paris: Minuit.

(1972) *Hermès II. L'interférence*, Paris: Minuit.

(1969) *Hermès I. La communication*, Paris: Minuit.

Further reading

Abbas, Nivan, ed. (2005), *Mapping Michel Serres*, Ann Arbor: University of Michigan Press.

Assad, Maria L. (1999), *Reading with Michel Serres: An Encounter with Time*, Albany: State University of New York.

Latour, Bruno (1990), 'Postmodern? No simply Amodern! Steps towards an anthropology of science', *Studies in the History and Philosophy of Science*, 21, 1 (March). Review of Serres's *Statues*.

PAUL VIRILIO (b.1932)

Paul Virilio is the theorist of the effects of increasing speed in post- or late-modernity. Of particular importance for him, in this regard, are information technology and technologies of vision, such as cinema and photography, especially in time of war. And, queries Virilio, is not this all the time? – peace being war by other means. The net result of the emergence of these prosthetic forces is the dominance of virtual reality and the disappearance of materiality (cf. Virilio 1991), of identities, of space as a definite place to be, of perception as contact with material reality, including the body. So, unlike some posthumanists, who see biology and technology (especially its cybernetic aspect) as being inextricably linked to positive outcomes, Virilio is a most trenchant critic of this. It remains to examine these aspects in more detail. But first, we turn to the Virilio biography.

Life and Intellectual Trajectory

Born in 1932 in Paris to an Italian communist father and French mother, Paul Virilio was evacuated at the beginning of World War II to Nantes, where he experienced at first hand the trauma of Hitler's *Blitzkrieg*. Trained at the École des métiers d'art in Paris, the future architect became an artist in stained glass who trained with Braque at Vargenville and with Matisse at Saint-Paul-de-Vence.

Also during the 1950s, after converting to Christianity through contact with 'worker priests', Virilio took up photography and photographed 15,000 German bunkers, stretching along the West European coast up to Denmark. Later, in 1975, he curated an exhibition called 'Bunker Archéologie', based on the images collected, and held at the Decorative Arts Museum of Paris (see Virilio 1994). The architecture of war, Virilio argues, makes palpable the power of technology. The study of bunker architecture is thus only the beginning. Later, in the 1960s, Virilio engaged in developing 'oblique architecture', which used physiological principles to develop more habitable buildings.

Briefly, Virilio's formal career includes the following appointments, showing that, despite his anarchist disposition, he did not reject access to power and influence. Thus in 1963 Virilio became the president and the editor of the *Architecture Principe* group's magazine. This group explored the idea of 'oblique' architecture, Virilio having noticed that people inhabit places with inclined, not horizontal, planes. He was also a teacher at the École Spéciale d'Architecture (ESA) until 1968, becoming its Director of Studies in 1973. That same year, he became the editor of the magazine, *L'Espace Critique*, published in Paris by Galilée. In 1975 he was appointed General Director of the ESA, and in 1989 became Chairman of the Board. In 1987, Virilio won the Grand National Prize for Architecture, and in 1989, he became the director of the programme of studies at the Collège International de Philosophie in Paris, under the direction of Jacques Derrida. He became a member, in 1992, of the High Committee for the Housing of the Disadvantaged and worked with the famous priest, Abbé Pierre. Among other projects, he is working on metropolitan techniques of time organization and the building of the first Museum of the Accident. Virilio, who retired from teaching in 1998, currently devotes himself to writing and working with private organisations concerned with housing the homeless in Paris.

The Thesis of War and Speed

To the extent that a general and distinct line of argument, or that a general theory of politics and society can be discerned in the wide dissemination of Virilio's thoughts, war, military organisation and power constitute the central and over-arching infrastructure of his thinking. Human life in the West has been dominated, since the nineteenth century, by speed, with the consequence that time and light (the ultimate speed) become the key ideas of the epoch. Although we are to understand that this kind of activity and organisation has been present in the life of humanity since time immemorial, it is the modern and post-modern periods – that is, from the eighteenth to the twentieth century and beyond – that become the particular focus of Virilio's theorising. In this epoch, there is a fundamental change from warfare based on the principle of space and position to one based on movement and time. The latest developments in information technology simply reinforce the dominance of the latter principle, even if its most recent incarnations result in war being based on mechanisms that are secretive, virtual and invisible. Because new technologies make possible secretive, virtual and invisible forms of warfare, war can quite easily be continued in periods of so-called peace.

Perception and Cinema

Particularly influential for Virilio have been Merleau-Ponty's phenomenological studies of perception, Virilio having been a student of the philosopher at the Sorbonne in the 1950s. New information technologies intervene first of all at the level of perception. These new forces in fact become a substitute for perception, especially in the context of war, where the supply of images becomes ammunition. This is starkly illustrated even by the time of the Great War of 1914–18. Thus, in one of his most telling books, Virilio shows how technology transforms perception, how weapons become tools of perception and how the battle becomes the 'rapidly changing fields of perception' (Virilio 1989: 6). Forces of productive power become the model of destructive power.

War, it transpires, is about captivating the enemy (Virilio 1989: 5), or of producing a magical spectacle, of instilling fear of death before death arrives. Weapons go hand in hand with psychological mystification. Representation is crucial.

At the same time as cinematic acceleration is applied to the real world, cinema becomes a training ground (like military training grounds). Ronald Reagan, for example, used cinema technology to further his political agenda. Indeed, no activity during or after the First World War escapes 'cinematisation'. War, battlefields, weaponry and technology are constant points of reference for Virilio, the aim being to show that cinema and war are now inextricably linked. Such a view is dependent on the shrinking of space and the emergence of time as the crucial element in all activity. Time goes with the emergence of the acceleration of all aspects of social life.

Warfare, with its use of information technologies, makes time fundamental. War is always connected to technologies, particularly to technologies of perception, which were used with such dedication and effect by Hitler and the Nazis. And yet, the Allied victory, it could be said, was due to undermining Hitler's charisma through film technology (Virilio 1989: 59).

In his later work, Virilio subscribes to the notion that war is going on in the time of peace: pure war is neither peace nor war. War is no longer identifiable with declared conflict. Peace is war by other means.

The issue is to understand the relationship between industrialised warfare and cinema.

Cinema technology, in a word, becomes the eyes and ears of armies. Face to face combat as the leading edge of warfare in a given territory becomes a thing of the past. The visible gives way to the invisible and secrecy. Neither side signals its intentions as, in order to instil fear in the enemy, it once might have. Deception at all levels becomes the name of the game.

During the Second World War, East Anglia in England was turned into a film set in order to deceive the enemy Luftwaffe bombers. 'At other key moments, look-alikes of Churchill and other military leaders embarked on aeroplanes to undertake bogus trips' (Virilio 1989: 64).

Optics of Speed

In war, 'eyesight and direct vision have gradually given way to optoelectrical processes, to the most sophisticated forms of "telescopic sight"' (Virilio 1989: 69). The camera's flow of images (which take the place of direct perception) ends the war of position, based on space, and inaugurates the war of movement based on time. Increasing speed – acceleration – transforms the nature of conflict. Tendencies take precedence over events in the Second World War, but can only be detected by computers and other technologies. Information technology itself is the incarnation of speed, as it is able to approximate the speed of light in its articulation. After the Second World War, survival depends on measures introduced during the War. Information technology and research in artificial intelligence – the backbone of cybernetics – began in the midst of the War. With the greater hold of information technology on society comes the greater dominance of speed, its inseparable accompaniment. As Virilio puts it in *The Information Bomb* (2000), the speed of information technology gives rise to chronopolitics (a politics of time), which is taking the place of a politics based on a territory. The computer screen enables the user not only 'to receive data' but 'to view the horizon of globalization, the space of its accelerated virtualization' (Virilio 2000: 16). As virtual reality takes over from material reality following the information technology revolution, the information bomb succeeds the nuclear bomb: space disappears along with bodies and every genre of object.

Disappearance and the Virtual and the Dark Side of the Enlightenment

Because technology today is increasingly becoming a force in its own right, the world of appearances gives way to the world of disappearances. Identity becomes virtual and multiple, implying movement between infinite substitutions. The result, if we are to believe passages from *Open Sky* (1997), is 'unprecedented temporal breakdown' that intimates a '*social crash*' the preliminary signs of which are structural unemployment and family breakdown (Virilio 1997: 71). This is the woe of the total immateriality of the city emblematised by American cinema, with Hollywood as its model.

People now engage in virtual interactions and perception changes, the body disappears (is not perceived as such) as does physical location. A landscape comes to be seen, if at all, only while travelling: through the car windscreen or window of a fast train. Soon, this vestige of appearance and materiality will also disappear to be replaced by virtual images on the internet.

Virilio, like Baudrillard, seems to focus on the dark side of the Enlightenment to the extent that light – the speed of light – the significance of which was starting to be seen at the start of the Industrial

Revolution at the end of the eighteenth century, is the element giving rise to the dominance of time over space, of virtuality over materiality. Yet Virilio is at pains to say that he is a realist, not a pessimist. It is just that there are so many believers in the whole of technology, and so few critics since the death of Virilio's mentor in 1994, the philosopher and theologian, Jacques Ellul. It is not that technology itself is evil; rather, taking a fundamentalist attitude towards it is. The latter consists in thinking that whatever technology prescribes must be followed to the letter.

Those who believe in Virilio see him as the prophet of the techno-speed-based millennium. Loss of time means greater acceleration: more speed. The nature and impact of this is the subject of 'dromology' – Virilio's invention – meaning: the study of speed. Relative speed is taken over by absolute speed, the speed of light. Einstein thus becomes so prescient.

Time, for Virilio, is the instant as much as duration. Cinema is a point in the development of electro-magnetic speed: cinema time is about putting movement into images. Everything accelerates.

Power

Power, for its part, becomes secret and invisible (exemplified by the lives of Howard Hughes and William Randolph Hearst, by the activities of the CIA, and by criminal activity). In the wake of an 'aesthetics of disappearance', the tangible version of power – power as the conscious and explicit implementation of the ruler's will – gives way to power as invisible and intangible. Foucault's ideas have been influential here. For Foucault as well, there is an historical change from visible forms of power, as exemplified by absolute monarchy, and power as it is articulated in modern democracies, where, following the panopticon model, power becomes invisible and integrated into a multitude of disciplinary practices. In a sense, the growing invisibility of power is also equivalent to its virtualisation, or, as Virilio would say, to its dematerialisation. And of course, Foucault also spoke in the same context about new *technologies* of power. Thus, for Virilio, the form of power changes and becomes invisible in light of the growing dominance of new technologies.

Virilio's theorising and descriptions are often of the moment. He is never short of examples to press home his point here, even if these often seem selective. Surveillance at airports and toll booths at all points of entry, change the city. Architecture gives way to functional, surveillance concerns.

Negative Aspects of Information Technology

A new technological space–time emerges in the era of hypo-modernity, which stretches into the beginning of the twenty-first century. Cities are becoming de-populated as post-industrialism takes hold. Speed dominates everything through new telecommunications.

The city no longer has gates; the 'face-to-face' disappears with the rise of the virtual. Substantial, homogeneous space in the Greek sense gives way to an accidental, heterogeneous space. The tyranny of distance gives way to the tyranny of real time. Space (e.g. office space) gives way to time. People live/work as disabled people do, using prosthetic gadgetry of all kinds. They become increasingly sedentary (see Virilio 1997).

In sum, the geographical environment is disappearing (space is disappearing). People no longer identify with a particular place, whether this be village, town or country. The result is often an indifference to neighbours while people profess a love for the other at a distance.

Time and space are always relative to human time and space, so it matters a great deal if these coordinates change. Virtual interaction at a distance, whether in the context of sexuality, politics or urban life, has a cybernetic dimension that, for Virilio, deprives people of free will in the sense that they become elements in a feed back and control system, the very opposite of freedom and democracy.

With regard to sexuality in particular, the risk for our theorist is that the contact at a distance of cybersex may lead to a preference for this kind of activity rather than activity in proximity with a partner. The very existence of the human race – or at least the most highly developed parts of it in the West – is then brought into question because it will no longer be able to reproduce itself. For reproduction is the result of proximity, not distance (Virilio 1997: 106–7).

Regarding the dominance of real time (over space and materiality), Virilio refers to Rodin's statement that the camera lies because time does not stand still. In response Virilio claims that photography (an older medium), while not being the same as time passing, is equivalent to the exposure of time, of time 'breaking the surface', and that when multiple images are shown in sequence, time does not stand still (Virilio 1997: 27–28). Not photographic time, but the time of media and television, the time of the live coverage, of what is happening 'now'. The real 'now' time, therefore, is not the time of photography, as Bergson once thought, but the time of the media revolution based on satellite and digital technology. 'Now' dominates over 'Here'.

The more technologies of seeing beyond the horizon become perfected the less we see of the world around us: 'tangible experience will diminish and be reduced to nothing, to less than nothing' (Virilio 1997: 42).

Economically, the collapse of the small firm shows the current irrelevance of a particular space; the workforce becomes mobile, decentralised, no longer located in cities or on urban outskirts (Virilio 1997: 75). The internet begins to take the place of shopping in the neighbourhood. However, buying on the internet is likely to result in mass unemployment. We are confronting 'information shock', which can bring a state to its knees with the collapse of the computer system. To believe totally in this technological revolution is equivalent to a technological fundamentalism, the result being that particular cultures come under threat with the emphasis on real time instead of space and community. What we have is industrialism (communications, transport) taken to the extreme. The virtualisation of politics leads to a loss of geographical sovereignty.

Cybersex entails the loss of the (use of) the body. It is a sexual diversion, where an erotics of distance and repulsion takes the place of intimacy and attraction.

In short, there a total disappearance of materiality due to digitalisation and the hegemony of the present moment (the now) over history and the time of community: the time of a past, present and future. Information technology signals, in Virilio's doomsday view, the loss of the past and the future.

In addition, in keeping with a growing immateriality, even units of measure have dematerialised. Objects are replaced by trajectories and this is a confirmation of the aesthetics of disappearance (Virilio 2005: 58–59). This leads to a post-objective perception: a 'trajective' perception (Virilio 2005: 59). Dromology takes over. Art becomes virtual. But this is a loss of art. For there is no art without analogy (against digitalisation) (cf. Virilio and Baj 2003: 51).

But is it All True ... ?

There is no doubt that Virilio succeeds in mounting a trenchant critique of technology. He is also astute in pointing out, against those who advocate a positive body–technology symbiosis (cyborg), that there are in fact negative consequences that, if ignored, may place the future existence of humanity at risk.

Although Virilio is often an astute observer of social and political life and has a plethora of examples to call upon to support the claims he makes regarding the negative effects of technology, his work is susceptible to the following criticisms.

1. As has been point out by Scott McQuire (1999), Virilio still works with an image and reality dichotomy, where the image is not real, and with a naïve notion of a natural human identity as being present to itself, thus by-passing the post-structuralist critique of the metaphysics of presence and the de-centring of the subject. Technology, in effect, brings a kind of fall from grace of the original, unified subject as part of a community and in touch with true materiality, including the body. However, it is also true that post-structuralism inhibits a critique of technology.

2. As technology, for Virilio, is essentially prosthetic, it cannot be an essential part of human identity. Indeed, it should always be the servant of humanity, never its master, which it is becoming in late-twentieth and early-twenty-first century society. This is also the lesson of earlier critiques of technology such as those of Mary Shelley in her book, *Frankenstein's Monster* and Fritz Lang's in his film, *Metropolis*. So the question arises as to how new Virilio's ideas really are.

3. Even though technology is not an essential part of what it is to be human, the human can be changed by technology. The risk is that technological determinism can creep in if technology alone, and by its very nature, is claimed to have deleterious effects on humanity. This becomes even more critical once war is seen as an essential aspect of the current social arrangements in the West, and technology – especially, information technology – is seen to be an inevitable component of war.

4. Because Virilio eschews a systematic approach to the history and theory of technology, relying instead on his own intuitive insights that often seem to be skewed by his Catholicism (cf. Virilio's promotion of the value of the traditional family), his claims about the negative impact of technology lack a certain credibility. In particular, he ignores the possibility that if technology inaugurates the loss of a certain sort of materiality, it also inaugurates gains in communication. In other words, like capitalism, technology is a two-edged sword.

5. Finally, Virilio steers clear of a detailed assessment of Artificial Intelligence (AI) and Artificial Life (AL), and about carbon and silicon life in biology (see N. Katherine Hayles 1999: 235–39), preferring instead to speak broadly about the negative effects of cyborg culture. This limits the plausibility of his critique.

Despite all this, Virilio, it has to be acknowledged, reminds us – often forcefully – that it is important not to become complacent with regard to the development and effects of new technologies, and that resistance and critique are key elements in any democratic politics worthy of the name.

References

Hayles, N. Katherine (1999), *How We Became Posthuman: Virtual Bodies in Cybernetics, Literature, and Informatics*, Chicago and London: University of Chicago Press.

McQuire, Scott (1999), 'Blinded by the (Speed of) Light', *Theory, Culture and Society*, 16, 5–6, 143–59.

Virilio, Paul (1989 [1984]), *War and Cinema. The Logistics of Perception*, trans. Patrick Camiller, London and New York: Verso.

—— (1991), *The Aesthetics of Disappearance*, trans. Philip Beitchman. New York: Semiotext(e).

—— (1994), *Bunker Archeology*, trans. George Collins, Princeton, NJ: Princeton Architectural Press.

—— (1997), *Open Sky*, trans. Julie Rose, London and New York: Verso.

—— (2000), *The Information Bomb*, trans. Chris Turner, London: Verso.

—— (2005), *L'Art à perte de vue*, Paris: Galilée.

Virilio, Paul and Baj, Enrico (2003), *Discours sur l'horreur de l'art*, Lyon, France: Atelier de creation libértaire.

See also: **Foucault, Haraway, Merleau-Ponty**

Virilio's major writings

(2005) *L'Art à perte de vue*, Paris: Galilée.

(2003) with Enrico Baj *Discours sur l'horreur de l'art*, Lyon, France: Atelier de création libértaire.

(2002 [1991]) *Desert Screen*, trans. Michael Degener, London and New York: Continuum.

(2000 [1998]) *The Information Bomb*, trans. Chris Turner, London: Verso.

(1997 [1995]) *Open Sky*, trans. Julie Rose, London and New York: Verso.

(1994a [1988]) *The Vision Machine*, trans. Julie Rose, Bloomington and London: Indiana University Press and British Film Institute.

(1994b [1975]) *Bunker Archaeology*, trans. George Collins. Princeton, NJ: Princeton Architectural Press.

(1991a [1984]) *The Lost Dimension*, trans. Daniel Moshenberg, New York: Semiotext(e).

(1991b [1988]) *The Aesthetics of Disappearance*, trans. Philip Beitchman, New York: Semiotext(e).

(1990 [1978]) *Popular Defense & Ecological Struggles*, trans. Mark Polizzotti, New York: Semiotext(e).

(1989 [1984]) *War and Cinema. The Logistics of Perception*, trans. Patrick Camiller, London and New York: Verso.

(1986 [1977]) *Speed & Politics: An Essay on Dromology*, trans. Mark Polizzotti, New York: Semiotext(e).

(1985) *L'Horizon négatif*, Paris: Galilée.

(1978) *La Dromoscopies ou la lumière de la vitesse*, Paris: Minuit.

(1976) *L'Insécurité du territoire*, Paris: Stock.

Further reading

Armitage, John (1999a), 'Paul Virilio: An Introduction', *Theory, Culture and Society*, 16, 5–6, 1–23.

Armitage, John (1999b), 'From Modernism to Hypermodernism and Beyond: An Interview with Paul Virilio', *Theory, Culture and Society*, 16, 5–6, 25–55.

McQuire, Scott (1999), 'Blinded by the (Speed of) Light', *Theory, Culture and Society*, 16, 5–6, 143–59.

VITALIST-INSPIRED THOUGHT

Thought of vitalist inspiration gives scope to the drive, or energy-based dimension of existence. Life is viewed as active and changing, not static and eternal. Issues of time and the body are addressed, as well as power and sacrifice. There is a concern to show that the most abstract, intellectual activities are affected by drives or vitalist energy.

Kristeva's idea of the drive-based semiotic is a good example of this. Another example is Deleuze's focus on revealing the nature of sensation and how it functions in various contexts such as art, cinema and thought.

GEORGES BATAILLE (1897–1961)

It is appropriate to begin an explication of Georges Bataille's work with biographical fragments for in an important sense Bataille's writing stands at the crossroads of fiction and biography.

Bataille was born at Billon in France in 1897. His father had gone blind before the birth of his son, and he became partially paralysed in 1900 when Georges was not yet three years old. Bataille claims in his autobiographical fragments that his father's condition was the result of syphilis. However, this was contested by his brother. Whatever the truth of the matter, Bataille claims to have retained from his childhood experience images of horror which he used in his fictional writing. In particular, there is the memory of the blank whites of the father's eyes, open wide while he urinated. This memory served, Bataille said, as a basis of imaginative transposition. Thus, in *Story of the Eye by Lord Auch*, the whites of the eye are transformed into egg whites and bull's testicles, and become associated with urination and death – specifically, the death of a matador, Granero, who was gored through the eye.

Horror and Obscenity

The horror which so often emerges in Bataille's fiction has its origin in the childhood memory of the slow and painful death of his father, and the periodic insanity of his mother. Whether this is true or not, Bataille's writing, both fictional and scientific, is often focused on horror and obscenity. In his book, *Eroticism*, for example, Bataille emphasises how the erotic is fundamentally a violation of the pure self; it is thus (unconsciously) linked with death. Similarly, in *The Tears of Eros* Bataille argues that the history of art shows that art has always been linked to horror. This is why it originated in caves, such as those discovered at Lascaux in France.

Bataille's fiction, in all its obscenity, has, like that of Sade, now been collected in the prestigious Pléiade collection published by Gallimard (see Bataille 2004). He is thus now part of the canon even if, for some, Bataille's focus on, or even obsession with, horror and obscenity in his fiction and, to a lesser extent, in some of his key theoretical works, seems to echo a certain mental instability. This, at any rate, appears to have been the view of André Breton in the *Second Surrealist Manifesto* when he referred to Bataille as a 'case' (Breton 1972: 184). And it is true that during 1927, and perhaps for longer, Bataille was in analysis with the liberal psychoanalyst, Dr Adrien Borel. Borel encouraged Bataille to put his obsessions on paper, and thereby gave a fillip to the writing career of his analysand.

Whether or not Bataille remained on the edge of insanity for much of his life – whether or not he was obsessed by horror and death – he has left an *oeuvre* which, it is now generally agreed, is of great theoretical profundity and intensity. For Bataille was indeed able to theorise the central themes of his obsessions; he was also able to bring his training in numismatics to bear in his intellectual enterprises – one of these being the creation of the ethnographic and art journal, *Documents*, edited by Bataille from 1929 to 1930. In 1946, Bataille established what was to become one of France's best-known journals: *Critique*. *Critique* presented the early work of Blanchot, Barthes, Foucault and Derrida to a wider audience.

Education and Intellectual Orientation

Intellectually, Bataille attended the Reims Lycée. In 1913 he left to become a border at Epernay College where, in 1914, he gained his first *baccalauréat*. In 1915 he passed his second *baccalauréat*, and after being demobilised from military service in 1917, was admitted to the École des Chartes in Paris, to study to be a Mediaevalist, from where he graduated in second place in 1922. In the same year, Bataille travelled to Madrid to attend the École des Hautes Études Hispaniques. In 1923, he read Nietzsche and Freud for the first time, and in 1924 was appointed as a librarian to the Cabinet des Médailles at the Bibliothèque Nationale in Paris.

For Bataille, Nietzsche is a writer as much as a philosopher, first, because he does not exclude autobiography (whether fictive or not) from his philosophical writings, and second, because in refusing to lend his voice to any cause, he condemns himself to solitude. Nietzsche's philosophy becomes a cry in the wilderness. The very notion of 'cry', along with tears, anguish and laughter assumes a fundamental place in Bataille's own philosophical outlook. The cry is part of a series of terms which mark the presence of the horizontal axis (the axis of difference) in Bataille's thought. Bataille's own explanation of the horizontal axis is to be found in his 1930 essay, 'The pineal eye'. Vegetation, Bataille says there, occupies a position exclusively on the vertical, while animal life tends towards the horizontal axis, although animals strive to raise themselves up and so assume a certain literal verticality.

The Vertical and the Horizontal

To capture the full force of the complex interaction between the horizontal and the vertical in Bataille's thought, we must consider Hegel's influence. Like a number of other important thinkers, Bataille learned his Hegel from Alexandre Kojève's idiosyncratic lectures on the *Phenomenology of Mind*, which he intermittently attended from 1933 to 1939. Hegel's system of Absolute knowledge, where even death is appropriated by consciousness, represents the end point of a kind of delirium of reason. The extreme point of illumination is so illuminating that it opens the way to a certain blindness, just as one can be blinded by looking directly into the sun, even though the sun is the source of illumination. Bataille's approach to Hegel had no doubt been anticipated in his 1930s article on Picasso, 'The rotten sun', where the myth of Icarus (who fell to the earth after flying so high because the sun had melted the wax of his wings) is used to illustrate the danger of too much enlightenment (illumination). Hegel, with his great idealist system, flies high, like Icarus. His philosophy would thus be the incarnation of the vertical axis, perhaps its most extreme manifestation. But, Bataille says, there is a point of blindness in the Hegelian system: it is that total illumination hides the very real obscurity of non-knowledge, of a base materialism, of the madness that Hegel himself feared was at hand in 1800 after the death of his father. What Hegel's system cannot state, let alone integrate, is that element in it which is equivalent to its own blindness, a blindness that foreshadows the fall of the all-seeing philosopher. Another way of putting it is to say that the Hegelian system, as the embodiment of the transcendental vertical axis, makes no room for horizontality. Just as the obelisk from Egypt, erected at Place de la Concorde in Paris in 1836, marks the place of the Revolutionary instrument of death – the guillotine – so Hegel's homogenising philosophical system hides a heterogeneous, material baseness.

Base Materialism, Sacrifice and the Sacred

A great deal of Bataille's writing is concerned with 'material baseness' – manifest in obscenity, in the case of his fiction, and in a series of practices, in the case of his theoretical writings. These practices open up the horizontal axis as the axis of sacrifice, loss, chance and eroticism. We will briefly examine each of these in turn.

Bataille's concern to show how highly intellectual productions often conceal an unassimilable base element, led him to ethnographies of societies whose social bond seemed to be founded on practices quite horrific to a modern Western sensibility. Thus, in *The Accursed Share* (Bataille 1988a), the theorist of expenditure as an excess argues that the magnificence of Aztec cultural artefacts has to be understood in conjunction with the practice of human sacrifice: the beautiful has to be linked to baseness. Wars provided the victims for the bloody ritual, where the priest would plunge an obsidian knife into the chest of the victim and pull out the still pulsating heart, which he would then offer to the sun, the supreme god of the Aztecs. Without in the least condoning Aztec sacrifice, Bataille shows that it does have a certain logic.

In the first place, human sacrifice is a way of introducing disequilibrium into a society dominated by utilitarian exchange values.

The degradation of utilitarian relations is embodied in slavery, where the slave is nothing but an object to be used by free people. The victim of Aztec sacrifice, by contrast, was often treated humanely, and even given special treatment; for there was an intimate link between the victim and captor. The victim in fact dies in the place of the executioner. He or she is their experience of death, an experience manifest in anguish as the executioners identify with the suffering of the victim. Sacrifice 'restores to the sacred world that which servile use has degraded, rendered profane' (Bataille 1988a: 55).[3] The sacred, then, lies beyond exchange-value; it has no equivalent: nothing, as a result, can be a substitute for the sacrificial act. In a society where exchange-value has almost completely taken over, sacrifice cannot be understood. However, it still has an echo in bodily mutilation (such as Van Gogh's), where the act ruptures the homogeneity of self, and introduces heterogeneity into social life.

By a somewhat paradoxical turn, the rupture of sacrifice and mutilation turns into a moment of continuity. For the witness who experiences the anguish of identification with the victim also communicates this to others, and so establishes a continuity with others. As a result, 'the sacred is only a privileged moment of communal unity, a convulsive form of what is ordinarily stifled' (Bataille 1985: 242).

The General Economy

Closely linked with sacrifice and the sacred is the notion of loss. For Bataille, Marcel Mauss's theory of potlatch does not show that exchange is essentially a system of reciprocity. Rather, potlatch should be seen as an instance of the general economy where excess and luxury are the central aspects. The general economy is an economy of loss, disequilibrium and expenditure without return. It cannot be analysed in terms of what Bataille calls the 'restricted' economy of production, equilibrium and balanced books: the economy of 'classical utility'. All forms of excess – which, by definition, do not have any equivalent – fall within the general economy. Excess and loss have no obvious function in social life; they stand for necessarily dysfunctional, heterogeneous elements.

In two texts in particular, Bataille discusses chance (Bataille 1988b: 69–86; 1992). However, chance is more than a concept in his writing; it is also part of a practice. Thus Bataille's text on Nietzsche is also an analogue of chance, in the same way that Surrealism often aimed to be an analogue of madness (Roudinesco 1990: 26). The element of chance has to be included in any analysis of Bataille's practice of writing; for it is as a practice that chance fully assumes its place on the horizontal axis. To appreciate chance in Bataille's theoretical writings, we recall that, since Laplace, chance has often been thought of as a symptom of the limitedness of human knowledge. Chance, in short, would be subjective rather than objective in nature. Moreover, causality, and the accompanying notion of determination, has been assumed to be the very basis of scientific explanation. Knowledge has always made chance an exception. Only since quantum mechanics emerged in the 1920s has this view been superseded.

Chance

Three of Bataille's most important books – *Inner Experience, Guilty,* and *On Nietzsche* – were written between 1941 and 1944, that is, during the Occupation in France. Chance figures, first and foremost, analogically in each one. Each has the air of a journal – the air of contingency that comes from the admixture of a transcription of day-to-day events, and personal recollection. Thus the 'shape' of each text is fortuitous rather than predetermined. In his introduction to *Guilty,* Denis Hollier reiterates that what he is introducing is not really a book, 'Bataille isn't concerned with giving thoughts a systematic form or developing a story' (Hollier 1988: vii). There is, though, a certain logic informing Bataille's writing here, one based on a desire to indulge in a kind of play which would enable a glimpse of chance. In *On Nietzsche* this is made clearer: the book is partly a day-to-day narrative of 'dice throws'. Chance then becomes the truth of life; it is equivalent to the disequilibrium brought to the vertical axis. More strongly, chance is explicitly linked to anguish. Anguish, like chance, is an impossible obscurity. 'Anguish says: "impossible": the impossible remains at the *mercy of chance*' (Bataille 1973: 134, Bataille's emphasis). Furthermore: 'Anguish alone defines chance entirely: chance is what the anguish in me regards as impossible. Anguish is the contestation of chance' (Bataille 1973: 134). The cry, laughter, tears, excrement (the waste products of the system), poetry – all these give rise to chance. Chance cannot be integrated into any system, for it is the 'other' of system. This is why chance does not exist for Hegel. Chance is Nietzsche's *amor fati* (love of fate) which is opposed to the grand equilibrium of the Hegelian edifice. Chance is linked to sacrifice, because like the latter, it is also a rupture with identity and the utilitarian experience based on the determination of events.

Eroticism

In eroticism, human sexuality obtains its zenith as a (regulated) transgression of taboos (Bataille 1987: 63–70). Eroticism becomes, in Bataille's theory, a way to the continuity of being in death. As an individual, each person is discontinuous. Eroticism, as a violation of this discontinuity, is a fundamental source of anguish; for this is also the violation, or transgression, of interdictions; the interdiction is made known by the transgression. Eroticism thus confirms the rupture of boundaries and frontiers, and leads to a fusion of beings, a fusion giving rise to the communication of anguish based on a loss of integrity. The erotic impulse has, for this reason, been appropriated for religious ends. And so, instead of being the very antithesis of the sacred, eroticism – as an opening up to otherness – is its very foundation. Through tears, wounds and the violation of boundaries, human beings are united. Eroticism, clearly, is located on the horizontal axis; however, a system of interdictions – the vertical axis – is the condition of possibility of this horizontality.

Analogue of Exhaustion

The thesis that progressively emerges from a reading of Bataille is that blindness is an essential element in knowledge – that the great heights of enlightenment are the correlate of the depths of non-knowledge and obscene laughter. Seeing – theory – cannot grasp its other, as Denis Hollier has rightly suggested (Hollier 1989: 87–88). Bataille shows that seeing, and all theoretical work, entails a vital component: the intellectual energy needed to sustain it. Thus the exhaustion and fatigue to which Bataille's texts constantly refer finds its analogue in the relatively fragmentary nature of the *oeuvre*: in the bursts of poetry, the prolific number of occasional pieces, and the essay style. These indices of an expenditure of energy are perhaps the closest a reader can get to an analogue of his or her own blindness.

References

Bataille, Georges (1973), 'Sur Nietzsche', in *Oeuvres Completes, VI*, Paris: Gallimard.
—— (1985), 'The sacred' in *Visions of Excess. Selected Writings, 1927–1939*, trans. Allan Stoekl, Minneapolis: University of Minnesota Press.
—— (1987), *Eroticism*, trans. Mary Dalwood, London and New York: Marion Boyars.
—— (1988a), *The Accursed Share*, Vol. I, trans. Robert Hurley, New York: Zone Books.

—— (1988b), *Guilty*, trans. Bruce Boone, Venice: The Lapis Press.
—— (1992), *On Nietzsche*, trans. Bruce Boone, New York: Paragon Press.
—— (2004), *Romans et écrits*, Paris: Gallimard, 'Bibliothèque de la Pléiade'.
Breton, André (1972), *Second Surrealist Manifesto in Manifestoes of Surrealism*, trans. Richard Seaver and Helen R. Lane, Ann Arbor: University of Michigan Press.
Hollier, Denis (1988), 'A tale of unsatisfied desire', Introduction to Bataille' in *Guilty*, trans. Bruce Boone, Venice: The Lapis Press.
—— (1989), *Against Architecture: The Writings of Georges Bataille*, trans. Betsy Wing, Cambridge, Mass.: MIT Press.
Roudinesco, Elisabeth (1990), *Jacques Lacan & Co. A History of Psychoanalysis in France, 1925–1985*, trans. Jeffrey Mehlman, Chicago: University of Chicago Press.

See also: **Agamben, Baudrillard, Kristeva, Mauss**

Bataille's major writings

(2004a) *The Unfinished System of Nonknowledge*, trans. Stuart Kendall and Michelle Kendall, Minneapolis: University of Minnesota Press.
(2004b) *Romans et écrits*, Paris: Gallimard, 'Bibliothèque de la Pléiade'.
(1992 [1945]) *On Nietzsche*, trans. Bruce Boone, New York: Paragon Press.
(1991a) *The Trial of Gilles de Rais*, documents presented by Georges Bataille, trans. Richard Robinson, Los Angeles: Amok.
(1991b [1947]) *The Impossible. A Story of Rats followed by Dianus and by The Oresteia*, trans. Robert Hurley, San Francisco: City Lights Books.
(1989a) *Theory of Religion*, trans. Robert Hurley, New York: Zone Books.
(1989b [1961]) *The Tears of Eros*, trans. Peter Connor, San Francisco: City Lights Books.
(1988a) *The College of Sociology, 1937–39*, trans. Betsy Wing, ed. Denis Hollier, Minneapolis: University of Minnesota Press. Contains texts by Bataille and other participants in the College.
(1988b) *Inner Experience*, trans. Leslie Anne Boldt, Albany: State University of New York Press.
(1988c [1966–1967]) *My Mother, Madame Edwarda, The Dead Man* (three novels), trans. Astryn Wainhouse, New York: Marion Boyars.
(1988d [1949]) *The Accursed Share*, Vol. I, trans. Robert Hurley, New York: Zone Books.
(1988e [1944]) *Guilty*, trans. Bruce Boone, Venice: The Lapis Press.
(1987 [1957]) *Eroticism*, trans. Mary Dalwood, London and New York: Marion Boyars.
(1986a [1935]) *Blue of Noon*, trans. Harry Mathews, New York: Marion Boyars.
(1986b [1957]) *Literature and Evil*, trans. Alastair Hamilton, London: Marion Boyars.
(1985) *Visions of Excess. Selected Writings, 1927–1939*, trans. Allan Stoekl, Carl R. Lovitt and Donald M. Leslie, Jr., ed. Allan Stoekl, Minneapolis: University of Minnesota Press.

(1982 [1928]) *Story of the Eye by Lord Auch*, trans. Joachim Neugroschal, Harmondsworth: Penguin Books.
(1950) *L'Abbé C*, Paris: Minuit.

Further reading

Gill, Carolyn, ed. (1994), *Georges Bataille: Writing and the Sacred*, London and New York: Routledge.
Hollier, Denis (1989), *Against Architecture: The Writings of Georges Bataille*, trans. Betsy Wing, Cambridge, Mass.: MIT Press.
Lechte, John, (1993), 'Introduction to Bataille. The impossible as (a practice of) writing', *Textual Practice*, 7, 2 (Summer).
Noys, Benjamin (2000) *Georges Bataille: A Critical Introduction*, London: Pluto.
Surya, Michel (2002) *George Bataille: An Intellectual Biography*, trans. Krzysztof Fijalkowski and Michael Richardson, London: Verso.

HENRI BERGSON (1859–1941)

Henri Bergson's philosophical trajectory is characterised by fame and obscurity. Almost a cult figure in his life-time, after the publication, in 1889, of works such as his doctoral thesis, *Essai sur les données immédiates de la conscience* (Essay on the Immediate Data of Consciousness, English translation *Time and Free Will*), *Matter and Memory* (*Matière et mémoire*) in 1896 and *Laughter* (*Le rire*) in 1900, his name disappears from the philosophical map after his death at the height of World War Two. Only after Gilles Deleuze's book, *Le Bergsonism* of 1966 (English translation *Bergsonism* 1991), and more surely after Deleuze's recourse to Bergson's theory of time in his cinema books of the 1980s does Bergson become a notable thinker once again.

Life and Intellectual Trajectory

Bergson was the second son of seven children. He was born in 1859 in Paris to an English mother and Polish father. Both parents were Jewish, and Bergson took out French citizenship in 1878, although he could also have chosen to become an English citizen.

Academically, Bergson was, like Husserl his direct German contemporary, an outstanding student in mathematics and won a prestigious prize in 1877 through solving a problem set by Pascal. Despite his proficiency in mathematics, Bergson chose to prepare for the humanities section of the École Normale Supérieure (rue d'Ulm) in Paris, and came second in his year in an *agrégation* in philosophy.

After the success of his publications, particularly *Matter and Memory*, Bergson was appointed, in 1897, to a chair at the Collège de France in Ancient Philosophy. In 1922, he was made president of the International Commission for Intellectual Cooperation, the same year that he debated, under the auspices of the *Société françaises de philosophie*, with Einstein on the notion of time and relativity. In 1927, Bergson was awarded the Nobel Prize for literature. Before his death in Paris in 1941, at the height of the Occupation, he was to publish two works of lasting significance: in 1932, *The Two Sources of Morality and Religion* (*Les deux sources de la morale et de la religion*) and a collection of essays in 1938 entitled, *La pensée et le mouvant* (English translation *The Creative Mind*). While *The Creative Mind* ranges over his early concerns with duration, intuition, the real and perception, in *The Two Sources of Morality*, Bergson, opposing Kant, develops a theory of 'closed' and 'open' morality. Closed morality could be that of the pre-modern community, where the maintenance of social cohesion is the dominant value and tradition and custom determine conduct and remain static in light of changing conditions. Closed morality is exclusively concerned with the survival of a particular society against other societies. It is thus always ready for war and cannot aspire to the universal. Open morality, by contrast, is creative and progressive; it aspires to be inclusive and universal, thus giving rise, where it is realised, to peace.

The Multiple, Time, Intuition

Three themes, then, dominate Bergson's thought: time, intuition and multiplicity. To focus on these implies as misguided the stereotypical idea of Bergson as a somewhat naïve vitalist who proposed the *élan vital* as an essential life force that explains everything human and natural. Rather, as Deleuze shows, the *élan vital* is 'movement and differentiation' and is therefore implicated in Bergson's synthetic, non-spatial, view of time. Indeed, in the same work that Bergson gives his most detailed account of the *élan vital*, the first chapter is devoted to duration, where a clear distinction is made between change as the passage from discontinuous, discrete and durationless states, and the opposite of this: change as the imperceptible, continuous flow of one state into another. Bergson argues that the lived state corresponds to the continuous transition from one state to another. In reality, there is no discrete state, only change (Bergson 1998: 3). The translation of change, or duration, into analytical knowledge based on the input of perception, leads to the privileging of discontinuity. Perception is thus at odds with duration.

The Multiple and Counting

If Bergson continues to address the question of duration in his explication of evolution and the *élan vital*, he had already signalled his intention in this area in his earlier work, based on his doctoral thesis, *Essai sur les données immédiates de la conscience* (1991). There, duration is linked to the idea of multiplicity (see Bergson 1991: 56–104). To explicate this, Bergson distinguishes between the one and the multiple, through distinguishing between counting and the sum total. Although deriving a sum total can serve obvious practical ends, it also neglects individual differences. In other words, a sum total is homogeneous and excludes difference, whereas counting includes differences. However, difference, and therefore counting, is infinite. Fifty sheep in a flock is not equivalent to fifty different sheep, but to one (sheep) repeated fifty times.

The mistake made with counting, Bergson says, is to believe that it is done in time – duration – rather than in space. Each counting figure becomes equivalent to a discrete moment on the way to the number (e.g. 1 to 50). There is, in other words, a spatialisation of time in play, not time as duration, not time as such. This insight will be repeated on numerous occasions throughout Bergson's *oeuvre*. The question here is: how does the notion of the multiple undermine this spatialising process?

The correct response is that the sum is also a multiple, but one that can be divided quantitatively, and is a product of analysis, while the counting multiple is qualitative and is a product of intuition. Moreover, qualitative multiplicities are found in emotions, such as love, hate and sympathy. Duration derives from this domain of intuition. Duration, in addition, is subjective and virtual, while space is objective and actual. Thus do we encounter the terms that are fundamental to Deleuze's engagement with cinema. These terms are elaborated at even greater length in Bergson's major work, *Matter and Memory*, which also addresses the nature of the image.

Intuition

Intuition, as Deleuze has said, is more than just a feeling, but is Bergson's key method for illuminating the major themes of his philosophy, such as time, consciousness, the self, memory (see Deleuze 1991: 13). The reason for this is that Bergson needed a way to go beyond, or to relativise a fully-fledged analytical method. While analysis is deductive and breaks things down into their basic elements, intuition is inductive and synthetic. While analysis is valid according to whether formal, step by step, procedures are correct, intuition is correct according to the insights it facilitates. Time as duration is essentially only accessible to thought through intuition because analysis, in dissection (both virtual and real) of things, privileges discrete and immobile elements, whereas time is fluid and continuous. Indeed, without intuition as method duration and memory would remain, as Deleuze says, 'indeterminate from the point of view of knowledge' (Deleuze 1991: 14). Furthermore, intuition alone makes possible access to the self in time, that is, to interiority. Analysis, by contrast, always takes up an external position and thus has recourse to a representation. But the latter is not adequate to the task in hand because it is an objectification. The essential meaning of a poem, or the notion of totality, are only available through intuition, which Bergson also calls metaphysics. Keeping this method of intuition in mind, let us look in more detail at time and memory as these are addressed in Bergson's key work, *Matter and Memory*.

Time in Matter and Memory

The Image

An image, Bergson says in the work in question, is neither a simple representation nor a thing, but is half-way between them. Images are linked to sense experience and may be perceived. More radically, Bergson says that the body is an image which acts like other images and one image influences another according to 'the laws of nature'. Interiority and exteriority are a relationship between images. In sum: the image is the mode in which things can be grasped. But a thing is not an image, nor is an image a representation (Bergson 1993: 21).

Subsequently, Bergson goes on to show that images relate to space and time, but that time is always grasped spatially because it is linked to perception which 'freezes' things, in the manner of photography. Thus in a key passage, Bergson writes:

> All of the difficulty of the problem which concerns us comes from the fact that we represent perception as a photographic view of things, which would be taken, from a predetermined position, with a special apparatus, such as the organ of perception, and which would then develop in the cerebral substance by I do not what kind of chemical and psychical process. But how can it not be seen that photography, if there is photography, is

already taken, already printed, in the interior of things and for all points in space?

(Bergson 1993: 35–36)

Memory

If perception is linked to space and the freezing of the image, as in photography, action gives access to time. What of memory? It is distinct from perception: there is pure memory; the memory-image; and perception. To be sure, the memory-image is implicated in perception, even if it is qualitatively different from it. Although perception is, in principle, related to space and the immediate exterior world, this is an analytical distinction. In fact, perception is always accompanied by affect and memory. There is no pure perception. On the other hand, memory is not a weaker version of perception, but is different in kind. To equate memory and perception is also to blur the difference between past and present. The mistake is to see only a quantitative (a difference of intensity) and not a qualitative difference between memory and perception. This is essentially because memory has to do with time, not space.

There are, Bergson says, two kinds of memory: one is the involuntary memory of an event; the second is learning by rote, habitual activities and voluntary memories. Only the first is memory proper. Memory as habit is contrasted with the memory-image, or a recollection image. A habit memory is constituted through repetition, whereas the recollection, or memory-image proper rarely has this aspect. Recollection memory is thus not just a representation of time, but is time – the past – as captured in intuition, once we are prepared to give up the idea that recollection is a past present and is, instead, the actual past. Or rather, memory is simultaneously virtual and actual: it is virtual to the extent that it is memory, but actual to the extent that it is also an intuition of duration and the past *as* past. The point is to avoid conceiving pure memory as a weaker form of perception and to see that memory and perception are qualitatively different. Memory as a weak perception leads to its materialisation and the idealisation of sensation. Perception, which is in the present, is sensory–motor. Memory leaves its pure state and becomes an image, which then relates it to perception. For its part, the 'image is of the present and cannot participate in the past other than through the recollection from which it derives' (Bergson 1993: 156). While perception appears continuously in space, and memory appears discontinuously in time, perception is always already penetrated by memory. In other words, there is no pure perception and this implies that human experience is never absolutely in the present (in space), but also in the past (in time).

Being, or the Individual?

Finally, Bergson discusses the indivisibility of movement and time: movement, 'as the passage from one point of rest to another is absolutely indivisible' (Bergson 1993: 209; Bergson's emphasis). Against Zeno's paradox, based on the idea of time as a sequence of immobile sections, Bergson proclaims that movement is indivisible and that time cannot be reduced to a series of points in space. Often, this is what perception does: it immobilises and condenses. Points in space also serve to contract immense periods of time into a few moments. There is also a tendency to think that a state of rest precedes a state of mobility.

Although Bergson's notion of time is innovative and his method of intuition productive, his main focus in relation to time seems to be the individual, whether psychological or rational. Indeed, the spatialisation of time occurs principally through perception, the medium of individual experience. In other words, it often appears as though access to an understanding of time is more or less dependent on the limitations or capabilities of the human intellect or psyche, rather than on the nature of being, or on the way things are. Deleuze argues strongly that Bergson's focus is being, that the illusion of time as space is in the nature of things, and that, therefore, his claims have an ontological status. To the extent that Bergson is working in philosophy rather than social science, this claim might have some force. However, to the extent that Bergson himself speaks of the importance of linking philosophy to life (= existence: the mode of life as lived), rather than being, Deleuze's argument looks much less plausible.

References

Bergson, Henri (1991), *Essai sur les données immédiates de la conscience*, Paris: Quadrige/PUF.

Bergson, Henri (1993), *Matière et mémoire*, Paris: Quadrige/PUF.

Bergson, Henri (1998), *La Pensée et le mouvant*, Paris: Quadrige/PUF.

Deleuze, Gilles (1991), *Bergsonism*, trans. Hugh Tomlinson and Barbara Habberjam, New York: Zone Books.

See also: **Deleuze, Husserl, Levinas, Merleau-Ponty**

Bergson's major writings

Note: French titles are also given because, in one or two cases, there is considerable divergence in the English title from a literal rendering of the French.

(2005) *Laughter: An Essay on the Meaning of the Comic*, ((1900) *Le rire: Essai sur la signification du comique*) trans. Cloudesley Brereton and Fred Rothwell, Mineola, New York: Dover Publications.

(2002) *Key Writings*, ed. Keith Ansell Pearson and John Mullarkey; 'Mélanges', trans. Melissa McMahon, New York: Continuum.

(1965) *Duration and Simultaneity*, ((1922) *Durée et simultanéité: A propos de la théorie d'Einstein*) trans. Leon Jacobson, Indianapolis: Bobbs-Merrill.

(1946) *Creative Mind*, ((1938) *La Pensée et le mouvant*) trans. Mabelle L. Andison, Westport, Conn.: Greenwood Press.

(1935) *Two Sources of Morality and Religion*, ((1932) *Les deux sources de la morale et de la religion*) trans. R. Ashley Audra and Cloudesley Brereton with the assistance of W. Horsfall Carter, New York: Henry Holt & Co.

(1920) *Mind-Energy*, ((1919) *L'Energie spirituelle*) trans. H. Wildon Carr, New York: Henry Holt & Co.

(1919) *Time and Free Will*, ((1889) *Essai sur les données immédiates de la conscience*) trans. F.L. Pogson, London: George Allen & Unwin; New York: Macmillan & Co.

(1911a) *Matter and Memory*, ((1896) *Matière et mémoire: Essai sur la relation du corps à l'esprit*) trans. Nancy Margaret Paul and W. Scott Palmer, London: George Allen & Unwin.

(1911b) *Creative Evolution*, ((1907) *Évolution créatrice*) trans. Arthur Mitchell, New York: Henry Holt & Co; (1944) New York: Macmillan & Co.

Further Reading

Ansell Pearson, Keith (2002), *Philosophy and the Adventure of the Virtual: Bergson and the Time of Life*, New York: Routledge.

Deleuze, Gilles (1991), *Bergsonism*, trans. Hugh Tomlinson and Barbara Habberjam, New York: Zone Books.

Gerlac, Suzanne (2006), *Thinking in Time: An Introduction to Henri Bergson*, Ithaca: Cornell University Press.

Muldoon, Mark (2006), *Tricks of Time: Bergson, Merleau-Ponty and Ricoeur in Search of Time, Self and Meaning*, Pittsburgh, PA: Duquesne University.

GILLES DELEUZE (1925–1995)

While it is true that he rejected 'master–disciple relationships' (see Lecercle 1985), Nietzsche and Bergson's role in Gilles Deleuze's philosophical trajectory must be acknowledged: if, like Nietzsche,

Deleuze has few, if any, imitators, there is, nevertheless, a definite logic to this inimitable bearing: the logic of a thinker whose thought is radically horizontal, or rhizomatic, always intent on dismantling hierarchies.

Deleuze was born in Paris in 1925 in the 17th arrondissement, which contains the Place de Clichy, haunt of Henry Miller, an author Deleuze read seriously. He attended the Lycée Carnot in Paris, and studied philosophy at the Sorbonne between 1944 and 1948, where he knew, among others, Michel Butor, Michel Tournier and François Châtelet. His main teachers were Ferdinand Aliquié (Descartes specialist, and explicator of the philosophy of Surrealism), Georges Canguilhem (Foucault's supervisor) and Jean Hyppolite (Hegel specialist). After gaining his *agrégation* in philosophy in 1948, Deleuze taught philosophy, until 1957, in various *lycées*. From 1957 until 1960, he taught the history of philosophy at the Sorbonne, and for four years from 1960 he was a researcher with the Centre National de Recherche Scientifique (CNRS). From 1964 until his appointment in 1969, at the behest of Michel Foucault, as professor of philosophy at Vincennes, Deleuze taught at the University of Lyon. Also in 1969, Deleuze defended his major thesis, published as, *Difference and Repetition*, and his minor thesis, published as, *Spinoza et le problème de l'expression*. He retired from teaching in 1987. He died in Paris in 1995.

Broadly speaking, the argument of *Difference and Repetition* rests on the view that, in the contemporary era, the play of repetition and difference has supplanted that of the Same and representation. Difference and repetition are, in effect, indices of one key aspect of Deleuze's approach to philosophy: a move towards non-representational, and radically horizontal, thought. Deleuze is the supreme practitioner of this.

Horizontal Thought

Although the terms, 'horizontal' or 'vertical', or their variants (the Deleuzian term, 'rhizome', as noted above, already evokes horizontality, but the latter is broader in scope), do not actually figure largely in any explicit sense in Deleuze's *oeuvre*, they tend to illuminate its structure, and thus have a certain explanatory power. Radically horizontal thought can only be compared to other forms of thought with difficulty; for the means of translation are difficult to formulate. Such thought operates largely according to its own norms and concepts. For this reason, Deleuze, significantly, never embraced the history of philosophy as it has been conventionally defined by the discipline in France. For him, a philosopher who thinks (i.e. one who creates an event in thought), separates him or herself from the history of philosophy and enters the desert, so to speak. This horizontality, perhaps paradoxically, does not lead to an order of sameness (everyone on the same level), but to the instability of differences. Radical horizontality, then, is the quasi-order of radical difference, where a basis of comparison becomes problematic.

Again, the horizontal axis does not entail the firming of boundaries between identities, as is the case with representational thought based on the Same, but leads instead to the permeability of all boundaries and barriers. This is why horizontal thought by-passes (it does not oppose) the vertical thought of everyday, bureaucratic hierarchy – the thought which entails the consolidation of identities.

Nietzsche is the philosopher most akin to Deleuze when it comes to horizontality; for, like Deleuze, he severed his connection with mainstream philosophy, but not with the history of philosophy, which he knew so well. Deleuze's reading of Nietzsche thus offers a way into the labyrinth of horizontality, even though Nietzsche talks of the virtues of hierarchy. Such a hierarchy emerges out of difference, not identity. It is a matter of which entities will have the strength (psychological, physical, artistic, moral) to set themselves apart and be a hierarchy to themselves.

Deleuze also makes substantial use of the principle of horizontality in his readings of Spinoza, Proust, Leibniz and Lewis Carroll. Thus for Spinoza, 'expression' is not an appearance through which an essence is expressed. Nor is morality a set of ideals to which one might aspire. Expression is rather a way of being and acting in the world, while morality is 'an ethics of joy' which enhances the power of acting (Deleuze 1988: 28). With Proust, the focus is on signs, not on signs as representations of objects, meanings, or truth, or – as one might have thought in the case of *In Search of Lost Time* (Proust 1992) – on signs as vehicles for memory, but on signs as entities which teach something. In Proust's writing, to interpret signs is to go through a fundamental learning process, which, in the case of the work of art, shows that signs are linked to essences, and that essences are constituted through differences (they are not unities, but singular qualities) within which subjects are implicated. Again, Deleuze shows that when Leibniz invented the concept of the 'fold' in philosophy – a concept inspired by the Baroque period in the history of art – he opened the way to a new practice of philosophy as the constitution of disjunctive figures. The fold is the mode of unity of these figures (e.g. the monad). More precisely, the fold is the relationship of difference with itself. Finally, the horizontal emerges in the reading of Lewis Carroll in a book – *The Logic of Sense* – constructed (or assembled) in series. Series can, by definition, proliferate; and, as Lecercle points out, 'proliferation is always a threat to order' (Lecercle 1985: 95). The horizontal would thus be equivalent to the proliferation of series.

In his collaborative work with Felix Guattari, the principle of horizontality which marks Deleuze's own philosophy is strikingly evident in the critique of Freud and psychoanalysis. For Deleuze and Guattari, Freud's theory of the Oedipus complex serves to confirm the dominance of hierarchical and 'tree-like' thought. The Oedipus principle, they say, inevitably leads to the notion of an original event, or trauma, which the authors of *Anti-Oedipus* find unimaginatively reductive. Phrases like, 'desiring machines' and 'body without organs' reinforce the theory's horizontality. We have seen that desire is not a desire based on lack – which is negative – but is always in movement and reforming itself: it is an affirmative process of flows and lines of flight The 'body without organs' (the term is borrowed from Antonin Artaud) is, perhaps predictably, not at all an organic body (a body with organs, 'the body of Oedipal reduction'), but a body like the body politic, one that is always in the process of formation and deformation. The body without organs is produced in a connective synthesis, and is neither an image of the body, nor a projection. In short, the body without organs is 'rhizomatic' and not engendered, or tree-like.

Horizontality, finally, is indicated in Deleuze's study of sensation in *Francis Bacon: The Logic of Sensation* (Deleuze 1992) on the painting of Francis Bacon. Here, the image is not understood as either representational or cerebral, but is a locus of intensities that Bacon paints prior to any model. The flux of sensation, in effect, throws up its own model.

Hume

The 'key' ideas which Deleuze develops in his first book on Hume carry through to his later works. These ideas are that: (1) subjectivity does not exist prior to experience; (2) experience, in the form of perceptions as ideas and impressions, is initially un-organised but becomes so, progressively; and, most importantly, (3) a relationship is external to its terms. Out of this we see that heterogeneous experience is made up of a multiplicity of perceptions, but that the relationship between these is external to the content of the individual perceptions themselves. In short: the content of perceptions does not enable one to predict the kind of subjectivity (or 'mind') that will emerge. The same applies with causality: causality is a relationship, the nature of which is independent of the nature of the elements which constitute it. On this basis, Hume can say that causality is contingent (derived from custom, or habit), and not an essential phenomenon. Even 'place' means 'taking place' (Deleuze 2001: 23). It is the event, the happening, which constitutes place. Place is not then an a priori principle, or model, which is endlessly available for conceptualising all the different versions of place.

Furthermore, representation has little to do with Hume's project because 'representations *cannot* present relations' (Deleuze 2001: 30, Deleuze's emphasis). A whole is made up of relations and therefore cannot be represented. The issue, then, is the relationship of the whole to its parts. Traditionally, two views have been supported on this question: one is that the whole is the outcome of the nature – or quality – of the parts themselves, the other is that a relationship between the parts, which is the whole, is different from the qualities attributable to each of the parts. Hume's position on this could not be clearer than when he is considering the nature of personal identity (Hume (1970 [1739]): 300–312). Each personal identity is a 'bundle or collection of different perceptions, which succeed each other with an inconceivable rapidity, and are in a perpetual flux and movement' (Hume (1970: 302). In other words, for Hume, there is no prior form (identity) to the totality of perceptions. The reality is difference; the desired outcome is identity. However, in classical empiricist style Hume denies that there is an essential identity in this diversity. Personal identity is a fiction – albeit a necessary fiction (cf. Hume 1970: 308). Because the volume and diversity of human perceptions is so great, memory, as essentially limited, becomes an arbitrary form imposed on this diversity. Memory, too, then participates in the fiction of identity.

But Hume's most telling point, as far as Deleuze's reading is concerned, is that 'identity is really nothing belonging to these different perceptions, and uniting them together, but is merely a quality which we attribute to them' (Hume 1970: 309). In Deleuze's language: a relation is external to the terms which make it up.

Deleuze thus finds that Hume is probably the first thinker of the modern era to take a synthetic approach to subjectivity. The subject is not given in advance, but is individuated. The subject is a set of relations and is thus external to the terms which make it up. It is explicable in terms of Hume's 'atomism', to the extent that the collection of ideas in the mind is a set of relations. Causality, famously, is a set of relations based on habit. Given this privileging of relations, we can say, in the language of complexity theory and that of artificial life, that the subject is emergent: it is not there as a blueprint in advance; instead it *becomes* what it is. The chapter, 'Empiricism and Subjectivity', which mirrors the book's title, offers further evidence of Deleuze's amazingly contemporary reading of Hume. For the subject is a 'collection of ideas' that form a system of relations – or, we could say, in order to maintain a contemporary language, that the subject is a specific mode of organisation.

Bergson

It is important to remember that Bergson was always the other contender for special attention, and not more so than in Deleuze's thinking about cinema.

Deleuze proposes that time is the essence of cinema – time being initially accessed through movement before it becomes directly apprehended in the time-image. In the wake of Bergson's discussion of the image and time, Deleuze argues that photography provided, and still provides, an analogy of analytical thought (the eternal moment) based in space, so cinema provides an analogy for synthetic thought based in time. Narrative which, to the extent that it is closed, is analytical, comes from images (rather than images from narrative) – just as written music is a denotation of sound, not the organiser of sound.

Deleuze finds his inspiration for a synthetic notion of time in the claim that the cinematographic 'method', which Bergson saw as a version of photography, not only gave us an intellectualist notion of time (time as a series of discrete units), but it also dominated 'perception, intellection, language' and science (Bergson 1998: 305 and 329). Were this to be the case, it would have important sociological and philosophical implications reaching far beyond the significance of cinema as a purveyor of values in modern society. For it would demonstrate that time as such, time as found in memory, has not yet been fully understood.

An implication of Bergson's approach is that time cannot be grasped analytically with the help of perception. Perception spatialises time and turns it into a present moment, whereas time, as an experience (in memory), cannot grasp itself as such. It can only be accessed through intuition. This is why Deleuze refers to a cinematic whole as synthetic:

> the whole must renounce its ideality, and become the synthetic whole of the film which is realised in the montage of the parts;

and, conversely, the parts must be selected, coordinated, enter into connections and liaisons which, through montage, reconstitute the virtual sequence shot or the analytic whole of the cinema.

(Deleuze 1986: 27)

The Time-Image

With the time-image in post-Second World War cinema, time ceases to be beholden to movement, which is an indirect presentation of time, and becomes pure presentation of time. After the movement-image – after the sensory-motor dimension is displaced in importance: the nature of the image itself (its sonorous and optical materiality) becomes the protagonist of the film. Movement derives from the time-image, not the reverse. The crystal image is a crystal of time. 'The eye is not the camera it is the screen' (Deleuze 1990: 78).

'The postulate of "the image in the present" is one of the most destructive for any understanding of cinema' (Deleuze 1989: 39). A *'pure optical and sound situation'* gives rise to a *'direct time-image.* Opsigns and sonsigns are direct presentations of time' (Deleuze: 1989: 41). Time is in the dispersal of the image. Chance events take over from organically organised events; thought is evoked.

On another level, the time-image has to by-pass a pure perception image based in space (the visuality of the image), and throw up something else. In order to arrive here, at this 'something else', it is first necessary to put aside some common attitudes towards film – attitudes which obscure the nature of Deleuze's approach.

In the first place, cinema cannot be understood as a medium. Instead, it has to be understood as a reality. Were it a medium, its contents would, in principle, be translatable into other media. The same idea could be available in a novel, a radio play or a philosophical treatise. Cinema must be connected to memory (time) in such a way that it becomes clear that the memory (time) itself is cinematic.

Secondly, cinema images are not representations. One reason for this is that cinema does not represent time – it is the unfolding of time itself. Another reason is that representation evokes the re-presentation of a present moment. This, in turn, is to understand cinema photographically as the re-capturing of a moment frozen in time.

The point made by Deleuze in his discussion of Resnais is revealing:

When we say that Resnais' characters are philosophers, we are certainly not saying that these characters talk about philosophy, or that Resnais 'applies' philosophical ideas to a cinema, but that he invents a *cinema of philosophy*, a *cinema of thought*, which is totally new in the history of cinema and totally alive in the history of philosophy.

(Deleuze 1989: 209, emphasis added)

Instead of thinking cinema – which could mean turning it into a photograph – thought becomes cinematic.

Creativity in Philosophy

Overall, there is no doubt that Deleuze was one of the most self-consciously creative philosophers of the contemporary era. Although he thought from the position of someone steeped in the history of philosophy, his philosophy seems to have struck a democratic chord in many English-speaking countries. In being synthetic in orientation (which, in the end, comprehends horizontal thought), Deleuze's thinking puts purely analytical thought in its place, while pursuing in philosophy an approach normally found in artistic endeavour. As Kant said of genius, this means that Deleuze can have no true imitator.

References

Bergson, Henri (1998), *L'Évolution créatrice*, Paris: PUF.

Deleuze, Gilles (1983), *Nietzsche and Philosophy*, trans. Hugh Tomlinson, New York: Columbia University Press.

—— (1986), *Cinema 1: The Movement Image*, trans. Hugh Tomlinson and Barbara Habberjam, Minneapolis: University of Minnesota Press.

—— (1988), *Spinoza: Practical Philosophy*, trans. Robert Hurley, San Francisco: City Lights Books.

—— (1989), *Cinema 2: The Time Image*, trans. Hugh Tomlinson and Robert Galeta, Minneapolis: University of Minnesota Press.

—— (1990), *Pourparlers, 1972–1990*, Paris: Minuit.

—— (1992 [1981]) *Francis Bacon: The Logic of Sensation*, 2 vols, trans. Daniel Smith, Cambridge, Mass.: MIT Press.

—— (2000), *Proust and Signs: The Complete Text*, trans. Richard Howard, Minneapolis: University of Minnesota Press.

—— (2001), *Empiricism and Subjectivity: An Essay on Hume's Theory of Human Nature*, trans. Constantin V. Boundas, New York: Columbia University Press, paperback edition.

Deleuze, Gilles and Guattari, Félix. (1984), *Anti-Oedipus: Capitalism and Schizophrenia*, trans Robert Hurley, Mark Seem and Helen R. Lane, London: Athlone.

Hume, David (1970 [1739]), *Treatise on Human Nature. Book I: Of the Understanding*, London and Glasgow: Fontana/Collins.

Lecercle, Jean-Jacques (1985), *Philosophy through the Looking-Glass: Language, Nonsense, Desire*, La Salle, Illinois: Open Court.

Proust, Marcel (1992), *In Search of Lost Time*, trans C.K. Scott Montcrieff and Terence Kilmartin, revised by D.J. Enright, London: Vintage.

See also: **Bergson, Lacan, Nietzsche**

Deleuze's major writings

(2007) *Dialogues II. Gilles Deleuze and Claire Parnet* (Revised Edition), trans. Hugh Tomlinson and Barbara Habberjam, New York: Columbia University Press.

(2006 [2003]) *Two Regimes of Madness: Texts and Interviews 1975–1995*, trans Ames Hodges and Mike Taorina, ed. David Lapoujade, Los Angeles: Semiotext(e); Cambridge, Mass.: Distributed by MIT Press.

(2004 [2002]) *Desert Islands and Other Texts, 1953–1974* trans Ames Hodges and Mike Taorina, ed. David Lapoujade, Los Angeles: Semiotext(e); Cambridge, Mass.: Distributed by MIT Press.

(2001a [1953]) *Empiricism and Subjectivity: An Essay on Hume's Theory of Human Nature*, trans. Constantin V. Boundas, New York: Columbia University Press, paperback edition.

(2001b) *Pure Immanence: Essays on a Life*, trans. Anne Boymen, ed. John Rajchaman, New York: Zone Books.

(2000 [1964 and 1970]), *Proust and Signs: The Complete Text*, trans. Richard Howard, Minneapolis: University of Minnesota Press.

(1997 [1993]) *Essays Critical and Clinical*, trans. Daniel W. Smith and Michael A. Greco, Minnesota: University of Minnesota Press.

(1994a [1991]) with Felix Guattari, *What is Philosophy?* trans. Hugh Tomlinson and Graham Burchall, New York: Columbia University Press.

(1994b [1990]) *Interviews, 1972–1990*, New York, Columbia University Press.

(1994c [1969]) *Difference and Repetition*, trans. Paul Patton, London: The Athlone Press.

(1993), *The Deleuze Reader*, ed. Constantin Boundas, New York: Columbia University Press.

(1992a [1988]) *The Fold: Leibniz and the Baroque*, trans. Tom Conley, Minneapolis: University of Minnesota Press.

(1992b [1981]) *Francis Bacon: The Logic of Sensation*, 2 vols, trans. Daniel Smith, Cambridge, Mass.: MIT Press.

(1990a 1968]) *Expressionism in Philosophy: Spinoza*, trans. Martin Joughin, New York: Zone Books.

(1990b [1969]) *The Logic of Sense*, trans. Mark Lester, ed. C.V. Boundas, New York: Columbia University Press.

(1988a [1981]) *Spinoza: Practical Philosophy*, trans. Robert Hurley, San Francisco: City Lights Books.

(1988b [1966]) *Bergsonism*, trans. Hugh Tomlinson and Barbara Habberjam, New York: Zone Books.

(1987a [1980]) with Felix Guattari, *A Thousand Plateaus: Capitalism and Schizophrenia*, trans. Brian Massumi, Minneapolis: University of Minnesota Press.

(1987b [1977]) with Claire Parnet, *Dialogues*, trans. Hugh Tomlinson and Barbara Habberjam, New York: Columbia University Press.

(1986 [1975]) with Félix Guattari, *Kafka: Toward a Minor Literature*, trans. Dana Polan, Minneapolis: University of Minnesota Press.

(1984 [1963]) *Kant's Critical Philosophy: The Doctrine of the Faculties* trans. Hugh Tomlinson and Barbara Habberjam, Minneapolis, University of Minnesota Press.

(1983 [1962]) *Nietzsche and Philosophy*, trans. Hugh Tomlinson, New York: Columbia University Press.

(1977 [1972]) with Félix Guattari, *Anti-Oedipus: Capitalism and Schizophrenia*, trans. Robert Hurley, M. Seem and H.R. Lane, New York: Viking Press/ A Richard Sever Book.

Further reading

Badiou, Alain (2000), *Deleuze: The Clamour of Being*, trans. Louise Burchill, Minneapolis: University of Minnesota Press.

Colebrook, Claire (2006), *Deleuze: A Guide for the Perplexed*, London and New York: Continuum.

Khalfa, Jean, ed. (1999), *An Introduction to the Philosophy of Gilles Deleuze*, New York and London: Continuum.

Lecercle, Jean-Jacques (1985), *Philosophy Through the Looking Glass*, La Salle, Illinois: Open Court.

Žižek, Slavoj (2004), *Organs Without Bodies: Deleuze and Consequences*, New York: Routledge.

SIGMUND FREUD (1856–1939)

Sigmund Freud was born into a Jewish family in 1856 in Freiburg. When he was four, his family moved to Vienna where Freud lived and worked until 1938, when he was forced to flee to England after the Anschluss. Although he always complained about the oppressiveness of Vienna, Freud not only lived there nearly all his life, but he lived with his family at the same address for nearly fifty years: the famous Berggasse 19.

Freud was a brilliant student, topping every year at the Gymnasium, and graduating with distinction in 1873. In 1881, he took his medical degree from the University of Vienna, and in 1885 won a scholarship to go to Paris to study under the great Jean Martin

Charcot, at Salpetrière. To Freud, Charcot not only opened the way to taking mental illness seriously, with his diagnosis of hysteria and the use of hypnosis; he was also a charismatic yet encouraging teacher for whom Freud had a lasting admiration. Upon his return to Vienna in 1886, Freud set up practice as a physician. He later died in London in 1939.

During his university years, the future psychoanalyst worked in the laboratory of the physiologist and positivist, Ernst Brücke. Brücke's contemporary and influential colleague, Hermann Helmholtz – who, among other things, wrote on thermodynamics – was also an early influence on the young Freud, as was the physicist and philosopher, Gustav Fechner. All three were representatives of the medical positivism and vitalism which reigned in Vienna and elsewhere during the last three decades of the nineteenth century. Their influence can be seen in particular in Freud's theory of 'bound' and 'unbound' psychical energy in the posthumously published, 'Project for a scientific psychology'. In the same year, 1895, Freud and Breuer, initially basing their work on the case of Anna O, published their *Studies in Hysteria* (Freud and Breuer 1895). Freud's research into psychical activity was thus pushed in a new direction. For what seemed to bring about Anna O's recovery through catharsis (release of tension), was, as the patient put it, the 'talking cure'. In effect, the 'talking cure' is the result of proceeding according to the physicalist or vitalist model of the psyche: tension is released (homeostasis is attained) through talking and interpretation – that is, through a manipulation of meaning(s).

The Challenge of Freud

It is a cliché to say that Freud was a man of his time – that he had the values of a nineteenth-century bourgeois, that he was influenced by scientific positivism and vitalism, that certain Victorian attitudes coloured his views about sexuality. From another angle, though, Freud is a thinker who was, and in all likelihood will remain, both controversial in what he had to say about sexuality and the psyche, and brilliantly disturbing in the way he founded psychoanalysis through the analysis of phenomena which were hitherto thought to be unanalysable – dreams, and slips of the tongue, for example.

Freud's text is more than challenging in what it says as a (relatively) discrete entity; it is also, and even primarily, challenging as the trace of a grand intellectual odyssey in which psychoanalysis undergoes a subtle transformation within a body of texts that is always evolving.

In part, this transformation results from Freud himself not being entirely in control of the concepts (e.g. life, death, drive, pleasure, ego, conscious, unconscious) he seeks to explicate, and this is because these concepts are often unstable in themselves. In short, Freud, who emphasised the importance of engaging continually in interpretation – Freud, who said that, ultimately, a psychoanalysis was interminable – this Freud must himself be interpreted in light of the notion of 'unlimited interpretation' that he inaugurated.

Consequently, perhaps one of the most interesting readings of Freud has been done by the French psychoanalyst, and student of Jacques Lacan, Jean Laplanche. Very briefly, Laplanche has suggested that, as concerns the concepts of life and death in particular, almost the whole of the Freudian corpus – from the 'Project for a scientific psychology', written in 1895 (Freud 1950), passing especially by *Beyond the Pleasure Principle* of 1920 (Freud 1920), to 'The economic problem of masochism' of 1924 (Freud 1924) – can be seen in terms of a chiasmus, where what was life (homeostasis) at the beginning becomes death (Thanatos), and what was death (unbound energy) in the beginning becomes life (Eros) (Laplanche 1976). Laplanche shows that there is indeed no substitute for actually reading Freud.

As Laplanche goes on to argue, the cross-over from the vitalist model of the psyche, witnessed in the analysis of hysteria, is more dramatically seen in a case study recounted in the 1895 'Project', a text which sets out most clearly the quantitative model of the psyche – the psyche as 'a kind of economics of nervous force', as Freud wrote in a letter to Fliess. The case in question concerns a young woman, Emma, who has a fear of going into shops alone. In analysis, Emma relates her symptom to the memory of going into a shop at the age of twelve, seeing two shop assistants laughing together, and fleeing in fright from the shop. Analytic investigation reveals that behind this scene, there is another: at the age of eight Emma went into a shop to buy some sweets, and the shopkeeper fondled her genitals through her clothes. At the time, however, Emma did not find the experience traumatic. What is significant about these two scenes is that the first is traumatic as a memory, but innocent as an event, whereas the second (chronologically the first) is potentially traumatic as an event but remains innocent as a memory – precisely because it was not experienced as traumatic. It was not until the intervening period of puberty had given the violation its full significance that it became traumatic in a psychical sense, but then only as a memory trace, only through displacement, we could say. The notion of displacement here is crucial, for it makes the categorical attribution of a trauma to a physical event impossible. Rather, it suggests that any notion of trauma in a human sense has to take account of its retrospective *meaning*. In other words, a physicalist or vitalist understanding of the psyche is inadequate. Such would be the way in which the very reality of displacement – which Freud outlined most fully in *The Interpretation of Dreams* (Freud 1900) – reveals itself within the structure of Freud's own text, when he is led to modify his positivistic theory of psychical life through an encounter with the facts of the psyche itself – those of his own psyche, encountered in self-analysis, as much as those of his patients.

The Psyche, Meaning and Dreams

The psyche is thus a meaning structure before it is a physical entity. It has to do with symbolic processes, and so calls for interpretation. Once the element of interpretation is seen to be crucial to psychical life, a quantitative – and more latterly, a behaviourist – model of the psyche becomes inadequate. Perhaps more than anything else, this apparent division in Freud's work between the physical-cum-biological level, and the symbolic level has been the centre of numerous debates and misunderstandings. With regard to sexuality, for example, many Anglo-American commentators have been moved to dismiss Freud's theory of sexuality because they read it in terms of biology – that is positivistically, not symbolically.

In the *Interpretation of Dreams*, Freud begins by clearly stating that in his effort to bring about a more profound understanding of dreams his method differs from earlier ones in that he will not be relying on a pre-existing dream code. He thus proposes to consider dream material on its own terms. Broadly speaking, Freud shows that dream interpretation has to be of a particular kind because a dream is the fulfilment of a wish – broadly, the wish that it not be understood at the level of its manifest content. A dream invariably contains a disguised message relating to the dreamer's sexuality. Taken literally, many people might think (many people have thought!) that this is an incredible claim. How is it possible to be sure that a dream is essentially about sexuality? The short answer is that sexuality is essentially disguised – has to be disguised, we could add. By this is meant that sexuality has to do with signs and the symbolic. It is not an animal urge (although Freud himself at times appears to be attracted to such a view), but permeates all the displacements of social and cultural life. Displacement here means circuitous path. In *The Interpretation of Dreams*, Freud defines displacement as one of the ways dream-work disguises the unconscious message of the dream. Together with condensation, it forms part of the primary process. Displacement refers to the way that an element, or elements, in the manifest content of the dream may be insignificant, or even absent in the latent content: the dream-thoughts. Condensation refers to the way the manifest content of a dream is meagre by comparison with the wealth of dream-thoughts which may be derived from it. Each dream element may give rise to multiple lines of association. This Freud called over-determination. Displacement and condensation therefore entail that a dream calls for interpretation (it cannot be equated with its manifest content). These two processes are, furthermore, two aspects of the dream-work which serve to disguise the dream's true meaning (inevitably sexual), and which thereby enable the fulfilment of a wish: the masking of unconscious thoughts.

As we noted earlier, Freud's point of departure is that there is no pre-given code for interpreting a dream. Each element (usually an image) must be interpreted as though for the first time. This is because a dream is less a product of linguistic processes, and more a language in its own might: it approximates an ideolect. It is perhaps because Freud showed how a dream stretched language and inter-pretation to the limit that his work has become influential in fields outside psychoanalysis dealing with the interpretation of texts.

The Unconscious and its Disguises

To understand the significance of disguise and distortion in dreams, Freud shows that it is also necessary to understand the role of repression. Repression, of course, is very closely linked to the unconscious. And unconscious dream thoughts are what are repressed. From one point of view, the dreamer – and, subsequently, the analysand – represses painful and traumatic memories of a sexual nature; repression, on this reading, is primarily a form of defence. However, in the wake of the work of Jacques Lacan, a more structural interpretation has been given to repression. Repression is now associated with the very formation of the subject in language and the symbolic. It would be what makes possible the very distinction between subject and object. But if this is so, why is it necessary to gain access to repressed material? If repression is a structural necessity, why does it have to be 'uncovered'? The answer in part is, as Freud showed, that repression can break down, resulting in a symptom (which Freud calls a compromise formation) and unconscious repe-tition. The former appears inexplicable to the subject, and the latter often escapes consciousness altogether. In both cases the aim becomes one of interpreting the symptom and the repetition, thereby confirming, and perhaps expanding, the domain of the symbolic. The unconscious *par excellence* is the sexual trauma: namely, that which cannot be said or symbolised, and which is known only by its effects in the symbolic. On this basis, obscenity would be the cross-over point between the symbolic and the unconscious (trauma).

Oedipus, Id, Ego and Superego

Freud, of course, is also known as the formulator of the concept of the Oedipus complex. Literally speaking, this is the phenomenon observed by Freud (and it figures in his own self-analysis) where the son (like Oedipus of the Greek myth) unconsciously wants to have done with his father in order to sleep with his mother. A related theme emerges in *Totem and Taboo* (1912–13), where Freud refers to the myth of the killing and devouring of the violent father in Darwin's primal horde. The sons, in an act of contrition and guilt, give up immediate access to the father's women, and so institute the symbolic order: the order of the law. Oedipus and the story of the primal horde both illustrate the way that the unconscious (the primary process) is always trying to avoid repression and thus by-pass the symbolic order (the secondary process). It leaves its mark in the symbolic as a symptom (such as slips of the tongue).

A strand of Freud's thought that has caused much debate is the notion of the ego. Freud defined the ego in relation to two other terms: the id – or reservoir of affective energy – and the super-ego – the ego-ideal, or the representative of external reality. A major point of contention has been over whether the ego is equal to the whole personality – in which case it would incorporate the id and the superego within itself – or whether the ego is an agency attempting to distinguish itself from the other two (id and super-ego). While the first view opens up the possibility of an ego ultimately identical with itself, the second renders problematic the very possibility of self-identity.

Another complicating factor in relation to the ego is narcissism. Here, the ego-subject makes itself an object to itself, once again bringing into question the notion of an entity identical with itself. For its part, American ego-psychology has tended to view the ego as the centre of perception and consciousness, thus opening up the possibility of an ego with a capacity for complete self-awareness. Whatever else one might say, Freud's text leaves no doubt as to the ambiguity which reigns throughout it in relation to the ego, and, we can add, in relation to a good many of the key concepts of psychoanalysis. And perhaps this is only to be expected from an *oeuvre* in continual evolution, one which, in the end, seeks to throw light on the very mechanisms of its own production.

Freud in the Twenty-First Century

Given Freud's apparent modesty and good faith in searching for the truth, we need to explain why psychoanalysis is not now lauded to the skies, if not for having solved problems related to understanding the psyche and human relations, at least for having placed things in a proper theoretical and research perspective. This is not the case for two main reasons.

The first is related to the ebb and flow of ideas in a discipline dealing with the nature of the psyche. Thus, at the moment, cognitive psychology is in the ascendency, which, in light of sophisticated computer modelling of the brain and the development of more effective psychotropic drugs for treating psychic dysfunction, means that psychoanalysis has had to take a back seat. Analysis is viewed as too time consuming and imprecise; the cure takes time; it is too much like an art, rather than a science. Moreover, the meaning of key psychoanalytic terms is continually contested. In short, psychoanalysis is not for today's fast, and increasingly faster, world. And it is true: psychoanalysis presupposes a certain kind of world in order to flourish.

Given this state of affairs, the hostility towards the perceived lack of scientific rigour in psychoanalysis is almost beyond belief. An example of this is to be found in Todd Dufresne's *Killing Freud* (2005).

The second reason for the difficulty of psychoanalysis in the popularity stakes – at least from an outsider's perspective – is the institutional crises that relate from everything from rules of clinical practice to who should be the custodian of Freud's word. Critics have a field day in pointing up the seemingly deep-seated and irreconcilable differences in the profession. Rather than defending this, we need to be bear in mind that such differences might have an impact on clinical practice, but they do not prevent anyone who chooses to read Freud and explore psychoanalysis themselves. Were they to do so, they might come to the realisation that when it comes to psychic life the battle of egos is 'normal', even if it is unpleasant for many of those closely involved.

A Broader View

More broadly, Freud left a wide-ranging and heterogeneous *oeuvre*: works based on a biological model of the psyche; meta-psychological works outlining key concepts; case studies derived from clinical practice; autobiographical and historical works; works based on anthropological and historical data; studies of everyday life, and didactic works which sought to explain psychoanalysis to a wider public. Perhaps what he left overall, however, is an *oeuvre* that does not conceal the process of its own evolution: the false starts, the discoveries, the continual modification of key concepts are all there. This means that for the contemporary reader, Freud's most enduring legacy is that his text, more than ever, calls for interpretation.

References

Dufresne, Todd (2005), *Killing Freud: Twentieth-Century Culture and the Death of Psychoanalysis*, London and New York: Continuum.
Freud, Sigmund (1962–75), *The Standard Edition of the Complete Psychological Works of Sigmund Freud* (hereafter, *SE*), trans. under the general editorship of James Strachey, London: Hogarth Press. Works mentioned in the above article with date of first publication and *SE* volume number are:
—— (with Joseph Breuer) (1895) *Studies in Hysteria*, SE, 2.
—— (1900), *The Interpretation of Dreams*, SE, 4–5.
—— (1920), *Beyond the Pleasure Principle*, SE, 18.
—— (1924), 'The economic problem of masochism', SE, 19.
—— (1912–13), *Totem and Taboo*, SE, 9.
—— (1950) 'Project for a scientific psychology [of 1895]' (posthumous), SE, 1.
Laplanche, Jean (1976) *Life and Death in Psychoanalysis*, trans. Jeffrey Mehlman, Baltimore: Johns Hopkins University Press.

See also: **Irigaray, Kristeva, Lacan, Žižek**

Freud's major writings

(1962–75) *The Standard Edition of the Complete Psychological Works of Sigmund Freud*, trans. under the general editorship of James Strachey, in collaboration with Anna Freud, assisted by Alix Strachey and Alan Tyson, London: Hogarth Press. This is the standard reference for all of Freud's works in English..

Further reading

Cohen, Josh (2005), *How to Read Freud*, New York: Norton.
Flieger, Jerry Aline (2005), *Is Oedipus on Line? Siting Freud after Freud*, Cambridge, Mass.: MIT Press.

Forrester, John (1997), *Dispatches from the Freud Wars: Psychoanalysis and its Passions*, Cambridge, Mass.: Harvard University Press.

Jones, Ernest (1953–57), *The Life and Work of Sigmund Freud*, 3 vols, New York: Basic Books.

Laplanche, Jean (1976), *Life and Death in Psychoanalysis*, trans. Jeffrey Mehlman, Baltimore: Johns Hopkins University Press.

Levine, Michael P., ed. (2000) *The Analytic Freud: Philosophy and Psychoanalysis*, London and New York: Routledge.

MacIntyre, Alasdair (2004) *The Unconscious: A Conceptual Analysis*, Rev. edition, New York: Routledge.

Sédat, Jacques (2005) *Freud*, New York: Other Press.

JULIA KRISTEVA (b.1941)

Julia Kristeva was born in 1941 in Sliven in Bulgaria and, as a student, came to Paris in 1965. She immediately became immersed in Parisian intellectual life, attending the seminars of Roland Barthes and becoming involved with the writers and intellectuals from the avant-garde literary journal, *Tel Quel*, edited by Philippe Sollers. *Tel Quel* at the end of the 1960s quickly became a leading force in the critique of representation – in writing as much as in politics – and this influence has been a lasting one.

Since arriving in Paris, Kristeva has achieved academic success, publishing her *Doctorat de 3e cycle* in 1971; defending, then publishing, her highly commended *Doctorat d'État* in 1974. Appointed as professor of linguistics at the University of Paris, Denis Diderot in 1973, Kristeva was elected as permanent visiting professor at Columbia University and the University of Toronto. She is also the recipient of eight honorary doctorates, and the winner, in 2004, of the prestigious Norwegian Holberg prize for her innovative work at the intersection 'between linguistics, culture and literature'.

Novel of the Self, Novel of the Subject

Despite the Holberg prize citation, Julia Kristeva is for many outside France best known as a feminist theorist. And while it is true that the psychoanalytic orientation of her work has led her to reflect upon the nature of the feminine (which she sees as the source of the unnameable and inexpressible), she has always maintained a clear interest in the nature of language and its manifestations. Indeed Kristeva demonstrated this interest in 1990 in a very practical way by publishing a *roman à clé*: *The Samurai* (*Les Samouraïs*). Like de Beauvoir's

Mandarins, which Kristeva's title recalls, *The Samurai*, too, is ostensibly a vivisection of the lives and loves of the Parisian intellectual avant-garde. This time, Kristeva's own generation – the one coming after Sartre – are the focus of attention.

After the publication of her most recent novel, *Murder in Byzantium* (2006) (her third detective novel), Kristeva indicated in an interview that she saw the novel today as a space where the imaginary could still find an outlet in a globalised, and therefore standardised, world. Furthermore, through the novel, a reformulation of psychic diversity might be possible (Kristeva 2005a: 84), but only provided if it is understood as a novel of the subject, and thus of the unconscious, not one of the self (a representation) or of the ego, of every-day consciousness. (Kristeva 2005b: 86–87). The subject is the actual process of language, of meaning, of the instantiation of identities, which are continually surpassed. Here we have an echo of the subject in process, made famous in *Revolution in Poetic Language* (1984).

More specifically, the detective novel, with its inevitable murder investigation, enables an exploration in society of violence and its ava-tars and of the articulation of the Freudian death drive of destruction. All this can be explored against the backdrop of the loss of religiosity and spirituality. Neither science nor philosophy can provide such an opportunity because they are more concerned with the level of the self and representation.

A predominant feature of Kristeva's work is its concern to bring the unanalysable into the experience of language: the inexpressible, heterogeneous, radical otherness of individual and cultural life. Although this could open the way to mysticism, bringing what is hitherto unanalysable into the symbolic prevents this. Kristeva's later writing, in particular, clearly alludes to the folly of any complete abandonment to otherness.

Language and the Semiotic

In the late 1960s Kristeva introduced the work of the Russian form-alist, Mikhail Bakhtin, to a European audience (see Kristeva 1986: 34–61). Freud and psychoanalysis were not then part of her intellec-tual universe when she highlighted Bakhtin's theory of the 'dialogical' novel, as well as his notion of 'carnival'. Soon after, Kristeva estab-lished herself as an important theorist of language and literature in her own right with the concept of 'semanalysis' (Kristeva 1969 and 1986: 24–33). Semanalysis focuses on poetics as the materiality of language (its sounds, rhythms and graphic disposition), rather than simply on its communicative function. As materiality, poetic language disrupts meaning, or at least opens the way to a range of new meanings, and even to new ways of understanding.

Kristeva's interest in analysing the heterogeneous nature of poetic language while she was still a student in Paris in the late 1960s and early 1970s, distinguished her from other semioticians, who were exclusively interested in formalising the conventional workings of language. It gave her a taste for grasping language as a dynamic, transgressive process rather than a static instrument, as the analyses of linguists implied. The static view is tied to the notion that language is reducible to those dimensions (such as logical propositions) that can be apprehended by consciousness, to the exclusion of the material, heterogeneous and unconscious dimension.

The Subject in Process and Poetic Language

Eventually, an interest in the unconscious leads Kristeva to develop her theory of the subject as a subject-in-process, a subject that is continually reforming itself. The subject, then, is never simply the static, punctual subject of consciousness: it is never simply the static phenomenon captured in a representation; it is also its unspeakable, unnameable, repressed form, which can only be known through its effects.

The connection between language and its importance in the formation of the subject led Kristeva, in 1974, to develop a theory of the 'semiotic' (le sémiotique) in her doctoral thesis, La révolution du langage poétique [Revolution in Poetic Language]. Here, she distinguishes le sémiotique from both la sémiotique (conventional semiotics) and the 'symbolic' – the sphere of representations, images, and all forms of fully articulated language. At the explicitly textual level, the semiotic and the symbolic correspond respectively to what are called the 'genotext' and the 'phenotext'. The genotext Kristeva says, 'is not linguistic' 'it is rather a process' (Kristeva 1984: 87). It is language's foundation. The 'phenotext', by contrast, corresponds to the language of communication. It is the level at which we normally read when searching for the meaning of words. Neither the genotext nor the phenotext exists in isolation, however. They always exist together in what Kristeva calls 'the signifying process'.

In her magnum opus, La révolution du langage poétique, Kristeva not only shows how the semiotic basis of language (its sounds and rhythms, and multiple bases of enunciation) is exploited by nineteenth-century avant-garde writers such as Mallarmé and Lautréamont, but she also demonstrates how poetic language has effects within a specific historical and economic formation, namely, the France of the Third Republic. In this work, too, Kristeva continues her development of a theory of the subject-in-process; but now she calls quite explicitly on Lacanian psychoanalytic theory. The semiotic thus becomes equated with the feminine *chora*, which is roughly the unrepresentable place of the mother. It is a kind of origin, but not one that is nameable; for that would place it squarely within the symbolic realm and give us a false notion of it. Like the feminine in general, the *chora* is on the side of the material, poetic dimension of language.

While the semiotic disposition of language may be observed in the work of poets like Mallarmé, it is important to recognise that what the artist makes explicit is also manifest during the child's acquisition of language. Thus in cries, singing and gestures, in rhythm, prosody and word-plays, or in laughter, the child presents the raw material to be used by the avant-garde poet. This is an extra-linguistic dimension linked to a signifying practice: that is, to a practice capable of shaking an existing, perhaps ossified, form of the symbolic, so that a new form may evolve.

Society and Culture with Freud

In 1980, the tenor of Kristeva's work changed. Gone were the very elaborate attempts to develop a general theory of language and the symbolic order, and in their place emerged a concern to analyse specific personal and artistic experiences (whether her own or those of her analysands), experiences which might, at the same time, offer a deeper understanding of social and cultural life. Thus in *Powers of Horror* (1982), Kristeva shows how abjection, as a point of ambiguity beyond what can be consciously coped with by either the individual or society, is evoked in an individual's vomiting because of the dislike of certain foods, or in social rituals dealing with pollution, or in works of art which either attempt to express, or repress abjection as horror and ambiguity.

Subsequently, Kristeva produced studies on love (*Tales of Love* 1987), melancholy and depression (*Black Sun* 1989), and on the history and experience of being a foreigner (*Strangers to Ourselves* 1991). Here, the importance for the individual subject of a successful entry into the symbolic predominates. Love, for example, is impossible without the capacity for idealisation and identification. This capacity is the precondition of identity formation and depends on the successful separation of the child from the mother: that is, on the successful assumption of individual autonomy. Given a more religious disposition, it would be easier for us to appreciate the notion of God as love (*agapē*) once played in the formation of subjectivity. *Agapē* is the power coming from the 'outside', the first tentative source of identification, the first tentative movement of separation from the mother. Without *agapē*, *eros* becomes a blind impulse on the road to destruction. Kristeva calls the equivalent of *agapē* in her psychoanalytic theory of the subject, 'the father of individual prehistory': the most elementary and indispensable basis of identity formation. The message here, perhaps, is not that identity is everything, but that a kind of harmony needs to be achieved between identity and the heterogeneous, poetic elements capable of tearing it apart. In contrast to love, melancholy is a severe impediment to the formation of symbolic and imaginary capacities. Typically, the one severely afflicted by melancholia is unable to love because of being unable to construct the necessary idealisations. Melancholics and depressives live in a kind of perpetual mourning for the mother. As Kristeva says: 'the speech of the depressed is to them like an alien skin; melancholy persons are foreigners in their maternal tongue' (Kristeva 1989: 53).

Writing Love

Kristeva's study of Colette examines the question of love as lived experience and as part of an insight into the psychology of love (Kristeva 2004). Studies, in the trilogy on the Feminine Genius, on Hannah Arendt and Melanie Klein, also devote considerable space to the theme of love. With Arendt's life (Kristeva 2001a) and *oeuvre*, love emerges, in particular, in Arendt's study of Saint Augustin, who is seen to open the way to love as action, a theme followed up by Duns Scotus in his theory of *haecceity* (singularity), which Arendt takes up in the context of the 'who'-subject of action (as opposed to the 'what' of the object). Arendt's notion of love also features the love of the other as an outsider of the community.

In Melanie Klein's case (Kristeva 2002a), love is the mediating force between parent (particularly the mother) and child, most of all in the context of childhood depression. Indeed, love in both Arendt and Melanie Klein, has a largely mediating, if not an instrumental, status.

Colette, for her part, shows that 'to write is to reinvent love' (Kristeva 2002b: 325). This, as it were, is a reiteration of love as an open system that Kristeva had proposed in *Tales of Love*. Consequently, Colette effectively reiterates that there is no fixed model of love, no form of it that cannot be changed. Love emerges as it is written and *in* the written, following the principle of transubstantiation. Writing (style and passion) gives access to the subject of enunciation (*énonciation*), not just the subject of the statement (*énoncé*). Moreover, Colette interprets love through the network of metaphors she uses in her 'reinvention', as well as in the descriptions of the feelings inscribed in the existential experience of everyday life.

In fact, Colette writes in a deluge of metaphors. Metaphor, in keeping with Kristeva's earlier formulations, enacts love in the writing of it. There is no love prior to metaphor. So, not only is metaphor not the 'language' of love, it is not the expression of love either.

Even though there is mourning for the love object, this does not plunge Colette or her heroines into melancholia, for the very possibility of infusing passion into words depends on avoiding the fall in melancholia. Colette is even different from many women here – who are often susceptible to depression – to the point of androgyny (Kristeva 2002b: 357).

Overall, love is present in Colette's work as the vitality of the imaginary, which is never near a point of collapse, even though the author writes of her suffering and the pain of human experience. This is always a form of working through to the other side. It is equivalent to keeping melancholia at bay.

Modes of Revolt

Chora is an 'experimental psychosis' (Kristeva 2002c: 10) of a subject-in-process/on trial. Revolt now ceases to be political as an overt transgression of the law ('world of action'), and assumes an intimate sense, taking the form of memory work and psychoanalysis, poetic language, writing fiction and any number of intellectual and artistic activities that have an impact on psychic life and that often imply some sort of crises of the self.

Revolt, then, is not revolution. Nor is it limited to explicit transgression. Rather, it includes all the ways in which there can be the equivalent of a 'psychical restructuring'. For Kristeva, psychical restructuring is equivalent to Freud, in his day, evoking the revolt of the sons in the myth of the primal horde.

In 'intimate' revolt, signs become the substitute for the mother. 'The depressive does not want to lose his object' (Kristeva 2002c: 23). The depressive in fact resists the return to the self through representation (signs). The mother, however, has become foreign, has become other. Thus Kristeva finds that, when curiosity about one's inner life is in full flower (something, she says, contemporary Information Society inhibits to an alarming extent), it will be found that intimacy, too, is an otherness, a foreign element. We discover a strangeness that haunts our most intimate selves. In fact, we have to make ourselves strangers to ourselves. Only by doing this can we combat 'our latent psychoses' (Kristeva 1998: 85). This is also the basis of revolt continuing when its overt political forms have ceased to have any currency. We need revolt with and against this otherness in us so that identity does not dissolve into the medium itself and become sheer nothingness.

The Subject and Art

There can be no *final* elaboration of the subject. Kristeva presents a subject which is never entirely analysable, but rather one always incomplete: a subject as the impetus for an infinite series of elaborations, a subject constituted by the materiality of language, of words, in a movement of transubstantiation, as Kristeva shows in her study of Proust (Kristeva 1996), where words and flesh, at the level of the imaginary, become one. Indeed, the mark of a rich imaginary is the capacity for transubstantiation. With the standardising procedures of, as Kristeva sees it, a mediatised 'society of the spectacle', the imaginary capacities – including the capacity to fantasise and to have an intimate life – are under threat.

Art participates in the dynamics of subject formation, and subjectivity is played out in the arts. The sense in which this is so is important; for it differentiates Kristeva from many other critics and semioticians. Thus while any artistic work must exhibit indications of human control and order for it to be identified as such, there is no complete subject prior to the work. Rather, artistic endeavour constitutes the subject as much as the subject constitutes the work of art. Moreover, because of the intimate link between art and the formation of subjectivity, Kristeva has always found art to be a particularly fruitful basis for analysis. Thus Mallarmé's poetry puts the 'semiotic disposition' in evidence, while *Romeo and Juliet* indicates the dynamics of love, and Dostoyevsky the structure of suffering and forgiveness in relation to a melancholic disposition. Given an open disposition, the recipients of the artistic message, or artistic effects, may have their symbolic and imaginary capacities expanded: that is, a work of art may become the basis of an authentic experience capable of opening the way to a change in personality. The problem today, Kristeva's work suggests, is that social life is increasingly characterised by subjects closed off from the qualities of works of art which do not conform to pre-conceptions and stereotypes. Or else people are simply fascinated and seduced by the play of images or acts – by the object – without being able to develop new symbolic capacities which would enable the object to be a new ingredient in social life. The aim, then, is to bring about a situation where subjectivity is an 'open system', or a 'work in progress', a becoming 'open to the other' which at the same time can bring about a revised form of one's own identity. This also gives rise to an ethics, but an ethics that now has to be fought for in the post-modern world of the spectacle, where the ego and representation blot out the signs of the working of the unconscious.

References

Kristeva, Julia (1969), *Séméiotiké. Recherches pour une sémanalyse*, Paris: Seuil.

—— (1982), *Powers of Horror. An Essay on Abjection*, trans. Leon S. Roudiez, New York, Columbia University Press.

—— (1984), *Revolution in Poetic Language*, trans. Margaret Waller, New York: Columbia University Press, a translation of the first part of: Kristeva, Julia (1974), *La révolution du langage poétique*, Paris: Seuil.

—— (1986), 'Word, dialogue, novel' in Toril Moi, ed., *The Kristeva Reader*, Oxford: Basil Blackwell.

—— (1987), *Tales of Love*, trans. Leon S. Roudiez, New York: Columbia University Press.

—— (1989), *Black Sun*, trans. Leon S. Roudiez, New York, Columbia University Press.

—— (1996), *Time and Sense. Proust and the Experience of Literature*, trans. Ross Guberman, New York: Columbia University Press.

—— (1998), *L'Avenir d'une révolte*. Paris: Calmann-Levy.

—— (2001a), *Hannah Arendt*, trans. R. Guberman, New York: Columbia University Press.

—— (2002a), *Melanie Klein*, trans. R. Guberman, New York: Columbia University Press.

—— (2002b), *Colette*, Paris: Fayard.

—— (2002c), *Intimate Revolt: The Powers and Limits of Psychoanalysis*, Vol II trans. Jeanine Herman, New York: Columbia University Press.

—— (2004), *Colette*, trans. J.M. Todd, New York: Columbia University Press.

—— (2005a), '*Meurtre à Byzance*, ou pourquoi "Je me voyage" en roman' [I], *L'Infini*, 92, Autumn.

—— (2005b), '*Meurtre à Byzance*, ou pourquoi "Je me voyage" en roman' [II], *L'Infini*, 91, Summer.

—— (2006), *Murder in Byzantium*, trans. C. Jon Delogu, New York: Columbia University Press.

See also: **Bakhtin, Barthes, Husserl, Joyce, Lacan, Merleau-Ponty**

Kristeva's major writings

(2006 [2004]) *Murder in Byzantium*, trans. C. Jon Delogu, New York: Columbia University Press.

(2005a) *La Haine et le Pardon.Pouvoirs et limites de la psychanalyse III*, Paris: Fayard.

(2005b) *L'Amour de soi et ses avatars. Démesure et limites de la sublimation*, Nantes: Pleins Feux, collection, 'authors and questions'.

(2004 [2002]) *Colette*, trans. J.M. Todd, New York: Columbia University Press.

(2002a [1997]) *Intimate Revolt: The Powers and Limits of Psychoanalysis*, Vol. II, trans. Jeanine Herman, New York: Columbia University Press.

(2002b [2000]) *Melanie Klein*, trans. Ross Guberman, New York: Columbia University Press.

(2002c) *Revolt, She Said*, Los Angeles, Ca.: Semiotext(e), [Distributed by MIT Press].

(2001a [1999]) *Hannah Arendt*, trans. Ross Guberman, New York: Columbia University Press.

(2001b [1998]) with C. Clément, *The Feminine and the Sacred*, trans. J.M. Todd, New York Columbia University Press.

(2000a [1996]) *The Sense and Non-sense of Revolt: The Powers and Limits of Psychoanalysis*, Vol. I, trans. Jeanine Herman, New York: Columbia University Press.

(2000b) *Crisis of the ~~European~~ Subject*, trans. S. Fairfield, New York: Other Press.

(1998 [1996]) *Possessions: A Novel*, trans. Barbara Bray, New York: Columbia University Press.

(1996 [1994]) *Time and Sense. Proust and the Experience of Literature*, trans. Ross Guberman, New York: Columbia University Press.

(1995 [1993]) *New Maladies of the Soul*, trans. Ross Guberman, New York: Columbia University Press.

(1994 [1991]) *The Old Man and the Wolves*, trans. Barbara Bray, New York: Columbia University Press.

(1993 [1990]) *Nations Without Nationalism*, trans. Leon S. Roudiez, New York: Columbia University Press.

(1992 [1990]) *The Samurai: A Novel*, trans. Barbara Bray, New York: Columbia University Press.

(1991 [1988]) *Strangers to Ourselves*, trans. Leon S. Roudiez, New York: Columbia University Press.

(1989 [1987]) *Black Sun*, trans. Leon S. Roudiez, New York: Columbia University Press.

(1987a [1983]) *Tales of Love*, trans. Leon S. Roudiez, New York: Columbia University Press.

(1987b [1985]) *In the Beginning Was Love – Psychoanalysis and Faith*, trans. Arthur Goldhammer, New York: Columbia.

(1986a) *The Kristeva Reader*, ed. Toril. Moi, Oxford: Basil Blackwell.

(1986b [1974]) *About Chinese Women*, trans. Anita Barrows, New York and London: Marion Boyars, paperback edn.

(1984a [1974]) *Revolution in Poetic Language*, trans. Margaret Waller, New York: Columbia University Press.

(1984b), *Desire in Language. A Semiotic Approach to Literature and Art*, trans. Thomas S. Gora, Alice Jardine and Leon S. Roudiez, Oxford: Basil Blackwell.

(1982 [1980]) *Powers of Horror. An Essay on Abjection*, trans. Leon S. Roudiez, New York, Columbia University Press.

(1977) *Polylogue*, Paris, Seuil, Eight of the twenty essays are in English in:

(1970) *Le Texte du roman. Approche sémiologique d'une structure discursive transformationnelle*, The Hague and Paris: Mouton.

(1969) *Séméiotiké. Recherches pour une sémanalyse*, Paris, Seuil.

Further Reading

Lechte, John (1990), *Julia Kristeva*, London and New York: Routledge.

Lechte, John and Margaroni, Maria (2004), *Julia Kristeva: Live Theory*, London and New York: Continuum.

Lechte, John. and Zournazi, Mary (2003), *The Kristeva Critical Reader*, Edinburgh: Edinburgh University Press.

McAfee, N. (2003), *Julia Kristeva*, London: Routledge (Routledge Critical Thinkers).

Nikolchina, M. (2004), *Matricide in Language: Writing Theory in Kristeva and Woolf*, New York: Other Press.

Oliver, K. (1993), *Reading Kristeva: Unraveling the Double Bind*, Bloomington, Indiana: Indiana University Press..

Smith, A.M. (1998), *Julia Kristeva: Speaking the Unspeakable*. London: Pluto Press.

Index

statements, true do not automatically result from existence of the referent 327
Stern, Gunther 226
Stiegler, Bernard 148–49
stochastics, perception of by Serres 350
story and memory, homologous with news and oblivion 265
structural coupling, language implicated in 341–42; living system's structures situated in and dependent on an environment 340
structuralism xvii 18, **58–59**, 139; Bakhtin distanced himself from and semiotics 15; Baudrillard worked through 301–2; began to subside in 1970s 142; Benveniste and 59, 64, 85; Bourdieu on 68–69, 121; Derrida 121, 132; Dumézil social sciences and 80, 84–85; early 3; first modern movement to challenge credibility of natural object 304; Genette and 88, 92, 121; hegemonic xix; history of science and 5; its place is both 'here and there' according to Serres 350; Jakobson 94; language and 104; Lévi-Strauss 68, 133; Lévi-Strauss and claiming Mauss for 22; Lévi-Strauss social sciences and 80; Mauss xvi; Saussure and 85, 180–81, 302; social science predominant vehicle of xix
structure, configuration of elements in given unity (or system) 340
'structure' and 'system', Dumézil and 85
style, Joyce and 288–89
subjectivation, notion of linked to the event 239–40
subjectivity, an a priori given in advance or enacted xvii; Cartesian version as elaborated by Lacan 252; element of always in play in human affairs 9; forms itself according to universal principles of Western philosophy 46; Lacanian psychoanalysis shows that consciousness or the ego not centre of 184; played out in the arts 401; in post-modernity takes

form of feature film 256; reduced to 'mere object' by exchange-value 221; subject prior to given historical formation 139
subject and object, distinction between 299
'substance', could be translated as what is manifest 166
'subversive bodily act', Butler challenges 186–87
surrationalism, enrichment and revitalisation of rationalism 7
Surrealism, often aimed to be analogue of madness 368; Sollers and 293
surrealists 102; Benjamin and 261; Lacan and 109; will has to do with semi-conscious day-dreaming (rêverie) 7–8
surveillance at airports and toll booths, change the city 359
suspension of law, suspension of Geneva conventions on conduct of war and Guantanamo Bay 212
Symbolic 107; both the 'pleasure principle' and the 'death drive' 253; Butler 187; domain of law founded on Name-of-the-Father 191–92; the father evokes 106; Kristeva 185–86; Metz and 11, 25–26; Peirce 174; realm of subjectivity 253; Saussure and Peirce 174; source of a priori principles Lacan 105
Symbolic Order, exemplified by Name-of-the-Father constitutes society 106; whole of is phallic according to Lacan 194
symbolic value, irreducible to either use- or exchange value 301
synthesis, Bachelard and 9
systems, work because they do not work 349

'talking cure' 388
tamogochi, the 257
technics, charged with insuring outcome of every action favourable to existence 29–30
technik, focus of Benjamin's interest 262, 264

Turner painting, interprets second
law of thermodynamics 349–38

Ulmer, Gregory, *Teletheory* xv
Ultimate man (equivalent to man in
general), reactive man 281
Ulysses, Leopold Bloom and series of
chance encounters 287–88; Molly
Bloom and monologue in last
chapter 289
unconscious, Adorno's view of 219;
Freud's work on 219, 264; is
discourse of the Other 253;
Kristeva and subject-in-process
397; Lacan 102, 104–5
unconscious *par excellence*, is the
sexual trauma which cannot be
said or symbolised 392
UN High Commission for Refugees
212
University, claim to be Master 108–9
Utopia, reverie of land of the good
life 205

Varela, Francisco J., colleague of
Maturana 339–40, 344; *Tree of
Knowledge, The* 340
Veblen, Thorstein 302
Verne, Jules 350
violence, legal weakens the law rather
than strengthen it 267
Virilio, Paul (b.1932) 235, **354–55**;
'Bunker Archéologie' 355; but is it
all true ... ? 361–63; criticisms of
his work 362–63; disappearance
and the virtual and the dark side of
the Enlightenment 358–59; forces
of productive power become
model of destructive power 356;
information technology and
technologies of vision 354, 361;
life and intellectual trajectory 355–
56; negative aspects of information
technology 360–61; 'oblique
architecture' 355; optics of speed
357–58; perception and cinema
356–57; photography is equivalent
to exposure of time, of time
'breaking the surface' 360; power
359; prophet of the techno-speed-
based millennium 359; says he is a
realist not a pessimist 359; tangible
experience will diminish and be
reduced to nothing 361; the thesis
of war and speed 356; editor of
Architecture Principe group's
magazine 355; editor of magazine
L'Espace Critique 355; *Information
Bomb, The* 358; *Open Sky* 358
virtual interaction, cybernetic
dimension that deprives people of
free will 360
virtualisation of politics, loss of
geographical sovereignty 361
virtual reality, code and 304; Virilio
354, 358
vita activa, comprised of labour, work
and action 230
vita contempletiva, realm of thought or
of contemplation of the eternal 230
vitalism xvii
vitalist-inspired thought **364**, 388
voice, Genette 90–91
void 237–38, 252, 254, 275; Sollers
293
Voloshinov, V.N., *Freusianism and
Marxism and the Philosophy of
Language* 11
Voltaire 292

war, about captivating the enemy or
producing a magical spectacle
357
weathercock, 'Dicent Sinsign' 174
Weber, Max 242, 324;
zweckrationalität 243
Webern, Anton 221
Western culture, related to condition
of feminine in society 194
Western philosophy, theology and
alterity 50; transcendence of 47
West, the, rich and one can expect to
live to 84 352
Whitaker, Randall, information from
web site 339–40
Whitehead, A.N. 335
Whitford, Margaret 194
'wildcat' discoveries, where
technology minimal can still take
place 325

eBooks – at www.eBookstore.tandf.co.uk

A library at your fingertips!

eBooks are electronic versions of printed books. You can store them on your PC/laptop or browse them online.

They have advantages for anyone needing rapid access to a wide variety of published, copyright information.

eBooks can help your research by enabling you to bookmark chapters, annotate text and use instant searches to find specific words or phrases. Several eBook files would fit on even a small laptop or PDA.

NEW: Save money by eSubscribing: cheap, online access to any eBook for as long as you need it.

Annual subscription packages

We now offer special low-cost bulk subscriptions to packages of eBooks in certain subject areas. These are available to libraries or to individuals.

For more information please contact webmaster.ebooks@tandf.co.uk

We're continually developing the eBook concept, so keep up to date by visiting the website.

www.eBookstore.tandf.co.uk